P9-CEC-637

SCHOLARS' GUIDE
TO WASHINGTON, D.C.
FOR EAST ASIAN STUDIES

華盛頓遠東學術資料指南

THE WILSON CENTER

SCHOLARS' GUIDE

TO WASHINGTON, D.C. FOR

EAST ASIAN STUDIES

(CHINA, JAPAN, KOREA, AND MONGOLIA)

HONG N. KIM

Consultants
FRANK JOSEPH SHULMAN
WARREN M. TSUNEISHI

Series Editor
ZDENĚK V. DAVID

WOODROW WILSON INTERNATIONAL CENTER FOR SCHOLARS

SMITHSONIAN INSTITUTION PRESS
WASHINGTON, D.C.
1979

Scholars' Guide to Washington, D.C. No. 3

© 1979 by the Smithsonian Institution. All rights reserved.
Printed in the United States of America.

Copyright is claimed until 5 years from date of publication. Thereafter all portions of this work covered by this copyright will be in the public domain.

This work was developed under a grant from the U.S. Office of Education, Department of Health, Education, and Welfare. However, the content does not necessarily reflect the position or policy of that Agency, and no official endorsement of these materials should be inferred.

Library of Congress Cataloging in Publication Data

Kim, Hong N
    Scholars' guide to Washington, D.C. for East Asian studies.

    (Scholars' guide to Washington, D.C.; 3)
    Bibliography: p. ___
    Includes indexes.
    1. East Asia—Library resources—Washington, D.C.
    2. East Asia—Archival resources—Washington, D.C.
    3. East Asia—Societies, etc.—Directories.
    4. Mongolia—Library resources—Washington, D.C.
    5. Mongolia—Archival resources—Washington, D.C.
    6. Mongolia—Societies, etc.—Directories.
  I. Woodrow Wilson International Center for Scholars. East Asian Program.
II. Title. III. Series.
Z3001.K49 [DS504.5] 950'.07'20753 79-17344
ISBN 0-87474-582-9
ISBN 0-87474-581-0 pbk.

Designed by Elizabeth Dixon and Natalie Babson.

CONTENTS

FOREWORD

This is the third in a series of *Guides* to the scholarly riches of the Washington area published by the Woodrow Wilson International Center for Scholars. The series exemplifies the Center's "switchboard function" of facilitating connections between the vast resources of the nation's capital and those with scholarly or practical needs—or simply curiosity. These *Guides*—like the Center's annual fellowship program—are designed largely to serve the national and international scholarly communities. Approximately 20,000 visiting scholars come annually to Washington from this country and abroad, and it is hoped that the *Guides* will be useful to this ever-growing constituency. We also hope that these *Guides* will inform scholars, many of them outside the major university research centers in the United States, about possibilities for engaging in research on particular topics in Washington.

The series of *Guides* is under the general editorship of Dr. Zdeněk V. David, the Wilson Center librarian, who has devised the basic format. Elizabeth Dixon is largely responsible for the design and the publication arrangements. The author of this particular volume, Dr. Hong N. Kim is professor of political science at West Virginia University.

The Center wishes to thank the U.S. Office of Education for its indispensable financial support of the *Guide's* preparation (under the authority of Title VI, Section 602, NDEA), as well as the Morris and Gwendolyn Cafritz Foundation for partially defraying the cost of its printing.

The first two Center *Guides* were designed for scholars in the Russian/Soviet and Latin American fields respectively. They were published in 1977 and 1979 by the Smithsonian Institution Press. Forthcoming volumes will include surveys of resources in the Washington area for scholars interested in the study of Africa, Central and Eastern Europe, the Middle East, South Asia, and of film and video materials.

James H. Billington, *Director*
Woodrow Wilson International Center for Scholars

INTRODUCTION

This volume was prepared as part of a series of *Scholars' Guides to Washington, D.C.* sponsored by the Woodrow Wilson International Center for Scholars. Like its companion volumes on other major regions of the world, the present volume on East Asia is designed to serve the specific needs of scholars who are interested in knowing the scope of research facilities and resources on the region available in the nation's capital.

It is well known that the Washington area contains by far the largest amount of research resources on East Asia in the United States. Not only are the Library of Congress and the National Archives here, but there are also many important government agencies, private and public research organizations, and academic centers dealing with East Asian affairs.

Although East Asia contains many political and ethnic units, the primary focus of this survey is on China, Japan, and Korea. In addition, comprehensive searches were undertaken to identify resources on the People's Republic of Mongolia (or "Outer Mongolia") and Tibet. Wherever possible, efforts were made to document available resources on Okinawa which was occupied and administered by the United States from 1945 to 1972. Other political units (e.g., Taiwan and Hong Kong) are treated as separate subject categories only when sufficient collections or holdings have justified such treatment. Siberian nationalities are not described in this survey; however, they are included in *Scholars' Guide to Washington, D.C. for Russian/Soviet Studies* compiled by Steven A. Grant (Washington, D.C.: Smithsonian Institution Press, 1977).

In preparing this volume, all subjects of scholarly interest have been considered. However, it was decided at the outset to treat the fields of science and technology in a much more limited way than those of the social sciences, arts, and humanities. Natural science and technology tend to be universalistic, usually defying demographic or regional boundaries. Nevertheless, it was an objective of this survey to identify at least the major resources for the study of East Asian science and its history. The subject index at the back of the book shows the scope of the materials sought. Similarly, the table of contents reveals the range of agencies, institutions, organizations, facilities, and collections investigated.

Though the survey of collections and organizations was fairly comprehensive, entries are selective. The *Guide* is designed neither to be a rudimentary directory of research facilities and collections, nor to document an exhaustive inventory of source materials. It is rather a descriptive and evaluative survey of research resources relevant for East Asian studies. In order to identify such resources, a comprehensive preliminary list was prepared for each section, relying on various sources of information which are listed in the bibliography at the end of this volume. From September 1977 to July 1978, the author contacted each organization thought to be of potential significance for research on East Asia. He has included those collections and organizations which, in his judgment, have the greatest significance for East Asian studies. In order to ensure the accuracy of the information, draft entries were sent whenever possible to the pertinent organizations and collections for review in November 1978.

In spite of every effort made to be accurate and fair in identifying and evaluating the scholarly resources, it is quite possible that the author has either overlooked or inadvertently slighted some important resources of the Washington area on East Asia. For possible future revision of this work, any suggestions by readers for additions, changes, and improvements will be greatly appreciated. Please notify the Wilson Center, Smithsonian Institution Building, 1000 Jefferson Drive, SW, Washington, D.C. 20560.

ACKNOWLEDGMENTS

A volume of this type would have been impossible without the generous co-operation and support provided by numerous institutions and people. The author gratefully acknowledges his indebtedness to the U.S. Department of Health, Education and Welfare for the grant which made this study possible, and to Dr. Jack L. Hammersmith (West Virginia University), who as the advisor for this project, has given generous support and invaluable editorial help. The author also wishes to acknowledge his indebtedness to: Dr. Zdeněk V. David, the series' editor, who worked closely with the author in carrying out the project, for his constant encouragement and advice; Mr. Frank Joseph Shulman and Dr. Warren M. Tsuneishi, co-consultants to the project, for their valuable suggestions and information as well as their meticulous reviews of the manuscript; and Ms. Lisa Garbern (Georgetown University) for her conscientious and able research assistance. Special acknowledgment and thanks are due also for the valuable information and materials provided by the following: Rev. Joseph Sebes (Georgetown University); Drs. Chi Wang, Key P. Yang, Thomas Kang, Sung Yoon Cho, and Messrs. Key Kobayashi, Peter Tseng, John McDonough, and Patrick Sheehan of the Library of Congress; Dr. and Mrs. Edward Griffin (U.S. State Department); Mr. Gary McCone (U.S.D.A. Technical Information Systems); Mrs. Ann Nottingham Kelsall (University of Maryland); and Dr. Tun Thin (International Monetary Fund). In addition, the author would like to thank the numerous staff members of the organizations and collections surveyed for this *Guide*. Without their cooperation, it would have been impossible to complete this survey. Most, if not all, are named in the main sections of this volume; however, it is impossible to acknowledge all of them individually here. Finally, it would have been impossible without the support and affection of my wife, Boohi, who was willing to assume additional chores and burdens created by my frequent trips to Washington, D.C., for the project.

HOW TO USE THE GUIDE

Format: The *Guide* is divided into 2 broad divisions: Collections and Organizations. Each division is sub-divided into sections, which correspond to specific categories of collections or organizations. Entries for each section are arranged alphabetically by the name of the collection or organization.

Libraries: The East Asian-related book holdings in most of the large and general collections, and in several smaller but specialized collections, are evaluated on a scale of A through C. These ratings are based on the quantity and quality of 14 major subject categories and 4 geographic categories. The Library of Congress (LC) holdings were taken as a standard for A collections, meaning comprehensive collections of primary and secondary sources. The B collections are defined as substantial collections (roughly one-tenth of LC's holdings) of primary and secondary sources, sufficient for original research. C collections contain substantial secondary sources (roughly one-half the size of a B collection) with some primary materials, sufficient to support graduate instruction. No ratings below the C level were noted.

The numerical strength of each collection is derived from measurements of library shelflists. The number of book titles was computed on the basis of 100 index cards per inch and 85 titles per 100 cards. As for the category of East Asian law, it was impractical to measure the legal holdings in many area collections, because of the unavailability of the LC classification schedule for East Asian law. Unavoidably, the word "unmeasured" appears in such instances. In short, as a consequence of inherent shortcomings in the method of measurement used, the size of collections may be understated rather than overstated.

Standard entry forms: Listed at the beginning of each section as well as in Appendix VIII, these forms indicate the categories and sequence of information contained for the entries included in each section. The numerical sequence of data presented within each entry corresponds to that of the standard entry form for that particular section. Where a number does not appear in an entry, it means that the point was irrelevant for that particular collection or organization.

Names, addresses, and telephone numbers: These data are subject to frequent change and should be treated accordingly. The most ephemeral data tend to be those relating to security-related government agencies and smaller private associations. All telephone numbers without an area code are located in the District of Columbia (area code 202). The area code for suburban Maryland is 301; and for northern Virginia, 703.

Indexes: The Name Index contains the names of organizations and institutions surveyed, but not of individuals. The Personal Papers Index includes only the names of individuals whose papers are located in the libraries and other depositories surveyed. The Library Subject Strength Index is based upon the method of evaluation explained above under the heading of "libraries." The Subject Index covers rather broad categories and such subjects as "Science" and "Technology" are not broken down by discipline or by geographic region for reasons explained in the introduction.

Transliteration: The transliteration system used in this book is essentially that of the Library of Congress. Certain seeming inconsistencies are inevitably due to the author's policy of spelling names and titles as they appear in the catalogs or other materials of the collections surveyed. Likewise, some organizations appear under names of their own transliteration.

Abbreviations:

FBIS   Foreign Broadcast Information Service
GPO   Government Printing Office
JPRS   Joint Publications Research Service
LC   Library of Congress
NARS   National Archives and Records Service
NTIS   National Technical Information Service
PRC   People's Republic of China
O.P.   Out of print
n.d.   No date

COLLECTIONS

A Libraries (Academic, Government, Public, Private, Special)

Entry Form for Libraries (A)

1. Access
   a. *Address; telephone number(s)*
   b. Hours of service
   c. Conditions of access (including interlibrary loan and reproduction facilities)
   d. Name/title of director and heads of relevant divisions

2. Size of collection

3. Description and evaluation of collection
   a. 18 subject categories
   b. Evaluation of subject strength on a scale from A to C

4. Special collections
   a. Periodicals
   b. Newspapers
   c. Government documents
   d. Books and monographs
   e. Archives and manuscripts
   f. Maps
   g. Films
   h. Tapes

5. Noteworthy holdings

6. Bibliographic aids (catalogs, guides, etc.) facilitating access to collection

A1 ACTION (Peace Corps) Library

1. a. *806 Connecticut Avenue, NW*
   Room M-407
   Washington, D.C. 20525
   254-3307 (Reference)

   b. 9:30 A.M.-4:00 P.M. Monday-Friday

    c. Open to the public for on-site reference use only. Interlibrary loan is available; however, there is no photoduplication service.

    d. Rita Warpeha, Chief Librarian
Victoria Fries, Reference Librarian

2-3. The library contains about 35,000 books and documents and is designed primarily for the use of the ACTION staff. It receives about 400 periodicals, 17 of which relate specifically to the Orient. Outside researchers wishing to utilize the facilities should be aware that reference services are limited due to the already heavy demands made on the small staff.

The Korean book holdings in the NANEAP section (North Africa, Near East, Asia, and Pacific) are, for the most part, English-language texts concerned with general information on history, culture, and economics. There is a card catalog for the book collection.

4. A major and unique collection of research materials is to be found in the library's vertical file information folders. They include miscellaneous documents such as Peace Corps project plans, and some articles, dating from 1961 to the present. A separate card catalog is available for this collection.

6. A listing of serials subscribed by the ACTION Library can be found in *Current Periodical Subscriptions* which can be consulted in the library.

Advanced International Studies Institute Library See entry M1.

A2 Agency for International Development (AID)—Development Information Center (DIC)

1.   a. *Development Information Center*
1601 North Kent Street, Room 105
Arlington, VA 22209
(703) 235-8936/1000

    State Department Branch
State Department
320-21 Street, NW (Room 1656)
Washington, D.C. 20523
632-8571/9345

  b. 8:45 A.M.-5:30 P.M. Monday-Friday

  c. The Development Information Center is designed primarily for the use of AID personnel and for contractors and grantees working under the auspices of AID. Scholars engaged in substantive research may gain access to the central DIC in Arlington and the State Department Branch by obtaining prior approval from the AID Office of Public Affairs (632-1850); from an AID technical or geographic bureau staff member; or from the DIC central or branch heads. Borrowing privileges are not extended to outside researchers. Photoduplication facilities are available.

  d. Joanne Paskar, Chief Librarian.

2.   DIC is a central collection point for program and technical documentation generated by AID and its predecessor agencies and, as such, functions as AID's "Memory Bank." In addition to AID materials, the Center selectively acquires appropriate technical and special documents produced by other non-AID government agencies and organizations and private research institutions and associations. Together these materials form the core of the development sciences information center.

The DIC's collection totals approximately 125,000 titles in microfiche and papercopy formats. The collection covers a broad spectrum of subject matters: agriculture/rural development, population/family planning, education, technical assistance methodology, urban development, and development administration. Included are both classified and unclassified reports.

3.   A survey of the listings in the geographic catalog for China, Japan, Korea, and Taiwan reveals the following approximate totals of titles: China, 33; Japan, 100; South Korea, 950-1000; North Korea, 1; and Taiwan, 350-400. The reason for the disproportionately larger figure for South Korea is to be found in the fact that it is the only country which still receives AID assistance. Studies and reports for the most part cover agriculture, economics, education, health/nutrition, population, and, more recently, energy. The materials maintained by the Information Center include reports, studies, and documents dating back to the late 1940s when AID had its beginnings as the Economic Cooperation Administration (1948) under the Marshall Plan. Sample titles on East Asia include: *An Analysis of New Land Development in Korea* (Michigan State University, 1973); *Korean Community Development Pilot Program* (Near East Foundation, 1957); *Korean Electric Company: Operations and Development* (1965); *Study of the Japanese Rural Health Delivery System* (Asia Foundation, 1974); *General Aspects of Fisheries in Japan* (Japanese Ministry of Agriculture and Forestry, 1956); *Town and City in "Pre-Modern" Japan* (Cornell University, 1964); *Land Reform in Free China* (Free China Review, 1953), and *Conference on Population and Economic Development in Taiwan* (Academica Sinica, 1975-1976).

6.   Access to the DIC's collection is provided through a bound catalog, AID's *Catalogue of Research Literature for Development,* and by browsing in the shelves of the central DIC. The DIC State Department Branch maintains a dictionary card catalog arranged by author, title, subject, geographic designation, and contract. Both branches are preparing for centralized on-line retrieval. At present, they have access to an automated data base containing a list of AID projects as well as the "ORBIT" and "DIALOG" data bases.

A3 Air Force Department—Office of Air Force History Library

1.   a. *Office of Air Force History*
Forrestal Building, Room 8E082
1000 Independence Avenue, SW
Washington, D.C. 20314

   b. 7:45 A.M.-4:00 P.M.   Monday-Friday

   c. Open to qualified researchers who make prior arrangements with the library. Many holdings are classified or restricted. Limited photoreproduction services are available. Microfilm copies of the holdings may be purchased from the Albert F. Simpson Historical Research Center, Maxwell Air Force Base, Alabama 36112, which holds the originals of most of the Library's microfilm collection (approximately 25,000 reels).

   d. Maj. Gen. John W. Huston, Chief
      Dr. Stanley L. Falk, Chief Historian
      William C. Heimoahl, Archivist

2-3.   The library contains about 3,000 volumes of books and journals, and over 25,000 microfilm reels of government documents as well as the personal papers of Air Force personnel. Approximately 1,000 microfilm reels are added annually. About 50 to 60 percent of the materials pertain to World War II or the pre-WWII period, while the remainder deal with the post-WWII period. Materials relating to WWII are the largest in number and the most comprehensive. The U.S. Air Force's activities in the Pacific theater of operations during WWII are well documented. Included are Air Force Intelligence and policy documents, unit histories, and histories of specific campaigns. In addition, the collection contains materials relating to "Strategic Bombing Survey (WWII);" "Occupation of Japan;" "India-Burma-China Theater—14th Air Force," including Gen. Claire L. Chennault's Flying Tigers; and some documents on "Japanese Aircraft."
      The Korean War collection (microfilms) contains the activities of the "U.N. Command," "Fifth Air Force," and an "unclassified statistical summary of the Korean campaign."

6.   The Library has a useful index to its microfilm holdings. In addition, a number of valuable reference tools are available for the researchers to locate pertinent material. They include: *United States Air Force History: A Guide to Documentary Sources* (1973); *United States Air Force History: An Annotated Bibliography* (1971); *Personal Files in the U.S. Air Force Historical Collection* (1975); and *U.S. Air Force Oral History Catalog* (1977).

American Association for the Advancement of Science (AAAS) Library See entry H1.

American Association of Museums Library See entry H3.

American Association of University Women Library See entry H4.

American Bar Association (Governmental Relations Office) Library See entry H5.

American Council on Education Library See entry H6.

American Enterprise Institute for Public Policy Research Library
See entry M2.

A4 American Federation of Labor and Congress of Industrial Organizations (AFL-CIO) Library

1. a. *815 Sixteenth Street, NW*
    Washington, D.C. 20006
    737-3000

    b. 9:00 A.M.-4:30 P.M. Monday-Friday

    c. Open to the public for on-site use.

    d. Photocopying facilities available for both printed and microfilmed materials.

    e. Dora Kelenson, Librarian

2. The library contains about 20,000 volumes, documents, and periodical titles with emphasis on American labor movements, economic and industrial developments, social welfare, and other related subjects. Its holdings on East Asia number no more than 100 titles. Nevertheless, the vertical file drawers have several folders of interest to East Asia specialists.

3. File materials (e.g., pamphlets, articles, and clippings) are arranged in part by date of publication and by subjects. Although most of them are in English, a few Japanese-language materials can be found in the 4 folders dealing with Japan. A copy of *Labor Movement in Japan* (Tokyo: Foreign Affairs Association of Japan, 1938) is contained in one of the 4 folders. One can also find a folder on South Korea, 1 on the People's Republic of China, and 1 on Taiwan.

4. This library is well stocked with literature and documents on the American labor movement. Of interest to East Asia specialists are microfilms of *International Correspondence (AFL and AFL-CIO), 1949-1967* (10 reels) that contain the correspondence between the AFL-CIO and its representatives in Asia and others during the period covered. A complete set of the *Reports of the Annual Convention of the AFL (1881-1954)* and the *Proceedings of the AFL-CIO* (1955-present) are available at this library.

American Film Institute Library See entry H7.

A5 American Institute of Architects Library

1. a. *1735 New York Avenue, NW*
Washington, D.C. 20006
785-7293

b. 8:30 A.M.-5:00 P.M.   Monday-Friday

c. Open to the public for on-site use. Limited interlibrary loan and photo-duplication services are available.

d. Susan Holton, Librarian

2-3. The library contains approximately 20,000 volumes on architecture, construction, urban planning, and related subjects. The emphasis of the collection is on American architecture and the practice of architecture, but it contains some materials on East Asia: 30-50 titles on China; 80-100 titles on Japan; and 3 titles on Korea. The texts are either in East Asian vernacular languages or combined with an English text. Its holdings on Japan and China deserve a "B" rating.

4. The library holds 2 photograph albums presented to the AIA by the Architectural Delegation of the People's Republic of China on their visit in September 1975. The first album contains interesting photographs of ancient architectural works (mostly pagodas and temples) and the Ming and Ch'ing Imperial Palaces. The second album features modern constructions including the T'ien-An-Men Square, the Great Hall of the People, and various other public buildings, parks, and residences in Peking, Shanghai, Taiyuan, and Nanking. The library also has a photograph album compiled by the Shanghai Architecture Society in April 1974. It contains more detailed photographs of architectural work in China than the 2 albums already mentioned. Several recent books on construction laws and urban planning from Taiwan are also available.

A number of Japanese books also contain excellent photographs of Japanese architecture, including the Japanese Imperial Palace, and the Soka Gakkai's head temple, Shōhondō (or "Palace of Peace").

American Psychological Association (APA) Library See entry H11.

American Society of International Law Library See entry H12.

American University—Foreign Area Studies Library See entry M3.

A6 American University Library

1. a. *Massachusetts and Nebraska Avenues, NW*
Washington, D.C. 20016
686-2325 (Reference)

b. Academic year:

8 A.M.-midnight   Monday-Friday
9 A.M.-6 P.M.   Saturday
1 P.M.-midnight   Sunday
Summer hours:
9 A.M.-11 P.M.   Monday-Thursday
9 A.M.-5 P.M.   Friday-Saturday

c. Open to the public for use of materials within the library, with borrowing privileges limited to the university community. Interlibrary loan and photoduplication services are available.

d. Donald D. Dennis, University Librarian

2. The library contains approximately 400,000 volumes, with East Asian holdings totaling some 6,500 volumes. The library also currently receives 3,100 periodicals and 50 newspapers.

3. b. Subject categories and evaluations (numbers represent tities):

Subject Category	China/Rating		Japan/Rating		Korea/Rating
1. Philosophy and Religion	71		90		4
2. History	385		669		140
3. Geography and Ethnography	24		40		3
4. Economics	176		196		12
5. Sociology	70	C	41		5
6. Government and Politics	89	C	58		11
7. Foreign Relations	122	C	58	C	8
8. Law	20		6		1
9. Fine Art	62	C	50	C	6
10. Education	31	C	15	C	3
11. Language	104		60		4
12. Literature	243		319		8
13. Military Affairs	4		5		43
14. Bibliography and Reference	3		18		0
15. Tibet	66	C			
16. Mongolia	23	C			
17. Okinawa			0		
18. Hong Kong	85	B			

4. d. THE CHARLES NELSON SPINKS COLLECTION

The collection consists of approximately 1,200 volumes recently donated to the American University Library by Dr. Charles Nelson Spinks who had collected these Japanese books, prints, and manuscripts since the late 1930s. These volumes, many of which are beautifully hand-bound, are devoted chiefly to the fields of Japanese local history, *Ukiyoe* (Japanese color prints), and the civilization of the Tokugawa period (1600-1868). Although they are not yet fully cataloged, a brief list of the authors, titles, and publication dates of the items included in the collection is available. See Yong Sun Chung, *The Manrakudo Library of Dr. Charles Nelson Spinks* (Washington, D.C.: The American University Library, 1977). 76 pp.

6. For more information about the AU library, see *Library Guide: The American University, Washington, D.C.* (1977).

Anderson House—The Society of the Cincinnati Library
See entry C1.

Archives of American Art and National Collection of Fine Arts Library See entry B2.

Arms Control and Disarmament Agency Library See entry K3.

A7 Army Library—Pentagon (Department of the Army)

1. a. *The Pentagon, Room 1A518*
    Washington, D.C. 20310
    697-4301

    b. 9:00 A.M.-4:00 P.M.   Monday-Friday

    c. Entrance to the Pentagon is restricted. Outside researchers who have access to the Pentagon may use the Army Library facilities at the discretion of its staff. Interlibrary loan and photocopying facilities are available.

    d. Mary L. Shaffer, Director

2-3. The Army Library contains approximately 280,000 volumes, one million documents, and 2,000 periodicals, covering such fields as military science, economics, geopolitics, social sciences, business administration, biography, technology, history, law, and the like.
   Holdings pertaining to East Asia total approximately 4,700 (i.e., China, 2,000; Japan, 1,500; Korea, 800; Mongolia, 100; and Okinawa and the Pacific islands in Second World War, 300). The strength of the collection lies in military affairs, international relations, and history. Its holdings on military affairs as well as Okinawa and Mongolia deserve a B rating.

4. The library subscribes to 2,000 periodicals, including about 20 journals specializing in East Asian affairs. Special collections include unit histories of World War II and Army publications.

6. The library has computer terminals with access to the Defense Documentation Center data base (see entry G3). In addition, it has access to a dozen or more bibliographic retrieval services including ERIC, and NTIS. The library's Research and Bibliography Section has published a

number of annotated bibliography surveys (e.g., *China: An Analytical Survey of Literature,* 1978 edition) that are sold through the U.S. Government Printing Office. The library also produces selective bibliographies on important topics (e.g., nuclear proliferation, terrorism, etc.). Copies of the following publications of the library can be obtained free on request: *Periodical Holdings of the Army Library* (1977); *Selected Current Acquisitions, the Army Library;* and *A Handbook: The Army Library Pentagon.*

Association of Asian-American Chambers of Commerce Library
See entry H19.

Brookings Institution Library See entry M5.

Bureau of Labor Statistics (Labor Department) Library
See entry K22.

A8 Catholic University of America—Mullen Library

1. a. *620 Michigan Avenue, NE*
   Washington, D.C. 20064
   635-5060/5155

    b. Academic year:

   9 A.M.-10:00 P.M. Monday-Thursday
   9 A.M.-5:00 P.M. Friday-Saturday
   1 P.M.-10:00 P.M. Sunday
   (Summer hours may vary considerably. For further information, call 635-5155).

    c. Open to the public for use of materials within the library. Visiting scholars may be eligible for temporary courtesy loans of books which may be available through the Office of the Director (635-5055). Interlibrary loan and photoduplication services are available.

    d. Dr. Fred M. Peterson, Director

2. a. The total collection numbers nearly one million volumes, with East Asian holdings of more than 3,000 volumes.

    b. Subject categories and evaluations (number represent titles):

Subject Category	China/Rating		Japan/Rating	Korea/Rating
1. Philosophy and Religion	143	C	82	0
2. History	452		191	66
3. Geography and Ethnography	32	C	7	1
4. Economics	55	C	40	3
5. Sociology	51		19	4
6. Government and Politics	39		27	1

Subject Category	China/Rating		Japan/Rating	Korea/Rating
7. Foreign Relations	108	C	26	1
8. Law	11		8	3
9. Fine Art	78	B	31	5
10. Education	21		20	2
11. Language	128		31	9
12. Literature	119		47	9
13. Military Affairs	5		6	16
14. Bibliography and Reference	9		1	0
15. Tibet	29			
16. Mongolia	50	C		
17. Okinawa			0	
18. Hong Kong	8			

4. a. The Institute of Christian Oriental Research library, housed in the basement of the Catholic University library building, has a complete set of the following periodicals: (1) *Journal of American Asiatic Society* (Vols. 1-96); (2) *Journal of the Royal Asiatic Society* (1934-1977); and (3) *Journal Asiatique* (1882-1977). For information, contact Br. Fitzgerald, Director of the Institute (635-5084).

   e. The Department of Archives and Manuscripts holds a number of valuable papers, including the "Labor Manuscripts." Of special interest to East Asian specialists is the Richard L. Deverall Papers, 1928-1959, which number 26 boxes, 127 bound volumes. Mr. Deverall was the editor of *Christian Front*, who later became the Chief of Education Branch, Labor Division, Supreme Commander of Allied Powers (SCAP) Headquarters in Tokyo from 1946 to 1948. From 1951 to 1956, he served as the representative of the American Federation of Labor (AFL) in Asia. Because of the sensitive nature of some of the materials included in the collection, use of the Deverall Papers is restricted. Anyone interested in using the post-1941 materials should secure permission from the Richard L. Deverall family through the Archives and Manuscript Division of the Catholic University Library. For further information, contact Dr. Anthony Zito, archivist (635-5065).

5. The Institute of Christian Oriental Research Library (Br. Fitzgerald, Director, 635-5084) holds over 100 rare books on East Asia, mostly travelogs written by Western travelers and missionaries from the 16th through 19th centuries. As these books have not been cataloged, one must rely heavily on the help provided by the Institute's staff, especially Br. Fitzgerald. Some of the rare books relating to East Asia that may be of interest to the East Asian specialists are: (1) Augustini Antonii Georgius, *Alphabetum Tibetanum Missionum Apostolicarum* (Rome, 1762); (2) Soucha de Rennefort, *Mémoires pour Servir A L'Histoire des Indes Orientales* (Paris, 1688); (3) Dequignes, *Histoire Générale des Huns, des Turcs, des Mongols, et des Autres Tartares Occidentaux* (Paris, 1756), 4 vols. in 5; (4) Louis le Comte, *Nouveaux Mémoires Sur L'Etat Présent de la Chine* (Paris, 1697); (5) Huc, *L'Empire Chinois* (Paris, 1857) 2 vols.; and (6) Charles Le Govien, S.J., *Histoire de L'Edit de L'Empereur de la Chine* (Paris, 1698). Also several hundred rare books are located at the Special Collections Section of the Catholic University's Mullen Library. However, most of the materials

have not been cataloged. Some of the noteworthy rare books that can be found at the special Collection Section are: (1) Joseph-Anne-Marie de Moriac de Mailla, *Histoire Générale de la Chine aux Annales de cet Empire* (Paris, 1777), 12 vols.; (2) Joachim Bouvet, *Istoria de L'Impreador de la Cina* (Padova, Italy, 1710); (3) Gabriel de Magalhaes, *Nouvelle Relation de la Chine* (Paris, 1688); (4) *(Jesuit, Letters from Missions) Nouvelles Letters Edifiantes de Missions de la Chine et de Indes Orientales* (Paris, 1818), 8 vols.; (5) Society for Propagation of the Faith, *Annales de l'Association de la Propagation de la Foi* (Paris, 1827), 101 vols.; (6) *(Jesuit, Letters from Missions), Lettres Edifiantes et Curieuses Ecrites des Missions Etrangères* (Lyon, France, 1819) 12 vols.; and (7) *(Jesuits Letters from Missions), Letters Edifiantes et Curieuses Ecrites des Missions Etrangères* (Paris, 1780), 24 vols. For information, contact Carolyn Lee (635-5088).

A9 Census Bureau Library (Commerce Department)

1. a. *Federal Office Building 3, Room 2451*
    Suitland, MD 20233
    (301) 763-5042 (Reference)
    763-5040 (Chief, Library Branch)

    b. 8:00 A.M.-5:00 P.M.   Monday-Friday

    c. Open to the public. Interlibrary loan and photoduplication services are available.

    d. Betty Baxtresser, Chief of the Library Branch

2. The library holds over 300,000 items on demography, economics, statistics, business, education, data processing, and other related subjects. Emphasis is given to statistical and census reports. Currently the library receives more than 3,000 serial titles.

3. The library's East Asian holdings include about 494 titles on Japan, 435 titles on China, 230 titles on South and North Korea, and about 100 titles on Taiwan. In sociology, this collection is a significant scholarly resource and deserves an A rating.

4. The library's extensive serials collection includes over 25 major Japanese demographic and economic indicators and statistical reports (e.g., *Monthly Foreign Trade Statistics, Japan Economic Indicators, Population Census of Japan, Monthly Statistics of Japan,* etc.); 23 South Korean serials (e.g., *Monthly Foreign Trade Statistics, Monthly Statistics of Korea, Monthly Economic Review,* etc.), and about 11 serials from Taiwan (e.g., *Monthly Bulletin of Statistics, Accounts and Statistics, Monthly Statistics of Transportation and Communication,* etc.).

6. The library maintains 2 separate dictionary card catalogs: an old catalog for holdings cataloged prior to March 1976; and a new catalog for post-March 1976 acquisitions. The contents of the old catalog have been published in *Catalogs of the Bureau of the Census Library, Washington,*

D.C., 20 vols. (Boston: G. K. Hall and Co., 1976). A *List of Periodicals Currently Received by the Census Library* is also available. Copies of monthly *Library Notes* listing new acquisitions can be obtained free on request.

Center for Chinese Research Materials (Association of Research Libraries) See entry M6.

Center for Defense Information Library See entry M7.

Center for International Policy Library See entry M8.

Center for Naval Analyses Library See entry M9.

Central Intelligence Agency Library See entry K4.

A10 Commerce Department Library

1.   a. *14th Street and Constitution Avenue, Room 7046*
   Washington, D.C. 20230
   377-5511

   b. 8:30 A.M.-5:00 P.M.   Monday-Friday

   c. Open to the public for on-site use. Interlibrary loan and photoduplication facilities are available.

   d. Stanley J. Bougas, Librarian

2-3. The library contains more than 300,000 volumes with emphasis on economics and related subjects. It receives about 1,400 current periodicals, including 27 serials from Japan, 15 from South Korea, and 3 from Taiwan. The library is designed to serve the needs of the Commerce Department staff. The collection contains numerous government publications (both U.S. and foreign) on commerce and trade.

   It is estimated that the library's holdings on East Asia number about 850 titles: 380 on China; 120 on South and North Korea; and 350 on Japan. Most of the books and journals on China, Japan, and Korea are concerned with trade, economic conditions and policies, and foreign relations. For economics, the library's holdings deserve at least a B rating.

6. Two card catalogs are maintained by the library: (1) an old card catalog for materials collected from 1914-1974; and, (2) a current catalog covering acquisitions since 1974. Occasionally, the library publishes the *Commerce Library Bulletin* (irregular) which lists selected recent acquisitions.

A11 Commerce Department—Bureau of East-West Trade—The PRC Affairs Division Collection

1. a. *14th Street and Constitution Avenue, NW, Room 4323*
      Washington, D.C. 20230
      377-4681

   b. 8:30 A.M.-5:00 P.M.   Monday-Friday

   c. Open to qualified researchers, by appointment. No interlibrary loan is available. On-site use only.

2-3.   The PRC Affairs Division maintains a small but highly specialized collection of approximately 300 books and reports on the Chinese economy, especially trade and industry. Materials are primarily in English. The office receives a handful of newspapers, journals, and East-West trade newsletters. For specialists in the Chinese economy, this collection may be highly valuable and important, for some of the materials (e.g., government reports, in-house studies and publications) are not readily available elsewhere. For further information, call William Clarke, Head of the Division (377-4681).

Commerce Department Export Information Reference Room
See entry K5.

A12 Commerce Department—Foreign Demographic Analysis Division Collection

1. a. *711-14th Street, NW, Room 702*
      Washington, D.C. 20230
      376-7695

   b. 8:00 A.M.-4:30 P.M.   Monday-Friday

   c. Open to serious researchers, by appointment. Limited interlibrary loan and photoduplication services are available.

   d. John S. Aird, Chief
      J. Philip Emerson, Analytical Statistician
      Florence L. Yuan, Research Analyst (China)

2-3.   The East Asian collection consists of about 500 titles (half in English and the other half in Chinese) dealing with the demography and economy of China, 243 Chinese periodicals, and over 80,000 research cards. Its holdings on Chinese sociology deserve an A rating.

4.   FDAD's East Asian collection contains incomplete series of about 40 Chinese national and provincial newspapers of the post-1949 period. Although most of them are on microfilm, copies of *Jen-min Jih-pao* (1958-present) and *Kwang-ming Jih-pao* (1972-present) are available in originals.

The FDAD collection also includes sets of the following serials: *Foreign Broadcast Information Service: Daily Report: The People's Republic of China* (1956-present); *Current Background* (1952-1977); and *Survey of Mainland China Press* (1952-1977). In addition, the collection contains *Weekly Information Report on Communist China* (1957-1963); *Weekly Report on North Korea* (August 1963-April 1965); and *Weekly Report on Mongolia* (September 1963-May 1966). Many of the JPRS publications on the PRC, North Korea, and the People's Republic of Mongolia are also available at FDAD.

5.   The FDAD collection contains over 80,000 research cards on the PRC; 1,000 on North and South Korea; and 1,000 on the People's Republic of Mongolia. These cards contain data and information on population, statistics, economics, and social structure (derived largely from the periodicals and other materials located at the FDAD) of the countries covered. The research cards on China are arranged under the following subject categories: agriculture, commerce and trade, economy, education, ethnic minorities, family and household, forests and lumbering, geography, health and medicine, life-style, housing, industry, labor force, language and language reforms, political parties, population, social security, wages, income, prices, and vital statistics. Each subject is then divided into more specific subcategories. For instance, under agriculture, subcategories include policy, plans and progress, organization, economics, labor force, development, research and training, production, and weather. Anyone desiring to utilize these research cards should contact Florence L. Yuan (376-7692).

6.   A Xeroxed classification scheme for the research cards on China is available at FDAD.

A13 Commerce Department—Patent Office Scientific Library

1.   a. *2021 Jefferson Davis Highway*
Arlington, VA
Mailing Address: Washington, D.C. 20231
(703) 557-2955
(703) 557-2957 (Reference)
(703) 557-3545 (Foreign Patent Services)

      b. 8:30 A.M.-5:00 P.M.   Monday-Friday
      c. Open to the public. Interlibrary loan and photocopying services are available.

      d. Elizabeth Pan, Librarian
Barrington Balthrop, Chief, Foreign Patent Services & Record Section.

2-3.   This library contains approximately 270,000 books, thousands of bound periodicals, and millions of foreign patents, in bound format and on microfilm. Currently, 1,700 periodicals are received.

    The library's holdings on East Asia number approximately 470: 350 titles on Japan; 80 titles on China, and 40 titles on Korea. Most of these deal with patents, patent laws, or other reference materials such as dictionaries.

4-5. The library receives 7 patent journals from Japan; 2 from South Korea, and 1 from Taiwan. In addition, it receives 25 nonpatent scientific and technical journals from Japan. The most significant and noteworthy collection consists of Japanese patents, which are believed to be the most comprehensive outside of Japan and date back to c. 1875. A near complete set of *Tokkyo Kōhō* listing examined patent applications is available at the library. In addition, the library has complete sets of *Kōkai Tokkyo Kōhō* which contain unexamined patent applications (1971-present) and *Kōkai Jitsuyō Shinan Kōhō* containing unexamined utility models (1971-present). To cope with the growing storage problems, the library has recently begun microfilming these patents (see entry K5).

In addition to the Japanese patents, the library also contains patents from South Korea and Taiwan. These, however, are relatively minor collections as compared to the Japanese collection.

6. The library has three card catalogs: (1) the main catalog is arranged by author, title, and subject; (2) the patent periodicals catalog is arranged geographically; and, (3) the general periodicals catalog is arranged alphabetically.

For patents, researchers should utilize the following indexes: *World Patents Indexes* (July 1974-), and *Central Patents Index* (February 1970-). For further information on the Japanese patent collection of the library, contact Paul Ishimoto (703/557-3193).

Commerce Department—U.S. Foreign Trade Reference Room
See entry K5.

Commerce Department World Trade Reference Room See entry K5.

Committee on Scholarly Communication with the People's Republic Of China (CSCPRC) **(National Academy of Sciences) Library** See entry J4.

A14 Congressional Quarterly Inc.—Editorial Reports Library

1. **a.** *1414 22nd Street, NW*
Washington, D.C. 20037
296-6800

b. 9:00 A.M.-5:00 P.M. Monday-Friday

c. Closed to the public. However, subscribers to *Congressional Quarterly* have permission to use the collection. Only limited photoduplication and interlibrary loan services are available.

d. Edna M. Frazier, Librarian

2.   The library contains over 9,000 bound volumes and 5,000 microforms. The major subjects covered are current events, international relations, and domestic politics.

3-4.   This library will be of immense help to researchers who want to gather information and data relating to postwar U.S. attitudes and policies toward China, Japan, and Korea. Congressional hearings and voting records, U.S. government documents and publications, plus information and data compiled by the *Congressional Quarterly* provide East Asian specialists with important source materials to work with.

5.   The library maintains an extensive vertical file collection on major regions of the world, including East Asia. A number of folders deal with China, Japan, Korea, Japanese-American and Sino-American relations, foreign trade, environmental problems, and nuclear power.

Energy Department Libraries See entry K9.

Environmental Protection Agency Library See entry K10.

Exotech Systems Library See entry M11.

Federal Aviation Administration (Transportation Department Library See entry K31.

A15 Federal Reserve System Research Library

1.   a. *Board Building*
      20th and Constitution Avenue, NW
      Washington, D.C. 20551
      452-3332 (Reference)

      b. 8:45 A.M.-5:15 P.M.   Monday-Friday

      c. Open to the public. Limited interlibrary loan and microfilm reader services are available.

      d. Ann Roane Clary, Chief Librarian (452-3398)

2-3.   The library's holdings total over 90,000 volumes in the field of banking, finance, monetary policy, and general economic conditions in the U.S. and abroad. Over 2,000 periodicals are received currently. It is difficult to determine the total number of the library's holdings on East Asia, as many titles are scattered in a number of subject fields. A sample count of the titles listed in the card catalog under China, Japan, Korea, and Taiwan indicates the following—China: 85-100 titles; Japan: 180-200 titles; Korea: 85-100 titles; and Taiwan: 8 titles. For scholars specializing in international economics and finance, this library can be a useful resource (i.e., B rating).

4. The library receives more than 70 periodicals emanating from East Asia: 45 from Japan; 14 from South Korea; 7 from Taiwan; and 5 from Hong Kong.

5. There is a card catalog, but no published catalog for the library's collection. Researchers should consult with the staff for further information.

Food and Agriculture Organization (of the United Nations) Library
See entry L4.

Foreign Claims Settlement Commission of the United States (FCSC) Library See entry K13.

A16 Freer Gallery of Art Library (Smithsonian Institution)

1. a. *12th Street and Jefferson Drive, SW*
    Washington, D.C. 20560
    381-5332

    b. 10:00 A.M.-4:30 P.M.   Monday-Friday

    c. Open to the public. There are no interlibrary loan services except for a slide collection of Oriental art; Xeroxing facilities are available.

    d. Priscilla P. Smith, Librarian

2. The Freer library contains approximately 24,000 volumes, over half of which (13,000) are Chinese and Japanese. The collection is designed to supplement the Freer Gallery's collection of art; it contains many important books relating to the objects in the Freer art collection and, to a lesser extent, to the civilizations that produce them.

3. This excellent collection is rich in the field of Near and Far Eastern art. The strength of the library's holdings on East Asia, mostly on Japan and China, can be illustrated as follows:

Language	Number of Titles (Estimated)	Mono-volumes
Chinese Collection	1,643	8,470
Japanese Collection	1,690	4,320
Western Collection	8,099	9,766
Periodicals (bound vols.)	—	1,089

Note: Uncataloged materials (e.g., sales catalogs and individual issues of periodicals) are not included in volume count.

The library's East Asian holdings cover such subfields of fine arts as paintings, ceramics, metalwork, drawings, glassware, graphics, and architecture. For fine arts as a whole (i.e., over 4,000 titles), its holdings represent one of the finest in the Washington area and deserve the rating of A. Its holdings in other fields are not as extensive as in fine arts; however, it has a sizable number of language and reference materials on East Asia that can be of immense help to East Asian specialists. Its holdings on Chinese and Japanese bibliography and reference as well as art history should be rated B.

4.   a. The library currently receives over 100 periodicals, including several journals emanating from East Asia and Europe such as: *Bijutsu shi; Ku-kung chou k'an; Toji;* and *T'oung pao.* It has a fairly comprehensive set of serial titles in the fine arts.

    g-h. The library contains about 38 microfilmed items, including correspondence of Charles L. Freer, Arthur Waley's *Notes on Chinese Alchemy* (1930-1932), and *Tōban Shinpin Zukan* ("Album of Sword Guard Masterpieces") (Tokyo, n.d.). A microfilm viewer is available. In addition, it has an equivalent number of tapes of lectures presented by scholars at the Freer Gallery from 1966 to March 1976. Unfortunately, however, the library does not provide equipment to utilize these audio materials. Until the library procures such equipment, scholars should work out special arrangements with the office for the use of these tapes.

5.   RARE BOOKS: The library has under its custody numerous rare books, including the following: (1) *Neng tuan chin kung pan jo po lo mi to ching* ("a well-cutting diamond *prajnaparamitra sutra*"), translated by Hsuan Tsang (n.p., n.d.). Titles and texts in Mongol, Manchu, and Tibetan languages are also available. (2) *Chi ku yin p'u*—compiled by Kan Yang in 1596; contains a collection of seals. (3) *Utai-bon* designed and published by Kōetsu Honami (1558-1637); one hundred "utai" for the No plays of the Kanze school are contained in 100 volumes in 6 lacquer boxes. (4) *Kansei go mizunoto-ushi nen dai sho*—a collection of "surimono" (or prints) made in 1793; it contains 172 "surimono" mounted on 46 pages.

SCROLLS: In addition to the rare books, the Freer library also possesses 56 scrolls, some of which are reproductions of objects in the Freer Gallery's collection. These scrolls are cataloged in the Shelf-list File located in the library.

REFERENCE COLLECTION: The library has an excellent collection of reference materials on East Asian art and art history (e.g., bibliographies, dictionaries, biographies, yearbooks, and encyclopedias, many of which are written in the Chinese or Japanese language). For example, one can find *Koga bikō* (Tokyo, 1912)—a 4-volume biographical dictionary of Japanese and Korean painters with illustrations of their seals and signatures; *Shu fa ta tzu tien* (Hong Kong, 1973)—a dictionary of different styles of Chinese writings; *Chung kuo ku chin ti ming ta tz'u tien* (Shanghai, 1931)—a dictionary of ancient and modern Chinese geographical names compiled by Li-huo Tsang et al.; and *Tōken tōsō kantei jiten* (Tokyo, 1936)—a dictionary for judging swords and their fittings.

6.   The Freer library does not use the LC classification scheme but the older Dewey Decimal system. In addition to *the Freer Catalogue* (Boston: G. K. Hall, 1968), the library maintains card catalogs which facilitate the researcher's access to the library's holdings. Also, scholars can count on excellent reference services provided by the staff of the Freer library.

General Research Corporation Library See entry M12.

A17 Geological Survey Library (Interior Department)

1. a. *12201 Sunrise Valley Drive, Fourth Floor*
    Reston, VA 22092
    (703) 860-6671 (Reference)

    b. 7:15 A.M.-4:45 P.M.   Monday-Friday

    c. Open to the public. Interlibrary loan and photoduplication facilities are available.

    d. George H. Goodwin, Jr., Librarian

2. The library contains over 600,000 bound and unbound monographs, serials and government publications; 300,000 pamphlets and reprints, doctoral dissertations and maps; and over 100,000 album prints, lantern slides, transparencies, and negatives. Currently, the library receives over 9,500 serial titles. The collection is devoted to various aspects of the geosciences with emphasis on geology, paleontology, petrology, mineralogy, geochemistry, geophysics, ground and surface water, cartography, and mineral resources. A significant number of books and periodicals reflect the Geological Survey's growing interest in the environment, earth satellites and remote sensing, geothermal energy, marine geology, land use, lunar geology, and the conservation of natural resources.

3. The bulk of the library's holdings on East Asia are in the geosciences and other physical sciences. A cursory survey of the shelflist reveals that the library contains at least 474 titles on China; 512 titles on Japan; 120 titles on Korea; and about 90 titles on Mongolia. The principal subjects covered are geology, economic conditions, mineral resources, paleontology, petrology, physical geography, water supplies, and languages (i.e., Japanese and Chinese). Its holdings on East Asia geography rate an A, while its holdings on Mongolia deserve a B rating.

    In addition, the library contains a fairly extensive collection of official geological surveys of East Asian countries: 90 titles from China; 180 titles from Japan; and 28 titles from South Korea.

    Unquestionably, the library's East Asian collection in the geosciences is one of the finest in the world and deserves an A rating.

4. The library's extensive serial collection is divided into 4 groups: the first is for all official geological survey publications (000-999) without letter prefixes; the second is for nonofficial geological publications (G); the third comprises nongeological official publications (P); and the fourth is for science serials other than geology (S). East Asian serials are measured as follows:

	China	Japan	Korea
(000-999)	90	180	20
G	45	90	3
P	7	22	1
S	72	261	2

6.   The library's card catalog is reproduced in book form: *Catalog of the United States Geological Survey Library* (Boston, G. K. Hall, 1964), 25 vols., and on-going supplements (21 vols., so far).

Also available at the library is a bibliography entitled *U.S. Geological Survey, Pacific Geological Survey—Military* compiled by Anna M. Blazer, Military Geology Branch, U.S. Geological Survey, in 1965. It lists over 1,000 Japanese scientific reports on East Asia and the Pacific region in the pre-1945 period prepared by Japanese geologists. These reports were subsequently translated into English for the Pacific Geological Survey Section, Military Geology Branch, U.S.G.S., in Tokyo, Japan, from 1946 to 1960.

A brochure entitled *U.S. Geological Survey Library* (1975) is available free on request.

George Washington University—Institute for Sino–Soviet Studies Library See entry M15.

A18 George Washington University Library

1.   a. *2130 H Street, NW*
     Washington, D.C. 20052
     676-6047 (Reference)
     676-6455 (Office)

 b. Academic year:

 8:30 A.M.-midnight   Monday-Friday
 10:00 A.M.-6:00 P.M.   Saturday
 10:00 A.M.-2:00 P.M.   Sunday
 (Library hours may vary during examination periods, holidays, and summer sessions. For information, call 676-6845).

 c. Open to the public for on-site use. Interlibrary loan and photoduplication facilities are available.

 d. Rupert C. Woodward, University Librarian

2.   The library holdings total approximately 500,000 volumes, with East Asian holdings numbering more than 7,000 volumes. The library currently receives 5,199 serials and over 60 newspapers (including 13 foreign newspapers), including the *Japan Times,* and *Jen Min Jih Pao.*

3.   a. A few thousand titles relating to East Asia are physically housed in the library of the Institute for Sino-Soviet Studies (ISSS) which is located at Room 601 of the library building. For details, see entry M15.

 b. Subject categories and evaluations (numbers represent titles):

Subject Category	China/Rating		Japan/Rating	Korea/Rating
1. Philosophy and Religion	87		55	1
2. History	1,109	C	355	85
3. Geography and Ethnography	28		11	3
4. Economics	157		127	18

Subject Category	China/Rating		Japan/Rating		Korea/Rating
5. Sociology	71	C	22	C	4
6. Government and Politics	108	C	55		8
7. Foreign Relations	229	B	54	C	10
8. Law	12		6		1
9. Fine Art	4		6		1
10. Education	20		14		0
11. Language	116		33		1
12. Literature	515	C	75		9
13. Military Affairs	7		10		47
14. Bibliography and Reference	48	C	12		4
15. Tibet	42	C			
16. Mongolia	13				
17. Okinawa			5		
18. Hong Kong	17				

4. a-f. Many periodicals, newspapers, and government documents relating to East Asia are located in the ISSS library. Recently, the George Washington University Library became the deposit library for Defense Mapping Agency Topographic Center maps for the Washington, D.C., Consortium of Universities. At least 450 maps on East Asia can be found here.

   g. The library's Audiovisual Department (676-6378) has been designed as a regional center for Vanderbilt University's Television News Archive. When it becomes fully operational, it is expected to supply video tapes of news stories on East Asia which have been aired by the three major commercial television networks in the United States. An annual index titled *Television News Index and Abstracts: A Guide to the Videotape Collection of the Network Evening News Programs* has been published by the Vanderbilt Television News Archive since 1968.

6.   For the Washington, D.C., Consortium of Universities, there is a *Guide to Library Resources* (September 1977).

A19 Georgetown University—Lauinger Library

1. a. *37th and O Streets, NW*
      Washington, D.C. 20057
      625-4175 (Reference)
      525-4095 (Office)
      625-4175 (Kay Won Lee, Oriental Materials Specialist)

   b. Academic year:

      8:30 A.M.-midnight   Monday-Thursday
      8:30 A.M.-10:00 P.M.   Friday
      10:00 A.M.-10:00 P.M.   Saturday
      11:00 A.M.-midnight   Sunday
      (For summer hours, call 625-3300)

   c. Open to scholars for on-site use. Interlibrary loan and photoreproduction facilities are available.

   d. Joseph E. Jeffs, University Librarian
      Kay Won Lee, Oriental Materials Specialist

2. The library collection numbers approximately 750,000 volumes, including East Asian holdings of at least 30,000 volumes. The library also currently receives 3,450 serials (an estimated 112 from East Asia) and 26 newspapers, including 3 from East Asia: *Asahi Shimbun, Chung Yang Jih Pao,* and *Jen Min Jih Pao.*

3. a. One of the finest university collections in the Washington area, its holdings are strong in religion, history, literature, language, and linguistics.

  b. Subject categories and evaluations (numbers represent titles):

Subject Category	China/Rating		Japan/Rating		Korea/Rating	
1. Philosophy and Religion	143	C	67		1	
2. History	736	C	473	C	106	C
3. Geography and Ethnography	31	C	11		3	
4. Economics	219	C	96		20	
5. Sociology	115	C	41		6	
6. Government and Politics	88	C	62		6	
7. Foreign Relations	257	B	111	B	9	
8. Law*	12		16		2	
9. Fine Art	6		13		0	
10. Education	23		9		2	
11. Language	2,529	B	1,106	B	43	C
12. Literature	3,376	B	3,081	B	62	
13. Military Affairs	46	C	36	C	64	C
14. Bibliography and Reference	44	C	48	C	27	

15. Mongolia	18	
16. Tibet	145	C
17. Okinawa	3	
18. Hong Kong	50	B

* Georgetown University's Fred O. Dennis Law Library, located at 600 New Jersey Avenue, N.W. (near Capitol Hill), has a Foreign Law Section containing about 21 East Asian titles.

4. c. Georgetown University Library is the only selective depository library for United States government documents among the Washington, D.C., Consortium of Universities. Its holdings total over 71,000 government publications. The library also has a complete set of the *U.N. Documents and Official Records* (1946-present) on microfilm.

  e. The Archives, Manuscripts, and Rare Books Division (625-4567/4160) holds a number of special collections, including the George Schwartz collection which contains correspondence and reports sent from Jesuit missions in North and South America and the Far East from 1675 to 1682, principally addressed to Rev. Mathias Tanner, S.J. A section of the collection deals with Jesuit activities in China.

  g-h. The Audio Visual Department of the library maintains 4 films and 7 slide collections on Japan and China; 9 film strips on Chinese and Japanese cultures; 4 video tapes on China; and several tapes. In addition, it has over 450 reels of microfilm on Asia: 375 reels on "Japan: Correspondence, 1856-1940"; 66 reels on "Japan: Correspondence, 1930-1940"; 16 reels on "Japan and Its Occupied Territories during World War II"; 6 reels on "Postwar Japan, Korea and Southeast Asia"; and 6 reels on "China and India."

A20 Georgetown University—Woodstock Theological Center Library

1. a. *37th and O Streets, NW*
    Washington, D.C. 20057
    625-3120

    b. 9 A.M.-5 P.M.   Monday-Friday

    c. Open to serious researchers for on-site use. Interlibrary loan and photo-duplicating facilities are available.

    d. Father Henry Bertels, S.J., Director
    Father William Sheehan, C.S.B., Assistant Librarian

2-3.   The 150,000-volume Woodstock Library, located in the lower level of Georgetown University's Lauinger Library, has strong holdings on theology, ecclesiastical history and law, and religious studies. Its collection of "Jesuitica" is believed to be as strong as any in the United States.

4.   d. It is within the collection of "Jesuitica" that one finds most of the items of interest to East Asia specialists. Scholars interested in the 16th- and 17th-century encounters between Europe and East Asia, or Christian missionary activities of the time, should find the Woodstock collection worthy of note, for its holdings tend to complement the far larger collections in the Library of Congress or the Catholic University of America. Those interested in the 19th- and 20th-century European involvements in China will find in the Woodstock Collection rare books written by Henri Havret, Louis Hermand, Joseph Hugon, and Louis Pfister. Among the works on China, Woodstock's Special Collection contains one of the rare surviving examples of the blockbooks printed under the direction of the Jesuits in 17th-century Peking: *Innocenta Victrix, sive Sententia Comitiorum Impeii Sinici pro Innocenta,* 1669, by Giovanni Lobelli, S.J. Most of the works related to Japan pertain to the Jesuit missions of the 16th and 17th centuries. Especially important among these are the *Fasciculus e Iaponicis Floribus suo adhuc Madentibus Sanguine* (Rome: Corbellete, 1646), by Antonia Francisco Cardim, S.J.; and a rare edition of letters from John Rodrigues and Matteo Ricci, addressed to the General of the Society of Jesus, Claudio Aquaviva, in 1611. The 8-volume *Histoire et description generale du Japon* (Paris: J. M. Gandouin, 1736), by Pierre Francois Xavier Charlevoix, S.J., presents Japan in all aspects of its culture and life as known in the 18th century. For a more detailed description and a selected list of early Jesuit accounts of China, Japan, and the Jesuit missionary activities and reports, see Ann Nottingham Kelsall, "Resources on China and Japan among the Jesuit Publications in the Woodstock Theological Center Library, Georgetown University," a paper presented at the 1977 Middle Atlantic Region Conference of the Association for Asian Studies, Princeton University, October 27, 1977. At least 40 different titles on China and 13 titles on Japan have been cited in the above-mentioned paper. In addition, 17 periodicals relating to Roman Catholic Missions in Asia (1836-1949) are also available at the Woodstock library.

Government Research Corporation Library See entry M20.

A21 Health, Education and Welfare Department (HEW) Library

1.   a. *330 Independence Avenue, SW*
      Washington, D.C. 20201
      245-6791 (Reference)

    b. 8:30 A.M.-5:30 P.M. Monday-Friday

    c. Open to the public for on-site use. Interlibrary loan and limited photo-duplication services are available.

    d. Charles F. Gately, Director

2-3.   The library contains approximately 600,000 volumes and currently receives about 5,000 periodicals and serials. The collection is strong on subjects pertaining to HEW; however, its holdings on East Asia are small and a relatively minor resource for East Asia specialists.

4.   The library subscribes to several periodicals published in East Asia (e.g., *Peking Review, Japan Quarterly*, etc.).

6.   The researchers can consult the *Author/Title Catalog of the Department Library* (Boston: G. K. Hall, 1965) in 29 volumes plus a 7-volume supplement (1973).

Hirshhorn Museum Library See entry C5.

A22 House of Representatives Library

1.   a. *Cannon House Office Building, B-18*
      New Jersey and Independence Avenues, SE
      Washington, D.C. 20515
      225-0462/0463

    b. 9:00 A.M.-5:30 P.M. Monday-Friday

    c. Open to the public, but stacks are closed. It is advisable to call before visiting. There are no interlibrary loan or photocopying services.

    d. Dr. E. R. Lewis, Librarian

2.   The House library is a legislative and legal reference library comprising over 100,000 volumes. It is the official depository of all published documents originating in and produced by the U.S. House of Representatives and its committees.

4.   Its principal holdings include: House and Senate *Journals* (1st Congress); *Congressional Record* (43rd Congress) and its predecessors such as the *Congressional Globe* (23rd Congress); House Reports and Documents (4th Congress); House Bills and Resolutions (6th Congress); House Committee Hearings (61st Congress); Senate Reports (30th

Congress) and Documents (79th Congress); Congressional Directories (40th Congress); and Precedents (Hinds & Cannon's, Deschlers). (Dates in parentheses indicate the beginning of each set.)

In addition to congressional documents, the House library also contains a number of other publications pertaining to federal law, and various documents of the Executive and Judicial branches of the United States government.

Materials of value to East Asia specialists include various documents relating to United States foreign relations with East Asia. For these materials, it would be easier, faster, and more convenient to use this library than the Library of Congress.

A23 Housing and Urban Development Department (HUD) Library

1. a. *451-7th Street, SW, Room 8141*
      Washington, D.C. 20410
      755-6370

   b. 8:30 A.M.-5:15 P.M.   Monday-Friday

   c. Open to the public. Interlibrary loan and photoduplication services are available.

   d. Elsa Freeman, Director

2-3. The library contains over half a million items, including about 1,800 current periodical titles. There are at least 400 titles pertaining to East Asia. By far the largest number of these titles deal with Japan; they include a collection of research papers published by the Building Research Institute, Japanese Ministry of Construction. The library also subscribes to several Japanese periodicals, such as *Japan Architect*. Researchers interested in utilizing foreign publications and documents acquired by HUD should check with its Office of International Affairs, which maintains a "foreign information retrieval system" that identifies foreign documents (including those from East Asian countries) available in the Office of International Affairs (see entry K15). For the category of Japanese architecture, its holdings deserve a B rating.

5. *The Dictionary Catalog of the United States Department of Housing and Urban Development Library*, 19 vols. (1972) plus two supplements are available. *Housing and Planning References* (bimonthly) indexes new publications, periodical articles, and documents published in the United States and abroad that have been acquired by the library every two months.

A24 Howard University—Founders Library

1. a. *500 Howard Place, NW*
      Washington, D.C. 20059
      636-7250/7251 (Circulation)
      636-7263 (Reference)
      636-7261 (Bernard B. Fall Collection)

    b. Open continuously from noon Sunday until 5:00 P.M. Saturday. Limited services, midnight-8:00 A.M.

    c. Open to serious researchers for on-site use. Interlibrary loan and photo-duplication facilities are available.

    d. Binford Conley, Director of University Libraries

2. The entire library system, which consists of the Founders and 10 smaller libraries, contains more than 1,000,000 volumes. East Asian holdings total approximately 9,000 volumes. Use of these library holdings is somewhat complicated due to the fact that the Founders Library collection is classified partly under the Library of Congress classification scheme (currently in effect) and partly under the older Dewey Decimal system.

3.   **b.** Subject categories and evaluations (numbers represent titles):

Subject Category	China/Rating		Japan/Rating		Korea/Rating
1. Philosophy and Religion	140	C	45		0
2. History	1,537	C	615		78
3. Geography and Ethnography	12		8		0
4. Economics	95		33		5
5. Sociology	49		15		2
6. Government and Politics	47		41		1
7. Foreign Relations	122	C	42	C	5
8. Law	13		8		4
9. Fine Arts	15		15		3
10. Education	19		15		0
11. Language	38		21		0
12. Literature	151		59		5
13. Military Affairs	5		15		20
14. Bibliography and Reference	12		3		1
15. Tibet	13				
16. Mongolia	10				
17. Okinawa			2		
18. Hong Kong	15				

4.   THE BERNARD B. FALL COLLECTION

Dr. Bernard B. Fall, a well-known scholar and author of many works on the Vietnam conflict, was Professor of Government at Howard University from 1958 to 1967. After his tragic death in Vietnam by a Vietcong mine in 1967, his wife, Dorothy Fall, donated a large number of materials from Dr. Fall's private collection to Howard University in 1968. In memory of his invaluable scholarly contributions to Howard University, the present collection has been named after him. It is located at room 300-A in the Founders Library building. The Bernard B. Fall Collection is a noncirculating collection of books, documents, pamphlets, and maps relating primarily to Indochina and to a lesser extent to East Asia. There are approximately 4,500 volumes, 2,000 vertical file items plus about 500 pamphets dealing with Indochina and East Asia. Dr. Fall's numerous works in English and in French, including those published by Hanoi and the National Liberation Front of South Vietnam, are included in the collection. The collection contains materials dealing with many diverse subjects on Asia, including those dealing with Sino-American relations (post-1949) and American involvement in the Indochina conflict.

a-b. Approximately 90 periodicals emanating from China (both active and inactive), 2 from Japan, and 6 from North and South Korea are available at the Bernard B. Fall Collection reading room. Also, the following materials are available in microform: (1) *Survey of China Mainland Press* (Beginning-1965); (2) *Current Background;* (3) *Extracts from the China Mainland Magazines;* (4) *Catalog of New Chinese Publication* (1950-1966); (5) *Joint Publications and Research Service* (1957-1969).

d. At least 376 titles on China, 42 on Japan, and 31 on Korea are included in the Bernard B. Fall Collection. In addition, some 60 pamphlets on China, 19 items dealing with Sino-American relations during the Vietnam conflict, 7 items with Japan, and 13 items on Korea are located in the vertical files.

THE KINDRIC N. MARSHALL COLLECTION

The Bernard B. Fall Collection also contains 2,300 books purchased recently from the Kindric N. Marshall Estate. Most of these books deal with China, Japan, and Korea; specifically, there are 1,400 titles on China, 544 on Japan, and 18 on Korea. Mostly out-of-print materials, one can find a number of rare books (at least 160 titles) which were published during the 19th century, including (1) Percival Lowell, *The Land of the Morning Calm* (1888); John H. Gray, *China, History of the Laws, Manners and Customs of the People* (1878), 2 vols.; Francis L. Hawks, *Narrative of the Expedition of an American Squadron to the China Seas and Japan, Performed in the Years 1852, 1853, & 1854 under the Command of Commodore M. C. Perry, U.S. Navy* (1856); and William Elliot Griffis, *The Mikado's Empire* (1877), 3 vols. For further information concerning the Bernard B. Fall Collection, contact Philip Wu, who is the curator of the collection (636-7261).

Institute for Defense Analyses Library See entry M22.

A25 Interior Department—Natural Resources Library

1. a. *Department of the Interior*
    C Street between 18th and 19th Streets, NW
    Washington, D.C. 20240
    343-5821 (Director's Office)
    345-5815 (Reference)

    b. 7:45 A.M.-5:00 P.M.   Monday-Friday

    c. Open to the public; however, circulation is limited to the department employees. Interlibrary loan and photoduplication service are available.

    d. Mary A. Huffer, Director

2. The library possesses over 775,000 volumes, including 4,000 current periodicals and 8,000 other serial titles which it subscribes to annually. The collection is devoted primarily to conservation and the development of natural resources, energy and power, land use and reclamation, fish and wildlife management, parks and recreation, mines and minerals, and administration of Indian and territorial affairs (U.S.).

3. The library's holdings of East Asian materials are relatively small. Altogether, it has about 400 titles on East Asia, 327 of which deal with "Fishes and Fisheries" (i.e., China—100; Japan—225; and Korea—2). In this category, its holdings on China and Japan should be rated B. In addition, there are several translations of East Asian materials.

6. The library staff has issued the following guides: *Abstracting and Indexing Services Received in the Department Library* (1968); and *Abstracting and Indexing Services in the Office of Library Services* (rev. ed., 1970). The library also publishes a *Bibliography Series* (over 30 titles so far), including No. 9, *Natural Resources in Foreign Countries; A Contribution Toward a Bibliography of Bibliographies* (1968) by Mary Anglemyer. *Dictionary Catalog of the Departmental Library,* 37 vols. (1967), 4 supplementary vols. (to date) are also available [N.B.: Geological Survey Library of the Interior Department (see entry A 17) contains more materials on East Asia.]

A26 International Communication Agency (ICA) Library

1. a. *1750 Pennsylvania Avenue, NW, Room 1011*
      Washington, D.C. 20547
      724-9214 (Librarian)
      724-9126 (Reference)

   b. 8:45 A.M.-5:30 P.M. Monday-Friday

   c. Closed to the public, but qualified researchers may obtain permission to use special materials. Interlibrary loan and photocopying facilities are available.

   d. Jeanne R. Zeydel, Librarian

2. The library's collection consists of about 60,000 volumes and over 5,000 reels of microfilm. Currently, the library receives over 360 periodicals.

3. East Asian holdings number about 970: 421 on China; 386 on Japan, and 160 on Korea. Since many of these titles are readily available in other libraries, the library's collection of books does not rank very high as a major source of information. However, the library maintains a number of special collections (see point 4).

4. General Documents Branch (Mary Woods, Chief, 724-5131) contains about 2,505,000 items in the collection, including material in the subject file as well as the biographic file. There are 900,000 items (20,000 entries) in the biographic file, and 1,605,550 items (30,000 subject headings) in the subject file. In the subject file, one can find at least 160 items on China and the Chinese; 12 on Taiwan; 136 on Japan and the

Japanese, and 87 on Korea and the Koreans. Included are unclassified U.S. government reports and press releases, materials issued by international organizations and clippings from major U.S. newspapers. The collection is organized by geographic areas and by subjects.

Agency Archives (Raymond Harvey, Archivist) maintains books, articles, congressional documents, and agency publications on the history and "pre-history" of ICA.

The Classified Documents Collection (Evelyn Hodges, Chief) includes about 67,000 classified documents, reports, and communiques of ICA and its predecesor (USIA) and other government agencies. Periodically, the materials are reviewed for declassification, and once declassified, they become accessible to researchers. For further information on declassified documents, contact the Director (Public Liaison), Room 1019, or call 724-9103.

6.   A brief guide, *The United States Information Agency Library* and *U.S. Information Agency Library: Periodical Holdings* (1976) can be obtained without charge.

International Food Policy Research Institute Library See entry M23.

A27 International Labor Organization (ILO)—Washington Branch Library

1. a. *1750 New York Avenue, NW, Room 330*
       Washington, D.C. 20006

    b. 8:30 A.M.-5:00 P.M.   Monday-Friday

    c. Open to the public; photoduplication facilities are available.

    d. Patricia S. Hord, Librarian

2.   The total collection consists of over 7,000 volumes plus 3,500 ILO documents.

3.   The strength and value of this library can be found in the fact that it contains about 90 percent of the entire ILO publications. The library's holdings are mostly in economics, sociology, and law and cover the following subjects: labor statistics; conditions, hours, and wages of labor; labor legislation; trade unions; health, safety, and welfare of wage earners; social policy and economic development; specific industries, such as aviation, coal mining, forestry; and employment, unemployment, and standards of living. Although the exact number of items on East Asia in the library's holdings cannot be ascertained, information and data pertaining to Japan, China, and Korea can be found in many ILO publications. Aids to finding relevant ILO publications and other materials relating to East Asia are listed in point 6 below.

4.   A number of important ILO serial titles are available, including: *ILO Record of Proceedings* (1919-present); *Minutes of the Governing Body* (1919-present); *Yearbook of Labor Statistics* (1935-present); *Interna-*

tional Labor Review (1921-present); *Official Bulletin of the ILO* (1919-present); *ILO Conference Reports* (1919-present); *(ILO) Legislative Series* (1919-present); and *ILO, Industrial and Labor Information* (1922-1939). Also, one can find such other ILO publications as *Poverty and Landlessness in Rural Asia* (1977); and a number of issues of *ILO Technical Assistance Report* dealing with Japan, Taiwan, and Korea. The library has a collection of about 2,000 photographs with an undetermined number on Japan and Korea. The library also has about 13 films produced by the ILO which may be borrowed by interested educational institutions and groups on a free-loan basis. For further information, write or call the ILO's Washington Office.

6. For the ILO publications, the following guides are indispensable: *Subject Guides to Publications of the International Labor Office, 1919-1964* (Geneva, 1967) and *ILO Catalogue of Publications in Print, 1975* (Geneva, n.d.). The former has a section on bibliographic contributions with a supplementary geographic index. Also useful is the *Legislative Series: Chronological Index of Laws and Regulations 1919-1967* (Geneva, 1969). The index can be updated by *Annual Supplements,* part 4: "Chronological List of Labour Legislation," which is organized alphabetically by country. *Legislative Series: General Subject Index 1919-1959* is also helpful in the use of ILO's *Legislative Series* that print the most important labor laws and regulations of the ILO member nations (translated into English) from 1920 to the present. The library also has *International Labor Documentation: Cumulative Edition, 1965-1969* (8 vols.), and *Cumulative Edition, 1970-1971* (2 vols.). The monthly *International Labor Documentation* contains information concerning new books cataloged by the ILO Library in Geneva, major new ILO publications, and labor-related abstracts from about 1,000 international journals. Each monthly issue includes approximately 250 short abstracts recorded in machine-readable form. Scholars should consult the staff on how to use these guides.

Japan–America Society of Washington Library See entry H29.

Japan Foundation Library See entry H30.

Johns Hopkins University—School of Advanced International Studies Library See entry M25.

A28 Joint Bank-Fund Library (Library of the International Monetary Fund and the International Bank for Reconstruction and Development)

1. a. *700-19th Street, NW*
    Washington, D.C. 20431
    477-3125 (Librarian)
    477-3167 (Reference)

b. 9:00 A.M.-5:30 P.M. Monday-Friday

c. Open to researchers for on-site use. Interlibrary loan and photoduplication services are available.

d. Charles O. Olsen, Librarian

2. The total collection numbers over 150,000 volumes and 3,000 serial titles, including 160 newspapers.

3. The library has a good collection of material on East Asian banking, commerce, finance, agriculture, industry, economic planning, and development, roughly divided as follows: China, 700 titles (including Taiwan); Japan, 1,300 titles; Korea, 500 titles; and Mongolia, 6 titles. For East Asian economics, the collection can be rated as B.

4. The library's serial holdings on East Asia are particularly strong in the fields of economics, trade, banking, industry, and agriculture. Currently, the library receives 3 from the PRC, 53 from Japan, 17 from South Korea, and 18 from Taiwan. Included are not only academic journals but also reports and surveys compiled by major banks (national as well as commercial), and statistical reports on trade, finance, and labor.

6. Useful reference tools for researchers at the library include: *Guide to the Joint Bank-Fund Library* (1976); *Economics and Finance: Index to Periodical Articles, 1947-1971*, 4 vols., (Boston: G. K. Hall, 1972) and a *First Supplement, 1972-1974; Current List of Periodicals Received by the Joint-Bank-Fund Library*, and *The Developing Areas: A Classed Bibliography of the Joint Bank-Fund Library: Vol. III, Asia and Oceania* (Boston: G. K. Hall, 1976).

A29 Labor Department Library

1. a. *New Department of Labor Building*
   200 Constitution Avenue, NW, Room 2439
   Washington, D.C. 20210
   523-6992 (Reference)

b. 8:15 A.M.-4:45 P.M. Monday-Friday

c. Open to the public for on-site use. Interlibrary loan and photoduplication services are available.

d. Andre C. Whisenton, Librarian

2. This library holds over 540,000 books, and receives more than 3,200 periodicals. The collection is particularly strong on labor and economics.

3. The library's holdings on East Asia number about 1,000 volumes with emphasis on labor and economics. Materials pertaining to China include a series of bulletins put out by various agencies and bureaus of the Chinese government in the 1920s and 1930s. They are mostly statistical in nature. With regard to the People's Republic of China, the library has various reports and documents issued by bureaus of the PRC government, covering economic conditions, trade relations, and others. In addi-

tion, the library has a collection of materials pertaining to American attitudes toward Asian immigrants dating as far back as the 1870s. The library's holdings on Japan include publications issued by the Japanese government on local, social, labor, and economic affairs since the late 1890s. Its holdings on Chinese and Japanese sociology should be rated C.

4.   The library receives about 40 periodicals from East Asia, including 7 from the PRC, 24 from Japan, and 6 from South Korea, many of which are published by government agencies, banks, universities, and research organizations of these countries (e.g., the Bank of Japan's *Wholesale Price Index Monthly, Fuji Bank Bulletin,* Korean *Monthly Economic Statistics, Taiwan Industrial Statistics Monthly*).

6.   A 38-volume U.S. Department of Labor Library Catalog (Boston: G. K. Hall, 1975) is available in the library. Also useful is *Journals Treating Foreign Countries Currently Received by the U.S. Department of Labor* (1973). A biweekly *Labor Literature* lists new acquisitions of the library and is available free of charge.

A30 Library of Congress

Because of the size and diversity of the LC's holdings, which make it by any standards the greatest research library in the Washington area for East Asia specialists, the format of this entry is modified from the standard one. Points 2 and 3 pertain almost exclusively to the main collections in the regular stack areas. The library's special collections, which are located in a particular division or are worthy of more detailed coverage, will be described under point 4. Under point 6 the reader will find those publications and reference materials pertaining to the entire library. Relevant publications and research aids issued by or available at the individual divisions are listed under those branches.

10-1st Street, SE
Washington, D.C. 20540
287-5000

b. General Reading Rooms, Library of Congress and Thomas Jefferson buildings 8:30 A.M.-9:30 P.M. (stack service to 9:00 P.M.), Monday-Friday
8:30 A.M.-5:00 P.M. (stack service to 4:00 P.M.)   Saturday
1:00 P.M.-5:00 P.M. (stack service to 4:30 P.M.)   Sunday and most holidays
Closed Christmas, Labor Day, and New Year's Day
Division hours are noted below

c. For on-site use, LC's facilities and staff service are available free to all scholars. Interlibrary loan service (except periodicals and newspapers) is available, though the process may require some waiting due to the volume of requests received. Photocopying machines are available for public use, and the library also has a photoduplication service.

d. Daniel J. Boorstin, the Librarian of Congress
Division heads are listed below.

2.   Total holdings of the LC exceed 75 million items. The Asian Division estimates that all East Asian language holdings come to about 1 million volumes, of which 800,000-900,000 are monographs and the rest are bound periodicals and pamphlets. No estimate is available on the LC's holdings of Western-language materials on East Asia. A partial breakdown of these holdings appears under point 3, which is based on the measurement of the main shelflist.

3.   a. The LC's holdings on East Asia (i.e., China, Japan, and Korea) are unquestionably the strongest outside of the countries themselves. The LC is regarded as one of the finest research libraries in the field of East Asian studies in the United States, and the best in the Washington area insofar as the library resources on East Asia are concerned.

    b. Subject categories and evaluation.
    The following figures are based on the measurement of the shelflist located in the Processing Services Department of the LC (Thomas Jefferson Building, Second Floor). They do not include the East Asian materials catalogued before 1958. Inevitably the figures represent far less than the actual LC holdings on East Asia and as such may reflect relative strengths at best rather than the actual numerical strength of each subject category.

Subject Category	China	Japan	Korea
1. Philosophy and Religion	2,361	2,633	760
2. History	18,913	21,242	4,011
3. Geography and Ethnography (excluding atlases and maps)	977	2,423	170
4. Economics	4,728	8,501	962
5. Sociology	1,163	1,905	201
6. Politics and Government	1,822	2,702	338
7. Foreign Relations	2,086	1,245	506
8. Law	U	U	U
9. Fine Art	579	1,886	58
10. Education	760	2,749	343
11. Language	5,705	2,974	803
12. Literature	16,883	21,810	3,963
13. Military Affairs	511	665	837
14. Bibliography and Reference	887	674	171
15. Tibet	1,167		
16. Mongolia	613		
17. Okinawa		451	
18. Hong Kong	446		

Rating: On the basis of size and quality, LC's East Asian collections rate an A for every subject category (1 through 18) surveyed.

Note: Atlases and maps of the Geography and Map Division are described separately in entry E3. Music materials are covered under point 4, and in entry D1. The East Asian materials which were catalogued before 1958 are described in connection with the Asian Division, for the shelflist as well as card catalogs for these materials are located at that division.

Divisions of the Library of Congress

ASIAN DIVISION (formerly Orientalia Division)

Thomas Jefferson Building, First Floor, Room A-1024
287-5420

Dr. Warren M. Tsuneishi, Chief (287-5426/5420)
Dr. Richard Howard, Assistant Chief (287-5426)

Chinese and Korean Section, Room A-1008
Dr. Chi Wang, Head (287-5423/5425)
Dr. Key P. Yang, Korean Area Specialist (287-5424)

Japanese Section, Room A-1010

Hisao Matsumoto, Head (287-5430)

8:30 A.M.-4:30 P.M.   Monday-Friday

8:30 A.M.-12:30 P.M.   Saturday

Closed Sunday

This division should be the first point of contact for East Asia specialists who want to find out what East Asian materials the LC has and how best to get hold of them. Staff members are of immense help to researchers in securing current bibliographic references and locating uncataloged or unclassified materials. The Asian Division takes an active role in the development of national library resources for research and the study of China, Japan, and Korea. It provides specialized reference services with respect to materials dealing with East Asia. Its facilities are used extensively by U.S. government agencies, research and educational institutions, as well as individual scholars. It handles reference inquiries by phone, by correspondence, and in person.

The division also maintains a reading room (Room 1016) where a number of basic reference materials are located. More specialized reference materials are located in each country section of the division.

Catalogs of Chinese, Japanese, and Korean books and publications are maintained in the respective sections of the Asian Division and in the division office. Printed cards for the East Asian publications currently cataloged are sold by the LC's Cataloging Distribution Service. These catalogs are indispensable tools for locating specific monographic titles or issues of periodicals held by the Asian Division.

EAST ASIAN LANGUAGE MATERIALS

Of the nearly one million volumes of East Asian language materials currently held by the Asian Division, about 550,000 volumes are written in Japanese, 430,000 in Chinese, and 60,000 in Korean. The East Asian collections are especially strong in the humanities, social sciences, and law. The Chinese collections are notable in works on communism, history, literature, law, and archaeology. The Japanese collections are noteworthy on national and local government publications acquired on exchange from the National Diet Library of Japan. The current strength of the Korean collections lies in history, literature, economics, politics, and law. It should be pointed out that East Asian materials cataloged since 1958 are included in the main shelflist and catalogs of the LC, while those cataloged before 1958 are not.

Works cataloged before 1958 by the former Orientalia Division (numbering approximately 57,000 titles—about 35,000 in Chinese, 20,000 in Japanese, and 2,000 in Korean) are represented in separate card catalogs maintained in the Asian Division and are not listed in the *Far Eastern Languages Catalog*. Many of the materials cataloged before 1958, the bulk of the Chinese collection, represent the traditional literature of the pre-modern period. This is especially true for Chinese and Korean works. In addition, a substantial body of pre-World War II and Occupation-period Japanese materials remain in semiprocessed form under partial bibliographical control.

PERIODICALS AND NEWSPAPERS

The Chinese and Korean Section holds approximately 8,000 periodical titles, including about 1,200 published in the People's Republic of China since 1949. More than 1,000 current periodicals are received regularly, including about 30 Chinese-language newspapers. The section is also responsible for maintaining about 2,800 serial titles on Korea which include about 1,400 active titles. Also over 160 Korean newspaper titles, including 39 current ones, are held by the Chinese and Korean Section. Serial titles held by the Japanese Section number about 12,000. Currently, it receives at least 20 newspapers.

SPECIAL COLLECTIONS: CHINA

Among rare items in the Chinese collection, the following should be mentioned: about 1,800 works printed before the Ch'ing dynasty, i.e., before 1644; 4,000 local histories, one of the largest collections ever assembled; fragments of eight Buddhist manuscript rolls made during and after the T'ang dynasty (A.D. 618-A.D. 906); 41 volumes of the original manuscript encyclopedia *Yung-lo ta tien;* and 1,072 reels of microfilms of 2,800 rare books of the National Library of Peiping. At least 1,777 items out of the above-mentioned rare books and manuscripts held by the Orientalia Division have been described in *A Descriptive Catalog of Rare Books in the Library of Congress* (1957), compiled by Chung-min Wang. The following listings are more detailed descriptions of some of the rare works held by the Asian Division:

(1) *Ku Chin t'u shu chi ch'eng.* Compiled under imperial auspices in the first quarter of the 18th century, this encyclopedia consists of 5,044 volumes in 528 cases. According to an estimate made by the eminent Sinologist, Professor Lionel Giles, this set contains between three and four times as much material as the 11th edition of the *Encyclopedia Britannica*. Only 64 original sets were printed in 1725.

(2) *Shih shih yuan liu ying hua shih chi.* This book deals with the origins of Buddhism and its development in China and was issued in 1486 under the auspices of the Emperor Hsien-tsung. It is in four vol-

umes, each volume containing 100 hand-colored paintings. Each painting is followed by a page of quotations from other works describing the episode depicted.

(3) *Yung-lo ta tien*. This is a handwritten encyclopedia compiled during 1403-07 in the reign of the third Ming emperor. To compile the set, over 2,000 scholars were employed. Only two manuscript copies, each comprising 11,095 folio volumes, were made. One of the two sets was entirely destroyed during the last days of the Ming dynasty. Subsequently, many volumes of the remaining set were lost. It is estimated that fewer than 500 volumes of this prodigious work are known to be extant; they are dispersed among various libraries and private collections all over the world. The LC has 41 original volumes.

(4) *Nung cheng ch'uan shu*. An encyclopedia on agriculture compiled by Kuang-ch'i Hsu (1562-1633), it consists of 24 volumes printed in 1837. This set was one of the 10 titles sent to the United States by the Chinese Government as a gift in 1869.

(5) *Tun-huang manuscript scrolls*. The Tun-huang manuscript scrolls, stored in a sealed chamber and unknown to the world for 1,000 years, were discovered at the turn of the century in the grottoes of Tun-huang in Kansu province. Made during the T'ang dynasty (A.D. 618-A.D. 906), they are the earliest surviving Chinese writing on paper and some of them antedate the use of block printing by several centuries.

(6) *The Buddhist Sutra, printed in 975*. One of the many scrolls recovered from the foundation of the famous Thunder Peak Pagoda in West Lake, Hangchow, which collapsed in a thunderstorm in 1924, this scroll constitutes the earliest example of Chinese printing in the LC.

(7) *The Moso pictographic manuscript*. The Moso (or Nashi) tribe is a minority group in Li-chiang in the southwestern province of Yunnan. Sorcery is practiced there, and for ceremonial chants the priests developed pictographic scripts. The LC has 3,000 volumes of Moso pictographic books.

(8) *The Tibetan Tripitaka*. The sutra is composed of two divisions, the *Kanjur* and the *Tanjur* with 318 fascicles. The *Kanjur* consists principally of teachings and sermons enunciated by the Buddha, while the *Tanjur* is a collection of expositions and treatises on such diverse subjects as history, language, logic, and medicine. The set was printed in the latter part of the 18th century. The wooden blocks, stored in a lamasery at Choni, Kansu province, were completely consumed by fire not long after the LC acquired this set in 1928.

(9) *Yen i pien*. A collection of 12 classical tales, each with an illustration; printed ca. 1600.

(10) *Keng chih t'u*. An album containing 46 original paintings by Court Painter Chiao Ping-chen (fl. 1662-1722); drawn in color on silk, the paintings depict various aspects of tilling and weaving. Each picture is accompanied by two poems, composed by Emperor Sheng-tsu whose reign period was known as K'ang-hsi (1662-1722) and transcribed by Yen Yu-tun (1650-1713).

(11) *Wu pei chih*. This treatise on military preparedness by Mao Yuan-i was written in 1621 and printed a few years later. It deals with weapons, firearms, and pyrotechnic stratagems.

(12) *The Caleb Cushing Collection*. The LC acquired the collection of Caleb Cushing, the American envoy who was sent to negotiate the first treaty between the United States and China in 1844, totaling 237 works in more than 2,500 volumes.

(13) *The Rockhill Collection*. The private library of basic Chinese litera-ture, collected by William W. Rockhill, United States Minister to China from 1905-1909, was donated to the LC after Rockhill's retirement from government service. It contains 6,000 volumes in the Chinese, Manchu, and Tibetan languages.

(14) *The Manchu Collection*. By far the most extensive collection in the United States, the LC holdings contain approximately 400 titles; each title has from one to 40 volumes. A useful catalog for the collection is compiled by Jun Matsumura and published in the Tōyō Gakuhō voL 57, nos. 1-2 (January 1976) ("A Catalogue of the Manchu Books in the Library of Congress").

(15) *Tibetan Materials*. In addition to the set of Choni *Kanjur* and *Tanjur* (described above), the LC has Derge *Kanjur;* a Narthang *Kanjur;* and the Peking "Red" edition (photoreproduction) of the *Kanjur* and *Tanjur*. In addition, the collection of Tibetan classical mate-rials includes about 200 xylographs.

(16) *The Mongolian Collection*. The Mongolian holdings are largely uncataloged and probably number a few hundred items; they include 3 manuscripts and 77 xylographs—valuable examples of Mongolian block-print literature on a variety of religious and other subjects. More detailed information on the Mongolian materials can be found in David M. Farquhar, "A Description of the Mongolian Manuscripts and Xylo-graphs in Washington, D.C.," *Central Asiatic Journal*, vol. 1, no. 3 (1955).

(17) *The Rare Books of the National Library of Peiping* (microfilms). 1,072 reels of microfilms of 2,800 rare works of the National Library of Peiping, which is now in custody of the National Central Library in Taipei.

SPECIAL COLLECTIONS: JAPAN

(1) *Crosby Stuart Noyes Collection*. In October 1905, Crosby Stuart Noyes of Washington, D.C., donated to the LC his entire collection of Japanese art, which included 12 watercolors, 145 original drawings, 331 wood engravings, 97 lithographs, 658 illustrated books, and 61 other items, representing works produced from the mid-18th century to the late 19th century. Single prints in this gift are now in the custody of the Prints and Photographs Division, while the illustrated books have been transferred to the Japanese Section of the Asian Division where they are kept as rare books in a separate "Noyes Collection." Included are "gachō," "gafu," and formats of a similar nature of 119 individual artists such as Beisen, Bunchō, Hiroshige, Hokusai, Kuniyoshi, Utamaro,

and 54 anonymous artists, as well as 31 titles of collected works. For details of the collection, see LC, *The Noyes Collection of Japanese Prints, Drawings, etc. Presented by Crosby Stuart Noyes* (Washington, D.C.: Government Printing Office, 1906).

(2) *Kan'ichi Asakawa Collection.* Commissioned by the Librarian of Congress, Professor Kan'ichi Asakawa of Yale University acquired in 1907-08 in Japan 9,072 volumes, representing approximately 3,160 titles. Approximately 75 percent of these works have been distributed among the present collections of the Japanese Section, while the remain- 25 percent is still shelved in the original shelflist order. The collection is particularly noteworthy for its comprehensive collection of volumes relating to Japanese Buddhist sects such as Jōdo-shū, Shin-shū, Nichiren sect, Tendai-shū, and Shingon-shū. Certain important works of the Zen sect are also included. In addition, there are 4 handwritten scrolls of a Buddhist canon made in the 8th century A.D.; 7 minutely illustrated handwritten scrolls of secret teaching of Ryōbu Shintō; and 37 scrolls in manuscript relating to swords collected by the late Ichirō Okubo. Although much of the collection remains uncataloged, more detailed description of the Asakawa Collection can be found in Andrew Y. Kuroda, "A History of the Japanese Collection in the Library of Congress, 1874-1941," *Senda Masao Kyōju Koki Kinen Toshokan Shiryō Ronshū* (Tenri: Senda Masao Kyōju Koki Kinenkai, Tenri Daigaku, 1970), pp. 297-306.

(3) *Shio Sakanishi Collection.* This collection includes a large number of books purchased by Dr. Shio Sakanishi of the LC in Japan in 1938. Numbering nearly 300 works of the so-called "kibyōshi," they include such authors as Kyōden Santō, Ikku Jippensha, and Harumachi Koika-wa; nearly 200 are volumes of "haiku," and there are a number of illustrated storybooks, books of flower arrangement, and of cooking of the late Tokugawa period. For a detailed description of the Sakanishi Collection, see *ibid.*, pp. 314-319.

(4) *South Manchurian Railway Co. Collection.* From 1907 to 1945, the South Manchurian Railway Company (SMR) research department published 6,284 research reports for the company, the Japanese Army, and other government agencies concerning natural resources, social and political conditions, and economic possibilities in Manchuria, China, Korea, the Soviet Union, etc. Out of 6,284 known pieces of research publications, 5,011 items are available at the LC. For an annotated bibliography of the SMR publications, see John Young, *The Research Activities of the South Manchurian Railway Company 1907-1945: A History and Bibliography* (New York: East Asian Institute, Columbia University, 1966).

(5) *Selected Archives of the Japanese Army, Navy, and Other Government Agencies, 1868-1945* (Microfilms). Some 400,000 pages of historical materials selected from the archives of the Japanese Army and Navy Ministries and of a small collection from the archives of the Home Ministry and other Japanese government agencies were microfilmed in 163 reels before the archives (seized after World War II) were returned to Japan in 1958. These documents deal mostly with events which took

place in East Asia from 1900 to 1945. For a checklist of the microfilms, see John Young, *Checklist of Microfilm Reproductions of Selected Archives of the Japanese Army, Navy, and Other Government Agencies, 1868-1945* (Washington, D.C.: Georgetown University Press, 1959).

(6) *Archives in the Japanese Ministry of Foreign Affairs, Tokyo, Japan, 1868-1945* (microfilms). Under the auspices of the U.S. Department of State, a team of specialists microfilmed for the LC over 2 million pages of archives of the Japanese Ministry of Foreign Affairs (covering from 1868 to 1945) in Tokyo from 1949 to 1951. These materials were then under the control of the Supreme Commander of the Allied Powers (SCAP). A total of 2,116 reels of microfilms are available at the LC. For a checklist of the microfilms, see Cecil H. Uyehara, *Checklist of Archives in the Japanese Ministry of Foreign Affairs, Tokyo, Japan, 1868-1945 (Microfilmed for the Library of Congress, 1949-1951)* (Washington D.C.: LC, 1954).

SPECIAL COLLECTIONS: KOREA

(1) *Yijo Sillok.* 849 vols. The "Annals of the Yi Dynasty" record the deeds of the Korean monarchs throughout the 5 centuries of the Yi Dynasty (1392-1910). All but 2 of the 27 (Kojong and Sunjong) annals have been published. These chronicles, originally contained in a set of over 1,700 volumes, were published in the fascimile edition by Keijo Imperial University during the Japanese colonial rule in Korea (1910-1945).

(2) *Old Books and Individual Literary Collections (Munjib).* These are about 4,500 volumes of early imprints of Korea, representing about 1,700 titles, which include such well-known works as *Samkang Haengshildo* (1432); *Hunmin Chŏngum* (ca. 1430); and *Munhŏn Pigo,* an encyclopedia which was originally compiled in 1588 and subsequently published in an enlarged edition of 51 volumes in 1908.

(3) *North Korean Collection.* The Chinese and Korean Section holds approximately 2,500 to 3,000 titles published in North Korea since 1945. In addition, it maintains about 290 periodicals and 40 newspapers emanating from North Korea. For details, see Key P. Yang, *Catalog for the North Korean Books,* (LC, 1971).

LC PUBLICATIONS: EAST ASIA

A number of publications are of great value to East Asian specialists.

(1) Shih-chia Chu, *Catalogue of Chinese Local Histories in the Library of Congress* (1942).

(2) *Far Eastern Languages Catalog* (Boston: G. K. Hall & Co., 1972). 22 vols. Publications cataloged between 1958 and 1971 are included).

(3) Chung-min Wang, comp.; T. L. Yuan ed., *A Descriptive Catalog of Rare Chinese Books in the Library of Congress* (1957), 2 vols.

(4) Han-chu Huang, *Chinese Periodicals in the Library of Congress* (forthcoming).

(5) Arthur W. Hummel, ed., *Eminent Chinese of the Ch'ing Period* (1943-44).

(6) *Chinese Cooperative Catalog* (1975-).

(7) Robert Dunn, *Chinese-English and English Chinese Dictionaries in the Library of Congress* (1977).

(8) *Draft Listing of Communist Newspapers Held by the Library of Congress* (1964-1965) 2 vols.

(9) *Union Card File of Oriental Vernacular Series: Chinese, Japanese and Korean* (1966).

(10) Cecil H. Uyehara, *Checklist of Archives in the Ministry of Foreign Affairs, Tokyo, Japan, 1868-1945* (LC, 1954).

(11) *Korea: An Annotated Bibliography of Publications in Far Eastern Languages* (1950).

OTHER BIBLIOGRAPHIC AND REFERENCE MATERIALS

(1) James Chu-yul Soong, *Chinese Materials on Microfilm Available from the Library of Congress* (Washington, D.C.: Center for Chinese Research Materials, 1971).

(2) James D. Pearson, *Oriental Manuscripts in Europe and North America: A Survey* (Zug, Switzerland: Inter Documentation Co., 1971).

(3) Association for Asian Studies, Committee on East Asian Libraries, *Library Resources on Asia* (Zug, Switzerland: Inter Documentation Co., 1967).

(4) Jun Matsumura, "A Catalogue of the Manchu Books in the Library of Congress, Washington, D.C.," *Tōyō Gakuhō*, vol. 57, nos. 1-2 (Jan. 1976).

(5) Tsuen-hsuin Tsien, "First Chinese-American Exchange of Publications," *Harvard Journal of Asiatic Studies*. vol. 25, 1964-1965.

(6) Harvard-Yenching Library, *Classified Catalogue of Korean Books* (Cambridge, Mass.: Harvard-Yenching Library, 1961).

(7) Thomas Hosuck Kang, "Korean Literature and Bibliography," *Encyclopedia of Library and Information Science* (New York: Marcel Dekker, 1977), vol. 21.

(8) William Sheh Wong, "Chinese Literature and Bibliography," From *Encyclopedia* (7).

(9) Hideo Kaneko, "Japanese Literature and Bibliography," From *Encyclopedia* (7).

(10) Theodore Besterman, ed., *A World Bibliography of Oriental Bibliographies;* rev. and updated by J. D. Pearson (Totowa, N.J.: Rowan and Littlefield, 1975).

(11) G. Raymond Nunn, *Asia: A Selected and Annotated Guide to Reference Work* (Cambridge, Mass.: MIT Press, 1971).

(12) Tsuen-hsuin Tsien, *A Guide to Reference and Source Materials for Chinese Studies* (University of Chicago, 1970).

(13) Endymion P. Wilkinson, *The History of Imperial China: A Research Guide* (Harvard University Press, 1973).

(14) John Young, *Checklist of Microfilm Reproductions of Selected Archives of the Japanese Army, Navy and Other Government Agencies* (Washington, D.C.: Georgetown University Press, 1959).

(15) John Young, *The Research Activities of the South Manchurian Railway Company, 1907-45: A History and Bibliography* (New York: East Asian Institute, Columbia University, 1966).

(16) Ping-kuen Yu et al., eds., *Materials on Twentieth Century China: An Annotated List of CCRM Publications* (Washington, D.C.: Center for Chinese Research Materials, Association of Research Libraries, 1975).

(17) Tung-li Yuan, *Russian Works on China, 1918-1960, in American Libraries* (Yale University Press, 1961).

(18) Ping-kuen Yu, comp., *Chinese Collections in the Library of Congress: Excerpts from the Annual Reports of the Librarian of Congress, 1898-1971* (Washington, D.C.: Center for Chinese Research Materials, Association of Research Libraries, 1974). 3 vols.

(19) David M. Farquhar, "A Description of the Mongolian Manuscripts and Xylographs in Washington, D.C.," *Central Asiatic Journal*, vol. 1, no. 3 (1955).

(20) Robert E. Ward and Frank J. Shulman, *The Allied Occupation of Japan, 1945-1952: An Annotated Bibliography of Western Language Materials* (Chicago: American Library Association, 1974).

(21) Norman D. King, *Ryukyu Islands, A Bibliography*. (Washington, D.C.: Department of Army, 1967).

FAR EASTERN LAW DIVISION

Law Library
Library of Congress Building, Second Floor
287-5065

Carleton W. Kenyon, Law Librarian (287-5065)

Dr. Tao-tai Hsia, Chief of Far Eastern Law Division (287-5085)

Dr. Sung Yoon Cho, Assistant to the Chief (287-5085)

Mya Saw Shin, Senior Legal Specialist (287-5085)

Phuong Khan Nguyen, Legal Specialist (287-5085)

8:30 A.M.-4:30 P.M.   Monday-Friday

By prior arrangement with a staff member of the Far Eastern Law Division (LL   FE), most materials in the division's collections may be used on reserve in the Anglo-American Law Reading Room of the Law

Library in the evening and on weekends. The Anglo-American Law Reading Room is open 8:30 A.M.-9:30 P.M. Monday-Friday; 8:30 A.M.-5:00 P.M. Saturday; 1:00 P.M.-5:00 P.M. Sunday. The Law Library contains over 1.5 million volumes. As one of the five divisions of the Law Library, the Far Eastern Law Division (LL FE) is responsible for the custody of materials dealing with the law of the nations of East and Southeast Asia, including Hong Kong, but excluding the Philippines, and for reference and research service involving their use. As of December 1977, the division's holdings totaled 91,000 volumes with the following distribution: China, 21,000 volumes; Japan, 57,000 volumes; Korea, 6,000 volumes; and Southeast Asia, 7,000 volumes.

While the holdings of Mongolian materials are insignificant, the Chinese, Japanese, and Korean collections are probably the best outside the countries themselves. At present, annual additions to the collections number 350 volumes of Chinese monographs; 850 volumes of Japanese monographs; and 280 volumes of Korean monographs.

Although the division's holdings cataloged during 1958-1971 are included in the LC's *Far Eastern Languages Catalog* (G. K. Hall, 1972), there is no separate published catalog of the Far Eastern Law Division's holdings, and no LC classification schedule has been devised for East and Southeast Asian legal materials. Cards for the division's holdings are filed in the dictionary catalog maintained in the Law Library and in the other main public catalogs of the Library of Congress. Entries for the division's microfilm materials, which number about 825 reels, have been made in the Law Library's microtext shelflist.

Like the other foreign law divisions of the Law Library, the Far Eastern Law Division uses its holdings to provide reference and research service to a varied clientele. Its staff of legal specialists and research assistants responds to all inquiries from the members and committees of Congress concerning East and Southeast Asian law. These responses often take the form of in-depth analyses of major legal topics. The division also prepares studies in anticipation of congressional requests. Second priority is given to requests from the executive and judicial branches for information on the law of the nations of East and Southeast Asia, which are necessary for the proper disposition of official business. Reference and bibliographic assistance is provided to those who come to the division and, insofar as policy and time allow, to those who address written requests to the Law Librarian or the Division Chief. Interlibrary loans may be arranged through the Loan Division of the Library of Congress. Requests for the photocopying of the division's materials should be addressed to the Chief, Photoduplication Service, Library of Congress, Washington, D.C. 20540.

A number of rare Chinese and Japanese titles are kept in the special collections of the Orientalia Division. However, there are several noteworthy collections located at the LL FE.

During a trip to the Far East in 1962, the chief of the division acquired *Ssu fa hsing cheng pu tiao ch'a chu so ts'ang Chung kung fa lu wen chien (Communist Chinese legal documents held by the Bureau of Investigation, Ministry of Justice, Republic of China)*. One of the most valuable bodies of materials on justice and law in Communist China, this collection consists of hand-copied documents bound in 28 volumes. Another noteworthy item in LL FE's collections is a complete set of *Hōrei zensho (Statutes at Large)* from 1868 to 1945 on microfilm. These films represent Japanese statutes arranged chronologically under various subject headings. Rare Korean holdings include 29 volumes of legal classics compiled during the Yi Dynasty (1392-1910). These are held in their original form, either handwritten with brushes or printed with wood-block letters.

Helpful information concerning the LL FE collections can be found in the following publications of the Far Eastern Law Division. Tao-tai Hsia's *Guide to Selected Legal Sources of Mainland China* (Washington, D.C.: Library of Congress, 1967) provides a listing of the laws and regulations contained in the two major statutory compilations of the People's Republic of China and translations of titles of Communist Chinese legal periodical literature. Sung Yoon Cho's *Japanese Writings on Communist Chinese Law 1946-1974; A Selected Annotated Bibliography* (Washington, D.C.: Library of Congress, 1977) comprises materials dealing with Communist Chinese law published in Japan in the Japanese language from 1946 to 1974. Paul Ho's *The People's Republic of China and International Law; A Selected Bibliography of Chinese Sources* (Washington, D.C.: Library of Congress, 1972) covers monographic materials and articles in periodicals and newspapers published in the Chinese language in the People's Republic of China.

RARE BOOK DIVISION

Library of Congress Building, Second Floor, Room 256

William Matheson, Chief (287-5434)

8:30 A.M.-5:00 P.M. Monday-Friday only

Since most rare books of East Asian origins are located in the Asian Division, there are only limited numbers of scattered items in Western languages relating to East Asia among this division's holdings which total more than 500,000 items and include 300,000 volumes and pamphlets, over 27,000 broadsides, and 44,000 title pages filed for copyright purposes from 1790-1870. In the card catalogs located in the division, one can find over 205 titles on China, about 200 titles on Japan and 4 titles on Korea. These materials are kept in the Rare Book Division for the following reasons: (1) age (mostly published before 1900); (2) special format—miniature books, broadsides, etc.; (3) notable examples of printing illustration; (4) ownership of the materials by famous individuals; or (5) presentation with inscription by well-known figures.

Regarding materials on China, one should mention the following: (1) *The Chinese Repository*, vols. 1-20 (1832-1851); (2) 1 portfolio containing 6 broadsides relating to China, including Sun Yat-sen's "Manifesto to Foreign Powers" signed on May 5, 1921 (printed); and (3) early travel books written by Western visitors and missionaries, including Juan Gonzalez de Mendoza, *Dell'historia della China* (Genova, 1586). Among the division's holdings on Japan, one should mention two books written by Emperor Hirohito of Japan: *Some Hydroids of the Amakusa Islands* (1969); and *A Review of the Hydroids of the Family*

Clathronidae with Description of a New Genus and Species from Japan (1969). Also, one can find a number of early travel books on Japan which were published in Europe in the 16th and 17th centuries.

In the Harrison Elliott Collection of Paperiana, there are some 2,500 specimen sheets (e.g., hand-made papers) from the Japan Paper Company and Stevens-Nelson Company. On Korea, one can find Basil Hall's *Account of a Voyage of Discovery to the West Coast of Korea and the Great Loo-Choo Island* (1818) in the Rare Book Division. For the division as a whole, two publications facilitate access to its holdings: The Rare Book Division: *A Guide to Its Collections and Services* (1965); and *Some Guides to Special Collections in the Rare Book Division* (1974). Both are available free on request.

MOTION PICTURE, BROADCASTING, AND RECORDED-SOUND DIVISION

Thomas Jefferson Building, Room 1046
287-5840

Erik Barnouw, Chief

8:00 A.M.-4:30 P.M.   Monday-Friday

This division maintains the LC's film collection for scholarly study and research. The collections contain over 75,000 titles, or more than 250,000 reels. Over 1,500 titles, including television films and video tapes, are added each year through copyright deposit, purchase, gift, or exchange.

For East Asia specialists, the division's holdings of nontextual materials on China, Japan, and Korea can be of real interest. Of particular importance to Japan specialists, for example, are about 4,500 Japanese records (78 rpm), mostly Japanese popular songs, produced before 1945. Also, there are materials of the Office of War Information (OWI), numbering 14-15,000 items, which were intended for the consumption of Japanese, Chinese, and Korean audiences during the World War II period (see entry D2 below).

In addition, the division maintains over 1,500 films, including a special collection on Japan. Included are over 1,400 Japanese documentaries, newsreels, and feature films (about 200) of the pre-1945 period, over 100 Chinese films, and about 60 Korean films. For a more detailed description of these films, see entry F5 below.

MUSIC DIVISION

Library of Congress Building, Street Level, Room G126
287-5507

Donald L. Leavitt, Chief (287-6321)

8:30 A.M.-5:30 P.M.   Monday-Saturday

The Music Division has custody of over 4 million items, including scores, sheet music, librettos, books, manuscripts, periodicals, and a variety of recordings.

The division's holdings are strong in Western music; however, one can also find some East Asian materials here. Since most of the holdings are not listed in the main public catalog, measurement of the shelflist (located in the Processing Department in the Thomas Jefferson Building) is an unsatisfactory method of ascertaining the division's holdings. In order to obtain a more accurate measurement, one may have to consult other tools located in the division's reading room (e.g., the class catalog, etc.).

Measurement of the main shelflist has revealed that there are at least 387 titles on Chinese music; 260 titles on Japanese music; 72 titles on Korean music; and 6 titles on Mongolian music.

A number of LC publications can facilitate access to the division's holdings: *The Library of Congress Catalog: Music and Phonorecords; a Cumulative List of Works Represented by Library of Congress Printed Cards,* which was issued as part of the *National Union Catalog,* has now been replaced by *Music, Books on Music, and Sound Recordings* (issued semiannually with annual and quinquennial cumulations). Although published as a part of the *National Union Catalog,* it is also available separately. The division also publishes a number of brochures, including the *Music Division: A Guide to Its Collections and Services* (1972).

AMERICAN FOLKLIFE CENTER—ARCHIVES OF FOLK SONG

Library of Congress Building, Ground Floor, Room G152

Joseph C. Hickerson, Head

8:30 A.M.-5:00 P.M.   Monday-Friday

The Archives of Folk Song houses over 225,000 sheets of manuscript material, including the 180,000 pages amassed in the fields of folklore, folk tales, oral history, and other types of folklore. It also houses over 30,000 recordings containing over 300,000 items of folksong, folk music, folk tales, oral history, and other types of folklore. The American Folklife Center maintains a reading room with over 2,500 books and periodicals dealing with folk music, folklore, and ethnomusicology, which are selected from the LC's collections. In addition to standard publications, it has also assembled a sizable collection of magazines, newsletters, and other serials of interest to folklorists and ethnomusicologists, as well as a number of unpublished theses and dissertations. For the archive's holdings on East Asia, see entry D1. The center's publications include *Folklife Center News* (monthly), and a brochure entitled *The Archive of Folk Song.*

SCIENCE AND TECHNOLOGY DIVISION

Thomas Jefferson Building, Fifth Floor, Science Reading Room
287-5639 (reference)
287-5687

Marvin W. McFarland, Chief (287-5674)
John F. Price, Assistant Chief for Reference and Referral
Thomas E. Hughes, Assistant Chief for Information Services

This division is primarily responsible for the LC's collections in science and technology, manages the Science Reading Room, and provides a variety of reference and bibliographic services. Although "science" means primarily the natural sciences, the division's National Referral Center covers some social sciences. The LC's holdings in these fields are quite extensive: over 3 million monographs, 20,000 current periodicals, and over 2.5 million technical reports.

The division provides reference service free of charge, except in cases of special or lengthy searches. Service hours of the Science Reading Room are the same as those for the Main and Thomas Jefferson reading rooms. Readers should note the presence of computer terminals in the Science Reading Room. Of particular interest to East Asia specialists are a series of bibliographic guides on a variety of subjects issued under the title *LC Science Tracer Bullet.* Several important subjects relating to East Asia dealt with as a part of this series include "Acupuncture" (1972); "Herbal and Folk Medicine" (1977); and "Ginseng" (July 1977). Each "tracer bullet" lists basic texts, handbooks, bibliographies, conference proceedings, government publications, and selected journal articles dealing with the particular subject. It also includes additional sources of information that a reader may look into. A typical "tracer bullet" ranges from 8 to 10 pages. So far, the division has published more than 100; free copies are available upon request. Also available is a brief guide to the division: *Mission and Services of the Science and Technology Division* (1973).

A bibliography entitled *Publications Prepared by the Science and Technology Division, 1940-1975* lists many titles, including the following:

(1) *Directories in Science and Technology; a Provisional Check List* (1963).

(2) *International Scientific Organizations: A Guide to Their Library Documentation and Information Services* (1962).

(3) *Directories Containing Descriptive Information on Nonbiographic Data Bases; A Selected Bibliography* (1973).

(4) *A Guide to the World's Abstracting and Indexing Services in Science and Technology* (1963).

(5) *Chinese Scientific and Technical Serial Publications in the Collection of the Library of Congress* (1961).

(6) *Journals in Science and Technology Published in Japan and Mainland China; a Selected List* (1961).

(7) *Nuclear Science in Mainland China; A Selected Bibliography* (1968).

(8) *Japanese Scientific and Technical Serial Publications in the Collections of the Library of Congress* (1962).

(9) *Academic and Technical Research Organizations of Mainland China: A Selective Listing* (1966).

For current information, or bibliographic assistance on questions of science and technology, the researcher should direct inquiries to the division (287-5639); by mail, address the inquiry to the division at the Library of Congress, 10   1st Street, SE, Washington, D.C. 20540.

NATIONAL REFERRAL CENTER: Operated by the Science and Technology Division, the center is open Monday through Friday, 8:30 A.M. to 4:30 P.M. A data base maintained by the center is a subject-indexed inventory that contains descriptions of about 12,000 "information resources" (i.e., organizations, institutions, groups, and some individuals) which are capable and willing to provide specialized knowledge and information in virtually any field, including the physical, biological, and social sciences. For anyone seeking advice on where to obtain information on specific topics, the center acts as an intermediary between those seeking information and the available "information resources" (e.g., organizations with expertise on the subject of inquiry). Inquiries may be made in person, by telephone, or by mail, and are generally handled within 5 days. The center can best provide service if inquiries include a precise statement specifying the desired information. It would also be helpful to include information on the resources already checked by the inquirer, plus the qualifications of the inquirer which may facilitate access to resources otherwise not open. Normally, the center's reply lists the name, address, and telephone number of information resources which are readily available. With regard to Japan, 21 scientific and research organizations (located both in the United States and in Japan) are registered with the National Referral Center; 19 organizations (mostly university-affiliated research organizations in the United States) are registered for China; and 6 are available for information on Korea. The center handled more than 32,000 inquiries during its first 10 years of existence (1964-1974).

Scholars desiring to utilize this referral service may be able to do so by contacting the division.

Telephone inquiries should be directed as follows: (202) 287-5670 for referral service; and (202) 287-5680 for registration of information resources.

Correspondence should be addressed to:

Library of Congress
Science and Technology Division
National Referral Center
10   1st Street, SE
Washington, D.C. 20540

The Referral Center distributes free copies of a 1978 folder entitled *National Referral Center.* Other publications of the center include a series of volumes under the general title, *A Directory of Information Resources in the United States.* Among the more general volumes are those subtitled as follows:

Social Sciences (rev. ed., 1973).
Federal Government, With a Supplement of Government-Sponsored Information Analysis Centers (1973).
Physical Sciences, Engineering (1971).
Biological Sciences (1972).

Additionally, the center has published a *Directory of Federally Supported Information Analysis Centers* (1974). The fourth edition (1979) is in press.

Also, *NRC Switchboard,* an irregular series of select lists of information resources registered with the Referral Center for specific subjects, can be secured from the center without charge while they last.

SERIAL AND GOVERNMENT PUBLICATIONS DIVISION

Newspaper and Current Periodical Room
Thomas Jefferson Building, First Floor, Room A-1026
287-5690

Donald F. Wisdom, Chief (of the Division)

8:30 A.M.-9:30 P.M.   Monday-Friday
8:30 A.M.-5:00 P.M.   Saturday
1:00 P.M.-5:00 P.M.   Sunday

This room in the Thomas Jefferson Building provides reader and reference service for all newspapers including those on microfilm, except for East Asian newspapers in vernacular languages which are processed and held by individual country sections of the Asian Division (e.g., newspapers by the Japanese section). All current Western-language periodicals and newspapers relating to East Asia are available here, provided that the LC receives them. Also, current governmental and nongovernmental serials of the United States and foreign countries are processed here.

Indexes covering Western-language periodicals, newspapers, and government publications are available for consultation.

Reference and consultative service on topics which are broadly international in scope is a major responsibility of the division's Senior Specialist in United Nations and International Documents, Robert W. Schaaf (287-5846). The international reference collection emphasizes guides, indexes, and catalogs relating to the United Nations and other intergovernmental organizations, whereas its specialized resources cover international nongovernmental groups and international conferences.

SERIAL AND GOVERNMENT PUBLICATIONS: The division receives over 1,500 newspapers currently, retaining approximately 1,200 permanently in its collection. The periodical collection includes unbound serials— foreign and domestic periodicals as well as federal, state, local, and foreign government publications. Approximately 70,000 titles of serial publications are currently received, and unbound pieces in the division's custody number close to 4 million. No unbound holdings serviced through the division date are more than 24 months old. Once bound or microfilmed, serial publications are serviced along with other items from the general collections of the library through the Main, Thomas Jefferson, or Microform reading rooms. Newspaper service for found titles often takes from 24 to 48 hours for materials to be delivered. Also, interlibrary loans may make some misfiled newspaper holdings temporarily unavailable. For these reasons, scholars are advised to write or call in advance to reserve materials they wish to use; the staff will be happy to accommodate such requests. Information about available foreign-language newspapers can be found in: (1) Henry A. Parson, *A Checklist of Foreign Newspapers in the Library of Congress* (Government Printing Office, 1929); (2) *Newspapers in Microform: Foreign*

Countries 1945-1972 (Library of Congress, 1973); (3) *Newspapers Received in the Library of Congress* (Library of Congress, 1978); and (4) *Newspapers in Microform: United States, 1945-1972* (Library of Congress, 1973), which includes Chinese, Japanese, and Korean language newspapers published in the United States.

GENERAL READING ROOMS DIVISION

Library of Congress Building, First Floor, Room 144 (287-5530)
Ellen Zabel Hahn, Chief

Main Reading Room Section (287-2116)
Josephus Nelson, Head

Thomas Jefferson Reading Rooms Section (287-4438)
Gary Jensen, Head

These sections provide reference service pertaining to almost any aspect of the LC's main holdings. Reference and bibliographic questions which do not fall within the expertise of one of the specialized divisions of the Library of Congress are fielded by the staff of these sections. Reference staff members are on duty in both sections during the regular hours of service.

Union Catalog Reference Section (287-6300)
Dorothy G. Kearney, Head

This section provides reference service on book locations and bibliographic information recorded in the *National Union Catalog* and in various auxiliary union catalogs, both published and unpublished. Parts of the unpublished catalogs are located on Deck 33 of the Library of Congress Building. The Union Catalog Reference Section (287-6300) is also located on this deck. Among other activities, this section issues the *Weekly List of Unlocated Research Books* and answers queries for information not contained in published catalogs.

Microform Reading Room Section
Library of Congress Building, First Floor, Room 140-B
287-5471

Robert V. Gross, Head of Microfilm Section

8:30 A.M.-5:00 P.M.   Monday-Friday
8:30 A.M.-9:30 P.M.   Tuesday-Thursday (stack service to 9:00 P.M.)
8:30 A.M.-12:30 P.M.   Saturday
Closed on Sunday

The section's holdings total over 1 million reels and other microfilms. Reading facilities are available for the microfilmed materials. East Asian holdings include 334 titles on Japan, 175 titles on China, and 40 titles on Korea. Of special importance to East Asia specialists are: John Young, *Checklist of Microfilm Reproductions of Selected Archives of the Japanese Army, Navy, and Other Government Agencies, 1868-1945* (Washington, D.C.: Georgetown University Press, 1959), 220 reels; and Cecil H. Uyehara, *Checklist of Archives in the Japanese Ministry of Foreign Affairs, Tokyo, Japan, 1868-1945* (Washington, D.C.: Photoduplication Service, Library of Congress, 1954), 2,116 reels. Also available at the reading room are a number of highly valuable U.S. government publications on microfilm: *Survey of the China Mainland Press; Current Background; Extracts from China Mainland Publications; Selections from China Mainland Magazines; Daily Summary of the Magazines;* and *U.S. Foreign Broadcasts Information Service Daily Reports.*

Other items of interest include some JPRS publications, League of Nations and United Nations documents, and a fairly comprehensive collection of doctoral dissertations microfilmed by University Microfilms International in Ann Arbor, Michigan. Nearly all the doctoral dissertations of the participating universities in the United States are available and can be readily identified by using the monthly volume of *Dissertation Abstracts International* (Ann Arbor, Michigan: University Microfilms International). Also useful are the following publications by Frank Joseph Shulman because they include the University Microfilms International order numbers which are identical with the LC Microform Reading Room's call numbers: *Japan and Korea: An Annotated Bibliography of Doctoral Dissertations in Western Languages, 1877-1969* (Chicago: American Library Association, 1970); *Doctoral Dissertations on Japan and Korea 1969-1974: A Classified Bibliographical Listing of International Research* (Ann Arbor, Michigan: University Microfilms International, 1976); *Doctoral Dissertations on China: A Bibliography of Studies in Western Languages, 1945-1970* (Seattle: University of Washington Press, 1972); and *Doctoral Dissertations on China, 1971-1975: A Bibliography of Studies in Western Languages* (Seattle: University of Washington Press, 1978). Also available at the Microfilm Reading Room is International Military Tribunal for the Far East, *Record of the Proceedings, Documents, Exhibits, Judgments, Dissenting Judgments, Interrogation, etc.* (mimeographed in Tokyo, 1946-1949).

Research Facilities Office
Bruce Martin
287-5211

For readers who plan to make extensive use of the Library, this division may make available special research/study facilities, including desks and shelves for reserving books for longer periods than the reading rooms permit. Scholars should check with the staff to obtain information about the facilities noted above. They should also inquire about the possibility of obtaining stack passes. The office is located in Alcove 8 of the Main Reading Room.

PHOTODUPLICATION SERVICE

Thomas Jefferson Building, Street Floor, Room G-1009
Charles G. LaHook, Jr., Chief (287-5654)
Carolyn Sung, Assistant Chief

8:00 A.M.-4:30 P.M.   Monday-Friday only (doors close at 4:15 P.M.)

For individuals and institutions requesting photoreproductions of the LC's holdings, this division provides photostats, photographs, slides, microfilm, and many other forms of copies at fixed fees. This branch also receives, duplicates, and sells materials from government agencies, including unclassified CIA reports, and, formerly, some scientific and technical reports of the Department of Commerce. Documents Expediting (DocEx) is the name of the program under which these documents are made available. The service also maintains the LC Master Negative Microfilm Collection, numbering more than 150,000 reels, which cover presidential papers, important manuscript collections, U.S. and foreign government documents, and many international periodicals. Of particular interest to East Asian specialists is *List of Circulars Currently Available from the Library of Congress Photoduplication Service,* which describes important items on sale. Included are: *Proceedings of the International Military Tribunal for the Far East; Hung Ch'i; The Trial of General Tomoyuki Yamashita; People's Republic of China—CIA Reference and Research Materials Available on Microfiche; A History of the Military Intelligence Division, 7 December 1941—2 September 1945; U.S. Military Government in the Mediterranean Theatre and Korea; AMMISCA File: The Magruder Mission to China (1941-1942);* and *History of the United States Armed Forces in Korea,* which is also known as "History of the Occupation of Korea August 1945-May 1948."

Information about other titles available at the Photoduplication Service may be found in the following publications: *National Register of Microform Master (1969),* annual, noncumulative; *Newspapers in Microform Foreign Countries, 1948-1972; Newspapers in Microform: United States, 1948-1972;Microfilm Clearing House Bulletin,* an appendix to the weekly LC *Information Bulletin;* and *Guides to Microfilms in Print.*

Readers may obtain an information brochure on the Photoduplication Service, a price list, and a flyer listing the catalogs of available materials without charge. Orders for photoduplication may be placed either in person or by mail.

Note: In addition to the divisions and sections described in this section, scholars should consult the entries in other sections of this *Guide* which deal with the LC's holdings on East Asia: the Manuscript Division (B5); American Folklife Center—Archive of Folk Song (D1); Geography and Map Division (E3); Motion Picture, Broadcasting, and Recorded Sound Division (D2, F5); and the Prints and Photograph Division (F6).

---

5. Most of the noteworthy LC holdings on important subjects have been described under appropriate divisions covered above. In fact, it may be fair to say that the library's collection is noteworthy for the following reasons.

a. Size—the LC collection of East Asian materials is the most extensive in the world outside of the countries of the region (i.e., China, Japan, and Korea).

b. All-inclusive nature—the comprehensiveness, breadth, and depth of the collection are outstanding insofar as the 18 basic subject categories covered in this survey are concerned. To be sure, for more specialized publications and titles on technical aspects of agriculture, health, and medicine, more materials can be found in the National Agricultural Library and National Library of Medicine respectively.

    c. Continuity of effort—the LC has been acquiring East Asian materials for over a century (1869-).

6.   In addition to the publications and other reference materials listed under the appropriate divisions above, scholars should consult the following publications which are more general in nature. Unless cited otherwise, these publications are for sale by the Superintendent of Documents, U.S. Government Printing Office, Washington, D.C. 20402 or by LC itself.

    a. LC publications:

The National Union Catalog, Pre-1956 imprints. Currently published by the Mansell Company in England, this catalog supersedes the following two titles; 610 vols. projected.

A Catalog of Books Represented by Library of Congress Printed Cards Issued (from August 1898 through July 1942), 167 vols. Supplement: cards issued August 1, 1942-December 31, 1947. 42 vols.

The Library of Congress Author Catalog: A Cumulative List of Works Represented by Library of Congress Cards, 1948-52, 24 vols.

The National Union Catalog: A Cumulative Author List Representing Library of Congress Printed Cards and Titles Reported by Other American Libraries. Cumulation for 1953-57, 28 vols., available in reprint form, Rowman and Littlefield; cumulation for 1958-62, 54 vols., o.p.; cumulation for 1963-67, 72 vols., available from J. W. Edwards, cumulation for 1956-67, 125 vols., available from Rowman and Littlefield; cumulation for 1968-72 available from J. W. Edwards; cumulations for recent years available from LC Cataloging Distribution Service Division. Currently in 9 monthly, 3 quarterly issues and an annual cumulation, the catalog covers some 1,100 United States and Canadian libraries.

Monographic Series, an aid to locating works published as a series but with various titles, are published in 3 quarterly issues and an annual cumulation.

Library of Congress Catalog—Books: Subjects, A Cumulative List of Works Represented by Library of Congress Printed Cards, for 1945 and later imprints, arranged alphabetically by LC subject headings and by author under subject headings. Cumulation for 1950-54, 20 vols., available in reprint from Rowman and Littlefield; cumulation for 1955-59, 22 vols., available from Rowman and Littlefield; cumulations for 1960-64, 25 vols., and for 1965-69, 42 vols., available from J. W. Edwards; cumulations for recent years available from LC Cataloging Distribution Service Division; and cumulation for 1970-74 being published by Rowman and Littlefield. Since 1975 this catalog is no longer being published under the title listed above, but is continued by the following title, *Subject Catalog.* This continues the preceding work and is published in 3 quarterly issues and an annual cumulation.

National Register of Microform Masters, annual, 1969 and volumes on later years are available from LC Cataloging Distribution Service Division.

In addition, the following LC publications are also useful: *The National Union Catalog: Reference and Related Services* (1973), available from the General Reading Rooms Division.

Information on the MARC System (4th ed., 1974), available free from LC Central Services Division.

Information for Readers in the Library of Congress (rev. ed., 1972), available free from the LC Central Services Division.

Special Facilities for Research in the Library of Congress (1975), available from the General Reading Rooms Division.

Foreign Newspaper and Gazette Report, irregular (formerly, Foreign Newspaper Report), available to libraries and institutions.

Digest of Public General Bills and Resolutions, published by LC Congressional Research Service in cumulations and supplements for current sessions of Congress.

b. Other publications, including both LC and non-LC:

New Serial Titles: A Union List of Serials Commencing Publication After December 31, 1949, based on reports from some 800 U.S. and Canadian libraries; cumulation for 1950-70, 4 vols., available from R. R. Bowker Co.: cumulation for 1971-74, available from LC Cataloging Distribution Service Division. Currently published in monthly and 4 quarterly issues with an annual cumulation (annuals cumulate up to 5- or 10-year periods). This work is a supplement to: *Union List of Serials in Libraries of the United States and Canada,* 5 vols., ed. Edna B. Titus (3d ed., 1965).

New Serial Titles—Classed Subject Arrangement is published in 12 monthly, non-cumulative issues.

Combined Indexes to the Library of Congress Classification Schedules, 15 vols., comp. Nancy Olson (Washington, D.C.: U.S. Historical Documents Institute, 1974-). These volumes are designed to serve as an aid to locating call numbers for materials by authors, names, geographic areas, subjects, and keywords.

Library of Congress Publication in Print, annual. Available free from the LC Cataloging Distribution Service Division.

Annual Report of the Librarian of Congress.

Quarterly Journal of the Library of Congress, particularly useful for the description of acquisitions of the various divisions.

A note on the LC computer systems:

The use of computerized data bases promises to revolutionize many aspects of scholarly research. LC has, since the 1960s, been using information in machine-readable form to automate more and more of its operations. Both on-line and off-line facilities are in use.

For researchers, the most important computerized tools to be aware of are MARC (Machine-Readable Cataloging) records and the retrieval systems, MUMS (Multiple-Use MARC) and SCORPIO (Subject-Oriented Retriever for Processing Information On-Line). These tools do not make obsolete such traditional aids as card catalogs, indexes, and bibliographies, but they certainly supplement them in invaluable ways. Already the systems have proven to be of tremendous use for East Asian studies.

While a lengthy description of all the LC computer systems is beyond the scope of this note, a few salient features can be indicated. For some bibliographic searches, the use of the LC retrieval systems can save scholars vast amounts of time and effort. The information desired can be obtained either on a computer terminal screen for note-taking purposes or in printed form. Individuals can perform many searches for themselves on terminals located off the Main Reading Room, in the Science Reading Room, and in other public reference facilities or they can request the Catalog Distribution Service staff to perform a search and produce a printed list for them. A standard fee is charged for such staff searches. (Reference staff will, however, show researchers how to use the computer terminals without charge). Available for on-line searching and display to scholars are bibliographic citations to all English-language books cataloged by LC and printed since 1968 or cataloged from 1969, and most Western European-language books printed or cataloged since the mid-1970s.

Bibliographic records concerning materials in East Asian languages are not yet available in machine-readable form. Searches can be performed by author, title, main entry, call number, subject, or added entries as well as by certain characterizing indicators such as country or area. Some examples of searches made in the past: books in translation published after 1969; translations of books in Class P (except juvenalia) published in 1974-75; discographies; and pre-1901 maps. For subject bibliographies, several subject headings and/or LC class numbers can be combined in a single search. Information about use of the LC retrieval systems can be obtained in the public reading rooms. Information about the fee searching service can be obtained from the Cataloging Distribution Service.

National Agricultural Library See entry A41.

A31 National Air and Space Museum Library (Smithsonian Institution)

1. a. *6th Street and Independence Avenue, SW*
       Washington, D.C. 20560
       381-6591

    b. 10:00 A.M.-5:15 P.M.   Monday-Friday

    c. Open to all interested persons. Circulation is limited to the staff of the Smithsonian Institution and its libraries on an interlibrary loan basis. Photocopying and microreproduction facilities are available for a fee.

    d. Catherine D. Scott, Librarian

2-3.   The National Air and Space Museum (NASM) library contains over 21,000 books, 4,600 bound periodicals, and 500,000 technical reports. The NASM library handles all types and levels of inquiries in the fields of aeronautics, astronautics, and related disciplines.

There is a small collection of books and articles dealing with aeronautics, aircraft, air force, aerospace industry, and the like in China. The library also has an atlas of the PRC. In addition, it contains a similar collection under the heading "Japan." Under a separate file entitled "German-Japanese Air Technical Documents WW II," an extensive collection of captured Japanese documents dealing with the engineering aspect of aeronautics in the pre-1945 period is available on microfilm. Some of the documents are translated, and the catalog is arranged by subject headings. In addition, the library has a small number of books pertaining to the Korean War.

4-5.   The historical archives of the museum contain over 19,000 files of aircraft photographs and drawings, astronautical photographs, and documents and biographical files of early and contemporary aerospace personalities. The archives may be consulted in the library, with restrictions for some classified materials.

In the Aero-Biographical files, one can find materials on such Chinese aviators as A. J. Chang, Fred Chang, and Yu-Lin Chang. The Aero-Transport list includes files on China Airline, China Civil Aviation, Japan Airlines, and Korean Airlines. The Aero-Military Index lists 1 file on China, 30 files on Japan. Finally, there is a file on the Korean War under the Aero-Wars list.

In addition, the library maintains the NASM photographic collection, which contains over 900,000 black-and-white photographs and drawings of aircraft and airmen, including pioneers in space flight. All aspects of the history of aeronautics and astronautics are covered (e.g., rocketry, balloons, airships, historic events, and personalities). Included in the photographic collection are several files of Japanese aircraft, especially those of World War II vintage (e.g., Kawasaki).

6.   A concise description of the organization and services of the NASM library can be found in *National Air and Space Museum Library* by Catherine D. Scott, originally published in the Bowker Annual of Library and Book Trade Information in 1976. Copies are available free upon request. A brief users' guide for the library is also available.

National Arboretum Library See entry C8.

National Association for Foreign Students Affairs Library
See entry H35.

National Council for U.S.–China Trade Library See entry H37.

National Defense University Library See entry K8.

A32 National Geographic Society Library

1. a. *1146-16th Street, NW*
    Washington, D.C. 20036
    296-7500
    857-7783 (Reference Library)

    b. 8:30 A.M.-5:00 P.M.   Monday-Friday

    c. Open to the public for on-site use. Interlibrary loan is available for the institutions located in the Washington area; no photocopying service is available.

    d. Virginia Carter Hills, Chief Librarian

2. This library is designed primarily to serve the staff of the National Geographic Society. Its holdings number more than 66,000 volumes with a strong emphasis on geography, natural history, travel, and exploration. Approximately 3,500 new volumes are added to the collection each year.

3. The measurement of the shelflist indicates that the library has over 1,150 titles on East Asia: 625 on China; 400 on Japan; 100 on Korea; and 30 on Mongolia. Most of the works are in English, but some are in the East Asian Languages (e.g., Chinese, Japanese). Although the collection covers a number of subject categories, most relate to geography and ethnography. For East Asian geography and ethnography, the collection deserves a B rating.

4. a. The library maintains more than 1,300 periodicals, including over 20 on or from East Asia (e.g., *Scientia Geologica Sinica, Scientia Sinica, Kexue Tongeao-Science Bulletin, Polar News* [Kyokuchi, Japan]).

    d. Virtually all maps of the National Geographic Society are kept in its Map Department, which is not accessible to the outside researchers without securing prior permission from the Department (857-1377).

    g. The Joseph F. Rock collection contains photographs on China; however, the collection is not accessible to outsiders.

5. The library contains several rare books on China, Japan, and Mongolia, including *Travels from St. Petersburg, Russia to Diverse Parts of Asia* by John Bell (1763); and *A Handbook for Travelers in Central and Northern Japan* by Ernest Mason Satow and U.A.G.S. Howes (1884).
    The library also maintains extensive vertical file materials, consisting mostly of clippings from American and British newspapers: China, 1½ drawers; Japan, 1½ drawers; Korea, ½ drawer; and Mongolia, 2 folders.

6. The library's card catalog is arranged in accordance with the LC's subject headings. However, the library uses its own classification scheme as well as call-number system instead of the LC's.
    For the *National Geographic*, the library maintains a special reference card index which lists every geographic area, country, city, or village

which has ever appeared in the magazine. The Public Reference Service (857-7059) gives prompt attention to inquiries concerning the magazine. Also useful to researchers is the *National Geographic Index*, which is published twice a year. Extensive cumulative index are also available for 1888-1946, 1947-1969, and 1970-1975.

A33 National Institute of Education (Health, Education, and Welfare [HEW] Department)—Educational Research Library

1. a. *1832 M Street, NW*
    Washington, D.C. 20208
    254-5060

    b. 8:00 A.M.-4:30 P.M.   Monday-Friday

    c. Open to the public. Interlibrary loan and photoduplication services are available.

    d. Patricia Coulter, Director

2-3.   The library contains approximately 130,000 volumes. The NIE collection is particularly strong in educational psychology, history of education, and urban education issues. However, its holdings on East Asia number no more than 100. Books dealing with international education, comparative education, etc., frequently contain sections dealing with East Asia. The library subscribes to over 1,200 periodicals, including *Chinese Education* and *Sae Kyo-Yuk* (or "The New Education," Korea).

6.   In addition to a card catalog (divided by author and subject), researchers should consult the *Subject Catalog of the Department Library* (Boston: G. K. Hall, 1965), 20 volumes plus a 4-volume supplement (1973). For the periodicals, the *Periodical Holdings List: Educational Research Library* (3d ed., 1977) is available.

A34 National Library of Medicine (NLM)

1.   a. *8600 Rockville Pike*
     Bethesda, MD 20014
     (301) 496-6095 (General Reference)
     (301) 496-5405 (History of Medicine Division)
     (301) 496-5560 (Oriental Area Reference)

     b. Regular Hours (Labor Day to Memorial Day)

     8:30 A.M.-9:00 P.M.—Monday-Friday
     8:30 A.M.-5:00 P.M.   Saturday
     Closed Sunday

     Summer Hours (Memorial Day to Labor Day)
     8:30 A.M.-5:00 P.M.   Monday-Saturday

     History of Medicine Collection
     8:30 A.M.-4:45 P.M.   Monday-Friday

c. The library is open to the public. Interlibrary loan and photoduplication services are available.

d. Martin M. Cummings, M.D., Director
Dr. Stephen Kim, Oriental Area Specialist (301) 496-5560

2. The main collection consists of about 2,500,000 items, including over 500,000 medical theses. Library holdings cover about 40 biomedical subjects and related fields. NLM, the largest collection of its kind in the world, receives over 20,000 serial titles annually.

3. NLM has one of the largest and finest collections of East Asian medical literature in the world. However, for a number of reasons, it is very difficult to estimate the size of the East Asian collection. The materials are primarily arranged by subject, making it difficult to determine the total number of items related to East Asia. According to a survey conducted by NLM staff in 1975, the library's East Asian language materials numbered about 25,000 volumes: Chinese language materials—7,000; Japanese language materials—16,000; and Korean language materials—2,000.

    Annual acquisition of East Asian materials is around 820 items (i.e., 170 Chinese, 600 Japanese, and 50 Korean titles).

4. NLM also receives over 1,350 East Asian serial titles. Specifically, it receives about 50 Chinese, 1,200 Japanese, and 100 Korean periodicals. It is estimated that, of the 20,000 current serials received by NLM, roughly 10 percent are either from East Asia or are concerned with East Asia. About 109 journals from East Asia are indexed monthly and included in the *Index Medicus* which surveys about 3,000 journals.

5. The History of Medicine Division has a sizable amount of East Asian material, some dating back at least to the Ming and Ch'ing dynasties. However, the materials are roughly cataloged at present and are incomplete. Some of these holdings will be found in the library's *Index Catalogue* (see point 6 below).

6. NLM has developed several computerized search systems:

    (1) MEDLARS (or Medical Literature Analysis and Retrieval System) was established in 1964 to facilitate rapid bibliographic access to NLM's vase store of biomedical information. MEDLARS contains some 3.5 million references dating from 1964.

    (2) MEDLINE (or MEDLARS On-Line) became operational in late 1971. It is available through a nationwide NLM network of about 800 universities, medical schools, hospitals, government agencies, and commercial organizations. It provides the ability to query the NLM's computer store of journal article references for instant retrieval. MEDLINE currently contains citations of approximately 600,000 items from 3,000 biomedical journals published in the United States and 40 foreign countries. Also included are a growing number of chapters and articles from selected monographs. One can search MEDLINE by keywords from article titles and/or abstracts or by some 14,000 medical-subject headings (MeSH).

(3) CATLINE (or Catalog On-Line) contains about 200,000 references to books and serials cataloged at NLM since 1965.

(4) SERLINE (or Serials On-Line) contains the journal titles and publishers of all serial publications received by NLM, which number approximately 20,000. For one-third of these, SERLINE has locator information that informs the user which library to consult for specific titles.

(5) AVLINE (or Audiovisual On-Line) contains citations to and abstracts of some 3,000 audiovisual teaching packages.

(6) CANCERLIT (or Cancer Literature) is sponsored by NIH's National Cancer Institute (NCI) and contains more than 140,000 references dealing with various aspects of cancer. In addition, NLM maintains other computerized data bases such as TOXLINE (Toxiology Information On-Line); CANCERPROJ (Cancer Research Projects); CHEMLINE (Chemical Dictionary On-Line); CLINICPROJ (Clinical Cancer Protocols); EPILEPSYLINE; and HISTLINE (history of medicine).

A number of published bibliographic tools are available to researchers using NLM facilities. *National Library of Medicine Current Catalog* is a fully computerized book catalog published quarterly, with annual and 5-year cumulations. For older materials in the History of Medicine Division, there is the *Index-Catalogue of the Library of the Surgeon General's Office.* Five multi-volume series of this catalog appeared between 1880 and 1961, covering books printed through 1950. It is arranged by author and subjects, and contains citations to periodical articles as well as books.

For periodical literature, researchers should consult *Index Medicus,* which is published monthly as a bibliographic listing of references to current articles from approximately 2,500 biomedical journals out of 20,000 received by NLM. It is arranged by author and subject with a separate *Bibliography of Medical Reviews.* An annual *Bibliography of the History of Medicine* is published which contains references to books and journal articles on this subject. Five-year cumulations are also published.

National Planning Association Library See entry M26.

A35 Naval Observatory Library (Navy Department)

1. a. *34th and Massachusetts Avenue, NW*
    Washington, D.C. 20390
    254-4525

    b. 8:00 A.M.-4:30 P.M.   Monday-Friday

    c. Researchers must call in advance to make arrangements for the use of the facilities. Limited interlibrary loan and photoduplication services are available.

    d. Brenda Corbin, Librarian

2.   The library has a collection of over 76,500 volumes, including bound periodicals, chiefly on astronomy, mathematics, physics, and geophysics. There are sets of publications from other foreign observatories as well as periodicals in the subject field.

3-4.   Materials of particular interest to East Asian specialists include a number of periodicals published in China, Japan, South Korea, and Taiwan. From the People's Republic of China, it has: *Acta Astronomica Sinica* (1955-); *Astronomical Observatory* (Peking), 1962-1963, and 1976-present; *Observatoire de Zi-ka-wei* (Zi-ka-wei, China), 1907-1942, and 1957. Publications from Japan include: *International Latitude Observatory* (Mizusawa, Japan)—annual report of research conducted by the Japanese observatory on meteorological and seismological studies (1966-present); *Japan Academy* (Tokyo), 1912-1936, 1944-1945; and *Institute of Physical and Chemical Research,* 1922-1941. The library receives *Nautical Almanac* (1955-present) compiled by the Navy Hydrographic Office, South Korea; *Astronomy Newsletter* (1957-present) published by the Taipei Amateur Astronomers Association; and *Report on Sun-spot Observatories During the Period from 1957,* prepared by the Weather Bureau, Taipei, Taiwan.

6.   *The Catalog of the Naval Observatory* (6 vols.) was published by G. K. Hall in 1976. Supplements are planned at 5-year intervals.

A36 Navy Department Library

1.   a. *Washington Navy Yard, Building 220*
         11th and M Streets, SE
         Washington, D.C. 20374
         433-4131/4132

      b. 7:30 A.M.-4:30 P.M.   Monday-Friday

      c. Open to public for on-site use. Interlibrary loan and photocopying services are available.

      d. Stanley Kalkus, Director

2.   The library contains more than 150,000 volumes with emphasis on naval history, naval biography, exploration, and naval science and technology. In addition, it maintains over 10,000 microfilm rolls, and receives more than 300 periodicals annually.

3.   The library's holdings on East Asia number nearly 2,000 titles: approximately 700 on Japan, 950 on China; and 300 on Korea. The strength of the library lies in its holdings for naval and general history and military affairs. For example, on the Russo-Japanese War of 1904-1905, there are roughly 80 titles. For World War II, there are several hundred titles, including about 70 monographs in Japanese on the history of the Pacific War. Other subjects include geography, international law, diplomacy, government and politics, and nearly all naval topics. Anyone interested in World War II in the Pacific region will find this library a rich source of materials.

4-5.   The library has a rare-book collection which numbers approximately 5,000 volumes, including about 70 Japanese and 6 Korean monographs and journals. The earliest imprint is Quintillianus's *Declamationes* (Venice, 1482). There are 140 titles printed in the 16th and 17th centuries. Included in the rare-book collection are various editions of Commodore Matthew C. Perry's expedition to Japan; James Burney's *History of the Voyages* and *Discoveries in the South Sea or Pacific Ocean* (London, 1813), 5 vols.; Charles Wilkes' *United States Exploring Expedition During the Years 1838-42* (Philadelphia, 1844), 23 vols.; John Pinkerton's *Narratives of Voyages and Travels* (London, 1808), 17 vols.; and James Cook's *A Voyage to the Pacific Ocean* (London, 1785), 3 vols. The collection also contains at least 200 atlases published in the United States and abroad, mostly before 1900.

     The library has custody over the Office of Naval Records and Library collection, which consists of about 1,000 historic manuscripts mostly dating from the 19th century. In addition, the library has a collection of graduate theses and dissertations in naval history, and a group of about 300 unpublished narrative histories dealing with virtually every aspect of the administration of the Naval Establishment and the roles it played during the wide-ranging operations of World War II.

     Finally, most of the microfilmed editions of naval documents in the National Archives (see *List of National Archives Microfilm Publications* for a complete description) are available at the Library. These reels may be borrowed through interlibrary loan.

6.   A copy of *The Navy Department Library: A Brief Description* is available upon request. Copies of its excellent *United States Naval History: A Bibliography* (1972) are available from the Superintendent of Documents, Government Printing Office, Washington, D.C. 20402. The price is 70 cents.

A37   Organization for Economic Cooperation and Development (OECD)—Washington Publications Center Library

1.   a.   *1750 Pennsylvania Avenue, NW, Suite 1207*
Washington, D.C. 20006
298-8755

     b.   9:00 A.M.-5:30 P.M.   Monday-Friday

     c.   Open to the public for on-site use; photoduplication facilities are available, but not interlibrary loan arrangements.

     d.   Eric N. Ekers, Head of the OECD Washington Publications Center

2-3.   The collection is primarily of its own publications which number approximately 1,500 volumes, plus about 18 periodicals. Holdings pertaining to East Asia are largely on Japan, for Japan is a member of the OECD.

4.   This library will be of value to Japanologists whose principal interests lie in the social sciences, such as economics, demography, the environ-

ment, energy, socio-political education, and statistics. Japan is covered in most OECD publications either directly or indirectly, and many of these works are rich in statistical data.

6. The OECD materials are not cataloged; however, they are collected together. *The OECD Catalogue of Publications,* published annually, is helpful in identifying the most recent OECD publications.

Overseas Development Council Library See entry M27.

Overseas Private Investment Corporation (OPIC) Library See entry K26.

Patent Office Scientific Library See entry A13.

Population Reference Bureau Library See entry M28.

Rand Corporation (Washington Office) Library See entry M30.

SRI International—Strategic Studies Center Library See entry M32.

A38 State Department Library

1. a. *State Department Building, Room 3239*
      2201 C Street, NW
      Washington, D.C. 20520
      632-0372 (Librarian)
      632-0535/1099/0486 (Reference)

   b. 8:45 A.M.-5:30 P.M.   Monday-Friday

   c. The library is open only to employees of the State Department, the Agency for International Development, and the Arms Control and Disarmament Agency. Outside researchers may be admitted to use specific materials not available elsewhere in the area. Non-employees cannot use the facility for in-depth research. Call in advance for clearance. Interlibrary loan and limited photocopying services are available.

   d. Conrad Eaton, Librarian

2. The library contains over 700,000 volumes, and currently receives about 1,100 periodical, including 50 journals from Japan, China, South and North Korea, and Taiwan. Annual acquisitions total about 16,000 volumes; and 30-40 percent of the new acquisitions are from foreign countries.

3. The library's East Asian holdings are strong in the fields of government and politics, foreign relations, economics, and the social sciences. On the average, 30 percent or more of the materials included in these categories is written in East Asian languages. Clearly, the library's emphasis is placed on contemporary works.

    The figures* listed below are provided by the staff that measured the library's shelflist for this survey:

Subject Category	China/Rating		Japan/Rating		Korea/Rating	
1. Philosophy and Religion	83	C	29		0	
2. History	3,014	B	1,162	B	419	C
3. Geography and Ethnography	13		3		0	
4. Economics	590	B	939	B	159	B
5. Sociology	349	B	80	C	10	
6. Government and Politics	338	B	351	B	37	C
7. Foreign Relations	503	B	577	B	36	C
8. Law	171		345		60	
9. Fine Arts	11		13		2	
10. Education	109	C	99	C	17	
11. Language	158	C	120	C	32	
12. Literature	72		22		2	
13. Military Affairs	29		43		208	B
14. Bibliography and Reference	88	C	110	C	33	C
15. Tibet	149	C				
16. Mongolia	25	C				
17. Okinawa			94	B		
18. Hong Kong	350	A				

    * The figures representing titles include the Oriental-language materials which comprise about 30 percent of the holdings in each category.

4. The library currently receives about 50 periodicals from East Asia. However, it does not subscribe to nor maintain any East Asian newspaper. East Asian newspapers and periodicals (other than those located in the library) can be found in other branches of the State Department (e.g., the Bureau of Intelligence and Research).

    The Map Library of the State Department (632-9674) is located elsewhere in the State Department building and is closed to outside researchers.

    In addition to the well-known State Department publications (e.g., *Foreign Relations of the United States* series) the library maintains the following materials which may not be readily available elsewhere: *AID Economic Data Book: Far East; Aid Status of Foreign Currency Funds; Background Notes; Biographic Register; Foreign Service List (1816-1975); Front Lines* (AID publication); *Geographic Notes; Schedule of International Conferences; Press Conferences of the Secretary of State;* and *State Department Telephone Directories* (1920s-present).

6. The library maintains two card catalogs: the first is a regular dictionary catalog, arranged alphabetically by author, title, and subject; and the second is a geographic catalog, arranged by geographic area and country. Area specialists can more readily utilize the geographic catalog.

The library publishes a monthly acquisition list as well as selected bibliographies on topics of current interest such as "Human Rights" and the "North-South Dialogue." In addition, it prepares a short bibliography on selected subjects which are published in the monthly *Department of State Newsletter*. A brief guide entitled *Department of State Library* (1976) can be consulted in the library.

Textile Museum Library See entry C13.

A39 Transportation Department Library

1. a. *Main Library:*

    400-7th Street, SW, Room 2200
    Washington, D.C. 20590
    426-2565 (Director)
    426-1792 (Reference)
    426-2563 (Law)

    Branch:

    800 Independence Avenue, SW, Room 930
    Washington, D.C. 20590

    b. Main Library: 7:30 A.M.-5:30 P.M.   Monday-Friday
    Branch Library: 8:30 A.M.-5:00 P.M.

    c. Open to the public for on-site use. Interlibrary loan and photocopying services are available.

    d. Lucile E. Beaver, Library Director

2. The combined holdings of the two libraries number over 550,000 hardcopy documents, 125,000 microform documents, and 2,170 current journal titles. The libraries also subscribe to over 100 abstracting services.

3. East Asian holdings of the libraries number about 200 volumes: approximately 80 on China and Taiwan; 100 on Japan; 18 on Korea; and 1 on Mongolia.

4. The main library has a collection of "backlog" material (largely uncataloged) from foreign countries. It is shelved in a designated area of the library, containing about 9 boxes of Chinese material dating from 1906 (no PRC material); and about 9 boxes of Japanese material dating from 1920 (including some English texts).

6. The library maintains an index file for periodical literature on many aspects of transportation published after the early 1920s. Over 800,000 cards are included in the file. This reference index file is available in a microfilmed edition entitled *Transportation Masterfile, 1921-1971* (140 reels), plus a supplement covering 1971-1974 (7 reels).

The library publishes *Transportation: Current Literature* (weekly); *Urban Transportation Research and Planning: Current Literature* (biweekly), and other bibliographies.

Researchers can also utilize the Transportation Research Information Service Network (or TRISNET) which includes TRIS-ON-LINE, a computerized data base. A growing amount of international material is stored in the system. Data on East Asia, however, is quite limited as of now. TRISNET information includes abstracts of transportation literature, photocopies of reports, résumés of planned and on-going research, references to numerical data bases and directories to transportation-related information centers. Outside researchers who wish to use TRIS-ON-LINE will be referred to a nongovernmental organization which will arrange a TRIS-ON-LINE search for a fee.

Treasury Department Library See entry K32.

A40 United Nations Information Centre

1. a. *2101 L Street, NW, Suite 209*
    Washington, D.C. 20037
    296-5370

    b. 9:00 A.M.-1:00 P.M. Monday-Friday

    c. Open to the public. Interlibrary loan service and photoduplication facilities are available.

    d. Vera P. Gathright, Reference Librarian.

2-3. The Centre's collection includes United Nations publications, records, and documents published since 1969. A monthly index is compiled for new materials received by the Centre, and an annual cumulative index is also compiled. The library's reference section is extensive. There is, howver, no card catalog for the Centre's collection.

4. United Nations' films are available for loans to educational institutions, organizations, and qualified researchers. The Centre has recently acquired a microfilm reading machine and is planning to increase its holdings of microfilm and microfiche in the future.

    Although it is difficult to assess the extent and significance of this library's holdings on East Asia, it seems a useful reference library for researchers interested in U.N. activities in East Asia, and the U.N. policies of the East Asian nations.

A41 U.S.D.A. (Agriculture Department) Science and Education Administration, Technical Information Systems (formerly National Agricultural Library [NAL])

1. a. *Main Library:*

    National Agricultural Library Building
    U.S. Route 1 and Interstate Route 95 (Beltway Exit 27 North)
    Beltsville, MD 20705

> *(301) 344-3778*
> *(301) 344-3755 (Reference)*
> *(301) 344-3761 (Interlibrary loan)*
> *(301) 344-3746 (Phone inquiry)*
>
> *D.C. Branch and Law Library:*
>
> *U.S. Department of Agriculture*
> *South Building, Room 1052*
> *Independence Avenue and 14th Street, SW*
> *Washington, D.C. 20250*
> *(202) 447-3434*

b. Main Library: 8:00 A.M.-4:30 P.M. Monday-Friday
   D.C. Branch: 8:00 A.M.-5:00 P.M. Monday-Friday

c. Open to the public. Paid photoduplication service (schedule of fees available on request) and coin-operated copying machines are available.

All photocopying requests should be sent to:

> Lending Division
> Attention: Photocopying Service
> Technical Information Systems
> National Agricultural Library Building
> Beltsville, MD 20705

d. Richard A. Farley, Deputy Director
   Gary McCone, Procurement Section (Oriental Serials)
   Edna Liu, Cataloging Section
   Wei-ping Liao, Indexing Section

2. The TIS's total holdings exceed 1.6 million volumes (monographs and serials). It receives over 23,000 periodicals and maintains 128,370 microforms. NAL's holdings are built around technical agricultural subjects and related topics of farming, botany, chemistry, entomology, forestry, soil science, food and nutrition, water resources and irrigation, rural society, geology, law, and economics as they pertain to agriculture.

3. This library represents a major resource, particularly for scholars specializing in East Asian agriculture, agronomy, rural sociology, and economics. The library has two different cataloging systems: the "Dictionary Catalog" contains all cards cataloged by the TIS from 1862 to 1965; author, title, and subject cards are interfiled. The LC classification system was adopted in 1966. The "Current Catalog" is divided into a Name Catalog (entries by personal authors, corporate bodies, etc.) and a Subject Catalog. The following figures are based on the cards from both cataloging systems. The first table emphasizes TIS holdings on non-agricultural subjects, whereas the second table deals with its holdings on agriculture and related subjects. The numbers in the following two tables represent titles.

Subject Category	China/Rating		Japan/Rating		Korea/Rating	
Economics	560	A	776	A	233	A
Geography	93	B	22	B	10	C
History	75		16		7	

Subject Category	China/Rating	Japan/Rating	Korea/Rating
Politics and Government	26	20	10
Foreign Relations	47	36	0
Sociology	91	234	95
Language	128	53	11
Literature	18	13	4
Bibliography	43	34	17
TOTAL	1,111	1,204	387

Subject Category	China	Japan	Korea
Agriculture	711	1,731	250
Botany	120	213	10
Forestry	43	739	37
Pomology	21	66	2
Sericulture	21	128	10
Soils	32	43	2
Zoology	21	22	4
Agricultural Statistics	24	128	0
Entomology	43	75	3
Geological Survey	11	128	2
TOTAL	969	3,273	320

TIS holdings on East Asia economics are exceptional. For non-economic subjects, however, the library's holdings are modest. The overall resources of the NAL can be more fully appreciated as one learns more about its special collections of East Asian language materials, which are unique and substantial, as can be seen from point 4 below.

4. EAST ASIAN LANGUAGE PERIODICALS

As of June 1962, the library's Japanese serial publications numbered 1,118. At least 200 new titles have been added since then, thus making Japanese serial publications in the library total more than 1,300 titles (both active and inactive combined). Also available are at least 242 Chinese periodicals, including over 132 Communist Chinese periodicals in the agricultural sciences. In addition, the TIS has more than 158 Korean serial titles.

CHINESE COLLECTION

For nearly a century the TIS has been a repository for Chinese publications. Today it maintains a Chinese collection of more than 25,000 books and serials in the biological and agricultural fields, surely one of the largest of its kind in the world. The collection also contains important reports, working papers, and other documents prepared by various technical missions and organizations, as well as reprints of some of the classical works on Chinese agriculture published several centuries ago. There are also materials published in mainland China before and after the Communist takeover and publications from Taiwan since 1949. Until recently, the Chinese collection at TIS was in the custody of Dr. Leslie T. C. Kuo, an agricultural economist by training, under whose supervision several bibliographies on Chinese, Japanese, and Korean agriculture were prepared and published by the TIS.

JAPANESE AND KOREAN MATERIALS

Japanese language materials number over 10,000 volumes, mostly in the biological and agricultural fields. The collection is especially strong in agricultural economics. The library also has many pre-1940 publications of Japanese agricultural research stations which are likely to be unique in the Western world. Korean publications in the TIS totaled nearly 200 titles in 1963, when *Korean Publications in the National Agricultural Library* was published. Subsequently, several hundred new titles have been added, bringing the library's total Korean publications to more than 1,000 volumes.

CHINESE, JAPANESE, AND KOREAN DICTIONARIES COLLECTION

According to a recent study by Gary K. McCone (a staff member), there are at least 253 different dictionaries in East Asian languages in the NAL. For details, see McCone's *Chinese, Japanese and Korean Dictionaries in the Collection of the National Agricultural Library* (1977).

6.   Several computerized information retrieval data bases are available at the TIS for service to researchers. The two most important systems are: 1) Serial Title Automated Record (STAR); and 2) Agricultural On-Line Access (AGRICOLA). STAR is a computerized data base containing serial records in machine-readable forms which began in 1971. Altogether some 35,000 records have been converted and stored in this computerized data base. There are presently 15 reports available from the STAR DATA base; however, the reports which are most frequently utilized by the TIS staff are STAR I which is in call-number order and STAR II which is filed by title. As of March 1978, STAR contained 880 Japanese, 242 Chinese, and 158 Korean serial titles in its data base. STAR also has on-line accessibility. AGRICOLA is a family of data bases which consists of indexes to general agriculture, food and nutrition, and agricultural economics. Approximately 5,000 journals worldwide are currently indexed. The total number of books and journal articles indexed as of January 1, 1977, was more than one million. AGRICOLA contains all items cataloged and indexed by the TIS since 1970. AGRICOLA can be searched using title words of monographs and journal articles. Other searching approaches include: author; category codes; corporate entries; date of indexing; date of publication; geographical codes; language; journal title abbreviations, etc. The East Asian language materials contained in the AGRICOLA data base are as follows:

Language	Total Items	From Monographs	From Serials
Chinese	2,846	113	2,733
Japanese	23,466	495	22,971
Korean	789	38	751

TIS also provides access to many other on-line systems: MEDLINE of the National Library of Medicine (see A34); JURIS, the retrieval and inquiry system of the Department of Justice (see K21); ERIC (or Educational Resources Information Center) (see G4); Lockheed Information Systems; Systems Development Corporation Search Service; and Bibliographical Retrieval Services.

As noted above, two distinct catalogs (the Dictionary Catalog and the Current Catalog) are maintained by the TIS. In addition, it also has a Translations File which contains entries for translations of individual articles in periodicals, chapters and extracts from books, and other publications. Only one entry appears for each translation, normally under the first author's name. Among many useful guides to the holdings of the library, the following should be mentioned: *Dictionary Catalog of the National Agricultural Library, 1862-1965* (Totowa, N.J.: Rowman and Littlefield, 1967-1970), 73 volumes; *The National Agricultural Library Catalog* (1966-); and the *Bibliography of Agriculture*. The last two are monthly publications which have annual cumulations with author and subject indexes. The *NAL Catalog* contains reproduced LC cards, while the *Bibliography of Agriculture* (AGRICOLA citations) includes more detailed information than the LC cards. For East Asia specialists, the following bibliographies compiled at the library should be of immense help: *Chinese Agricultural Publications from the Republic of China since 1947* (1964); *Communist Chinese Monographs in the USDA Library* (1961); *Communist Chinese Periodicals in the Agricultural Sciences* (1963); *Publications on Chinese Agriculture Prior to 1949* (1966); *Japanese Serial Publications in the National Agricultural Library* (1962); *Korean Publications in the National Agricultural Library* (1963); and *Chinese, Japanese, and Korean Dictionaries in the Collection of the National Agricultural Library* (1977) compiled by Gary K. McCone. See also Gary K. McCone's 1978 conference paper, "Historical and Contemporary East Asia Resources in the Department of Agriculture Library."

The following TIS brochures are available free on request: *The National Agricultural Library: A Guide to Services* (1974); *The Card Catalogs of the National Agricultural Library: How to Use Them* (1976); and *AGRICOLA* (n.d.).

United States–Japan Trade Council Library See entry H46.

A42 University of Maryland (College Park Campus)

1. a. *College Park, MD 20742*
       (301) 454-5704 (Reference, McKeldin Library)
       (301) 454-4316 (Architecture Library)
       (301) 454-4737 (Undergraduate Library)
       (301) 454-2819/5459 (East Asia Collection)

    b. 8:00 A.M.-11:00 P.M.   Monday-Thursday
       8:00 A.M.-6:00 P.M.   Friday
       10:00 A.M.-6:00 P.M.   Saturday
       12:00-11:00 P.M.   Sunday

    These hours are for the McKeldin Library during the regular academic year and summer sessions. For other schedules, call the above-listed telephone number.

    c. The libraries and the book stack are open to all; however, only university-affiliated people may check out library materials. Interlibrary loan service and photoduplication facilities are available (including microfilm and microfiche copiers).

    d. Dr. H. Joanne Harrar, Director of Libraries
    Berna Neal, Librarian of the Architecture Library
    J. Donald Thomas, Head of the Undergraduate Library
    Frank Joseph Shulman, Head of the East Asia Collection

2.   Campus libraries hold about 1,465,000 volumes, 875,000 microfilm units, 240,400 United States and foreign documents, and 58,950 other items (including cassettes and films) for a total of over 2,639,400 pieces. Libraries subscribe to approximately 15,000 serials.

3.   Subject categories and evaluations (numbers represent titles):

Subject Category	China/Rating		Japan/Rating		Korea/Rating	
1. Philosophy and Religion	118	C	1,517	B	5	
2. History	3,876	B	6,138	B	172	C
3. Geography	186	B	358	B	5	
4. Economics	272	C	2,340	B	21	
5. Sociology	88	C	655	B	15	
6. Government and Politics	217	B	792	B	25	C
7. Foreign Relations	513	B	424	B	32	C
8. Law	*unmeasured*		*unmeasured*		*unmeasured*	
9. Education	434	A	410	B	4	
10. Fine Art	143	B	581	B	10	C
11. Language	538	B	286	B	8	
12. Literature	1,564	B	7,215	B	3	
13. Military Affairs	19		275	B	70	B
14. Bibliography and Reference	276	B	474	B	9	

15. Mongolia	59	C				
16. Tibet	260	C				
17. Okinawa			21	C		
18. Hong Kong	45	B				

    Phonograph records are located in McKeldin's Fine Arts Room while some art/architecture items are located in the Architecture Library. Many art volumes are expected to be transferred to a new Art Library in 1979.

    This is a very good collection, probably ranking after LC as the second best general collection in the Washington, D.C., area. The strength of the McKeldin Library's holdings on East Asia, particularly on Japan and China, can be illustrated further by its strong East Asia Collection which contains over 80,000 volumes (or an estimated 48,000 titles), mostly in Japanese and Chinese, and which subscribes to over 320 East Asian language periodicals and newspapers. As described more in detail in the following section (4), the Japanese language materials from early years of the Allied Occupation period (1945-1952) constitute a truly remarkable collection.

4. SPECIAL COLLECTIONS

The East Asia Collection and the *Gordon W. Prange Collection:* The East Asia Collection (offices in Rooms 3111 and 3115E of the McKeldin Library) contains approximately 48,000 titles (or over 80,000 volumes) in East Asian languages. Specifically, the numerical strength of the collection is as follows:

Collection	Number of Titles (Estimated)	Mono-volumes
Chinese Collection	6,048	10,281
Japanese Collection	41,819	70,000
Korean Collection	60	150

These collections as a whole are strong in the social sciences and the humanities. Also, over 8,000 volumes of scientific and technical books (many of them are textbooks) published in Japan between 1945 and 1949 are included in the Japanese portion of the collection. The East Asia Collection also contains a fairly large number of East Asian language periodicals; the researcher can count with some assurance on the availability of many basic journals in such subjects as history, economics, art, literature, statistics, and political science, published in China and Japan. Specifically, the East Asia Collection maintains over 160 different Chinese periodicals (including some which are no longer published) and newspapers. Most of the important journals published in Peking, Taipei, and Hong Kong are available at the East Asia Collection. Also, approximately 160 Japanese periodicals and newspapers are subscribed to and maintained by the East Asia Collection. Such Japanese newspapers as *Asahi, Nihon Keizai Shimbun* and *Akahata* are available in reduced-size monthly editions. Only limited numbers of Korean periodicals are kept by the East Asia Library: 7 journals and one newspaper.

Over the years, the portion of the McKeldin Library's East Asian Collection (recently renamed as the "Gordon W. Prange Collection") has become widely known as a repository for published and unpublished materials from the Allied Occupation of Japan. Obtained through the good offices of Dr. Gordon W. Prange (Professor of History at the University of Maryland), this collection of over 60,000 publications includes a copy of items published in Japan between 1945 and 1949. Copies of all such publications were automatically deposited with the Civil Censorship Detachment of SCAP (Supreme Commander for the Allied Powers). Every book, periodical and newspaper, monograph, movie magazine, news dispatch, piece of fiction, and even children's literature, came under SCAP scrutiny during the early part of the occupation period. The process of sorting and analyzing this unique collection has been under way since the mid-1960s. As of November 1978, the scope and nature of these materials were described as follows:

(1) Periodicals (i.e., magazines)

Processed holdings consist of approximately 13,000 periodical titles. A holdings card has been prepared for each one. Arranged in alphabetical order, cards containing basic bibliographical information form the basis of a reference work that is scheduled to be published in Japan as part of the university's efforts to make these materials more accessible.

(2) Newspapers

The East Asia Collection has runs of approximately 11,000 daily and non-daily local and national newspapers. Approximately 225 linear feet of these newspapers have been fully processed; they represent titles beginning with the letters A through Na. Approximately 582 linear feet of newspapers (letters Ni through Z) remain to be cataloged. Holdings cards are being prepared for all of the newspapers.

Also, there is a large collection of NEWS SERVICE DISPATCHES (Tsūhin) from the Japanese counterparts of AP and UPI e.g., Dōmei, Kokusai, Kyōdō, Jiji, Rengō, etc.): approximately 363 linear feet have been processed, and holding cards are available for the processed materials.

(3) Books and Monographs

(a) Over 13,000 monographs as well as hundreds of reference works have been cataloged. The cataloged collection is especially strong in the areas of Japanese history, Japanese literature (especially first editions of the post-World War II fiction), economics, education, government, and religion and philosophy; (b) Approximately 25,000 (estimated) volumes of books occupying 2,000 linear feet of shelf space are yet to be cataloged, including an estimated 8,100 volumes on technology and science; 3,780 textbooks (estimated); and over 6,400 volumes (estimated) of children's books.

(4) Censored Materials

Consisting mainly of book-length manuscripts and selected periodical articles submitted for prepublication or postpublication censorship, these items are accompanied by English-language documents describing and translating offensive passages within each item and outlining the action taken by the SCAP's Civil Censorship Detachment on each item. The bases for censorship were predominantly political, and the suppressed materials range from publications expressing militaristic, ultra-nationalistic, or rightist views to those advocating militant communism. Some censored materials, however, involved criticism of General MacArthur and various policies or programs instituted by SCAP. The documents are almost entirely intact and are not duplicated elsewhere. The total holdings of censored materials are: 5 (4-drawer) file cabinets of manuscripts and related materials; and 14 (4-drawer) file cabinets of periodical articles and news dispatches.

(5) Related English-Language Materials

The East Asia Collection also contains ancillary or related materials in the English language which date from World War II and the occupation years and which make the holdings of the McKeldin Library even more convenient or self-contained for researchers. There are, for instance, the ATIS Papers (translations of Japanese documents taken in battle within the Southwest Pacific area, and press translations dating mainly from 1945 to 1948 of leading newspapers), summaries prepared by SCAP of nonmilitary activities, civil affairs handbooks prepared by the United States Army, stenographic records of meetings of the Allied High Command in Japan, United States Office of Strategic Bombing Survey materials on the interrogation of Japanese officials in 1945, a set of the

Tokyo War Crimes Tribunal Records, incoming American and European news service dispatches (which were censored), and extensive runs of the *Pacific Stars and Stripes,* the *Osaka Mainichi,* the *Nippon Times,* and the daily newspaper of the British Commonwealth Occupation Force. The University of Maryland has supplemented some of these newspaper holdings by purchasing microfilm reels for earlier and later periods.

(6) Maps

Approximately 3 linear feet of uncataloged maps can be found here. All of the above-mentioned materials (1-6) are housed in the McKeldin Library. Censored publications may be found in the "Documents Room" (Room 3115A); the Occupation magazines, newspapers and cataloged books are in Room 3115; and with a few exceptions, all remaining materials are presently being kept in the basement of the library (Room B-130). Further information concerning the Japanese-language materials from the occupation period (1945-1952) can be obtained by calling or writing to Frank Joseph Shulman, head of the East Asian Collection, McKeldin Library, University of Maryland, College Park, MD 20742. Tel. (301) 454-2819.

(7) Photograph Albums

Over 100 albums containing photographs (many of them unpublished) from the Russo-Japanese and Sino-Japanese Wars. These albums originally belonged to a Japanese naval institute library. (See also, entry F15.)

(8) Microfilms

A large number of Japanese and Chinese newspapers, periodicals and serials are available in microfilms: Chinese, 581   35-mm reels; Japanese, 901   35-mm reels.

(9) Audio-visual materials

In the Undergraduate Library, there is an extensive audio-visual facility and materials. A quick survey of materials there revealed at least 35 video-tapes (some documentary types) on China, Japan, and Korea. Also, nearly 100 tapes dealing with Chinese folk songs, Japanese popular songs, special lectures on China and Japan, and Japanese and Chinese language training, etc., are available at the Language Media Center, Division of Arts and Humanities. For further information, contact Dr. James E. Royalty, Director, at (301) 454-5728. (See also, entry D4.)

5.   The items mentioned above, especially 1-7, constitute noteworthy collections. In addition, some rare Chinese books of the East Asia Collection should be mentioned: *Ta fang pien fo pao en ching* (published in 1593); *Shan hai ching kaung chu* (published in 1667); *Yuan shih* (published in 1659), 50 volumes; and *Ming shih* (published in 1739), 112 volumes.

6.   There are no published catalogs or descriptions of the Maryland libraries. A brief printed guide to the McKeldin Library and 1-page fliers describing certain features of the library are free on request. For the East Asia collection, however, a few helpful guides and reports are available:

(1) Frank Joseph Shulman, "Publications and Unpublished Materials from the Allied Occupation of Japan Within the East Asia Collection,

McKeldin Library, University of Maryland, College Park" *Committee on East Asian Libraries Bulletin*, No. 55, (March 1978); also available in mimeographed form at the Collection's office.

(2) Frank Joseph Shulman, "Rengōkoku Nihon Senryōki no kankōbutsu to mikankō shiryō" *Kokuritsu Kokkai Toshokan geppō (National Diet Library Monthly Bulletin)*, No. 204, (March 1978), a translation into Japanese of the above.

(3) *Microfilm Holdings of the East Asia Collection, McKeldin Library, University of Maryland* (July 1976).

(4) A forthcoming mimeographed holdings list of current East Asian language periodicals in the University of Maryland's East Asia Collection.

Also, the University library's newsletter occasionally carries news from the East Asia Collection (e.g., *Library News*, vol. 5, nos. 3/4, April/May 1976). (See also, private collections, Frank Joseph Shulman; and also, academic programs, University of Maryland in entries M33 and M34.)

Washington Post **Library** See entry N16.

Washington Star **Library** See entry N17.

Woodrow Wilson International Center for Scholars Library
See entry M35.

A43 Private Collection

1.   *Frank Joseph Shulman*
College Park, MD
Mailing Address:
East Asia Collection, McKeldin Library
University of Maryland
College Park, MD 20742
(301) 454-2819

2-3.   As a part of a rapidly growing personal library collection on Asia as a whole, Shulman (Head of the University of Maryland's East Asia Collection(owns 4,000-5,000 books and volumes of periodicals relating to China, Japan, and Korea. Areas of particular strength include: Western-language bibliographies and other types of reference works on East Asia; and Japanese-language publications on the Middle East and on Jewish subjects (e.g., nearly complete sets of *Chūtō tsūhō* and *Gekkan kibbutz*) and Hebrew-language books and magazines on East Asia.

In addition, Shulman maintains for archival purposes very extensive vertical files of Western-language newsletters and information bulletins published during the 1960s and the 1970s in the area of East Asian

Studies (e.g., *Chinese Republican Studies Newsletter, Bulletin of the European Association for Japanese Studies*) and comprehensive bibliographical files for complete worldwide doctoral dissertations on Asia. An unpublished card catalog (arranged alphabetically by author) exists for the book collection. Many of the newsletters have been listed in Shulman's "Newsletters and Association Bulletins on Asia: An Annotated Guide to Current Academic Resources" (*Asian Studies Professional Review,* vols. 4 (1974-75) and 5 (1975-76)).

The dissertation files, in turn, form the basis for such bibliographies as Shulman's *Doctoral Dissertations on Japan and Korea, 1969-1974* (Ann Arbor, Mich.: University Microfilms International, 1976) and his *Doctoral Dissertations on China, 1971-1975* (Seattle: University of Washington Press, 1978), as well as for the journal *Doctoral Dissertations on Asia* (published by the Association for Asian Studies in Ann Arbor, Michigan). The entire collection is available, by appointment, for scholarly use at Shulman's home in College Park.

B Archives and Manuscript Depositories

Entry Form for Archives and Manuscript Depositories (B)

1. Access
   a. *Address; telephone number(s)*
   b. Hours of Service
   c. Conditions of access
   d. Reproduction services
   e. Director; heads of relevant divisions

2. Size of holdings pertaining to East Asia

3. Description of holdings

4. Bibliography of materials facilitating access to the collection (inventories, finding aids, catalogs, guides, descriptions)

B1 American Red Cross Archives

1. a. *17th and D Streets, NW* (Entrance to library on 18th St.)
      Washington, D.C. 20006
      857-3712

   b. 8:30 A.M.-4:45 P.M.   Monday-Friday

   c. The archives are open to scholars.

   d. Limited free photoduplication service; more extensive copying for a fee.

   e. Irma Lucas, Archivist

2. The archival materials of the American Red Cross (ARC) are arranged by subject in 5 record groups. East Asian holdings can be found in each record group. However, the first 3 groups, spanning the years 1881-1946, have been transferred to the National Archives and Record Service (NARS). A list of folder captions of these 3 record groups is available at the American Red Cross Archives. Included are files on the China Famine Relief of the early 1900s, and the American Red Cross activities in East Asia during World War II. The last 2 record groups,

RG 4 (1947-64) and RG 5 (1965-present), are still located at the ARC Archives. Included in these record groups are files on such topics as "Formation of the Korean Red Cross Society" and "The Visit by the Emperor and Empress Hirohito to the American Red Cross National Headquarters, October 1975."

3. These archival materials deal with American Red Cross activities both in the United States and abroad, including East Asia. They are rich in information about Chinese famines, Japanese earthquakes, and wars in the Pacific and East Asia.

4. No published research tools are available, but the list noted in point 2 above are useful to researchers.

**B2 Archives of American Art/National Collection
of Fine Art (NCFA)—National Portrait Gallery
(NPG) Library (Smithsonian Institution)**

1. a. *Fine Arts and Portrait Gallery Building*
    8th and F Streets, NW
    Washington, D.C. 20560
    381-6174 (Archives)
    381-5118 (Library)

    b. 10:00 A.M.-5:00 P.M.   Monday-Friday

    c. Open to researchers, who should secure a pass from the entrance guards. Some archival items are restricted.

    d. Photoduplication service is available.

    e. Archives:

    William Woolfenden, Director (in New York)
    Garnett McCoy, Deputy Director
    Arthur Breton, Curator of Manuscripts

    Library:
    William B. Walker, Director

2. The library contains approximately 15,000 volumes relating to the fine arts, mostly in the United States.

3. Historians, especially those studying émigrés from East Asia, may find in the archives materials on East Asian artists now in the United States (e.g., Dong Kingman of Hawaii).
    The focus of the art collections as well as reference materials at NCFA and NPG is on American art, and the number of items relating to East Asia is extremely limited. The National Portrait Gallery, which collects only portraits of Americans, has in its collection two Japanese portrait print—one is of Commodore Matthew C. Perry; and the other is of President Ulysses S. Grant and his wife. Both were made during their visits to Japan.

4.   In addition to the card catalogs, the following guides are available: *Archives of American Art: Directory of Resources* by Garnett McCoy (New York: R. R. Bowker, 1972); and *Archives of American Art: A Checklist of the Collection* compiled by Arthur J. Breton et al. (Washington, D.C.: Smithsonian Institution, 1975).

B3 Army Center for Military History (CMH)

1.   a. *Forrestal Building, Room 6A015*
1000 Independence Avenue, SW
Washington, D.C. 20314
693-5002

    b. 8:00 A.M.-4:30 P.M. Monday-Friday

    c. Most of the collection is open to serious researchers for on-site use. Prior arrangements with the office are needed to use the archives.

    d. Photoduplication service is available through the Library of Congress.

    e. Brig. Gen. James L. Collins, Jr., Chief of Military History
Dr. Maurice Matloff, Chief Historian
Hannah Zeidlik, Chief, Historical Records Branch

2-3.   The Army Center of Military History has custody over approximately 900 linear feet of archival materials including about 5,000 unpublished historical manuscripts dealing with the U.S. Army's activities from 1941 through 1978. The materials in this collection dealing with East Asia are substantial and include (1) materials relating to the Allied Occupation of Japan (1945-1952); (2) manuscripts dealing with the China and Burma Theater of operations during World War II; (3) "Japanese monographs" (i.e., 180 monographs on Japanese military activities during World War II and 13 studies on Japanese operations in Manchuria (1931-1945); (4) a history of the U.S. occupation of Korea (1945-1948); (5) records of U.S. Army operations in the Korean War (approximately 200 items); (6) a series of studies on China undertaken under the auspices of the Military History Division of the U.S. Department of the Army; (7) materials on the Vietnam conflict (unprocessed); and (8) miscellaneous documents dealing with U.S. Army activities in Asia.

    More specifically, the Center archives contain the following materials relating to East Asia.

MATERIALS ON CHINA

(1) "History of the China-Burma-India Theater, 21 May 1942 to 25 October 1944." 4 vols.
(2) "History of Service of Supply China-Burma-India, 11 June 1942 to 24 October 1944." 38 vols.
(3) "History of India-Burma Theater: 25 October 1944 to 23 June 1945; 24 June 1945 to 31 May 1946." 28 vols.
(4) "Photographs—History of Northern Combat Area Command, India-Burma Theater." 3 albums.

(5) "History of China Theater." 3 vols.
(6) "Army Advisory Group Unit History, Nanking, China, 1946."
(7) "History of Army Section, MAAG, Taiwan: 1946-1955."
(8) Headquarters, U.S. Forces China Theater, Chungking, China, "Basic Study of a Proposed Organization of the Chinese Department of National Defense (1945)."
(9) "Yenan Observer Group, Dixie Mission (1944-1946)." 4 vols.

MATERIALS ON WORLD WAR II

(1) Tenth Army. 1st Information and Historical Service, "XXIV Corps in the Conquest of Okinawa 1 April to June 22 1945." 4 vols.
(2) ———, "The Battle for Saipan." 980 pp.
(3) ———, "The Attu Operation, 7th Division, Reduction of Attu Islands Supported by Troops of the 4th Infantry Regiment of Alaska Defense Command."
(4) Far East Command, General Headquarters. General Staff, Military History Section, "History of the United States Army Forces in the Far East, 1943-1945."
(5) Various U.S. Army staff studies of Japanese operations on "Jolo Islands," "Leyte and Cebu," "Mindanao Island," "Negros Island," the "Batangas Area," "Panay Island," "Luzon," and others.
(6) Middle Pacific and Predecessor Commands, United States Army Forces. Historical Sub-Section, G-2. War Department Histories, "United States Army Forces, Middle Pacific and Predecessor Commands World War II, 7 December 1941-2 September 1945." 33 vols.

MATERIALS ON JAPAN

At least three major collections on Japan are contained in the Army archives: (1) "History of the Non-Military Activities of the Occupation of Japan" (prepared at GHQ, Supreme Commander for the Allied Powers) 55 items; (2) "List of Japanese Monographs and Studies" 185 items; and (3) "List of Japanese Studies on Manchuria, including Japanese Night Combat Study" 13 vols. Finding aids for these collections are available at the Army Center of Military History. In addition, the Center's archives contain records of the U.S. Eighth Army in Japan during the Occupation period. Some of the more significant titles included in these collections are as follows:

(1) *History of the Non-Military Activities of the Occupation of Japan* (as listed in sequence in the CMH's "Historical Manuscript Accession List" issued on July 1, 1952).
 2. "Administration of the Occupation, 1945 through 1951."
 4. "Population, 1945 through January 1951."
 5. "Trials of Class 'B' and 'C' War Criminals."
 6. "The Purge, 1945 through 1951."
 7. "Constitutional Revision, 1945 through December 1951."
 8. "Election Reform, 1945-November 1951."
10. "Development of Political Parties, 1945 through November 1951."
11. "National Administrative Reorganization, 1945 through 1949."
12. "Reorganization of Civil Service, 1945 through 1951."
13. "Local Government Reform, 1945 through December 1950."
14. "Legal and Judicial Reform, 1945 through October 1951."

15. "Police and Public Safety, 1945 through October 1951."
16. "Freedom of the Press, 1945 to January 1951."
17. "Radio Broadcasting, 1945 through 1951."
19. "Treatment of Foreign Nationals, 1945 through 1950."
20. "Education, 1945 through September 1949."
21. "Religion, 1945 through June 1951."
22. "Public Welfare, 1945 through December 1949."
23. "Social Security, 1945 through March 1950."
25. "Reparations, 1945 through March 1950."
26. "Foreign Property Administration, 1945 through September 1949."
28. "Elimination of Zaibatsu Control, 1945 through June 1950."
29. "Deconcentration of Economic Power, 1945 through December 1950."
31. "Development of the Trade Union Movement, 1945 through June 1951."
33. "The Rural Land Reform, 1945 through June 1951."
37. "National Government Finance, 1945 through March 1951."
38. "Money and Banking, 1945 through June 1951."
39. "Local Government Finance, 1945 through March 1951."
40. "Financial Reorganization of Corporate Enterprise, 1945 through December 1950."
41. "Agriculture, September 1945 through December 1950."
42. "Fisheries, 1945 through 1950."
46. "Expansion and Reorganization of the Electric Power and Gas Industries, 1945 through March 1950."
48. "Heavy Industries, 1945 through 1950."
50. "The Light Industries, 1945 through March 1951."
51. "Reorganization of Science and Technology in Japan, 1945 to September 1950."
52. "Foreign Trade, 1945 through December 1950."
53. "Land and Air Transportation, 1945 through March 1951."
55. "Communications, 1945 through December 1950."

[*Note:* Entire set of 55 reports on microfilm is available for purchase from the Washington National Records Center, Washington, D.C. 20409.]

(2) *List of Japanese Monographs and Studies:* Following are selected items included in the list of monographs and studies (185 items) prepared by the Japanese Research Division of the Military History Section, General Headquarters, Far East.

1. "Philippines Operations Records."
2. "Homeland Operations Records."
3. "Southeast Area Operations Records."
4. "Burma Operations Records."
5. "The Invasion of the Netherlands East Indies."
6. "Army Operations in China." (1938-August 1945).
7. "The Kwantung Army in the Manchurian Campaign (1941-1945)."
8. "Sources of Materials Used in the Preparation of Japanese Monographs (Army)."
9. "Malaya Invasion Naval Operations (December 1941-April 1942)." (revised)

10. "China Area Operations Records" (August 1943-July 1944).
11. "Japanese Preparations for Operations in Manchuria (January 1943-August 1945)."
12. "Political Strategy Prior to Outbreak of War (September 1931-December 1941)." Parts.
13. "Outline of Naval Armament and Preparations for War." 6 parts.
14. "Records of Operations Against Soviet Russia, Eastern Front (August 1945)."
15. "Records of Operations Against Soviet Russia, Northern and Western Fronts (August-September 1945)."
16. "North China Area Operations Record (July 1937-May 1941)."
17. "Central China Area Operations Record (1937-1941)."
18. "South China Area Operations Record (1937-1941)."

(3) *List of Japanese Studies on Manchuria, Including Japanese Night Combat Study:*

Vol. 1: "Japanese Operational Planning Against the USSR (1932-1945)."
Vol. 2: "Imperial Japanese Army in Manchuria (1894-1945)."
Vol. 3: "Strategic Study on Manchuria: Military Topography and Geography."
Vols. 4-6: "Air Operations," "Infantry Operations," & "Armor Operations."
Vols. 7-9: "Supporting Arms and Services," "Logistics in Manchuria," & "Climatic Factors."
Vol. 10: "Japanese Intelligence Planning Against the USSR Army (1934-1941)."
Vol. 11: "Small Wars and Border Problems." (e.g., the Changkufeng Incident, 1938, the Nomonhan Incident, 1939, etc.)
Vol. 12: "Anti-Bandit Operations (1931-41)."
Vol. 13: "Study of Strategical and Tactical Peculiarities of Far Eastern Russia and Soviet Far Eastern Forces (1931-45)."

(4) *Other Materials on Japan:*

1. Eighth Army, Headquarters. 10th Information and Historical Service. "Special Study of the Yokohama War Crimes Trials, December 1945-September 1947."
2. ———, "Eighth Army Military Government System in Japan."
3. Eighth Army, Headquarters. Historical Section, "Occupational Monographs of the Eighth U.S. Army in Japan, August 1945-December 1948," 4 vols.

MATERIALS ON KOREA

(1) United States Armed Forces in Korea (USAFIK), U.S. Army Military Government in Korea, Statistical Research Division of the Office of Administrative Headquarters, "History of U.S. Army Military Government in Korea, Period of September 1945-30 June 1946." 3 vols.
(2) Historical Manuscripts on Korean Conflict: the Center of Military History's archives contain various records relating to the U.S. Army's combat operations and activities in the Korean War (1950-1953), including the following:
1. Far East Command, Headquarters, Military History Section, "History of the Korean War."

2. Far East Command, Headquarters. Eighth U.S. Army in Korea (EUSAK), "Special Problems in the Korean Conflict."

3. Far East Command, Headquarters. Military History Section, "History of the Korean War Chronology, 25 June-31 December 1951."

4. Far East, U.S. Army Forces, Headquarters. 3rd Historical Detachment, "EUSAK Combat Propaganda Operations, 13 July 1950-1 September 1952."

5. Republic of Korea (ROK), *Military History of Korea*. Translated by Headquarters, U.S. Army Forces, Far East 500th Military Intelligence Service Group.

6. Various records pertaining to major battles in Korea (e.g., "Heartbreak Ridge," "Bloody Ridge," etc.).

7. "U.N. Military Operations in Korea."

8. "P.O.W.'s Repatriation."

9. "Armistice Negotiations."

4. There is no published catalog for the holdings of the Historical Record Branch of the Center of Military History. There are, however, finding aids for the major collections. Also useful are a number of "Historical Manuscript Accession Lists" prepared by the Center of Military History, such as: "History of the Non-Military Activities of the Occupation of Japan;" "Korean Conflict;" "History of the U.S. Army Forces in the Far East, 1943-1945;" "List of Japanese Monographs and Studies;" and "List and Description of Japanese Studies on Manchuria, including Japanese Night Combat Study."

For the publications of the center, see *Publications of the U.S. Army Center of Military History* (Government Printing Office, 1977). It lists and describes those works that have been published by the Center either in book form, photoprint, or microfilm, including those available from the National Archives and Records Service.

[*Note:* To stimulate unofficial scholarly research in the field of military history, the CMH offers two "Dissertation Year Fellowships" to qualified doctoral candidates writing dissertations in American military history. For further information, write to the Chief Historian, Center of Military History, Department of the Army, James Forrestal Building, Washington, D.C. 20314.]

Catholic University of America Library See entry A8.

B4 Freer Gallery of Art Library (Smithsonian Institution)

1. a. *12th Street and Jefferson Drive, SW*
    Washington, D.C. 20560
    381-5332

    b. 10:00 A.M.-4:30 P.M.   Monday-Friday

    c. Open to the public. No interlibrary loans are possible except for the slide collection on Oriental art.

d. Photocopying and microfilming facilities.

e. Priscilla P. Smith, Librarian

2-3.   The library has custody over personal papers, albums, and manuscripts donated by a number of distinguished artists and scholars; including the following:

CHARLES LANG FREER CORRESPONDENCE COLLECTION

This includes 30 volumes of letters (carbon copies) from Freer to various people on a wide range of topics, including Freer's acquisition activities on behalf of the Oriental art collection preserved at the Freer Gallery. A microfilmed version is also available. It also contains some original letters of Freer.

CARL WHITING BISHOP COLLECTION

It contains 11 albums and 2 unpublished manuscripts ("Archaeological Finds in China" and "Archaeological Research in China, 1923-1934") prepared by Bishop, a former staff member of the Freer Gallery, who worked in China from 1930 to 1933. The photographic collection consists of over 2,600 photos on various subjects, local scenes, customs, and artifacts in China.

XYLOGRAPHS COLLECTION

The library has a number of xylographed sutras in Chinese, and at least one in the Manchu, Mongol, and Tibetan languages, including one of the oldest of its kind entitled "I chieh ju lai hsin pi mi chuan shen she li pao chieh yin to lo ni ching" from the Lei-ku-t'a or Thunder Peak pagoda in Hangchou, China, which was printed in A.D. 975.

4.   No published catalog for these collections is available; however, xylographic collection can be located in the library's card catalog under "Sutras." For further information, researchers should consult with staff members.

Georgetown University Library See entry A19.

B5 Library of Congress—Manuscript Division

1.   a. *Room 3004, Thomas Jefferson Building*
Library of Congress
10 1st Street, SE
Washington, D.C. 20540
426-5383

b. 8:30 A.M.-5:00 P.M.   Monday-Saturday (stack service ends of 4:15 P.M.)

c. Open to serious researchers; registration required. Use of some holdings may be restricted.

d. Photocopying service is available.

e. John C. Broderick, Chief

2.   No accurate estimate of size of East Asian holdings is possible, but materials are extensive. Total holdings, about 35-40 million items; organized in about 10,000 collections.

3.   There is no established method of locating items relating to East Asia by subject or geographic approach. Inevitably, one has to rely heavily on the help provided by the reference specialists of the Manuscript Division. To be definitive, one would have to check the division's card catalogs and computerized listings of its collections against lists of all United States presidents, secretaries of state, diplomatic mission chiefs to China, Japan, and Korea, etc., and then examine finding aids for these collections and the collections themselves. The following list is divided along the lines just mentioned; however, it is selective, not exhaustive, in nature.

Papers of the following individuals contain materials relating to East Asia:

	Containers	Items	Period Covered
PRESIDENTS			
Andrew Jackson	192	26,000	1775-1860
Martin Van Buren	75	6,000	1787-1868
John Tyler	8	1,400	1691-1918
James K. Polk	156	20,500	1775-1891
Zachary Taylor	10	631	1814-1931
Franklin Pierce	26	2,300	1820-1869
James Buchanan	4	1,500	1829-1887
Abraham Lincoln	213	42,100	1833-1916
Andrew Johnson	251	40,000	1814-1900
Ulysses Simpson Grant	185	47,236	1844-1922
James Abram Garfield	524	80,354	1831-1881
Grover Cleveland	600	100,000	1859-1945
William McKinley	424	131,000	1847-1901
Theodore Roosevelt	1,148	276,000	1759-1920
William Howard Taft	1,633	675,000	1810-1930
Woodrow Wilson	1,607	278,540	1786-1944
Calvin Coolidge	750	179,000	1921-1929
SECRETARIES OF STATE			
Henry Clay	37	4,500	1770-1910
Daniel Webster	17	2,500	1800-1895
Edward Everett	6	150	1858-1864
William Learned Marcy	94	15,000	1806-1857
Jeremiah Sullivan Black	81	10,000	1813-1904
William Henry Seward	1	40	1801-1872
Frederick Theodore Frelinghuysen	1	700	n.d.
Hamilton Fish	360	60,000	1732-1914
William Maxwell Evarts	62	12,000	1835-1908
James Gillespie Blaine	49	7,000	1777-1945
Thomas Francis Bayard (Contains materials relating to the Japanese conflict over the vassalage of Korea.)	239	60,000	1780-1899
John Watson Foster	1	175	1872-1917
Walter Quintin Gresham	51	12,000	1857-1930
Richard Olney	162	28,000	1830-1924
John Sherman	619	111,000	1836-1900

	Containers	Items	Period Covered
John Hay	113	11,290	1785-1914
Elihu Root	262	66,000	1863-1937
Philander Chase Knox (Contains extensive materials relating to China and the Chinese revolution of 1911-1912.)	75	8,450	1796-1922
William Jennings Bryan	66	18,000	1877-1940
Robert Lansing	81	12,000	1890-1933
Bainbridge Colby	28	2,500	1888-1950
Charles Evans Hughes	260	61,000	1876-1939
Cordell Hull	265	70,000	1908-1956

DIPLOMATIC CHIEFS TO CHINA

	Containers	Items	Period Covered
James Burrill Angell	1	—	1829-1916
John Ross Browne	1	2	1821-1875
Anson Burlingame	6	550	1810-1937
Caleb Cushing	421	120,000	1785-1906
Edward Everett	6	150	1858-1864
Nelson Trusler Johnson	66	22,400	1916-1954
Alan Goodrich Kirk	1	125	1919-1961
Louis McLane (Louis was not a minister to China. His son, Robert, was, and Robert is represented in Louis McLane papers.)	—	—	1795-1894
John Russell Young	44	28,000	1843-1898

DIPLOMATIC MISSION CHIEFS TO JAPAN

	Containers	Items	Period Covered
Chauncey Mitchell Depew	1	150	1865-1928
William Cameron Forbes	11	2,500	1904-1946
Lloyd Carpenter Griscom	4	900	1898-1951
Townsend Harris	2	11	1856-1862
Richard Bennett Hubbard	1	—	1832-1901
Roland Slector Morris	15	5,000	1910-1943

DIPLOMATIC MISSION CHIEFS TO KOREA

	Containers	Items	Period Covered
Horace Newton Allen	1	2	1858-1932

NAVAL OFFICERS: EAST ASIA

	Containers	Items	Period Covered
Mark Lambert Bristol (Correspondence relating in part to his command of the U.S. Asiatic Fleet in late 1920s.)	98	40,000	1887-1939
George Dewey (Contains materials relating to his service as naval commander in the Far East during the Spanish-American War.)	8	25,000	1820-1943
Alfred Thayer Mahan	24	1,000	1824-1914
Harry Ervin Yarnell (Correspondence and papers relating to Sino-Japanese conflict in 1937-1938, including an account of the Panay incident.)	8	3,500	1936-1939
William D. Leahy	23	27	1893-1959

NAVAL OFFICERS: EMPHASIS ON CHINA

	Containers	Items	Period Covered
Montgomery M. Taylor (Much of the collection relates to Taylor's role as com-	4	1,200	1800-1936

	Containers	Items	Period Covered
mander-in-chief of the U.S. Asiatic Fleet, 1931-1933, and concerns Japanese expansion into China and the Shanghai incident [1932].)			
Joseph Strauss (Served as the commander-in-chief of the U.S. Asiatic Fleet.)	1	25	1881-1922
Thomas Kearny	1	3	1931-1936
Colville Terrett	1	6	1850-1859
Albert Gleaves (Correspondence shows Gleaves' dealings with Russian, Chinese, and Japanese governments. Also records of the U.S. Asiatic Fleet.)	21	6,000	1803-1946
George Eugene Belknap	4	1,400	1857-1903
Franklin Dillen (Reports on military and political conditions in China.)	1	45	1925-1927
Purnell Frederick Harrington	1	100	1861-1885

NAVAL OFFICERS: EMPHASIS ON JAPAN

	Containers	Items	Period Covered
John Glendy Sproston (Journal [February-March 1854] written during Perry's expedition to Japan.)	1	1	
Theodore Stark Wilkinson	1	200	1942-1945
William Reynolds	1	2	1877-1880
Louis Ashfield Kimberly	1	200	1889-1896
Wood Family	1	28	1836-1906
Matthew C. Perry (Printed matter from the American-Japanese Society.)	2	200	1838-1933
Silas Casey (Collection includes materials on (1) USS *Niagara* and its cruise to Tokyo in 1860-1861 with Japanese diplomats; (2) USS *Colorado* and Casey's command of the landing force in the Korean Punitive Expedition of 1871, including printed matter on the capture of Fort McKee on Kanghua Island, Korea.)	6	300	1771-1941
Edward John Dorn	5	1,000	1868-1936
Herbert Bain Knowles	9	—	1941-1945
William Sterling Parsons	3	1,500	1943-1953
John Franklin Shafroth (Commander of the South Pacific Force; materials primarily on World War II [1943-1945].)	7	1,800	1926-1945
Charles Andreas Lockwood	7	7,000	1904-1967

NAVAL OFFICERS: EMPHASIS ON KOREA

	Containers	Items	Period Covered
William Alexander Marshall	1	100	1876-1906
George Clayton Foulk	1	300	1872-1951
Robert Wilson Shufeldt	37	15,000	1836-1910
Harry S. Elseffer (Contains an account of the signing of the U.S. treaty with Korea in 1883).	1	80	1874-1886

ARMY OFFICERS

	Containers	Items	Period Covered
Tasker H. Bliss	496	80,000	1870-1937
Charles J. Bonaparte	262	80,000	1790-1921

	Containers	Items	Period Covered
Claire Lee Chennault (Army officer/aviator. Basically pertains to war efforts in China—"Flying Tigers.")	12 (reels)	–	1941-1954
Henry Clark Corbin (Including materials on the Boxer Rebellion.)	22	2,000	1864-1938
Frank Ross McCoy (Including subject files on Far Eastern-American Relief Mission to Japan [1923] and Lytton Commission [1932].)	106	36,750	1847-1954

STATESMEN, SCHOLARS, JOURNALISTS, MISSIONARIES, FINANCIERS, ETC.

	Containers	Items	Period Covered
Chandler P. Anderson	101	–	1894-1953
Joseph Wright Alsop (Journalist—correspondence relating to almost all major events and personalities of late 1940s through early 1960s with emphasis on China.)	127	46,000	1699-1970
Wharton Barker (Financier/publisher—papers relating to Chinese and Russian trade.)	29	5,000	1870-1920
William Edgar Borah (Senator/politician—includes materials dealing with the Kellogg Briand pact [1928-1929].)	881	260,000	1905-1940
Josephus Daniels (Secretary of Navy/ambassador)	931	330,000	1806-1948
Norman H. Davis (Economist/diplomat—was a delegate to the Washington Conference of 1921-1922).)	93	43,000	1918-1942
Dutilh & Wachsmuth (Philadelphia) (Business papers—China trade.)	2	517	1784-1800
Herbert Feis (Scholar/historian — mainly correspondence; some regarding China and Japan; and also research materials utilized for Feis's various books.)	120	26,000	1893-1972
Henry Prather Fletcher (Diplomat—served in Peking.)	28	6,500	1898-1958
Francis Dunlap Gamewell (Missionary—some materials on missionary works in Peking during the Boxer Rebellion [1900].)	1	200	1900-1937
Mary W. Gribble (Diary of voyage from San Francisco to Japan in 1866.)	1	1	1866
George Kennan (Explorer/author—correspondence pertaining to travels in Russia, Japan, and other parts of East Asia [1865-1923].)	119	60,000	1840-1937
Lafcadio Hearn (Author/physician who lived in Japan.)	9	2,700	1877-1931
John R. Latimer (Merchant—contains letters, invoices, insurance policies, and accounts on the opium trade between India and China as conducted by foreign mer-	41	2,800	1805-1844

	Containers	Items	Period Covered
chants in Canton during the decades immediately preceding the Opium War [1839-1842].)			
Charles William LeGendre (Army officer/ diplomat—materials relating to LeGendre's career in both the United States and Japanese foreign services, 1866-1875. Also some materials relating to Korea, 1891-1893.)	15	1,790	1866-1893
Abiel A. Low and Mills E. S. Low (Family papers—correspondence of the family relating to Chinese and Japanese trade.)	21	4,000	1795-1959
Henry Luce (Editor/publisher—materials relating to Luce's organizational efforts for the China Institute in America; United Board for Christian Higher Education in Asia; United China Relief; United Service to China; Yale-in-China Association, etc.)	110	35,000	1917-1967
David Murray (Educator/scientist—materials dealing with education, government, history, social conditions in Japan during 1870-1879, which were written while serving as advisor on educational reforms in Japan.	4	500	1872-1904
Maurice F. Neufeld collection (Contains 2,000 papers relating to Allied military government in Italy and to World War II, including materials on German-Japanese technical cooperation.)	7	2,000	1943-1945
J. Robert Oppenheimer (Some correspondence with prominent Chinese and Japanese physicists, such as Shuichi Kusaka, Tsung-dao Lee, Chen-ning [Frank] Yang, Hideki Yukawa.)	293	74,000	1927-1967
Willard P. Phillips (Merchant-trader—correspondence relating to trade with the Philippines and China.)	1	184	1837-1887
Key Pittman (Congressman—contains materials on commercial relations with China and the Far East.)	191	55,000	1898-1951
Thomas Pitkin (Artist—notes pertaining to Japan.)	1	60	1865
Robert Porter Patterson (Secretary of war. Covered in collection—Marshall Plan, the United Nations, etc.)	107	47,800	1940-1951
Edmund Roberts (Merchant/diplomat—papers provide descriptive portrait of the people, customs, languages, religions, and arts of East Asia and South America.)	5	1,000	1803-1905
Russell & Co. (Considerable materials bearing on Russell & Co.'s activities in China.)	21	4,200	1816-1835

	Containers	Items	Period Covered
Rufus Harvey Sargent (Geologist/cartographer—some materials relating to expedition in North China.)	1	17	1903-1904
Francis Bowes Sayre (Diplomat—some materials relating to Japan.)	27	8,100	1861-1961
Henry Agard Wallace (U.S. vice president/secretary of agriculture.)	99	24,600	1934-1944
James Harrison Wilson (China trade; industrialization of China, especially railroad production.)	53	–	1865-1920
OTHERS			
American Council of Learned Societies Records (Records of the Council include materials relating to international intellectual cooperation and programs supporting research on East Asia—China and Japan.)	548	184,250	1919-1946
Henry Alfred Kissinger (Papers not yet available to the public.)	–	290,000	1969-1976

4. The most important guide to archives and manuscripts in the United States is the ongoing publication of *The National Union Catalog of Manuscript Collections* (1959-). So far, 15 volumes have been published. NUCMC describes many LC holdings. Useful information can also be found in earlier publications, such as Philip Hamer's *A Guide to Archives and Manuscripts in the United States* (New Haven, Conn.: Yale University Press, 1961) the *Handbook of Manuscripts in the Library of Congress* (1918); Curtis W. Garrison, *List of Manuscript Collections in the Library of Congress to July 1931* (1932); and C. Percy Powell, *List of Manuscript Collections Received in the Library of Congress, July 1931 to July 1938* (1939). Manuscript accessions are described in the *Annual Report of the Library of Congress* (1898-) and in the *Quarterly Journal of the Library of Congress* (1943-).

The most complete list of holdings is unpublished; it is the computerized descriptive listing kept at the Manuscript Reading Room desk. It is updated every six months and shows the size of collections, the availability of finding aides, etc. This is indispensable for scholars who want to utilize the division's holdings.

Since 1958 the Manuscript Division has been publishing "registers" for some of its holdings. However, the majority of collections do not have published registers, but usually have finding aids or unpublished registers. All presidential papers have a published index.

The Manuscript Division provides without charge two brief guides to readers: "Manuscript Division: Library of Congress" and "Catalogs, Indexes, Finding Aids."

Library of Congress, Orientalia Division See entry A30.

B6 Marine Corps (Navy Department)—History and Museum Division

1. a. *Washington Navy Yard, Building 58*
   9th and M Street, SE
   Washington, D.C. 20374
   433-3840

   b. 8:00 A.M.-4:30 P.M. Monday-Friday

   c. Researchers should call ahead to arrange a visit.

   d. Photoreproduction facilities are available.

   e. Brig. Gen. E. H. Simmons, Director of Marine Corps History and Museums

   Col. John E. Greenwood, Deputy Director for History
   Henry I. Shaw, Jr., Chief Historian
   Benis M. Frank, Director of the Oral History Program
   Col. Franklin B. Nihart, Deputy Director for Museums
   Jack B. Hilliard, Chief Curator
   Charles Anthony Wood, Curator of Personal Papers
   Capt. Judson E. Bennett, Jr., Curator of Military Music
   Ken Smith-Christmas, Registrar
   John T. Dyer, Jr., Curator of Art

2. The division's total holdings pertaining to East Asia are difficult to estimate. Clearly, however, the division does possess a number of items of interest to East Asian specialists. An aviation museum branch of the Washington museum is located at the Quantico Marine Base in northern Virginia. The Quantico museum, however, is not covered by this guide.

3. The History and Museum Division has a collection of over 600 Marine Corps personal papers. The "Manuscript Collection" is housed in Building 58, Washington Navy Yard. Researchers wanting access to the collections may use them on the premises. A written request for access should be addressed through the Curator of Personal Papers at least one week in advance. Some of the more important personal papers are listed below.

   INDIVIDUAL COLLECTIONS

   Personal Collection (or PC) 51: *Col. Luther A. Brown Collection* is built around a photostatic copy of Brown's diary of the Shanghai incident of 1932; and materials gathered during his incarceration in a Japanese Prisoner of War camp during World War II. Included in the collection is a 6-page transcript carbon copy of an interview conducted by Marine Corps historians regarding Colonel Brown's experiences in North China and the Prisoner-of-War Camps, 1941-45.
   PC 227: *Major Roscoe Ellis Collection.* Most of these materials deal with Ellis's tours of duty in Shanghai in the late 1930s and include 59 Chinese newspapers covering unrest in and the problems of China in 1937.

PC 198: *Lt. Gen. Merwin H. Silverthorn Collection* which, in addition to a manuscript entitled "Men in Battle" (1936), contains 12 photograph albums which vividly cover the general's long career in the Marine Corps. Of note are the photo albums on the Okinawa campaign, April-June 1945; and assignments at Mare Island, Tinian, Peleliu, and Guadalcanal during World War II.

PC 178: *Maj. Gen. William W. Stickney Collection.* During World War II General Stickney participated in the Guadalcanal-Tulagi landings, the Eastern New Guinea and Bismarck archipelago operations, Saipan, and the postwar Occupation of Japan.

PC 122: *Lt. Col. Mclane Tilton.* As Senior Marine Officer with the Asiatic squadron from 1870-1872, he led the U.S. Marine contingent in the Korean Expedition of 1871. He also escorted the American Minister, Frederick Low, to Peking in 1870.

PC 224: *Brig. Gen. Littleton W. T. Waller, Jr. Collection* contains materials pertaining to Waller's father, especially his personal photograph album of the relief expedition in the summer of 1900 to aid the foreign residents in Peking during the Boxer Rebellion.

GROUP COLLECTIONS—CHINA PAPERS, 1900; 1912; 1937-1939

PC 3: *Master Sgt. Wesley M. Baker Collection* includes materials pertaining to Baker's late 1930s tour with the Mounted Detachment, Peking, China.

PC 48: *Lt. Gen. James C. Breckinridge Collection* contains a 13-page letter written by Breckenridge to Col. Jesse F. Dyer on November 17, 1931, on the situation in China, plus the general's personal opinions regarding the Chinese and Japanese gained during his 2-year tour in Tientsin in the 1930s.

PC 56: *Brig. Gen. Evans F. Carlson Collection* includes a 10-page report entitled "Observations of the Sino-Japanese Armies during the battle of Taierchwang (Shantun)" by Carlson.

PC 452: *Captain Richard Dalton Collection* contains a Xerox copy of Maj. Evans F. Carlson's article entitled "The Chinese Army . . . Its Organization and Military Efficiency" (64 pages) published in mimeograph form by the Institute of Pacific Relations in 1939.

PC 16: *Captain John H. Reilly Collection* contains a letter from a Marine officer who participated in the 1900 expedition against the Boxers.

PC 35: *Maj. Gen. John H. Russell, Jr. Collection* includes a logbook of the Marine Detachment, American Legation, Peking, and other materials from 1912 to 1919.

PC 442: *Miss Helen Stote Collection* centers on materials relating to the Marine Corps' role in the siege of Peking, 1900.

GROUP COLLECTIONS—TWENTIETH-CENTURY MARINE CORPS

PC 31: *Col. Oscar T. Jensen Collection* includes a printed document on the Korean Armistice agreement of 1953 and a few related materials.

PC 444: *Staff Sgt. Werner H. Claussen Collection* is a miscellaneous collection of documents and artifacts gathered by Claussen during World War II, including an envelope containing Japanese currency, a photograph album of World War II with South Pacific battle scenes, and various Japanese artifacts.

PC 8: *Sgt. Samuel Cosman Collection* includes printed matter pertaining to Sergeant Cosman's World War II duty in the Pacific (e.g., a quantity of captured Japanese occupation money obtained on Guadalcanal).

PC 453: *Platoon Sgt. Thomas R. O'Neill Collection* contains a Xeroxed copy of a diary compiled by O'Neill following the assault and capture of Guam during World War II.

PC 33: *Gen. Lewis W. Walt Collection* contains typescript copy of translated documents entitled "Instruments to Imperial Japanese Army for Defense of Guadalcanal Island" and "Address of Instruction" (issued in October 1942).

For a detailed description of these papers, see *Marine Corps Personal Papers Collection Catalog* (1974) compiled by Charles Anthony Wood, the division's curator of manuscripts.

THE ORAL HISTORY COLLECTION

The collection of Marine Corps oral histories includes extended interviews with more than 150 prominent, retired Marine Corps' officers. By special arrangement with the Oral History Office of Columbia University, edited transcripts of these interviews have been made available at the division. Many of these documents are open for research. In addition, the Marine Corps has tapes of approximately 4,000 interviews with active-duty personnel conducted by Marine Corps' historians. Most of these materials relate to the Vietnam War. Some are security classified and restricted.

4. The History and Museum Division has published a number of bibliographic guides, including the *Marine Corps Personal Papers Collection Catalog* (1974) and *Marine Corps Oral History Collection Catalog* (1975) compiled by Benis M. Frank. Other useful publications of the division include: *The United States Marines in the Occupation of Japan* (1962) by Henry I. Shaw, Jr.; *One Hundred Eighty Landings of United States Marines 1800-1934* (1974) by Capt. Harry A. Ellsworth; *Special Marine Corps Units of World War II* (1977, reprinted) by Charles L. Updegraph, Jr., and *The United Marines in North China 1945-1949* (1968) by Henry I. Shaw, Jr.

B7 National Anthropological Archives (Smithsonian Institution— National Museum of Natural History)

1. a. *Constitution Avenue and 10th Street, NW*
       Washington, D.C. 20560
       381-5225

    b. 9:00 A.M. to 5:00 P.M. Monday-Friday (except for national holidays).

    c. It is advisable to notify the Archives in advance of a visit and to inquire about specific material, since the collection is diverse and access to some material is restricted.

    d. Photoreproduction facilities are available; prints can be purchased at the office.

e. Herman J. Viola, Director
James R. Glenn, Deputy Director

2-3. The National Anthropological Archives was established in 1965 as part of the Smithsonian Institution's Department of Anthropology, National Museum on Natural History (see entry C 10). Its purpose is to serve as a depository for the records of the Department of Anthropology and its antecedents; and to collect private papers relating to world cultures and the history of anthropology. There are two main collections: Records and Manuscripts and Photographs.

RECORDS AND MANUSCRIPTS COLLECTIONS

Official records and manuscript collections in the Archives amount to approximately 3,500 cubic feet with most of the materials dating between 1847 and 1970. In addition to various official records, it contains a number of private papers of well-known anthropologists (e.g., W. J. McGee, William Duncan Strong, John P. Harrington). Eleven manuscripts pertain to East Asia, 5 to China, and 6 to Japan.

Those dealing with China include:

(1) "The Hua Miao of Southwest China" (1967) by William Harrison Hudspeth.
(2) "On Sign Language in China" (1882) by J. T. Gurlick; and (3-5) manuscripts on Chinese vocabulary.

Those manuscripts on Japan include:

(1) "Water Color Drawings of Japanese Textile Workers" by A. Zeno Shindler.
(2) "Manuscripts of the Matsuri, Religious Festival of the God Anwa, Patron Diety of Nagasaki."
(3) "Sign Languages (Gesture Speech) in Japan 1883-1894" by J. T. Gurlick, including field notes, descriptions of gestures and meanings.
(4-6) "Japanese Language, and the Japo-Peninsula Group." In addition, the NAA maintains the papers of Sister M. Inez Higler who worked among the Ainus (ca. 1965-71).

Included in the collection are typed copies of notes complied by Sister Inez and her Japanese assistants on the customs, traditions, history, language, and arts of the Ainus. The Archives also has a manuscript entitled "Ezo Kiko (an account of a journey through the Island of Ezo [among the Ainus])" which is translated into English (ca. 18th century). Finally, the Archives has recently received the papers of Dr. Eugene Knez, the curator for Asian ethnology, National Museum of Natural History. The Knez collection has not yet been processed; however, it contains papers (mostly administrative in nature), photographs, and other materials that will be of interest to researchers. For further information, contact James R. Glenn, the Archivist (381-5225).

PHOTOGRAPHIC COLLECTIONS

The photographic holdings of the NAA are estimated at 90,000 items, and most of them are dated between 1860 and 1930. NAA's collection of photographs on East Asia is, while not as extensive as its other holdings, generally well organized and quite fascinating. Scenes of everyday life as well as famous individuals are included. A list of the NAA's collection of photographs on East Asia has been compiled and is in the process of being printed.

Some of the more important collections are:

(1) *McCartee Collection* includes 10 black and white photos of various individuals and scenes from Japan and China, including portraits of a Chinese bride and bridegroom, a botanist, a samurai, and a Buddhist priest, which were collected by Divie Bethune McCartee, M.D. (1820-1900). McCartee served as a medical missionary for three decades in China and later spent several years in Tokyo, first as a professor of law and science at the Tokyo Imperial University and later as a curator of the Tokyo Botanical Gardens.

(2) *Shufeldt Collection* has approximately 100 hand-colored and sepia-tone photographic prints of various individuals, scenes, localities, and buildings taken in China, Japan, and Korea by Adm. Robert Wilson Shufeldt around 1878-1887. Admiral Shufeldt visited East Asia to negotiate a treaty of amity and commerce with Korea in 1882. This collection relates primarily to his diplomatic activities in the 1880s. Photographs of Japan and China pertain mainly to architectural and scenic views.

(2) *Goward Collection* contains about 50 photographs of Japanese subjects (ethnographic and historic) donated by Gustavus Goward who had served in the U.S. Legation in Tokyo from 1882-1887. Over half seem to be studio portraits of priests, warriors, and court figures, while the remainder show the destruction wrought by an earthquake in the Gifu-Nagoya area in 1891, and scenes of the Japanese Exhibit at the World Columbian Exposition.

(4) *Graham Collection* consists of about 90 photographs made by David Crockett Graham, a zoological collector for the Smithsonian Institution, during his fieldwork in China's Szechwan province from 1919-1930. Graham photographed native scenes and ruins, people, and especially subjects relating to native religious practices, temples, shrines, and pagodas. Detailed captions are provided for each photographic print.

(5) *Hrdlička Collection* has approximately 30 black and white photos of Korean subjects collected by Dr. Aleš Hrdlička, Curator of Physical Anthropology at the U.S. National Museum (USNM) during his research trips to Japan, Korea, Manchuria, and Hawaii in 1920. The Korean photos vividly reflect the socio-political conditions of the country, especially the northern provinces, in the aftermath of the Korean uprisings of March 1, 1919, against Japanese colonial rule.

(6) *Jouy Collection* contains about 40 photographic prints depicting Korean life in city and village, and individual and group portraits taken by Pierre Louise Jouy in the Pusan and Seoul vicinities around 1890. Jouy went to Korea in 1883 with Lucius H. Foote, the first U.S. Minister to Seoul. Subsequently, he worked for the Korean government.

(7) *Bernadon Collection* includes photographs showing various styles of Korean household furniture and folk graphics typical of home decoration in Korea; they were collected by Ens. John Bernadon of the U.S. Legation in Seoul from 1884-1886. Bernadon collected a number of Korean ethnological specimens in consultation with Dr. Spencer F.

Baird, then Secretary of the Smithsonian, during his service in Korea. (8) *Dall Collection* contains small collection of photos from a series titled "Celebrated Men of the World" (ca. 1860-1866); it was donated by Dr. William Healey Dall.

(9) *Foulk Collection,* taken in Korea and the United States around 1883-1887, consists of 13 sepia-tone photographic prints which include individual and group portraits of the members of the first Korean diplomatic mission to the United States, and views of monuments, buildings, palace grounds, and cities in Korea. These pictures were collected by Ens. George Clayton Foulk who escorted the Korean diplomatic mission to Washington in 1883 and returned with them to Korea in 1884 to serve as naval attaché (and later as chargé d'affaires) of the U.S. Legation in Seoul.

(10) *Miscellaneous Collection* contains several photographs of China, Japan, and Korea, such as photographs of the U.S. Legation in Peking (1904), the Ainu in Japan, one of the first Korean women to visit the United States, and Empress Dowager Tz'u Hsi.

FILM COLLECTION

The Archives has a documentary film entitled "Chi'an Miao people, West China" (1936) which was donated by David C. Graham.

B8 National Archives and Records Service (NARS) (General Services Administration)

1. a. *8th Street and Pennsylvania Avenue, NW*
    (Entrance from Pennsylvania Avenue only)
    Washington, D.C. 20408

    Central Research Room (Room 203, Second Floor)   523-3232
    General Information   523-3099

    Records Information (Room 201, Second Floor)   523-3218

    General Archives Division   (301) 763-7000/7410
    Washington National Records Center
    Suitland, Md. (4205 Suitland Road)
    Mail: Washington, D.C. 20409
    (301) 763-7000

    Machine-Readable Archives Division
    711 14th Street, NW
    Washington, D.C. 20408
    724-1080

    b. Central Research Room (and Microfilm Reading Room)
    8:45 A.M.-10:00 P.M.   Monday-Friday
    8:45 A.M.-5:00 P.M.   Saturday

    Branch Research Rooms:
    8:45 A.M.-5:00 P.M.   Monday-Friday

c. Research at the NARS may be conducted by serious scholars. However, in order to use the NARS' facilities and resources, one must obtain a researcher identification card issued by the NARS. Applicants for the card must have proper identification. The identification card functions as a pass to the 6 research rooms in the National Archives Building as well as other Washington-area research facilities operated by the NARS (e.g., Federal Records Center, Suitland, Maryland). It is valid for 2 years and can be renewed.

Declassified materials are readily available, but classified and restricted materials require either security clearance or special permission from the originating agency. Scholars should contact the staff concerning access to whatever records they plan to utilize.

d. Photocopies of unrestricted documents can be obtained in the Central Research Room, and Xerox copies of microfilm materials in the Microfilm Research Room for a nominal fee. For reproduction services in research areas other than the Central or Microfilm Research Rooms, payment must be made to the cashier in Room 605. The NARS laboratories can provide microfilm copies, photostatic copies, black-and-white or color slides, and color transparencies. The staff can also copy black-and-white or color motion pictures, silent or sound, 16mm or 35mm; tape or disc recordings; aerial photographs; and still photos. These services are provided in accordance with existing copyright laws.

For East Asian and other materials readily available on microfilm, see the *Catalog of National Archives Microfilm Publications* (1974; reprinted 1975).

e. James B. Rhoads, Archivist of the United States
The NARS has the following divisions and branches, each of which has materials relating to East Asia:

Civil Archives Division
Jane Smith, Director   523-3239
Diplomatic Branch
Milton Gustafson, Chief   523-3174
Industrial and Social Branch
Jerome Finster, Chief   523-3119
Legislative, Judicial, and Fiscal Branch
Clarence Lyons, Chief   523-3059
Natural Resources Branch
Harold Pinkett, Chief   523-3238

Military Archives Division
Meyer Fishbein, Director   523-3089
Navy and Old Army Branch
Robert Krauskopf, Chief   523-3229
Modern Military Branch
Robert Wolfe, Chief   523-3340

General Archives Division
Daniel Goggin, Director   (301) 763-7410

Audiovisual Archives Division
James Moore, Director   523-3236

Motion-Picture and Sound-Recording Branch
William Murphy, Chief   523-3267
Still-Picture Branch
Joe Thomas, Chief   523-3054

Cartographic Archives Division
Ralph Enrenberg, Director   523-3062

Machine-Readable Archives Division
Charles Dollar, Director   724-1080

Records Declassification Division
Edwin Thompson, Director   523-3165

Office of Presidential Libraries
Daniel Reed, Director   523-3212

Special Projects Division
A. H. Leisinger, Director   523-3032
Center for Polar Archives
Franklin Burch, Director   523-3223

Regional Archives Coordinator
Charles South 523-3081

2.   The National Archives houses the records of the United States government from the first meeting of the Continental Congress in 1774 through
the first half of the 20th century. These records come from executive,
legislative, and judicial branches of the United States government as
well as most of the independent regulatory commissions and agencies.
There are billions of pages of textual material; 6 million still pictures;
100.000 reels of motion-picture film; 80.000 sound recordings including
congressional hearings; and nearly 5 million maps, charts, and aerial
photographs.

All materials preserved are important to the workings of the United
States government, or have long-term research worth. However, not all
of the noncurrent records of the United States government are housed
in the National Archives. Many are housed in the Federal Records Center, where they are administered by the NARS. The papers of Presidents
Hoover, Roosevelt, Truman, Eisenhower, Kennedy, and Johnson are
preserved in presidential libraries located throughout the country and
also administered by the NARS.

Generally, records in the NARS are arranged not by subject matter,
but by provenance. They are kept in the order in which they were compiled by the federal agency, department, or bureau that produced them.
The combined records of a particular government unit, such as the
Department of State, are referred to as a record group. Altogether,
there are more than 450 such record groups in the NARS. Understanding these records groups will greatly facilitate the work of a researcher.

Each record group has a finding aid which outlines its scope and
nature. The scholar who comes in person should consult with NARS
staff members for advice and guidance concerning holdings, finding aids,
reference tools, and the like.

Given the abundance of East Asian materials at the NARS, the exact extent of the NARS' holdings on East Asia is unknown. In this section, materials are described under the record groups to which they have been allocated. The greatest concentrations of East Asian holdings can be found in the Records of the Department of State (RG 59), the Records of the Foreign Service Posts of the Department of State (RG 84), in those groups directly related to wars, the military, defense, and intelligence (e.g., RGs18, 38, 80, 94, 111, 127, 153, 160, 165, 179, 208, 210, 218, 238, 242, 243, 262, 319, 330, 331, 332, 333, 335, 338, 340, 341, 342, 349, 389, 395, 407, etc.) Other important record groups include the General Records of the United States government (RG 11), Records of the United States Participation in International Conferences, Commissions and Expositions (RG 43), National Archives Gift Collection (RG 200), Records of the American Commission for the Protection and Salvage of Artistic and Historic Monuments in War Areas (RG 239), National Archives Collection of Foreign Records Seized, 1941- (RG 242), Records of the Bureau of Foreign and Domestic Commerce (RG 151), and a number of other records compiled by various United States government agencies (e.g., Department of Agriculture, Justice, the U.S. Tariff Commission, etc.), which can be found in over 20 different record groups.

What follows is the barest outline of East Asian materials readily identifiable through the use of the *Guide to the National Archives of the United States* (1974). While not an exhaustive inventory, it briefly describes selected record groups which contain significant materials on China, Japan, Korea, and Mongolia.

MATERIALS ON CHINA

RG 16: *Records of the Office of the Secretary of Agriculture* contain reports and letters concerning the collection of tea seeds in China.

RG 18: *Records of the Army Air Forces* contain "Security-Classified Correspondence Relating to Foreign Countries, 1942-1944," some of which pertain to East Asia.

RG 26: *Records of the U.S. Coast Guard* contain "Records of Revenues—Cutter Service, 1790-1915," which deals with enforcement of laws forbidding the importation of unskilled Chinese laborers into the United States.

RG 36: *Records of the Bureau of Customs* contain case files and reports relating to investigations of customs employees, Chinese immigration, etc.

RG 40: *General Records of the Department of Commerce* contain a substantial number of documents relating to Chinese excursion, immigration problems and policies, 1903-7; the China Trade Act, 1923-27; and the Chinese Nationalist Government 1948-50.

RG 59: *General Records of the Department of State* contain extensive materials relating to East Asia in general and China and Japan in particular. Included are: "Records of the American War Production Mission in China, 1944-45;" "Records of the Marshall Mission to China, 1945-47;" "Records of the Pauley Reparations Mission, 1945-48;" and "Records of the Wedemeyer Mission to China, 1947."

RG 84: *Records of the Foreign Service Posts of the Department of State* contain materials that were compiled by the diplomatic posts (e.g., embassies and legations) in China (1843-1945), Japan (1855-1936), and Korea (1882-1907). In addition, "Foreign Service Post Records" (at Suitland, Maryland) include records of China (1936-55), Japan (1936-41, 1950-55), and Korea (1948-55).

RG 85: *Records of Immigration and Naturalization Service* contain "Chinese Immigration Records, 1882-1925," documenting the administration and regulation of Chinese immigrants and residents in the United States from 1882-1925.

RG 76: *Records of Boundary and Claims Commissions and Arbitrations* contain such historical documents as "Convention of 1858 (China);" and "Protocol of 1901-Boxer Rebellion Claims and Indemnity Fund."

RG 118: *Records of U.S. Attorneys and Marshals* included are "Records of U.S. Marshals, 1845-1941;" records on "District of China" such as case files relating to investigations of complaints involving United States citizens in China, 1935-41.

RG 127: *Records of the U.S. Marine Corps* include "Records of Expeditionary Forces and Detachments Abroad, 1898-1944" containing the general correspondence of U.S. Marines in China, 1930-1934. RG 127 also has "Reports Relating to Engagement of Marine Corps Personnel in the Philippines and China, 1899-1901."

RG 151: *Records of the Bureau of Foreign and Domestic Commerce and Successor Agencies* contain various documents and reports pertaining to economic and financial situations in China from 1919 to 1956.

RG 160: *Records of Headquarters Army Service Forces* contain records of the United States military missions to China 1942-1945.

RG 165: *Records of the War Department General and Special Staffs* contain "Records of the Office of the Director of Service, Supply and Procurement (G-4), 1914-1917," including records relating to the Chinese officer-training program in 1946.

RG 166: *Records of Foreign Agricultural Service* contain materials relating to Chinese agriculture, agricultural products, land, policies, and relief, 1918-1938.

RG 200: *National Archives Gift Collection* includes Leslie R. Groves's letters, written as Army chaplain from China, 1898-1901.

RG 170: *Records of the Bureau of Narcotics and Dangerous Drugs* contain records (1915-40) relating mainly to applications and permits allowing the importation and exportation of narcotics, violations of narcotics laws, etc., including 14 reels of film relating to drug traffic and enforcement of narcotics laws in China and the United States.

RG 266: *Records of the Office of Strategic Services* contain the OSS' Far Eastern Division correspondence with its outposts, 1942-46, and reports relating to China and Taiwan, 1941-1946: The "Field Office Records" has correspondence of the China Theater of Operations, 1944-45.

RG 256: *Records of the American Commission to Negotiate Peace* contain extensive materials pertaining to China, including "The Present Status of Far Eastern Inquiries (1918);" "Preliminary Report on Far Eastern Policy (1918);" and "Commercial and Financial Activities of the Foreign Powers in China (1918)."

RG 319: *Records of the Army Staff* contain "Records of the Assistant Chief of Staff, G-2, Intelligence, 1939-55." The records consist of general correspondence, incoming and outgoing messages, intelligence document (ID) file, and intelligence library ("P") file. RG 319 also contains "Records of the Office of the Assistant Chief of Staff, G-3, Operations, 1943-54" which consist of memorandums of the Joint Chiefs of Staff Secretariat, 1942-1951, and correspondence relating to the China aid program, 1945-49. (163 rolls of microfilm are available.)

RG 262: *Records of the Foreign Broadcast Intelligence Service* contain "Daily Reports of Foreign Radio Broadcasts, 1941-45," including broadcasts by Japan and China; and "Daily Reports, Far Eastern Section," 1946, relating to China and Japan.

RG 265: *Records of the Office of Foreign Assets Control* include materials relating to the assets of China and North Korea frozen by the United States after the Chinese intervention in Korea in 1950 and orders issued under the amended Trading with the Enemy Act.

RG 319: *Records of the Army Staff* contain "Records of the Office of the Assistant Chief of Staff, G-3, Operations, 1943-1954," which cover the academic training of foreign nationals, 1943-54, and the China aid program, 1945-49.

RG 332: *Records of U.S. Theaters of War, World War II* include "Records, 1939-50" of materials relating to the China-Burma-India theater. Included are the correspondence and messages of Gen. Joseph W. Stilwell and office files of his successor, Gen. Albert C. Wedemeyer, 1941-1946.

RG 338: *Records of U.S. Army Commands, 1942-* contain "Records of Other Army Field Commands, 1940-52" with materials on the U.S. Army in Korea, the China-Burma-India theater, etc.

RG 395: *Records of U.S. Army Overseas Operations and Commands, 1898-1942* contain records of the China Relief Expedition, 1900-1905; and records of U.S. troops in China, 1917-38.

RG 395: *Records of U.S. Army Overseas Operations and Commands, 1898-1942* contain records of China Relief Expedition, 1900-01, and of U.S. Army troops in China, 1912-1938.

MATERIALS ON JAPAN

RG 32: *Records of the U.S. Shipping Board* contain statistical and accounting records of the special representatives of the Fleet Corporation in Japan and China regarding vessels built in these countries for the corporation (1917-28).

RG 43: *Records of International Conferences, Commissions, and Expositions* contain records of the Far Eastern Commission, 1945-1951; the Allied Council for Japan, 1946-52, and the Sino-Japanese disputes, 1930-32. There are also records of the Yalta Conference (2/1945) and Potsdam Conference (7/1945) in RG 43.

RG 59: *General Records of the Department of State* contain extensive materials on Japan, including materials relating to the revision of the Treaty of Yedo (1860-62 and 1872); records of the Office of the Assistant Secretary of State for Occupied Areas, 1946-49; reports on the Japanese Economy, 1938-46; and proceedings of the Japanese Peace Conference held at San Francisco in 1951 together with documentary films of the conference.

RG 60: *General Records of the Department of Justice* pertain to Japanese propaganda and security matters, particularly with reference to the activities of the Japanese in Hawaii before December 7, 1941.

RG 85: *Records of the Immigration and Naturalization Service* include administrative records and internee case files of 16 alien enemy internment facilities, 1941-1948.

RG 131: *Records of the Office of Alien Property* contain records of the Alien Property Division of the Justice Department which had jurisdiction over the property in the United States owned by Germany and Japan or their nationals; and records of a research project on Japanese economic operations, inventories, and reference materials (1941-51).

RG 153: *Records of the Office of the Judge Advocate General (Army)* include "Records of the War Crimes Division, 1942-51," consisting of case files for war crimes trials held by military commissions in the European theater of operations and copies of trial records of the International Military Tribunal for the Far East.

RG 160: *Records of the Headquarters Army Service Forces* contain the Army Intelligence Division's reports and studies on Japanese balloons, 1942-45.

RG 165: *Records of the War Department General and Special Staffs* contain Pearl Harbor investigation records, 1941-46.

RG 166: *Records of the Foreign Agricultural Service* contain extensive materials relating to Chinese agriculture from 1918 to 1938; Japanese agriculture from 1913 to 1938; and Korean agriculture from 1918 to 1938.

RG 210: *Records of the War Relocation Authority* document the activities of the War Relocation Authority (WRA) which oversaw the internment of approximately 110,000 persons of Japanese ancestry from 1942-1945.

RG 218: *Records of the U.S. Joint Chiefs of Staff* contain instruments of surrender of the Japanese forces signed in Tokyo Bay on September 2, 1945; and similar surrender documents of Japanese forces in South Korea, Okinawa, and other areas in 1945.

RG 226: *Records of the Office of the Strategic Services* contain still and motion pictures pertaining to Japanese industry, the Japanese attack at Pearl Harbor on December 7, 1941, and the OSS' Far Eastern Division correspondence with its outposts from 1942-46.

RG 238: *National Archives Collection of World War II War Crimes Records* contain records of the International Military Tribunal for the Far East, established on January 19, 1946, to try persons charged with war crimes. Included are the partially indexed transcripts of proceedings, miscellaneous records, the court journal, and other documents, 1946-48; defense documents with indexes, 1900-1945; and a review of the sentences by Gen. Douglas MacArthur. (62 rolls of microfilm are available).

RG 239: *Records of the American Commission for the Protection and Salvage of Artistic and Historic Monuments in War Areas* contain documents entitled "The Records, 1943-46" (1,489 items), consisting of a set of maps and identification lists of items collected from foreign countries including Japan and Korea.

RG 242: *National Archives Collection of Foreign Records Seized, 1941-* contains "Japanese Records, 1928-47." The records include studies on aeronautics, aviation, medicine, and electronics of the Aeronautical Research Institute of Tokyo Imperial University, 1928-44; records of the Japanese Army and Navy High Commands; Japanese Army and Navy orders and reports to the emperor; casualty reports; records on war-material production and national economic strength; stenographic records of the Imperial Diet; plans for negotiations with the Soviets and a report on the Soviet entry into the war, 1937-47; and Japanese newspapers and private papers of prominent figures (366 rolls of microfilm are available). Also, it contains "Records of Axis Cultural and Research Institutions, 1914-45" (available in 551 rolls of microfilm) and "Records of Embassies and Consulates, 1919-45" (available in 78 rolls of microfilm). The former covers materials primarily relating to Japanese and Manchurian industrial and export companies engaged in transactions with Germany and other Asian countries, 1924-1945, whereas the latter pertains to Japanese diplomatic and consular activities in selected countries, 1919-1945.

RG 243: *Records of the U.S. Strategic Bombing Survey* contain information and data pertaining to the direct and indirect effects of the strategic bombing of Japan, based on interviews with political, military, and industrial leaders in 1945-46. Also included are "Records of the European and Pacific Survey, 1937-47" (available in 411 rolls of microfilm), consisting of reports and photographs of Allied air attacks and their effects on Germany and Japan and areas occupied by the Axis powers, 1937-47.

RG 335: *Records of the Office of the Secretary of the Army* contain records relating to postwar occupied areas including the United States occupation of Japan, Korea, and the Ryukyu Islands; and records of the Office of Occupied Areas, 1951-52.

RG 338: *Records of U.S. Army Commands, 1942-* include "Records of the U.S. Army Pacific, 1942-52," with case files of the Sugamo Prison Supervisory Detachment, 1945-52, and "Records of the Western Defense Command, 1941-46" (available on 620 rolls of microfilm) which include documents on the removal of the Japanese and Japanese-Americans to war relocation centers.

RG 331: *Records of Allied Operational Occupation Headquarters, World War II* contain "Records of General Headquarters, Supreme Commander of the Allied Powers (SCAP), 1945-52." The records totaling some 10,214 cubic feet include general records of such administrative units as the Office of the Chief of Staff, 1949-51, and the Deputy Chief of Staff, 1945-51; the Allied Council for Japan and the Public Information Section, 1946-50; and the Soviet Liaison Office, Office of the Comptroller, and the Adjutant General Section, 1945-52. In addition, the records of General Staff sections, 1945-52, and other records relating to the operation of General Staff Sections G-1 to G-4 are included together with the records of Special Staff sections, such as the records of the International Prosecution Section (part of which is available on 162 rolls of microfilm), 1945-48, and the Judge Advocate Section's records, 1945-49, pertaining to war-crimes trials in Japan. Other documents contained in the records are correspondence and other records of the following sections: the Legal Section; the Civil Affairs Section; the Civil Communications Section, Civil Historical Section; Office of the Civil Property Custodian; Civil Informaton and Education Section; Civil Transportation Section; Natural Resources Section; Public Health and Welfare Section; and Provost Marshal's Section; the Economic and Scientific Section; and the Civil Intelligence Section (1945-49). For further information, see Helene Bowen, "Preliminary Inventory of the Records of Allied Operational and Occupation Headquarters, World War II (Record Group 331), Part II: Records of General Headquarters, Supreme Commander for the Allied Powers (SCAP)" (Washington, D.C.: Office of Military Archives, 1962).

RG 353: *Records of Interdepartmental and Intradepartmental Committees (State Department)* contain "Records of the State-War-Navy Coordinating Committee, 1944-49 (SWNCC)" consisting of the minutes, agenda, decisions, rosters, reports, memorandums, letters of subcommittees, and indexes to the records. The committee was established to reconcile the views of the three major departments in formulating United States occupation policies for Japan and Germany. Other relevant documents can be found in "Japan-Korean Files" and "Northeast Asian Affairs Files" (1950-53) in the same RG.

RG 389: *Records of the Office of the Provost Marshal General, 1941-* contain records relating to American prisoners of war, 1941-56, including a card file of Americans interned by Germany and Japan during World War II and civilian alien internee case files, 1941-45.

MATERIALS ON KOREA

RG 43: *Records of International Conferences, Commissions, and Expositions* contain "Records of the American Delegation, U.S.-USSR Joint Commission on Korea," and "Records relating to the U.N. Temporary Commission on Korea, 1947-48."

RG 45: *Naval Records Collection of the Office of Naval Records and Library* contains "Letters from Commodore Robert W. Shufeldt, 1878-1880" concerning his voyage to Africa and Asia (especially Korea). In addition, it contains "Registers Maintained by Asiatic Squadron, 1/1900, 2/1902" and other naval records.

RG 59: *General Records of the Department of State* contain "Records of the Office of the Assistant Secretary of State for Occupied Areas, 1946-49;" "Records of the Office of Assistant Secretary and Under Secretary of State—Dean Acheson, 1941-1950;" and four Korean War newsreels, produced in the United States during 1950-51.

RG 153: *Records of the Judge Advocate General (Army)* contain records concerning the Korean conflict which include historical reports of the War Crimes Division of the Korean Communications zone, case files for investigation of war crimes in Korean Communications zone, case files for investigation of war crimes in Korea, and investigation records of returned American prisoners of war following a prisoner exchange with North Korea.

RG 218: *Records of the U.S. Joint Chiefs of Staff* contain "Instruments of Surrender and Armistice, 1942-53" (available in 1 roll of microfilm) with instruments of surrender of the Japanese forces in South Korea, Japan, Okinawa, etc.; and the Korean Armistice Agreement of 1953.

RG 242: *National Archives Collection of Foreign Records Seized, 1941-* includes "Records Seized by U.S. Military Forces in Korea, 1921-1952." The records, consisting of 6,983 items totaling over 1,608,-000 pages plus an undetermined number of photographs, are contained in about 1,343 boxes. These constitute probably the most valuable collection of records available outside of North Korea itself concerning the political, economic, and military affairs of North Korea from 1945 to 1950. Included in the collection are administrative and personnel files, books, periodicals, and bulletins dealing with science, agriculture, literature, economics, geography, politics, propaganda; the Chinese People's Volunteer Army in Korea; the history and activities of the North Korean Communist Party; North Korean-Russian trade; North Korean Army; and the U.N. forces in Korea. Although the materials are mostly in the Korean language, the collection contains about 300,000 pages of Japanese materials, 10,000 pages of Russian materials, and 3,000 pages of Chinese materials. For a detailed analysis and description of the records, see Thomas Hosuck Kang, "North Korean Captured Records at the Washington National Records Center, Suitland, Maryland," a paper presented at the 7th annual meeting of the Mid-Atlantic Region of the Association for Asian Studies, held at George Washington University, Washington, D.C. on October 28-29, 1978.

RG 256: *Records of the American Commission to Negotiate Peace* contain a report entitled "The Trouble in Korea (1919)" which deals with the March First uprisings staged by the Koreans against Japanese colonial rule. Another report deals with "Trade and Economic Change in Chosen [Korea] during the War (1918)."

RG 330: *Records of the Office of the Secretary of Defense* contain documents entitled "Records of the Assistant Secretary of Defense (Supply and Logistics), 1941-55" which relate to programming materials for the Department of Defense, 1954-55, and tabulations of World War II and Korean War reports on the dollar value of industrial shipments, 1941-52.

RG 332: *Records of U.S. Theaters of War, World War II* contain documents entitled "Historical files of U.S. Armed Forces, Korea, 1945-48;" and a subject file of the U.S. Army Military Government in Korea, 1945-1948.

RG 333: *Records of International Military Agencies* contain documents entitled "Records of the Headquarters, United Nations Command, 1950-57," consisting of an orders file; a U.N.-Japan administrative working file, 1952-53; and correspondence, publications, and Korean armistice agreement documents. "Records of the U.N. Command Military Armistice Commission (UNCMAC)" include records relating to negotiation and implementation of the Korean armistice, 1951-1957, while "Records of the UNC Repatriation Group" consist of correspondence, journals, and publications, 1953-1954.

RG 335: *Records of the Office of the Secretary of Army* contain records of Under Secretary Archbald S. Alexander's tour of the Far East Command, 1951; records of Senate hearings on Korean ammunition shortages, 1951-54. "Records Relating to Postwar Occupied Areas, 1948-52" include general records of the Office of the Occupied Areas, 1951-52; files relating to the occupied-areas programs, 1949-52; and correspondence of the Office of the Food Administrator for Occupied Areas, 1948-50.

RG 338: *Records of U.S. Army Commands,* 1942-   contain "Records of Other Army Field Commands, 1940-50" with records of the U.S. Army Forces in Korea, 1945-1949.

RG 341: *Records of Headquarters, U.S. Air Force* contain "Records of the Office of the Deputy Chief of Staff, Operations, 1941-57" that include "Korean Daily Reports, 1951-53" and "Field Photographic Intelligence Reports of Korea, 1950-56."

RG 349: *Records of the Joint Commands* contain documents relating to Korean armistice negotiations, 1951-53; and "Records of the Combined Command for Reconnaisance Activities, Korea (CCRAK), 1952-53" consisting of intelligence reports of CCRAK which supervised clandestine operations supporting American combat operations in Korea during 1952-53.

RG 407: *Records of the Adjutant General's Office* contain "Korean Command Reports, 1949-54," consisting of after-action reports, war diaries, reports of combat and service units, and journals on the U.S. Army operations in Korea.

MATERIALS ON EAST ASIA (CHINA, JAPAN, KOREA)

RG 20: *Records of the Office of the Special Adviser to the President on Foreign Trade* contain "files of the Secretariat of Records" which relate to economic conditions abroad including East Asia (1933-1935) and "Records of the Division of Research and Statistics" which include analyses of United States trade with other countries in East Asia.

RG 23: *Records of the Coast and Geodetic Survey* contain scientific observations made in the South Pacific Islands, Japan, Korea, and the Philippines.

RG 243: *Records of the U.S. Strategic Bombing Survey* contain extensive materials relating to Japan such as "Japanese Resources Reference Notebooks, 1945," "Reports of Japanese Responses to Questionnaires Relating to Japanese Air Strength, 1945-1946," and "Security-Classified Pacific Survey Reports and Supporting Records, 1928-47." RG 243 also contains "Security-Classified Joint Army-Navy Intelligence Studies (JANIS), 1944-45" which pertain to China, Japan, and Korea.

RG 40: *General Records of the Department of Commerce* contain extensive materials relating to China and Japan. The materials compiled from 1903-12 deal largely with the Chinese exclusion and immigration problems and policies. The records compiled from 1913 to 1942 cover mostly the administration of the China Trade Act, whereas the records of 1948-1950 relate to the Chinese Nationalist government. Records on Japan relate to problems of Japanese immigration, 1903-07; Japanese Railway Mission, Japanese Relief Fund, Japanese competition and fisheries, 1913-1942; and some correspondence dating from 1943 to 1947. As for Korea, RG 40 contains limited information on the post-WWII period.

RG 43: *Records of International Conferences, Commissions, and Expositions* contain "Records of WWII Conferences, 1943-1945" which consist of communiques, declarations, reports, etc., relating to the conferences of the Allied leaders at Moscow, Tehran, Cairo, Yalta, Dumbarton Oaks (Washington, D.C.), San Francisco, and Potsdam.

RG 59: *General Records of the Department of State* contain "Notes from Foreign Missions, 1789-1906" and "Notes to Foreign Missions,

1793-1906" which cover China from 1868 to 1906. RG 59 also contains extensive materials relating to the internal situation in Japan in the pre-1945 period. In addition, RG 59 contains a list of special agents of the State Department who served in China, Japan, and Korea (mostly in the 19th century), including William W. Rockhill, Caleb Cushing, Matthew C. Perry, George F. Seward, and Robert W. Shufeldt.

RG 84: *Records of the Foreign Service Posts of the Department of State* contain records compiled by U.S. diplomatic posts (e.g., embassies and legations) which include China from 1843-1945; Japan from 1855-1936; and Korea from 1882-1907. The more recent "Foreign Service Post Records" (located at Suitland, Maryland) cover China from 1936-55; Japan from 1936-41 and 1950-55; and Korea from 1948-55.

MATERIALS ON MONGOLIA

RG 54: *Records of Bureau of Plant Industry, Soils, and Agricultural Engineering* contain "General Records of the Bureau of Plant Industry, 1900-53" which include documents relating to the Roerich expedition to Mongolia and North Manchuria to survey drought-resistant grasses, 1934-37.

4. An indispensable reference tool for anyone interested in conducting research in the National Archives is the *Guide to the National Archives of the United States* (1974). It describes the origins, scope, nature, and content of each record group and its subgroups. At the end of each entry, the *Guide* lists published finding aids (e.g., inventories, special lists) available for the particular record group or subgroup and contains information on which records have been microfilmed. In addition, it stipulates specific restrictions governing access to materials which have not yet been declassified.

Also highly useful is the finding-aid folder containing inventories, special lists, and other reference materials for each record group. These folders are constantly updated and are shelved in Room 200-B of the National Archives.

To help researchers, individual branches and divisions of the NARS also maintain inventories, guides, and other reference materials for the record groups which come under their administrative supervision. For example, finding aids available at the Diplomatic Branch (NARS) include the following:

RG 11:*United States Government Documents Having General Legal Effect,* PI 159 (1964).

RG 43: *Preliminary Inventory of the Records of United States Participation in International Conferences, Commissions, and Expositions,* PI 76 (1955).

RG 59: *Preliminary Inventory of the General Records of the Department of State,* 157 (1963).

List of Documents Relating to Special Agents of the Department of State, 1789-1906, SL 7 (1951).

RG 76: *Preliminary Inventory of the Records Relating to International Boundaries,* PI 170 (1968).

Records Relating to International Claims, PI 177 (1974).

Preliminary Inventory of Records Relating to International Arbitrations, NC 155 (1969).

RG 84: *List of Foreign Service Post Records in the National Archives,* SL 9 (1967).
Preliminary Inventory of the Records of Selected Foreign Service Posts, PI 60 (1953).
RG 256: *Records of the American Commission to Negotiate Peace,* Inventory 9 (1974).
RG 353: *Preliminary Inventory of the Records of Interdepartmental and Intradepartmental Committees (State Department),* (1967).

For a list of "Inventories," "Preliminary Inventories," and "Special Lists" available for each record group, see the *Select List of Publications of the National Archives and Records Service,* General Information Leaflet No. 3 (1977).
Other useful brochures and publications of the NARS include:

Regulations for the Public Use of Records in the National Archives and Records Service. General Information Leaflet No. 2 (1977).
Location of Records and Fees for Reproduction Services in the National Archives and Records Service. General Information Leaflet No. 14 (1976).
List of Record Groups of the National Archives and Records Service (October 1976). This publication is highly useful in locating divisions wherein individual record groups are maintained.
Military Service Records in the National Archives of the United States (1977).
A Researcher's Guide to the National Archives. General Information Leaflet No. 25 (1977).
Catalog of Machine-Readable Records in the National Archives of the United States (1977).

For the NARS records available in microfilm, researchers should consult the *Catalog of National Archives Microfilm Publications* (1974) and a supplement published in 1978. For further information about NARS publications, reference tools, and finding aids, researchers should consult with the staff of the particular branch or division which specializes in the area of the researcher's interest. Also useful is the NARS quarterly entitled *Prologue: The Journal of the National Archives* which describes NARS accessions.

Note: NARS collection of East Asian maps is described in entry E4, its film and photo collection in entry F8, and its music and sound recordings in entry D3.

B9 Naval Historical Center (Navy Department)—Operational Archives Branch

1. a. *Washington Navy Yard, Building 200*
      9th and M Streets, SE
      Washington, D.C. 20374
      433-3171

    b. 7:30 A.M.-4:30 P.M.   Monday-Friday

c. Most of the Center's pre-1955 archives are open to the public for on-site use.

d. Photoduplication service is available.

e. Dr. Dean C. Allard, Director

2. The Naval Historical Center, with custody over the operational archives of the U.S. Navy, was created in 1942 to centralize and organize the basic records documenting the combat activities of naval fleet units. The Operational Archives Branch continues to collect documents on fleet operations as well as official records of the Office of the Chief of Naval Operations and other operational headquarters of the U.S. Navy. The records amount to approximately 10,000 feet (or over 200,000 items) and date primarily from 1940 to the present. Although most of the recent holdings are classified and restricted, archival materials before 1955 have been declassified and can be used by serious scholars on the premises. It is estimated that more than half of the materials preserved at the center pertain to the Pacific region (i.e., western, central, and southern).

In addition, the Operational Archives Branch holds groups of Japanese and German naval records seized after World War II and the personal papers of some recent naval figures.

3. The collections listed below are either declassified or accessible through special accession permission for United States citizens undertaking bona fide research. To request such permission, scholars should write for the necessary forms to the Director of Naval History, Washington Navy Yard, Washington, D.C. 20390. Additional information on specific holdings and available finding aids can be obtained upon request:

RECORDS ORGANIZED BY THE OPERATIONAL ARCHIVES

Title	Dates	Volume
(1) *Action and Other Operational Reports of Naval Forces* (contains approximately 100,000 battle reports of World War II and the Korean War, as well as reports of peacetime deployment, training exercises, and foreign visits.)	1937-45 1946-53	1,028 ft. 175 ft.
(2) *War Diaries of Naval Forces* (included are day-by-day diaries submitted by all major naval units and commands in World War II and the forces actually involved in the Korean War.)	1941-45	833 ft.
(3) *Records Relating to the U.S. Asiatic Fleet and the Asiatic Campaign*	1939-42	2 ft.
(4) *Miscellaneous Record Material and Publications* ("Command File"—some of the documents included in the collection pertain to histories of commands, tactical doctrine publications, fleet organization lists, naval conference reports, monthly operational summaries, and transcripts of approximately 400 interviews with World War II naval personnel.)	1933-45 1946-54	524 ft. 200 ft.

RECORDS OF NAVAL COMMANDS AND OFFICES—components of the Office of the Chief of Naval Operations; the Headquarters of the Commander in Chief, U.S. Fleet; and other commands and offices.

Title	Dates	Volume
(1) *Central Security-Classified Files of the Office of the Chief of Naval Operations*	1940-47	1,063 ft.
(2) *War Plans Division*	1935-45	85 ft.
(3) *Fleet Operations Division*	1944-50	16 ft.
(4) *Base Maintenance Division* (contains histories and other data on the U.S. Navy's overseas bases.)	1939-57	25 ft.
(5) *Aviation History Unit* (contains primarily histories of Naval and Marine air units and commands.)	1943-52	169 ft.
(6) *Naval History Division* (includes source materials collected in connection with the compilation of administrative histories of naval commands in World War II and other historical projects.)	1934-63	191 ft.
(7) *Central Security-Classified Files of the Headquarters, Commander in Chief, U.S. Fleet*	1942-45	984 ft.
(8) *Top Secret Control Office*	1941-47	349 ft.
(9) *Operations Division*	1941-47	10 ft.
(10) *Seventh Fleet*	1942-44	2 ft.
(11) *Amphibious Corps, Pacific Fleet*	1921-42	22 ft.
(12) *Naval Group China*	1942-47	41 ft.
(13) *Naval Analysis Division, U.S. Strategic Bombing Survey*	1940-47	12 ft.
(14) *Reference and Evaluation Branch, Navy Office of Information*	1941-62	20 ft.

PERSONAL PAPERS

Title	Dates	Volume
(1) Adm. Daniel E. Barbey, USN	1943-69	22 ft.
(2) Adm. George Dewey, USN	1893-1942	3 ft.
(3) Fleet Adm. William F. Halsey, USN (transferred to LC Manuscript Division.)	1906-59	25 ft.
(4) Adm. Thomas C. Hart, USN	1897-1945	1 ft.
(5) Adm. Harry W. Hill, USN	1942-50	8 ft.
(6) Fleet Adm. Ernest J. King, USN	1918-55	8 ft.
(7) Adm. Alan G. Kirk, USN	1937-45	16 ft.
(8) Capt. Tracy B. Kittredge, USNR	1941-50	5 ft.

Title	Dates	Volume
(9) Adm. Charles A. Lockwood, USN (transferred to LC Manuscript Division.)	1925-67	10 ft.
(10) Adm. William V. Pratt, USN	1905-62	7 ft.
(11) Adm. Dewitt C. Ramsey, USN	1914-49	6 ft.
(12) Adm. Richmond K. Turner, USN	1939-61	13 ft.
(13) Adm. Harry E. Yarnell, USN	1897-1960	10 ft.

(14) Adm. Milton Miles: Included in the *Naval Group China* collection, the Miles Papers cover guerrilla warfare conducted against the Japanese troops in China during World War II.

(15) Diary of Vice Adm. Newton A. McCully (2 vols.): McCully was a naval attaché in the U.S. Legation in St. Petersburg in 1904-05. He was an observer with the Russian forces in the Russo-Japanese War and witnessed the seizure and fall of Port Arthur and the Battle of Mukden.

(16) Other memoirs of naval officers as compiled by the Oral History Research Office, Columbia University and the U.S. Naval Institute.

COLLECTIONS OF NAVAL RADIO-MESSAGE FILES

Title	Dates	Volume
(1) *Chart Room, Commander-in-Chief, U.S. Fleet*	1940-46	79 ft.
(2) *Convoy and Routing Division, Office of the Commander in Chief, U.S. Fleet*	1941-45	336 micro-film reels
(3) *Pacific Fleet and Pacific Ocean Areas*	1941-45	832 micro-film reels
(4) *Commander in Chief, Southwest Pacific Area*	1942-44	2 ft.
(5) *Submarines, Pacific Fleet*	1942-45	7 ft.

RECORDS FROM FOREIGN SOURCES

Title	Dates	Volume
(1) *The Imperial Japanese Navy* (contains 230 reels of microfilms of selected operational records of World War II (in Japanese), plus translations of miscellaneous Japanese records and related studies, histories, and essays. Mostly records of the Japanese Naval Ministry, they were seized in Japan by the SCAP during the Occupation period (1945-1952).)	1940-51	230 micro-film reels

4.   Various finding aids and indices have been compiled by the staff of the Operational Archives to facilitate research in the archives. Researchers should consult with staff members for such reference tools and other assistance. The following reference materials are also useful: *Declassified and Unclassified Groups and Collections in the Operational Archives* (1977); *U.S. Naval History Sources in the Washington Area and Suggested Research Subjects* (1970) by Dean C. Allard and Betty Bern; *Guide to United States Naval Administrative Histories of World War II*

(1976); and *World War II Histories and Historical Reports in the U.S. Naval History Division: Partial Checklist* (1977). For the microfilmed Japanese naval records, the Operational Archives has compiled an unpublished index which is indispensable for microfilmed material. Also useful for East Asian specialists are two microfilm publications of the Operational Archives: *Bulletin of the Intelligence Center, Pacific Ocean Area, Joint Intelligence Center, Pacific Ocean Area and the Commander in Chief, Pacific and Pacific Ocean Area, 1942-1946* (1976); and *Reports of the U.S. Naval Technical Mission to Japan, 1945-1946* (1974). Finally, copies of "Information for Visitors to the Operational Archives" (1978) are available free upon request.

B10 Smithsonian Institution Archives (SIA)

1. a. *900 Jefferson Drive*
    Washington, D.C. 20560
    381-4075

    b. 9:00 A.M.-5:00 P.M.   Monday-Friday

    c. Open to the public.

    d. Photoduplication facilities and microfilm viewers are available.

    e. Richard H. Lytle, Archivist

2. The Smithsonian Institution Archives contain over 6,000 cubic feet of materials, most of which pertain to the development of American science and the broad range of activities undertaken by various branches of the Smithsonian Institution (entry K29). The following information and data have been gathered through the SIA Subject Index which specifies the subject headings of Asia, China, Japan, and Korea. Undoubtedly, this approach has its limitations as there may be pertinent information on East Asia under other subject headings. Furthermore, it should be pointed out that the SIA Subject Index is by no means comprehensive, for nearly 80 percent of the Archives collections have not been indexed. However, the following listings would indicate that East Asian specialists can find rich source materials in the archives.

3. Generally, records in the SIA are arranged by Record Unit (RU). Altogether, there are more than 400 such units. A description of the listings in each RU can be found in the *Guide to the Smithsonian Archives* (1978).

    RU 74: *National Zoological Park, 1887-1965, Records* concern animals acquired from the Tokyo Zoo.
    RU 161: *Division of Reptiles and Amphibians, 1873-1968, Records* contain material on Chinese herpetology and some correspondence with Asian herpetologists.
    RU 189: *Assistant Secretary in Charge of United States National Museum (USNM) 1860-1908* consists mostly of incoming correspondence; Box 17, Folder 6, deals with the "Capron Collection" of Japanese Works of Art (1868, 1886, 1891 and undated).

RU 192:*USNM 1877-1975: Permanent Administrative Files* contain, among other materials, documents on museum accessions, participation in expositions, Smithsonian expeditions and field trips. The "Accession Records" contain data on the "Herbert R. Bishop Jade Collection" (1895-1905); the "Herbert G. Squires Collection" of Chinese jades, porcelains and lacquers (1907-1908); and the "Hippisley Collection" of Chinese porcelains, 1909-1912. The "Records Related to Smithsonian Expeditions and Field Work" include the correspondence of Carl Whiting Bishop of the Freer Gallery regarding his archeological field work in China in 1932. Also included in this unit are records pertaining to Arthur deC. Sowerby's Expeditions to China from 1909 to 1922; several boxes of materials from David Crockett Graham's acquisition trips to China from 1920 to 1940, including correspondence relating to his activities for USNM in Szechwan Province from 1927 to 1940; Charles M. Hoy's collecting work on China from 1923-24 and the Henry Weed Fowler correspondence regarding his study of USNM's collection of Formosan fishes; and the National Geological Survey of China, 1915-1927.

RU 208: *Division of Mammals, circa 1882-1971, Records* contain correspondence of Arthur deC. Sowerby and Charles M. Hoy and a discussion of mammals of China.

RU 218: *Office of International and Environmental Programs, 1962-1975* contains over 21 cubic feet of material, some of which concerns the rapid urbanization of Seoul, Korea.

RU 223: *Division of Plants, 1899-1947, Records* contain correspondence regarding William Ralph Maxon's expedition to China.

RU 229: *Division of Grasses, 1884, 1888, 1899-1963, Records* include material regarding the political and economic conditions during the Chinese Civil War.

RU 7074: *Leonhard Stejneger Papers, 1867-1943* include a significant amount of material on Chinese and Japanese herpetology.

RU 7113: *Charles Fuller Baker Papers, 1913-1927* contain correspondence regarding entomology of Southeast Asia and Australia.

RU 7117: *William Louis Abbott Papers, circa 1890-1917* include correspondence while collecting natural history and ethnological specimens for the Smithsonian.

RU 7118: *Joseph Harvey Riley Papers* (ca. 1930s) concern Riley's research interests in the Avifauna of Asia; he published many articles based on the collections of William Louis Abbott in Southeast Asia, Joseph Francis Rock in China, F. R. Wulsin in Mongolia, and David C. Graham in China and Tibet.

RU 7165: *International Whaling Conference and International Whaling Commission, 1930-1968* include several interesting items. For example, Box 6, Folder 3, contains Japanese whaling charts showing Antarctic whaling ground from 1935-1941; Box 7, Folder 5 ("U.S. Department of Navy, Office of Naval Intelligence, 1938"), includes correspondence relating to Japanese factory ships; Box 11, Folder 4, contains data pertaining to the Japanese ship, "Hashidate Maru," from 1946-1947; Folder 7 of Box 11 ("Commonwealth of Australia") has materials relating to Japanese Antarctic whaling operations in 1948-1949; and Box 15, Folder 7, and Box 16, Folders 1-3 ("Tokyo Sixth International Whaling Commission Meeting, 1954") contain conference documents, statistical data, and material submitted by the Bureau of International Whaling Statistics.

RU 7176: *United States Fish and Wildlife Service, 1860-1961, Field Reports* include a report on Chinese production and trade in musk, 1931, and a report on wildlife in Malaya, 1938.

RU 7179: *Edmund Heller Papers (ca. 1898-1918)* concern this well-known naturalist, who participated in several Smithsonian expeditions as well as other explorations. One of these included an expedition to China (1916-1917) with the American Museum of Natural History team to make a zoological study of Southern China, especially Yunnan province. The collection includes photos and other materials on China, Korea, and Japan.

RU 7183: *Austin H. Clark Papers, 1883-1954* include material on Asian birds.

RU 7217: *Collected Notes, Lists, Drawings, and Catalogs on Mammals, circa 1825-1972* contain field notes of William Louis Abbott.

RU 7232: *Charles Elmer Resser Papers, 1912-1942 and Undated* contain correspondence regarding Chinese fossils.

RU 7234: *Ray S. Bassler Papers, 1875-1961, and Undated* contain correspondence regarding Asian paleontology.

RU 7263: *Arthur deC. Sowerby Papers, 1904-1954, and Undated* include mostly photographs of Chinese flora, fauna, and inhabitants, but also include photographs of Japanese art objects, tombs, and mausoleums from China, and photographs and lantern slides from Shanghai Museum.

RU 1010003: *Egbert Hamilton Walker Papers, 1938-1961* include material for *Bibliography of Eastern Asian Botany*.

RU 1010004: *Rolla Kent Beattie Papers, circa 1928-1947* contain correspondence and other materials relating to botany of Japan and China.

RU 1050101: *Joseph A. Cushman Papers, circa 1862-1977, and Undated* include correspondence concerning the identification and exchange of Asian foraminifera.

RU 1050102: *T. Wayland Vaughan Papers, 1908-1947, and Undated* include correspondence concerning the identification and change of Japanese foraminifera.

4. a. *Guide to the Smithsonian Archives* (Washington, D.C.: Smithsonian Institution Press, 1978) is useful for researchers; however, personal contact and consultation with the staff for unpublished research tools are essential.

C Museums, Galleries, and Art Collections

Entry Form for Museums, Galleries, and Art Collections (C)

1. Access
   a. *Address; telephone number(s)*
   b. Hours of service
   c. Conditions of access
   d. Reproduction services
   e. Director; heads of relevant divisions

2. Size of holdings pertaining to East Asia

3. Description of holdings

4. Bibliography of materials facilitating access to the collection (inventories, catalogs, guides, descriptions)

5. Exchange programs and fellowships

American University Library—The Charles Nelson Spinks Collection See entry A6.

C1 Anderson House—The Society of the Cincinnati

1. a. *2118 Massachusetts Avenue, NW*
      Washington, D.C. 20008
      785-2040

   b. 2:00 P.M.-4:00 P.M.   Tuesday-Sunday (Museum Collection)
      10:00 A.M.-4:00 P.M.   Monday-Friday (Library)

   c. Open to the public.

   d. Xerox duplication services are available.

   e. John D. Kilbourne, Director

2-3. Approximately 250 Oriental art objects are included in the museum collection. The objects are predominantly from China and Japan and are comprised of the following: (1) a Chinese single color and decorated porcelain; (2) Japanese decorated porcelains; (3) Japanese folding screens; (4) Chinese folding screens; (5) "Ming" or Jade Tree as well as other carvings; (6) Chinese and Japanese ivory carvings; (7) Chinese wall plaques; (8) Chinese jade and other semiprecious mineral carvings; (9) a Chinese red carved lacquer; (10) Japanese lacquers and Inrō; (11) Japanese Buddhist images; and (12) Chinese Buddhist images.

This collection of Oriental art objects is mostly from the 18th and 19th centuries, but includes at least one Han dynasty vase. The art collection as well as the house belonged originally to Ambassador and Mrs. Larz Anderson who became interested in Oriental art collecting during Ambassador Anderson's tenure as the head of the U.S. Embassy in Tokyo from 1912-1913. Upon the ambassador's death, his widow presented the house together with their art collection to the Society of the Cincinnati to be used as its headquarters and museum.

4. To aid researchers, especially on the Oriental collection, the museum has published a reference tool entitled *Oriental Art—Anderson House* (n.d.). In addition, in its library there is an inventory list of the museum's collection with detailed descriptions of each item. The library also has a small collection of reference books pertaining to Oriental art, primarily designed for the use of the staff.

Archives of American Art and National Collection of Fine Arts Library (Smithsonian Institution) See entry B2.

Army Audiovisual Agency (Army Department) Japanese Painting Collection See entry F3.

C2 Corcoran Gallery of Art

1. **a.** *17th Street and New York Avenue, NW*
    Washington, D.C. 20006
    638-3211

    b. 11:00 A.M.-5:00 P.M.   Tuesday-Sunday
    (Closed Mondays and major holidays)

    c. An appointment is necessary to view items within the collection (either art objects or reading materials) for scholarly use.

    d. Black and white photographs or color transparencies of the paintings may be ordered from the registrar.

    e. Peter Marzio, Director of the Corcoran Gallery and School of Art
    Jane Livingston, Associate Director
    Edward J. Nygren, Curator of Collections

2-3. With the exception of 2 18th-century vases and 1 or 2 carpets on loan to the Textile Museum, there is nothing in original works of art from China. As for Japanese art, there are one or two photographs by William

Heine of Commodore Perry's expedition to Japan in 1853-54. The gallery also has a small collection of about 50 drawings by Japanese children presented to an American admiral visiting Japan in the late 19th century.

C3 Freer Gallery of Art—Smithsonian Institution

1. a. *12th Street and Jefferson Drive, SW*
    Washington, D.C. 20560
    381-5332 (Library); 381-5344 (Administrative Office)

    b. 10:00 A.M.-4:30 P.M.   Monday-Friday (Library)
    10:00 A.M.-5:30 P.M. daily (Museum)

    c. Open to the public. No interlibrary loan is available except for the slide collection of Oriental art.

    For those who desire to work in the gallery, adequate provision has been made. All objects in the collection (except those on exhibition) are available for researchers during office hours from Monday through Friday. Anyone desiring to photograph objects on exhibition or to see objects not on exhibition should make arrangements through the Administrative Office.

    d. Photocopying facilities are available; and prints and slides of major objects in the collection are available for purchase.

    e. Thomas Lawton, Director

2. The Freer Gallery of Art contains one of the finest collections of Oriental art in the world. This remarkable collection began with some 9,500 objects that Charles Lang Freer of Detroit collected during his lifetime (1856-1919) and subsequently donated as a gift to the people of the United States in 1906. When the Smithsonian Institution assumed custody of the collection, which was transferred from Detroit to Washington in 1920, it included, besides works by James MacNeill Whistler (1,189 objects), a sizable collection of East Asian art: 3,400 Chinese, 1,863 Japanese, and 451 Korean objects. Since then, almost 2,000 additional Oriental objects have been added by purchase, bringing the total to nearly 12,000 objects. This collection also contains a large number of artifacts from the Middle East, India, and Southeast Asia.

3. Because of its extensive size and scope, it is almost impossible to provide a comprehensive review of the Freer collection of East Asian art. The following table may give the readers some ideas as to the magnitude of the collection:

Categories	Chinese Items	Japanese Items	Korean Items
Bamboo	2	–	–
Bone	6	–	–
Bronze	842	43	164
Calligraphy	6	7	–
Cloisonné	2	–	–

Categories	Chinese Items	Japanese Items	Korean Items
Furniture	20	2	–
Glass	17	–	1
Ivory	7	–	–
Jade	588	1	1
Lacquer	37	85	1
Marble	2	–	–
Metalwork	76	18	25 (*Tibet:* 1)
Paintings	890	1,060	14
Pottery	670	876	240
Prints	–	97	–
Rubbings	20	–	–
Shell	1	–	1
Stone and Stone/Bead	116	94	–
Stone Sculpture	178	3	2
Textiles	180	100	–
Wood boxes/blocks	–	20	–
Wood carving/Sculpture	19	46	–
TOTAL	3,679	2,452	449

Note: These are not exact numbers but approximations.

STUDY COLLECTION

In addition to the main collection, there is an ever-growing study collection, which consists mostly of shards of pottery and porcelain (estimated to total over 5,000). The study collection also includes what may be the most complete group of shards from Japanese kiln sites assembled outside of Japan. Furthermore, it also contains a number of fragments of ancient Chinese ceremonial bronzes. These materials are not used for exhibition, but are kept in the study rooms for comparative study and analysis.

4. The Freer Gallery publishes a number of excellent guides for its collection. Of many Freer publications, the following are especially helpful: *Masterpieces of Chinese and Japanese Art: Freer Gallery of Art Handbook* (Washington, D.C.: Smithsonian Institution, 1976); *The Freer Gallery of Art, I: China* (1971); *The Freer Gallery of Art, II: Japan* (1971); *Ukiyo-e Painting* by Harold P. Stern (1973); *Chinese Figure Painting* by Thomas Lawton (1973); and *The Freer Chinese Bronzes*, vols. 1 and 2 (1967 and 1969). (These last two volumes were published as parts of the Freer Gallery's monograph series on Oriental arts, *The Freer Gallery of Art Oriental Studies*.) *The Freer Gallery of Art Occasional Papers* (1947-present) also carries scholarly works on East Asian arts. Also highly recommended is "The Freer Gallery of Art" by John A. Pope in *Records of the Columbia Historical Society of Washington, D.C.* (1969-1970). In addition to these publications, there is a card catalog listing all the objects located in the Freer Gallery. It is arranged primarily by medium and then by country and chronology. In addition, there are notations for objects with no attribution, and for those with attributions, by the artists' names in alphabetical order. There is also a file of "Folder Sheets" for the gallery's objects. Generally, a "folder sheet" will contain a more detailed description of each object than its corresponding catalog card. Finally, scholars and researchers can contact the staff for further information and guidance.

5.   The Freer Gallery of Art administers fellowship and scholarship programs in cooperation with the University of Michigan. The fund is derived from an endowment provided for in Charles Lang Freer's bequest. The Freer Fellowships are awarded on an occasional basis to graduate students at Michigan writing doctoral dissertations on material in the Freer collections. The Freer Scholarships provide for tuition and other expenses for such students on the Ann Arbor campus; and some of the fund is used to bring Michigan graduate students in Oriental art to Washington, D.C., for visits to the Freer Gallery.

C4 Hillwood Museum

1.   a. *4155 Linnean Avenue, NW*
Washington, D.C. 20008
686-5807

    b-c. The collection is open by appointment only.

    d. Most of the items have been photographed; copies may be purchased.

    e. Roy D. R. Betteley, Director
Katrina V. H. Taylor, Assistant Curator
The museum is operated by the Marjorie Merriweather Post Foundation of the District of Columbia.

2.   The museum's collection consists primarily of French and Russian art and artifacts. However, there are also about 130 Chinese hardstone carvings, the majority in jade, and about 60 Chinese snuff bottles. In addition, there are about 20 decorative Chinese porcelain vases. Objects from Japan include several porcelains.

C5 Hirshhorn Museum and Sculpture Garden (Smithsonian Institution)

1.   a. *Independence Avenue at 8th Street, SW*
Washington, D.C. 20560
628-4422

    b. April 1-Labor day: 10:00 A.M.-9:00 P.M.
Remainder of year: 10:00 A.M.-5:30 P.M.

    c. Open to the public. Many of the museum's holdings are not on permanent display but in storage. To examine these items, researchers must make arrangements in advance with the Department of Painting and Sculpture (381-6708).

    d. The museum sells black and white prints of some of its holdings. For a $50 fee the staff will take black and white photos of specified objects in the collection. (To make arrangements, call 381-6760.) If they prefer, visitors may take their own nonflash, hand-held camera photo of any item on exhibit.

    e. Abram Lerner, Director

2-3. The museum's permanent collection of approximately 6,500 works (primarily 19th- and 20th-century painting and sculpture) contains a small group of antiquities that includes two Japanese works. Also in the collection are works by a few contemporary artists who immigrated to the United States from East Asia.

4. Although no comprehensive listing of the museum's collection is available, a useful guide to representative works is *Selected Paintings and Sculpture from the Hirshhorn Museum and Sculpture Garden* (1974). Also, researchers may consult computer printouts of the museum's collections available by appointment at the Hirshhorn Library (381-6703).

C6 Luther Whiting Mason Collection of the Music Educators National Conference Historical Center

1. a. *Music Educators National Conference (MENC) Historical Center*
   McKeldin Library
   University of Maryland
   College Park, MD 20742
   (301) 454-5611

   b. 10:00 A.M.-5:00 P.M.   weekdays (except Thursday)
   2:00 P.M.-9:30 P.M.   Thursday

   c. Open to researchers.

   d. Bruce D. Wilson, Curator

2-3. The MENC Historical Center serves as both the official archives of the Music Educators National Conference and a special reference collection devoted to the general history of music education. In addition to MENC documents, manuscripts, books, pamphlets, periodicals, and oral history interviews, the Center houses the Luther Whiting Mason collection which consists of approximately 250 items of Japanese art and artifacts, books, papers, photographs, and rare Japanese musical instruments presented to Luther Whiting Mason (n.d.-1896) by Japanese Court musicians during Mason's stay in Japan as an advisor for music education to the Japanese government from 1880-1882. The collection is on an indefinite loan to the center by Mason's great-granddaughter.

   Perhaps the most noteworthy items contained in the Mason collection are several Japanese music instruments such as a flute used in the Imperial Palace orchestra, presented to Mason by its first flutist, 1 smaller flute, 1 "shō" (or a pan pipe), 2 "koto," 1 "biwa" (or lute), and 1 "shamisen." In addition, the collection also contains scroll hangings (10 items), fans (14 items), photographs (25 items), music textbooks and charts (29 items), clothing, cloth, and embroidery (26 items), other miscellaneous artifacts (35 items), and letters and documents (83 items).

4. b. No reservation is required; however, appointments are recommended.

   c. Free of charge.

    d. Pictures of the musical instruments may be taken with the permission of the curator.

5.   Although there is no published catalog for the collection, researchers may consult a guide to the collection entitled "Inventory, Luther Whiting Mason Collection" at the MENC. Also available free on request is a brochure entitled "Special Collections in the MENC Historical Center (March 1978)."

C7 National Air and Space Museum (Smithsonian Institution)

1.   a. *6th Street and Independence Avenue, SW*
Washington, D.C. 20560
381-6264

    b. April 1-Labor Day: 10:00 A.M.-9:00 P.M.
Remainder of year: 10:00 A.M.-5:30 P.M.

    c. Open to the public free of charge.

    d. Photocopying services are available.

    e. Dr. Noel W. Hinners, Director
F. C. Durant, Assistant Director, Department of Astronautics
Donald Lopez, Assistant Director, Department of Aeronautics
Howard Wolfe, Assistant Director, Department of Science and Technology

2-3.   In the museum's collection, there is one display of a Japanese flying suit from World War II. Also, several incendiary balloons made by the Japanese in the early 1940s are on display. Unquestionably, the most important part of the museum's collection on East Asia is its Japanese aircraft. NASM owns the world's largest collection of pre-World War II and World War II Japanese aircraft, even surpassing holdings in Japan. A famous Mitsubishi "zero" fighter plane used by the Japanese in the World War II is displayed at the museum. Most of the Japanese aircraft, however, are in storage at the Silver Hill Museum of NASM (Old Silver Hill Road, Suitland, Maryland), which is located near exit 36 of the Capital Beltway in suburban Maryland.

    On continually changing display in the Silver Hill's Museum are more than 100 aircraft, spacecraft, power plants, and related objects from the reserve collection of the NASM. Both military and general aviation aircraft are exhibited and often more planes can be seen at the Silver Hill Museum than in the NASM's main museum in Washington, D.C. Trained guides conduct free tours of the exhibit areas (which now consist of 24 buildings) for the visitors who may also see a large shop where technicians work on a variety of flight vehicles and other historical objects in need of restoration.

    The Silver Hill Museum is open by appointment only:

Wednesday	10:00 A.M.
Friday	10:00 A.M.
Saturday	10:00 A.M. and 2:00 P.M.
Sunday	10:00 A.M. and 2:00 P.M.

For tour reservations call (202) 381-4056 at least 2 weeks in advance. Reservations can be made from 9:00 A.M. to 4:00 P.M. Monday through Friday.

4.   For the most up-to-date information about museum programs and theater and Spacearium schedules, check at the information desk in the South Lobby located on the Independence Avenue side.

C8 National Bonsai Collection (Department of Agriculture— The National Arboretum)

1.   a. *24th and R Streets, NE*
Washington, D.C. 20002
399-5400

     b. Open to the public from 10:00 A.M.-2:30 P.M. Anyone under 16 must be accompanied by a parent or other responsible adult.

     c. Visitors may take pictures of the collection.

     d. Dr. John L. Creech, Director
Robert Drechsler, Curator

2.   The National Arboretum was established by an act of the United States Congress in 1927 and was placed on the National Register of Historic Places in 1973. In addition to over 500,000 dried plants preserved in a herbarium, the arboretum maintains numerous plants arranged in different combinations throughout its 444-acre garden. The arboretum's primary activities are concerned with educating the public regarding trees and shrubs as well as conducting research on these plants. It is an educational "outdoor museum" in which one can study many kinds of trees, shrubs, and plants.

3.   The National Arboretum houses the National Bonsai Collection, consisting of 53 rare and priceless bonsai which were presented to the American people by the Nippon Bonsai Association in commemoration of the 200th anniversary of the United States in 1976. The 53 bonsai, assembled by the association, are 30 to 350 years old and represent 34 different species. About half the plants were donations from private sources (e.g., Takeo Fukuda, Takeo Miki). One, a 180-year-old Japanese Red Pine, comes from the Imperial Household and represents the first bonsai sent abroad from the Imperial Collection. The remainder were purchased by the association with funds provided by the Japan Foundation (see entry H30).

     These precious bonsai are housed in the Bonsai Pavillion (built by Masao Kinoshita of the Sasaki Associates, Watertown, Massachusetts) together with 6 unique viewing stones that are part of the Bicentennial gift from Japan.

     Bonsai represents one of Japan's oldest and highest unique art forms. It has been developed by the Japanese for centuries to bring the beauty of nature nearer to their homes. The same love for natural beauty expressed in bonsai is also in *suiseki*, or stone viewing. The 6 stones on display are outstanding examples of this art.

4.   A highly informative and illustrated brochure for the collection, *The National Bonsai Collection* (February 1978), is available free on request. It lists vital information for each of the bonsai in the collection (e.g., age of the plant, botanical as well as common name) and names for the 6 viewing stones. Copies of the *United States National Arboretum* are also available without charge.

It should be noted that the National Arboretum has a reference library containing over 5,000 titles plus about 1,300 bound volumes of periodicals. The library maintains a special collection of reference materials and books on bonsai (i.e., about 35 English and 15 Japanese titles). On-site use of these materials is available to the public from 8:00 A.M. to 4:30 P.M. on weekdays. An annotated bibliography entitled *Bonsai: A Selected Booklist* compiled by Jayne T. MacLean (Washington, D.C.: National Arboretum Branch, National Agricultural Library, 1976) is available at the library. For further information, call Jayne T. MacLean, the librarian, at 399-5400, extension 43.

C9 National Museum of History and Technology (MHT) (Smithsonian Institution)

1. a. *Constitution Avenue between 12th and 14th Streets, NW*
    Washington, D.C. 20560
    628-4422

    b. April 1-Labor Day: 10:00 A.M.-9:00 P.M.
    Remainder of the year: 10:00 A.M.-5:30 P.M.

    c. Open to the public. Many pertinent items are not on permanent display. To see these items, researchers must make arrangements in advance.

    d. Visitors may take their own photographs of MHT holdings. However, photos intended for publication must be cleared with the Public Affairs Office.

    e. Roger G. Kennedy, Director

2.   The museum contains some interesting items relating to East Asia. However, it is difficult to determine the exact number of East Asian materials located in this museum. Many such items have been transferred to other branches of the Smithsonian Institution (e.g., the Department of Anthropology of the National Museum of Natural History, and the Freer Gallery of Art).

3.   The following departments or divisions have some materials on East Asia:

Department of National History—Dr. Vladimir Clain-Stefanelli, Chairman (381-6230)—and the Division of Postal History (381-5024). Among the approximately 13 million items in this fascinating collection are a sizable number of postal history materials from East Asia, including postal stamps and stationery. Materials from Japan are particularly rich and impressive.

With the exception of a few Japanese samurai swords, most of the original items in the collections of the Division of Political History (381-5532) and the Division of Military History (381-5115) relating to East Asia were transferred to the Department of Anthropology in the National Museum of Natural History (NHM), or to the Freer Gallery of Art.

Except for an exhibit of a Chinese chain bridge made in the 19th century and a model of a war chariot, there is almost nothing pertaining to East Asia in the Department of the History of Technology, Dr. John T. Schlebecker, Chairman (381-6169).

4.　There is no comprehensive guide to the museum as a whole. Perhaps the most complete listing of MHT holdings is the bicentennial exhibition catalog, *A Nation of Nations* (1976), edited by Peter Marzio.

C10　National Museum of Natural History (Smithsonian Institution)

1.　a. *Constitution Avenue at 10th Street, NW*
　　Washington, D.C. 20560
　　628-4422

　b. June 1-Labor Day:　10:00 A.M.-9:00 P.M.
　　Labor Day-April 1:　10:00 A.M.-5:30 P.M.

　c. Exhibits are open to the public. Arrangements must be made in advance to see items not on permanent display. Such items are available to researchers Monday through Friday between 9:00 A.M.-4:00 P.M.

　d. Visitors may take photographs of the exhibits. Photographic services of the museums are also available.

　e. Dr. James F. Mello, Acting Director

2.　Since many divisions of the museum do not arrange their holdings geographically, it is difficult to determine the exact amount of East Asian materials among the approximately 60-million separate items in the museum's collections. The most important office that deals with East Asia in the museum is its Department of Anthropology (Dr. William W. Fitzhugh, Chairman, 381-5626). Dr. Eugene I. Knez, Curator, Asian Anthropology (381-4051) is especially knowledgeable about the department's collection of East Asia.

The card catalog for East Asian entries in this department is in the Processing Laboratory located in Room 311. It is available to researchers from Monday through Friday (9:00 A.M.-5:00 P.M.). Arranged geographically as well as numerically in accordance with each object's catalog number, the numerical catalog also contains descriptions of the items.

CHINESE COLLECTION

Objects from China range from the mundane to the unusual and rare. Included in the collection are Chinese food, clothing, instruments, utensils, snuff bottles, opium smoker's lamps and boxes, Buddhist objects, embroideries, jades, porcelain, cloisonné jewelry and ornaments, farming implements, ivory and stone carvings, an ancient bronze vessel, and even human scalps. There are more than 4,100 Chinese entries.

JAPANESE COLLECTION

This collection also contains a wide variety of objects, 4,934 entries in all, with 183 on the Ainu and 910 on various prefectures of Japan. About 400 items were collected by Commodore Matthew C. Perry during his expedition to Japan (1853-1854). Included in the Perry Collection are Japanese silks, lacquerware, fans, porcelain, musical instruments, farming tools, and clothing. The Perry Collection was the first ever acquired by the Smithsonian Institution and was cataloged in 1859.

KOREAN COLLECTION

This is particularly noteworthy for its collection of Shaman objects such as musical instruments, charms, and knives. Altogether there are 1,640 entries under Korea, including some 140 on Shaman.

TAIWAN COLLECTION

This is subdivided into various tribal groups (aborigines) and is arranged alphabetically. These objects also cover a wide range of daily life of special interest to anthropologists. Altogether there are 762 entries, nearly half deal with the aboriginal tribes.

Aside from the Department of Anthropology, the national museum contains a Department of Mineralogy with holdings of interest to East Asia specialists. The department has an impressive jade collection on exhibit in the Gems and Mineralogy Hall, including the Maude Monell Verleson Collection of Chinese Jade Carvings of the 16th to 19th centuries which was presented to the Smithsonian Institution in 1958.

For other fields of research, scholars should contact such individual departments as botany, vertebrate, and zoology for further information.

4. No published catalogs or inventories exist for the museum's collection. There are, however, different card catalogs to aid researchers and, for the staff, a computerized inventory.

C11 National Rifle Association Firearms Museum

1. a. *1600 Rhode Island Avenue, NW*
   Washington, D.C. 20036
   783-6505, Extension 227

   b. 10:00 A.M.-4:00 P.M.   seven days a week; closed on major holidays.

   c. Open to the public.

   d. Visitors must obtain prior permission for photographing any item in the collection.

   e. Dan R. Abbey, Jr., Curator

2-3. The museum has over 1,500 items "under glass" (or on exhibition), including the following firearms and swords from East Asia.

   Chinese collection consists of 2 "jingle" (or Rampart) rifles (ca. 1900), 3 or 4 handguns of World War I vintage, and 5 or 6 semiautomatic and bolt-action rifles of the World War II period.

Japanese Collection is comprised of 5 or 6 handguns (1920s-1940s), 18 World War II rifles, 3 temple rifles (manufactured in the 17th and 18th centuries), and 1 Japanese Garand rifle (altogether 12 are known to exist in the world today). In addition, the collection includes 1 Nambu pistol (early 1920s), 1 baby Nambu pistol (1920s), and 4 other pistols, plus 3 samurai swords (including one dating back to the Edo period).

Korean Collection contains half a dozen semi- and bolt-type rifles used in the Korean War (1950-1953).

C12 Navy Memorial Museum (Navy Department)

1. a. *9th and M Streets, SE*
   Washington, D.C. 20374
   433-2651

   b. 9:00 A.M.-4:00 P.M.   Monday-Friday
   10:00 A.M.-5:00 P.M.   weekends and holidays (except Thanksgiving, Christmas, and New Year's Day)

   c. Open to the public without charge.

   d. Visitors may take their own pictures with the permission of the museum office.

   e. Comdr. T. A. Damon, Director

2-3.   The U.S. Navy Memorial Museum depicts the history of naval service in war and peace from the American Revolution to the space age. More than 4,000 objects are on display in the museum building and nearby waterfront parks. All exhibits are on ground level.
   Of particular interest to East Asian specialists are Japanese weapons and equipment captured during World War II; these include:

   (1) Japanese 26-inch turret face plate for a Yamato-class battleship;
   (2) World War II Japanese field mortar, 120 mm, type 2;
   (3) World War II Japanese two-man submarine;
   (4) World War II Japanese Y-gun, depth-charge thrower;
   (5) World War II Japanese medium tank, type 97 (modified 1937, with 47 mm gun)—the only one available in the world;
   (6) World War II Japanese field gun, 150 mm;
   (7) World War II Japanese projectile, 18.1-inch (46 cm) for a Yamato-class battleship.

   These items are on permanent display in Willard Park, located near the museum.
   Other museum objects of interest are as follows:

   (1) A trainer model of "Oka" (or "Suicide Bomb") which was used by the Japanese Navy in World War II (only 10 are known to exist in the world today);
   (2) The builder's models of Japanese naval vessels, World War II variety (several on display);

(3) Approximately 20 identification models of Japanese naval ships (World War II variety);

(4) A Korean "Turtle Boat" model;

(5) One Japanese samurai sword;

(6) A Japanese vase which was a gift of Admiral Isoroku Yamamoto to P. P. Power in the pre-World War II period;

(7) One Japanese magnetic compass;

(8) A panel of exhibits on Commodore Matthew C. Perry's expedition to Japan (1853-54). It contains 2 lithographs of the original watercolor pictures drawn by William Heine, one of the expedition artists who accompanied Perry; "Portrait of Perry, a North American"—a modern wood-block copy of a contemporary print by a Japanese artist; and 2 bundles of Japanese pattern cloth brought back by the Perry expedition.

4. Copies of *Navy Memorial Museum* (brochure) and *The Navy Memorial Museum's Guide to Willard Park* are available free on request. Researchers may consult with the previous director, Capt. Roger Pineau, who is very knowledgeable about the museum's collection in general and its Japanese objects in particular. He may be reached at his home: 9403 Holland Avenue, Bethesda, Maryland 20014.

C13 Textile Museum

1. a. *2320 S Street, NW*
       Washington, D.C. 20006
       667-0441

    b. 10:00 A.M.-5:00 P.M. Tuesday through Saturday. Curators are available Tuesday through Friday only.

    c. Open to the public; no admission fees.

    d. Limited photoduplication service is available.

    e. Andrew Oliver, Jr., Director
       Patricia Fiske, Assistant Curator

2-3. The museum features exhibits of its collection on a rotating basis. In the spring 1978, an exhibit of "Chinese Looms Resplendent" was presented. The museum's holdings are kept in storage for the most part, but can be seen by appointment.

The collection of textiles from China is fairly sizable, dating back to the T'ang dynasty (A.D. 618-907) with the majority of the holdings from the Ch'ing period (1644-1912). The holdings are cataloged chronologically first and then, within each time period, are further classified by either type of weave or function of the holding (cushion, covers, robe, etc.). The textile holdings from China include: T'ang, 4; Sung, 2; Ming, 22; Ch'ing, 89; undated holdings, 61; and scrolls, 8. In addition, there are about 27 rugs from China, dating back to the Ming period (1368-1644).

As for Japanese textiles, the museum's holdings are not as extensive as on China; nor are they as thoroughly cataloged. There are, however, at least 83 textile items and 1 rug made in Japan.

In addition, there are 2 textile items from Korea; 2 from Taiwan; and 7 rugs from Turkestan manufactured during the 18th and 19th centuries.

4.   There is no published catalog on the museum's East Asian collection. However, a card catalog for the museum's holdings is available in the reference library of the Textile Museum, which contains about 6,000 titles, including about 200 on East Asia. Katherine Freshley is the librarian. Most titles are on the subjects of rugs, embroidery, the textile industry and fabrics, and tapestry in China and Japan. An appointment must be made with the curators to use the catalog.

Note: Every Saturday, at 10:30 A.M., the museum holds "rug mornings." An expert explains the textiles or rugs of some geographical area, including East Asia. The public is invited to attend free of charge. The museum also sponsors occasional lectures, some of which may be of interest to East Asia specialists.

In addition to the galleries and museums listed above, several local commercial art galleries and shops sponsor occasional exhibitions of East Asian arts (e.g., paintings). Interested scholars should consult the *Calendar of Events* (monthly) published by the Asia Society's Washington Office (see entry H17). Some of the more active ones include:

Atlantic Gallery
1055 Thomas Jefferson Street, NW,
Washington, D.C.
333-1040

Gallery Amerasia
2142 F Street, NW,
Washington, D.C.
331-0129

Daly & Reed, Inc.
2903 M Street, NW,
Washington, D.C.
338-6717

Hendricks Art Collection, Ltd.
9101 Old Georgetown Road,
Bethesda, Md.
(301) 365-1234

East-West Art Associates, Ltd.
1553 Rockville Pike,
Rockville, Md.
(301) 881-5920

Shogun Gallery
1083 Wisconsin Ave., NW,
Washington, D.C.
965-5454

D Collections of Music and Other Sound Recordings

Entry Form for Collections of Music and Other Sound Recordings (D)

1. Access
   a. *Address; telephone number(s)*
   b. Hours of service
   c. Conditions of access; special requirements or restrictions on use
   d. Director; heads of relevant divisions

2. Size of collection pertaining to East Asia

3. Description of holdings

4. Facilities for study and guidance for use
   a. Listening equipment
   b. Reservation requirements
   c. Fees charged
   d. Copies available for purchase

5. Bibliography of materials facilitating access to the collection (inventories, catalogs, guides, descriptions)

Chinese Opera Society of Washington, D.C. See entry H21.

Freer Gallery of Art Library See entry A16.

D1 Library of Congress—American Folklife Center—Archive of Folk Song

1. a. *Library of Congress Building, Ground Floor, G152*
      Library of Congress
      10   1st Street, SE
      Washington, D.C. 20540
      287-5510

   b. 8:30 A.M.-5:00 P.M.   Monday-Friday

    c. Open to the public.

    d. Joseph C. Hickerson, Head

2.   The Archive of Folk Song was established within the LC's Music Division in 1928 as a national repository for documentary manuscripts and sound recordings of American folk music. On July 31, 1978, it merged with the American Folklife Center to form a new administrative body within the LC.

        The Archive houses over 30,000 recordings (i.e., cylinders, discs, wires, and tapes) containing over 300,000 items of folksong, folk music, folk tale, oral history, and other types of folklore. Every region and every state of the United States is represented in the Archive.

        In addition to materials from the United States, the Archive maintains representative collections of traditional music and lore from foreign countries, including China, Japan, and South Korea.

3.   The Archives of Folk Song contains 7 records on Japanese music, and about 25 records on Korean vocal and instrumental music. In addition, it maintains the following field recordings of Chinese music: (1) 5 records (33 rpm) of flute and lute (ch'in) pieces played by C. H. Cha, Soochow, China, in 1945; (2) 120 cylinders of folk music from the Eric von Hornbostel collection of the University of Berlin, which was deposited by Dr. Walter Bingham in 1949, including a number of East Asian examples recorded early in the 20th century; (3) duplication of 3 cylinders from a collection in Museé de l'Homme, Paris, made available by John Schwarz (assistant director) who visited the LC in 1970. It contains music played by the delegations from Hanoi and China at the Paris World Fair (1900); (4) 1 record made by Helen and Virginia Moshang at the LC Recording Laboratory in 1943, with accompaniment on the Chinese moon harp by Helen Moshang; (5) 7 12-inch records and 3 10-inch records made at the 5th Catskill Folk Festival held at Phoenicia, New York, by Charles Hofmann and B. A. Botkin in 1944 including some Chinese selections; and (6) 5 12-inch records of Chinese songs recorded by Chao Rulan, Margaret Speaks, and students and faculty of the former California College in China.

4.   a. Listening equipment is available free of charge.

    b. Researchers should call for appointment.

    c. There is no charge or fee for using the materials in the collection.

    d. Duplication is available through a special order with the LC's Recording Laboratory.

D2 Library of Congress—Motion Picture, Broadcasting, and Recorded-Sound Division

1.   a. *Library of Congress Building, G152*
Library of Congress
10   1st Street, SE
Washington, D.C. 20540
287-5508/5509 (Recorded Sound)

    b. 8:30 A.M.-5:00 P.M.   Monday-Friday

    c. Open to the public.

    d. Robert Carneal, Head of Recorded Sound

2.   No accurate measurement of the division's East Asian materials can be made, for most of them are uncataloged. Nevertheless, one can say that there are at least 20,000 items relating to East Asia, including 4,500 Japanese records produced in the pre-1945 period.

3.   The Recorded Sound Section of the division (located in the Library of Congress Building G152) holds about 950,000 items. The collection can be divided into 3 components: (1) approximately 600,000 non-commercial recordings; (2) 190,000 pre-LP commercial recordings; and (3) 160,000 commercial LP recordings, both domestic and foreign. Annual acquisition of recorded sound items number around 85,000-90,000. As most of these materials are uncataloged, one must rely heavily on the staff. Discussions with them have revealed the existence of the following materials relating to East Asia:

JAPANESE RECORDS COLLECTION

The division has custody of approximately 4,500 Japanese records of the pre-1945 period which were acquired by the United States forces during the occupation period (1945-1952) and were transferred to the division from the Special Service Unit of the U.S. Department of Army. Mostly popular songs of the prewar period, these records constitute a unique collection that can be invaluable to scholars interested in Japanese popular music of the pre-1945 period. To inspect these materials, special arrangements must be made with the Recorded Sound Section, because they are stored in a warehouse located in the Washington suburbs.

THE OWI COLLECTION

The MBRS Division also has custody of approximately 15,000 records (mostly 33 rpm) of music, propaganda materials, and news broadcasts relating to East Asia by the Office of War Information (OWI) during World War II. The OWI produced these materials for the consumption of Japanese, Chinese, and Korean audiences as a part of the psychological warfare conducted by the United States against Japan. Approximately 10,000 items were designed for the Japanese audience, 3,000 for the Chinese, and 2,000 for Koreans. The division also has copies of the entire OWI collection as well as transcripts of the Voice of America productions.

THE U.N. COLLECTION

The division also has acquired a huge amount of United Nations recordings, mostly the proceedings of the General Assembly and the Security Council, from 1945 to the present. For example, the recordings of the U.N. Security Council are almost complete from 1946 to 1977 (all in original languages).

4.   **a.** Listening equipment is available without charge for virtually every form of recorded sound (e.g., tapes, phonodiscs, etc.).

b. Audio facilities are available for 3 hours between 9:00 A.M.-12:00 noon. Serious scholars who make reservations may use them for a longer period.

c. There is no fee for listening to the items in the collections.

d. The Recorded Sound Section has its own recording laboratory where all forms of recorded sound can be reproduced. A substantial fee is charged for this service. Phonodiscs can also be purchased.

5. The cataloged recorded-sound holdings appear in the comprehensive catalog entitled *Music, Books on Music, and Sound Recordings,* which is published as a part of the *National Union Catalog.* It is issued semi-annually with annual and quinquennial cumulations. Also helpful is a brochure entitled *The Music Division: A Guide to its Collections and Services* (1972). Substantial additional information is available from the staff of the respective sections and from internal files and catalogs.

D3 National Archives and Records Service (NARS) (General Service Administration)—Motion Picture and Sound-Recording Branch

1. a. *8th Street and Pennsylvania Avenue, NW*
   (Entrance from Pennsylvania Avenue only)
   Washington, D.C. 20408
   523-3267

   b. 8:45 A.M.-5:00 P.M.   Monday-Friday

   c. Open to researchers. Users must have a pass ("research identification card") issued by the NARS to work in this branch. Some materials may be restricted.

   d. William T. Murphy, Branch Chief
   Les Waffen, Archivist
   Don Rae, Archivist

2. Altogether, the NARS holds over 100,000 sound recordings with an undetermined number of items on East Asia.

3. The many sound recordings on East Asia readily identifiable in the *Guide to the National Archives of the United States* (1974) will be described along the record groups. Most recordings are of speeches and broadcasts either emanating from East Asia or concerning East Asia.

   RG 59: *General Records of the Department of State* contain recordings of radio broadcasts by Secretaries of State Cordell Hull, John Foster Dulles, and Christian Herter. In addition, there are 31,509 memovox recordings of broadcasts of the International Broadcasting Division of the Office of Information and Education Exchange (formerly the Office of War Information) to foreign countries from 1946 to 1949.
   RG 111: *General Records of the Office of Chief Signal Officer* include the sound track of a recorded interview with "Tokyo Rose" (Iva D'Aquino) on September 20, 1945.

RG 118: *Records of U.S. Attorneys and Marshals* contain 16 disc recordings of broadcasts by Radio Tokyo and other Japanese stations during World War II; all relate to "Tokyo Rose" who was later tried and convicted of treason by the United States government.

RG 165: *Records of the War Department General Staff* contain miscellaneous recordings collected by the Radio Branch of the Bureau of Public Relations of the War Department from 1942 to 1949 relating to the war in the Pacific, including Gen. Douglas MacArthur's arrival in Melbourne from the Philippine Islands in 1942; the American surrender in the Philippines in 1942; and the Japanese surrender in the Philippines in 1945. Also, it contains recordings of press conferences of Gen. Robert L. Eichelberger concerning the occupation of Japan; a recording of the farewell ceremonies of General MacArthur at Haneda Airport, Tokyo, in 1951; and many recordings in German, Japanese, and Chinese that were used by the Axis in their psychological warfare efforts during World War II.

RG 178: *Records of the U.S. Maritime Commission* contain sound recordings, 1941-45 [128 items]. Included are a dramatized history of the merchant marine, with such recreated events as the arrival of the *Franklin* at Nagasaki in 1799, the voyage of the *Margaret* from Salem to Nagasaki in 1801, and the landing of a liberty ship on the beach of Okinawa in 1945.

RG 179: *Records of the War Production Board* contain recordings of speeches broadcast by prominent public figures, such as Joseph C. Grew, former United States Ambassador to Japan (1932-1941).

RG 200: *National Archives Gift Collection* contains sound recordings (1892-1966) of speeches, interviews, and panel discussions by prominent figures such as Gen. Douglas MacArthur and Mme Chiang Kai-shek [1,973 items]. It also contains 8 tapes recorded from 1951 to 1954 by the Longine-Witnauer Watch Co.; most are speeches by prominent American and East Asian leaders pertaining to the Korean war. In addition, there are 15 tape recordings of speeches made by John Foster Dulles on the Japanese peace treaty, Senators John Sparkman and Joseph McCarthy on the Korean war, and Dean Rusk on the Korean ceasefire.

RG 208: *Records of the Office of War Information* contain sound recordings [1,115 items] of radio broadcasts concerning the defeat of Italy, Germany, and Japan; and international conferences such as Yalta (1945), Dumbarton Oaks (1944), and San Francisco (1945). There are 45 overseas broadcasts on East Asia, most pertaining to Japan.

RG 210: *Records of the War Relocation Authority* contain 28 radio broadcasts covering the activities of the War Relocation Authority which administered the internment of Japanese and Japanese-Americans during World War II and the war records of Japanese-Nisei soldiers.

RG 243: *Records of the U.S. Strategic Bombing Survey* contain 366 recorded interviews with Japanese civilians concerning the effects of American bombing on several Japanese cities, including Hiroshima and Tokyo.

RG 262: *Records of the Foreign Broadcast Intelligence Service* contain foreign broadcasts (mostly 1941-1945) in Japanese, German, and other languages monitored by the FBIS. Included are 86 cylinders of Japanese broadcasts covering speeches by Hideki Tojo, Mamoru Shigemitsu, and others, and English-language news broadcasts from Tokyo.

RG 306: *Records of the U.S. Information Agency* contain recordings made by or for the "Voice of America" for overseas release. At least 13 tapes relating to East Asia can be found here, mostly recordings of speeches by prominent American leaders on the Korean war.

RG 330: *Records of the Office of the Secretary of Defense* contain approximately 136 items pertaining to the Korean war. Under the "Time for Defense" series all phases of the military operations in Korea are summarized, usually during the first segment of the show.

4. a. Tape recorders are available for listening to the tapes; and phonographs can be used for disc-recorded materials.

    b. Researchers should make reservations in advance for the use of the necessary equipment.

    c. There is no fee for listening to items in the collection; and researchers may use their own tape recorder for duplication. There is a charge for duplicating services by the staff.

5. The following published and unpublished guides to the division's holdings are available:
    Sound Recordings in the Audiovisual Archives Division of the National Archives by Mayfield S. Bray and Leslie C. Waffen (1972), a preliminary draft is available to readers free of charge while the supply lasts;
    Sound Recordings: Voices of World War II, 1937-1945 (1971) and *The Crucial Decade 1945-1954 (1976)*.
    In addition, partial card catalogs, arranged by subject, name, and title, exist for much of the collection; and there is a card file of titles for record groups arranged in numerical order.

D4 University of Maryland Language Media Center

1. a. *Language Media Center*
       1204 Foreign Language Building
       University of Maryland
       College Park, Maryland 20742
       (301) 454-5728

    b. 8:00 A.M.-10:00 P.M. during regular school days; closed on holidays and weekends.

    c. Open to researchers.

    d. To duplicate the tapes, researchers must secure permission from the Center's director.

    e. James E. Royalty, Director

2. The Language Media Center holds about 410 tapes relating to China and Japan.

3. The collection may be divided into three categories: (1) 17 cassette tapes recording Chinese and Japanese music and folk songs; (2) 60

tapes of speeches by prominent Chinese leaders and lectures by specialists on Chinese and Japanese art, culture, religion, history, literature, and foreign relations. Some of the significant items include recordings of speeches by Chinese foreign ministers (i.e., Chiao Kuan-hua and Huang Hua) at the United Nations; an interview with Yukio Mishima; Dr. Sayo Yotsukura's lectures on the "Japanese Way of Thinking"; and others (e.g., lectures on Japanese Noh drama, Kabuki, and Zen Buddhism); and (3) 340 cassette tapes for language training (i.e., 200 for Chinese and 140 Japanese).

4. a. Tape recorders are available for listening to the tapes.

    b. Researchers should call ahead to reserve the necessary material and equipment.

  c-d. No fees are charged for listening.

University of Maryland Undergraduate Library See entry A42.

E Map Collections

Entry Form for Map Collections (E)

1. Access
   a. *Address; telephone number(s)*
   b. Hours of service
   c. Conditions of access
   d. Reproduction services
   e. Director, heads of relevant divisions

2. Size of holdings pertaining to East Asia

3. Description of holdings

4. Bibliography of materials facilitating access to the collection (inventories, guides, descriptions)

Central Intelligence Agency Map Collection See entry K4.

Commerce Department, National Oceanic and Atmospheric Administration, National Marine Fisheries Service See entry K5.

E1 Defense Mapping Agency Hydrographic/Topographic Center (Defense Department)

1. a. *6500 Brookes Lane*
      Washington, D.C. 20315
      227-2000
      227-2006/2007 (Public Affairs)

   b. 7:00 A.M.-4:00 P.M.   Monday-Friday

   c. The Defense Mapping Agency (DMA) map collections are not open to the public. Security clearance or special permission is necessary for researchers wishing to gain access to the collections. Further information may be obtained from the Public Affairs Office (227-2006/2007).

d. Copies of a few unclassified maps may be purchased from the State Department.

e. William R. Lund, Director

2-3. The map collections of the Defense Mapping Agency's Topographic Center are, for the most part, classified. The collections consist of approximately 1.7 million maps, nearly 700,000 books, periodicals, and documents on cartography, geodesy, and geography, and several hundred thousand photographs including some on East Asia. These materials are housed in the Information Resources Division (also known as the Department of Defense Library of Maps, Geodetic Data, and Foreign Place Names). Unclassified maps produced by the DMA are distributed to DMA repositories which include the Library of Congress—Geography and Map Division (see entry E3) and the George Washington University Library (see entry A18), the National Geographic Society (see entry H39), and the University of Maryland's McKeldin Library (see entry A42). The Defense Mapping Agency Hydrographic Center maintains a public sales office (763-1530) where navigational charts and publications relating to East Asia can be purchased.

4. There is no published inventory to the DMA map collections. The center maintains a 5-volume *Catalog of Maps, Charts, and Related Products* (in loose-leaf form), the use of which is restricted. Permission to gain access must be obtained from the Director of DMA.

E2 Geological Survey Library (Interior Department)

1. a. *12201 Sunrise Drive, Fourth Floor*
      Reston, Va. 22092
      (703) 860-6679

   b. 7:15 A.M.-4:45 P.M.   Monday-Friday

   c. Open to the public.

   d. The library's Map Section has a very limited capacity to copy maps. Researchers seeking copies are directed to local photoduplication firms which provide such services for a fee.

   e. Barbara Chappell, Head of Reference and Circulation (including Maps)

2. The library's map collection consists of approximately 275,000 sheet maps, including about 500 maps on China, 2,150 on Japan, and 150 on Korea. These are filed together in 59 map drawers (i.e., 13 on China, 43 on Japan and 3 on Korea). In addition, there are 4 drawers containing maps of Asia in general.

3. Maps are arranged by geographic area, subject, scale, and date. Coverage include general topographic, geological, and geophysical features, and other subject categories (e.g., mineral resources including petroleum and mining maps), water, soils, volcanoes, vegetation, etc.

4. The library is currently utilizing the on-line computerized cataloging system operated by OCLC (Ohio College Library Center). No published catalog or inventory for the map collection is available. However, a bibliographic record of thematic maps published by the Geological Survey, which constitute a large part of the collection, is provided by the following catalogs: *Publications of the Geological Survey, 1879-1961* and *Publications of the Geological Survey, 1962-1970.* Both are available free from the U.S.G.S. Distribution Center, 1200 South Eads St., Arlington, VA 22202. A similar record for current U.S.G.S. maps is available in *New Publications of the Geological Survey* issued monthly with annual cumulations. This publication is available without charge from the U.S. Geological Survey, National Center, Reston, Va. 22092.

George Washington University Library See entry A18.

E3 Library of Congress—Geography and Map Division

1. a. *845 South Pickett Street*
    Alexandria, Va.
    (703) 370-1335
    Mail: Washington, D.C. 20540
    Note: The Geography and Map Division is scheduled to move into the new Madison Memorial Building (the Library of Congress) between 1979 and 1980.

    b. Reading Room:
    8:30 A.M.-5:00 P.M.   Monday-Friday
    8:30 A.M.-12:30 P.M.   Saturday
    Closed Sundays and holidays

    c. Open to the public; visitors must register. Limited interlibrary loan service is available.

    d. Photoduplication facilities

    e. John A. Wolter, Chief

2. The Geography and Map Division has custody of the world's largest and most comprehensive cartographic collection, which includes more than 3.6 million maps and charts, 41,000 atlases, 275 globes, and some 2,500 3-dimensional relief models. East Asian materials amount to at least 21,000 items.

3. The division's resources may best be described under 3 separate rubrics: Maps, Atlases, and Cartography.

    MAPS

    Approximately 55 percent of the 3.6 million maps are individual sheets of large- and medium-scale series maps and charts published during the 19th and 20th centuries. Included are official topographic and geologic series, and soil, mineral, and agricultural resource maps plus nautical and aeronautical charts for most countries of the world and its various geographical and political entities, divisions, and subdivisions. Three different map collections form the whole: (1) MARC map file; (2) the titled collection (single- and multi-sheet thematic maps); and (3) set maps and series collections. The MARC Map file consists of thematic maps cataloged by the LC computer system (MARC). Almost all of the cartographic items contained in the MARC cataloged map-data base have been acquired since 1968. The titled collection also involves single-sheet (large) maps, but only a few of these maps appear in the shelflist; most are unclassified and uncataloged. Both of these map files are arranged basically in G classification order. The titled collection is first arranged by gross geographic area, then by geographic subdivision, subject, and finally by geographic subdivision of the country (e.g., region, administrative division, city, etc.). Within the subdivisions, chronological and subject classifications are again maintained. The series collection is predominantly cataloged and included in the master shelflist (arranged in G classification). The division also maintains extensive indexes for map series showing extent and date of coverage.

The following is an approximate indication of the division's holdings based on shelflist measurement which include all of the MARC and set maps, but not the titled collection (pre-MARC single maps):

Call Numbers	Countries	Number of Titles
G 7800-7824	China	723
7830-7834	Manchuria	181
7850	Inner Mongolia	1
7860	Outer Mongolia	7
7880	Sinkiang	7
7890	Tibet	3
7895	Outer Mongolia (MPR)	15
7910-7914	Taiwan	199
7900-7904	South Korea	261
7905-7909	North Korea	44
7950-7964	Japan	1,148
7962-06 & R9	Okinawa	26
	Total	2,616

As a supplement to these measurements, a simple drawer count of the titled collection (uncataloged) yields the following figures:

Category	China (drawers)	Japan (drawers)	Korea (drawers)
By date	13	13	3
By regions	4	40	½
By provinces	21	49	½
By cities	22	172	9½
By subjects	25	52	4
Manchuria	16		
Mongolia	1		
Taiwan	12		

Total number of drawers counted in the titled collection: 457.5 drawers. A very rough estimate of maps per drawer is 40. Thus, the title map file would hold approximately 18,300 maps. If one combines these two totals, the division's holdings on East Asia come to a minimum of 20,916 single- and multi-sheet thematic maps.

ATLASES

Atlases represent a smaller portion of the division's holdings. There are altogether 41,000 atlases. The following shelflist measurements reveal the size of the East Asian materials in this category:

Call Numbers	Countries	Number of Titles
G 2300	East Asia	22
2305-2313	China	435
2315-2317	Mongolia	4
2320-2324	Sinkiang	8
2325-2326	Tibet	5
2340-2344	Taiwan	25
2330-2334	Korea	48
2335	Okinawa	1
2353-2359	Japan	978
	Total	1,526

CARTOGRAPHY

The division maintains a card catalog for articles and books dealing with cartography—the *Bibliography of Cartography*. The bibliography is arranged by author and subject/geographic heading. Entries listed in the *Bibliography* do not necessarily represent the division's own holdings, nor those of the Library of Congress as a whole. The number of East Asian titles included in the bibliography can be listed as follows: China, 238; Mongolia, 10; Tibet, 6; Taiwan, 7; Japan, 246; and Korea, 28.

SPECIAL COLLECTIONS

The division holds early maps of China, Korea, and Japan in the Hummel, Warner, and miscellaneous Oriental map collections.
(1) *The Hummel Collection.* In 1930 Andrew W. Mellon, then U.S. Secretary of the Treasury, purchased for the Library of Congress a collection of 38 rare Chinese maps and atlases. The collection had been carefully assembled by the distinguished Orientalist Arthur W. Hummel for more than 15 years while he was a resident of China. The initial purchase included the following items: 2 manuscript atlases of China, each containing 20 maps, drawn in the Ming period (A.D. 1368-1644); an atlas of China, printed before 1662, comprising 20 maps; a large manuscript wall map of China (ca. 1673); a map of the world printed in Peking in 1674 by the Jesuit priest Ferdinand Verbiest; 2 wall maps of China, one printed in 1821, the other in 1831; a large 18th-century manuscript wall map of South China; a manuscript scroll map of the territory bordering the Great Wall; 2 mariner's charts; a rare manuscript road map of the highways from Sian to Chengtu; an 18th-century manu-

script atlas of Chekiang province; a manuscript atlas of Fukien province (ca. 18th century); old manuscript maps of Shantung, Honan, and Chihli provinces; a manuscript map of Nanking (ca. 1864); an old painted map of the Ming Tombs; 3 manuscript military maps of South China; a printed atlas of Formosa before the Japanese occupation; plus several other items. While serving as the Chief of the LC's Orientalia Division, Dr. Hummel purchased 31 additional early Chinese maps and atlases in China in 1934. In 1962, after retirement, Dr. Hummel presented to the Geography and Map Division a group of 16 rare manuscript maps from his personal collection. These materials are briefly described in the September 1962 issue of the *Quarterly Journal of the Library of Congress.*

(2) *The Warner Collection.* In 1929 a number of manuscript maps and atlases of Korea and China were acquired from Mr. Langdon Warner of the Fogg Art Museum, Harvard University. Among the items are an undated manuscript atlas of China which was drawn probably during the Ming period; an atlas of the 8 provinces of Korea; and an undated atlas of Chung-Chŏng Province, Korea; a map of Manchuria, 1733-1858; a map of Chŏlla province, Korea, printed on a fan; a wood-engraved map of Korea (ca. 1822); a complete set of maps of the 8 provinces of Korea; a set of 7 maps showing administrative divisions of Korea; and a complete set of maps of the 8 provinces of Korea (all Yi Dynasty).

(3) *Others.*

In recent years, the Asian Division (formerly Orientalia) of the LC has transferred to the Geography and Map Division an assortment of early Chinese and Japanese maps. Supplementing these and the above-mentioned items are a number of distinctive maps which were selected from the division's general collection of Oriental maps for preservation in the vault. Several hundred rare maps of China, Japan, and Korea are kept in the vault, with more than half of them being fully cataloged.

The following publications help facilitate access of the collections: *A List of Geographical Atlases in the Library of Congress, with Bibliographical Notes,* 8 vols.; *Bibliography of Cartography* (Boston, G. K. Hall, 1973), 5 vols.; and *The Geography and Map Division: A Guide to Its Collections and Services* (rev. ed., 1975).

E4 National Archives and Records Service (NARS) [General Services Administration (GSA)]—Center for Cartographic and Architectural Archives

1.   a. *8th Street and Pennsylvania Avenue, NW*
     (Entrance from Pennsylvania Avenue only)
     Washington, D.C. 20408
     523-3062

     b. 8:45 A.M.-5:00 P.M.   Monday-Friday

     c. Open to all researchers. In order to use the NARS's facilities and resources, one must get a "researcher identification card" issued by NARS. Use of some holdings may be restricted.

d. Various types of photoduplication services are available for fixed fees.

e. Ralph Ehrenberg, Director

2. A large number of East Asian maps are scattered in many different record groups.

3. The maps, covering different subjects and time periods, can be found in the following record groups:

RG 11: "General Records of the U.S. Government" contain a manuscript map of the harbor of Shimoda in 1854, which was compiled by surveyors with Commodore Perry's fleet, to accompany the first American treaty with Japan.

RG 37: *Records of the Hydrographic Office* contain many items of survey records from U.S. Navy surveys, including 17 charts from the Perry Expedition to Japan (1953-54), approximately 70 original coast charts of Japan, Siberia, and Pacific islands from the North Pacific Survey Expedition (1853-58), and several 19th-century maps of Korea.

RG 38: *Records of the Office of the Chief of Naval Operations: Office of Naval Intelligence, 1884-1943* contain maps illustrating the Sino-Japanese War, 1894-1895. Charts of harbors and ports including Yokohama, Japan, are included in "Around-the-World Cruise 1907-1912." Also included in the group are "maps of the world" published in 1929 showing naval bases, stations, and other installations of the British Empire, Japan, the United States, France, and Italy; 5 general maps of Asia, 1894-1919; 13 maps and other records relating to Japan, 1901-1940; 1 map of Korea; and 3 maps of Manchuria.

RG 59: *General Records of the Department of State* contain published maps of Japan showing United States consular districts; maps of China and Manchuria showing railway, caravan, and motor routes; and an atlas of Japan with administrative subdivisions.

RG 77: *Records of the Office of the Chief of Engineers* contain a subgroup titled Fortifications Map File which includes maps of China, Japan, the Philippines, and Korea and plans of fortifications and military equipment (1845-1942). The War Department Map Collection includes approximately 2,300 maps of the Philippines, China, Japan, Korea, and Taiwan which pertain to the Russo-Japanese War, the China Relief Expedition, the Philippine pacification program, and the Battle of the Yalu River (1904). A series of published topographic maps of China and the Philippines are also included. The U.S. Army Map Service (AMS) contains about 12,000 topographic maps of East Asian countries published from 1940 through 1970. The larger scale AMS maps cannot be viewed by non-United States citizens without prior approval of the creating agency. Other holdings include topographic models of Japan, China, North Vietnam, and eastern Russia.

RG 83: *Records of the Bureau of Agricultural Economics* contain 4 maps published 1930-1947, showing the distribution of Japanese-Americans in the Pacific coast states.

RG 120: *Records of the American Expeditionary Forces World War I (1917-23)* contain a subgroup entitled "AEF, Siberia, 1918-19," which includes manuscript, blueprint, and photo-processed maps of parts of Russia, Siberia, China, and Japan.

RG 127: *Records of the U.S. Marine Corps* contain 16 general maps of China (1927-1937); 71 maps of North China, including the Peking region; 29 maps and related records pertaining to South China, Shanghai, and Tientsin; 23 maps of Chinese cities (e.g., Tsingtao, Soochow, and Ningpo); and 1 map of Korea.

RG 165: *Records of the War Department and General Staffs* include published town plans of Korea, land survey maps of Japan, and other published maps of China and Manchuria for the early 20th century. World War II records include photocopies of topographic models of Burma, the Philippines, Okinawa, and other locations in the Pacific Theater of Operations showing terrain features and some military operations. Approximately 25 maps of Asia; 45 maps of China; 4 maps of Japan; and 2 maps of Korea (1904-1946).

RG 169: *Records of the Foreign Economic Administration* contain an incomplete series of numbered maps published by the Cartographic Section, including a map showing mining and metallurgical enterprises in Southwestern China. Also a number of industrial maps of Japan, China, Korea, and Mongolia (1943-45) are included in this record group.

RG 226: *Records of the Office of Strategic Services* have several maps covering East Asia which are included in this record group. These maps are primarily thematic in nature, depicting information relating to transportation systems, population distribution, mineral deposits, agricultural and industrial activities, and the like.

RG 239: *Records of the American Commission for the Protection and Salvage of Artistic and Historic Monuments in War Areas* contain a set of maps and identification list, including those of Japan and Korea.

RG 256: *Records of the American Commission to Negotiate Peace: Economics and Statistics Division, 1917-1919* contain 5 maps showing power resources and mineral deposits of Asia (e.g., coal, oil, gold, copper, lead, iron, tungsten, etc.) in 1913; "Inner Asia Division, 1917-1919" contains maps of Sinkiang (n.d.), illustrating communication networks, population density, and linguistic distribution in Sinkiang province; and "Far East and Pacific Division" records with several annotated and printed maps of China prepared in 1918.

RG 324: *Records of the Board on Geographic Names* contain about 20 outline maps prepared in 1943-47 for Board publications showing political boundaries in Sakhalin, racial distribution in Burma, the Burma Road, prefecture and district boundaries in Taiwan, Japanese oil and coal fields, local administrative centers and place names in Thailand, provinces in Korea and Manchuria, and local place names along the Russian-Chinese borders.

RG 332: *Records of U.S. Theaters of War, World War II* include general and theaterwide maps of East Asia and the Pacific region showing airfields and seaplane bases, outline maps of East Asia showing air distance to industrial centers of Japan from various points, and maps of Japan, East China, Korea, and Siberia. In addition, there are 11 maps of China and Taiwan; and 20 maps of Japan and Korea, showing airfields, railways, highways, and anchorage charts.

RG 341: *Records of the Army Air Force* contain a subgroup entitled "Assistant Chief of Air Staff-Intelligence, 1942-44" which includes relief maps of parts of Japan and Taiwan and also maps of cities and towns in Manchuria showing road patterns and military targets. "Aeronautical Chart Service, 1939-47" includes special maps prepared for the strategic air planning chart of the Asiatic Pacific Theater, 1942-45. Included in this record group is a subgroup entitled "Army Air Force Commands, 1942-45" that contains a series of maps, target charts, and target areas in Japan and the South Pacific.

RG 395: *Records of U.S. Army Overseas Operations and Commands 1898-1942* include 2,239 maps from both tactical and directional units, relating chiefly to the Spanish-American War and the Philippine Pacification (1889-1902).

4.　a. As there is no single comprehensive catalog listing of the NAR's East Asian map collection, researchers should consult the following: *Guide to the National Archives of the United States* (1974); *Guide to Cartographic Records in the National Archives*, by Charlotte M. Ashby et al. (1971); and various preliminary inventories and special lists of NARS Record Groups. Researchers should also consult with the staff of the Cartographic Division for assistance in locating maps and other cartographic records.

National Geographic Society Map Collection See entry A32.

University of Maryland Map Collection See entry A42.

F Film and Still-Picture Collections

Film and Still-Picture Collections Entry Form (F)

1. General Information
   a. *address; telephone number(s)*
   b. hours of service
   c. conditions of access
   d. name/title of director and key staff members

2. Size of Holding Pertaining to East Asia

3. Description of Holdings Pertaining to East Asia

4. Facilities for Study and Use
   a. availability of audiovisual equipment
   b. reservation requirements
   c. fees charged
   d. reproduction services

5. Bibliographic Aids Facilitating Use of Collection

F1 Agency for International Development (AID) Photo Collection

1. a. *Office of Public Affairs*
      State Department Building, Room 4894
      320 21st Street, NW
      Washington, D.C. 20532
      632-8194

   b. 8:45 A.M.-5:30 P.M. Monday-Friday

   c. Open to researchers by appointment. Call ahead for clearance.

   d. Carl Purcell, Photographer

2-3. The collection contains over 20,000 recent photographs (predominantly black and white, but some color pictures are included) covering AID's foreign aid projects, dams, hospitals, people, and living conditions in the host countries. About 1,000 items pertain to AID activities in South Korea and Taiwan.

4.   Photographic prints can be ordered for a fee. Researchers must make the requests in person at the office. No phone calls or written requests can be processed.

F2 Air Force Central Still-Photographic Depository (Air Force Department)

1.   **a.** *1361st Audiovisual Squadron*
     HQ Aerospace Audiovisual Service
     1221 South Fern Street
     Arlington, Virginia 22202
     (703) 695-1147/1148/1149

    b. 7:45 A.M.-4:30 P.M. Monday-Friday

    c. Open to the public

    d. Margaret Livesay, Chief

2.   The entire collection numbers over 300,000 photographs. Approximately 60,000 still pictures deposited here pertain to the Far East, including about 30,000 on Vietnam and the Vietnam conflict. Over 4,000 new pictures are added annually. The collection includes both color and black and white prints.

    Almost all items at the depository are unclassified, including the East Asian materials. Particularly significant among its holdings on East Asia are pictures highlighting the U.S. Air Force's participation in World War II: 2,250 photos on the China theater of operations; 1,200 photos on Japan during World War II; 1,000 on Okinawa; and about 8,000 photos on various campaigns in the South and Southwest Pacific (e.g., Marshall, Marianas, Carolines, Bonins, Solomon islands). The depository also has over 15,000 photos relating to the Korean War. In addition, it contains about 700 photos on post-World War II; 1,100 items on postwar South Korea; and about 300 photos on Taiwan.

4.   **c.** Staff members charge a fee for any research or searching required by outside requests. No fees are charged, however, for work done on the premises by researchers themselves.

    d. Copies of all holdings are available for a fee.

5.   The depository maintains a visual print file arranged by subject and geographic area. These file prints are kept in binders on open shelves for the use of visitors. Each photo has its own identification number plus a brief caption citing the background as well as the date and location of the picture taken. Also, the depository maintains a valuable cross-indexing system. Free copies of the "Information Sheet" for the depository are available on request.

American Institute of Architects Library See entry A5.

F3 Army Audiovisual Agency (Army Department)

1.   a. *Reference Library*
The Pentagon, Room 5A486
Washington, D.C. 20310
697-2806
Film Library
The Pentagon, Room 5A1058
Washington, D.C. 20310
695-5320

   b. Reference Library: 10:00 A.M.-4:00 P.M. Monday-Friday
Film Library: 8:30 A.M.-4:30 P.M. Monday-Friday

   c. Access to the Pentagon is restricted. Visitors to these two libraries must phone from the Pentagon entrance to secure permission to use the facilities and get escorts to accompany them to the libraries. Some of the motion pictures in the Film Library are open to the public; however, many are restricted to military or government personnel. A film catalog is available for the convenience of the users of the facility.

   d. Lt. Col. Melvin Russell, Commanding Officer, U.S. Army Audiovisual
      Support Activity and Director of the Film Library
Thomas Bresnahan, Chief, Audiovisual Support Branch
Vickie Destefano, Chief of Reference (Reference Library)

2.   The Reference Library contains over one million photos; approximately 250,000 of these pertain to East Asia. The Film Library's total holdings come to approximately 2,600 films, including about 13 on Korea, 3 on Japan, 1 on Taiwan, plus about 30 on the World War II campaigns in the Pacific. Approximately 20,000 new photos are added to the Army collection each year.

3.   Almost all photos located at the Reference Library are unclassified. The Reference Library contains an extensive collection of photos relating to World War II (including various campaigns in the Pacific and the China-Burma-India theater of operations; the Allied Occupation of Japan and Korea; and the Korean War. In addition, it contains a collection of about 153 Japanese war paintings seized during and after World War II. Insofar as the photographs of the post-WW II and post-Korean War periods are concerned, there are approximately 35,000 items on Japan, 45,000 photos on Korea, and about 1,320 on Taiwan.

      The subjects covered by these photographs include not only military operations and activities, but also other non-military subjects, such as farming, floods, Red Cross relief activities, factories, aerial views, maps, and charts.

      Titles of the available motion pictures include the "History of the Korean War," "Korean Armistice," "Chinese Reds Enter War," "The Eighth Army—Shield of the Free World," "Korea Revisited," "Evacuation of Kweilin," (Combat Bulletin No. 25, 1944), and several documentary films depicting the famous battles of the Second World War in the Pacific.

4.   a. The Reference Library has a viewer for its microform collection, and viewing equipment is available for the motion pictures.

      b. The library requires reservations, at least one day in advance.

      c. No fees are charged for the use of the facilities.

      d. For a fee, copies of all photo holdings are available.

5.   Although no published inventories or guides are available for the still picture collection, there is a card index broken down by geographic areas, types of equipment, Army units, and other categories. As for the film collection, copies of *Index of Army Motion Pictures for Public Non-Profit Use* (September 1977) are available free upon request. Requests for the use of the Army films by the educational institutions in the Washington area should be directed to Thomas Bresnahan (695-5320). For those located outside the Washington area, such requests should be addressed to: Training Material Support Detachment, Tobyhanna Army Depot, Tobyhanna, Pa. 18466, or to Henry Strano (717) 894-8301, extension 9941.

Central Intelligence Agency Film Collection See entry K4.

Embassy of Japan Film Collection See entry L1.

Embassy of the People's Republic of China Film Collection See entry L2.

Freer Gallery of Art Library See entry A16.

Georgetown University Library See entry A19.

F4 International Bank for Reconstruction and Development (World Bank) Photo Library

1.   a. *801 19th Street, NW*
        Washington, D.C. 20433
        676-1585

      b. 9:00 A.M.-5:30 P.M.   Monday-Friday

      c. By appointment.

      d. Yosef Hadar, Photo Editor

2-3.   The World Bank Photo Library contains approximately 10,000 black-and-white prints and 30,000 color slides dealing primarily with economic development projects funded by the World Bank. The photo library's holdings on East Asia pertain largely to South Korea and Taiwan, and do not exceed 1 percent of the total collection.

4.   A limited number of black-and-white print copies and color slides are available free on request.

International Communication Agency Film Collection
See entry K17.

International Labor Organization Library See entry A27.

Japan Foundation Film Collection See entry H30.

Korean Information Office, Embassy of the Republic of Korea
See entry L3.

F5   Library of Congress—Motion Picture, Broadcasting, and Recorded-Sound Division

1.   a.   *Thomas Jefferson Building, Room 1046*
Library of Congress
10 First Street, SE
Washington, D.C. 20540
287-5840

b.   8:00 A.M.-4:30 P.M.   Monday-Friday

c.   Open to the public.

d.   Erik Barnouw, Chief

2.   The Motion Picture, Broadcasting, and Recorded-Sound Division maintains the library's film collections for scholarly study and research. The collections contain over 75,000 titles, or more than 250,000 reels. Over 1,500 titles, including television films and video tapes, are added each year through copyright deposit, purchase, gift, or exchange.

3.   Of particular interest to East Asia specialists are films seized during World War II, including a special collection on Japan. There are over 1,400 Japanese documentaries, newsreels, and feature films (about 200) of the pre-1945 period, over 100 Chinese films, and about 60 Korean films.

JAPANESE COLLECTION

Approximately 1,400 films, produced in Japan primarily during the 1930s and early 1940s, constitute this special collection. Specifically, it includes 200 features, 700 short documentaries, and 450 newsreels. Mostly in the Japanese language, there are only a small number of films which use English. Though uncataloged, titles can be found in a shelflist located in the reading room; and a more detailed description of each title is kept in separate file boxes maintained by the reference librarian of the division. The collection became available through arrangements made between the United States Government and the Tokyo National Film Center in the early 1960s when the United States returned the original films confiscated by the United States forces during the occupation period (1945-1952). In return, the National Film Center agreed to donate reproduced copies of the original films. The feature-films collection contains most of the well-known popular films of the 1930s and the early 1940s, including such feature films as: "Miyamoto Musashi," "Shina no Yoru," "Kurama Tengu," "Byakuran no Uta," and "Tange Sazen." Also, one can find "Sugata Sanshiro" (1945), one of the earliest films directed by Akira Kurosawa, among the collection. Most of the short documentary films deal with such subjects as Japanese military activities in Manchuria, China, and Southeast Asia, popular Japanese sports (e.g., judō, sumō, etc.), and Japanese war efforts both at home and abroad. Inevitably, these contain much propaganda. The newsreel collection includes partial runs from the following productions: *Asahi News* (1935-1940), *Daitōa News, Daimai Movie News Special, Dentsu News, Dōmei News, Nippon News, Nichiei Foreign News* (1932-1940). *Shōchiku News, Tōa News,* and *Yomiuri News* (1934-1940). Unquestionably, these film collections constitute rich treasures for scholars interested in the Japanese cinema of the 1930s and 1940s or in Japanese propaganda films in the prewar period.

KLEINE COLLECTION

A number of prints and negatives made around 1904-1905 are a part of the George Kleine Collection. Included are the following items pertaining to East Asia:

(a) "Scenes and Incidents, Russo-Japanese Peace Conference, Portsmouth, N.H., 1905" which consists of 342 feet (16 mm) of duplicate negatives and prints on the peace conference.

(b) "Battle of Chemulpo Bay (Korea)," which consists of 2 reels totaling 143 feet (16 mm) of duplicate prints and negatives of this battle of the Russo-Japanese War (1904-1905). This is a reenactment, not actuality footage. These films were originally produced by Thomas A. Edison, Inc., in 1904-1905. Finally, there is an American film made in 1918 which is titled "Banzai." This is an anti-German movie produced in conjunction with the 4th Liberty Loan Campaign during the World War I, and features Sessue Hayakawa.

PAPER-PRINT COLLECTION, 1894-1912

The Motion Picture Division has collected a large number of short paper-print reproductions of motion pictures made at the turn of the century. Among these, one can find the following items relating to East Asia:

Street Scene in Yokohama
The Forbidden City, Peking
Theatre Road, Yokohama

Arrival of Tokyo Train
Chien-Men Gate, Peking
Landing Wharf at Canton
Ricksha Parade (Kyoto), Japan
Street Scene, Tokyo, Japan
General Chafee in Peking
Launch of the Japanese Man-of-War 'Chitose'
Canton River Scene and Canton Steamboat Landing Chinese Passengers
Li Hung-chang and Suite: Presentation of Parlor Mutoscope
Asakusa Temple, Tokyo, Japan
Japanese Village
Japanese Sampans
Panorama of Kobe Harbor, Japan
Japanese Fencing
Chinese Procession

The length of these paper prints varies from 20 to 100 feet. For detailed descriptions of the LC's holdings, see Kemp R. Niver, *Motion Pictures from the Library of Congress Paper Print Collection* (Berkeley: University of California Press, 1967).

THE CHINESE COLLECTION

The LC's film collection on China is not as rich as on Japan. There are, however, over 100 films of various types on China, including some produced in the People's Republic of China (e.g., "The East is Red"). Among the items of particular interest to China specialists are copies (from paper prints registered for copyright) of films made by two American cameramen working in China for Biograph in 1901. Made by Ackerman and Bonine, they include what is possibly the first stage film in China.

THE KOREAN COLLECTION

On Korea, the LC's film collection consists of about 60 films on the Korean War (1950-1953) and 15 Korean feature films presented by the Motion Picture Promotion Corporation of Korea in 1974.

4. For motion pictures, the facilities, which consist of several 16-mm and 35-mm viewing machines, may be used free of charge by serious researchers. Viewing times must be scheduled in advance.

The facilities may not be used by high school students; undergraduate college students must provide a letter from an instructor endorsing their project. Copies of film footage not restricted by copyright, by provisions of donations or transfer, or by physical condition, may be ordered through the Motion Picture Section.

The reference tools available for motion pictures are: *Library of Congress Catalog—Films and Other Materials for Projection* (formerly Library of Congress Catalog—Motion Pictures and Filmstrips) issued quarterly and in annual editions and appearing as volumes in the quinquennial cumulation of the LC's *National Union Catalog;* and as computer tapes produced monthly in a machine-readable cataloging (MARC) format. These three items are for sale by the LC's Card Division, Building 150, Navy Yard Annex, Washington, D.C. 20541. In addition, the Copyright Office of the LC prepares a semiannual *Catalog of Copyright Entries: Motion Pictures and Filmstrips,* which list all such materials registered for copyright in the United States and five cumulative catalogs entitled *Motion Pictures,* which together cover registrations for films for the years 1894-1969.

For paper-print collections (from the motion pictures), see Kemp R. Niver, *Motion Pictures from the Library of Congress Paper Print Collection* (Berkeley: University of California Press, 1967). For information concerning East Asian films, call the reference librarian (287-5840).

F6 Library of Congress—Prints and Photographs Division

1. a. *Thomas Jefferson Building, Room 1051*
    Library of Congress
    10 1st Street, SE
    Washington, D.C. 20540
    287-5836

    b. 8:30 A.M.-5:00 P.M. Monday-Friday

    c. Open to the public

    d. John Kuiper, Chief

2. This is unquestionably one of the largest still-picture collections on East Asia in the Washington, D.C., area. Although there is no way to measure accurately the total amount of East Asian materials located here, one can derive a rough estimate from the following: there are at least 174 collections of photographs and prints on China, 150 collections on Japan, 28 collections on Korea, and 6 collections on Mongolia. Each collection consists of anywhere from 25 to 2,500 items (e.g., photographs and negatives, prints, and slides). Also, there are over 2,800 stereographs produced in the early part of the 20th century: 860 on Japan, 1,730 on China, and 210 on Korea. In addition, there is a large number of unprocessed materials (e.g., Japanese and Chinese prints) that is yet to be sorted and cataloged.

3. It should be pointed out that it is not easy to locate the still pictures on East Asia through any single approach. The division's catalogs are of some help, but many photographs and prints are not grouped under geographic headings. Furthermore, many materials on Japan and China are dispersed among different collections or listed in ways not obvious to the East Asia specialists. The Vanderbilt's guide to the division's collections, listed in point 5 below, is helpful in locating major collections cataloged before 1955. However, it is of no help for scholars in locating most collections added since 1955. For these reasons, staff help is indispensable. Most collections, especially the large ones, can be found either by lot numbers or the names of the collections. For the smaller ones, one must know the lot numbers, for there is no other way to locate them.

COLLECTIONS ON CHINA

(1) *Chien Lung, Emperor of China, Collection.* Engravings produced in China and in France in the late 18th century, celebrating the military victories of the Chinese Emperor, Chien Lung (1736-95). There are 72 engravings with 18 plates of text, several duplicate prints, and 1 bound volume of collotype reproductions of the first series.

(2) *Turner Collection.* Hand-colored photographs of Chinese and Japanese costumes and scenes of daily life of the period 1900-10. Presented by L. M. Turner of Baltimore in 1926.

(3) *Janse Collection.* Photographic negatives, corresponding captioned proofs and photocopies of views and activities in Indochina, with similar materials in Southwest China and Japan. Approximately 1,000 photoprints with notes.

(4) *Pung Wo Company Collection.* Photographs of the hand manufacture in China of pieces used in playing the game Mah Jong received as copyright deposits in 1924. 38 prints.

(5) *Chu Min-i Collection.* Photographs of and relating to Chu Min-i, former head of the Nanking puppet regime established by Japan (1940-45). Apparently personal albums of Chu Min-i seized and transferred in 1947 to the LC. Approximately 1,000 photoprints in 13 albums.

(6) *Gilman Collection.* Chinese paintings on "rice paper" representing the Chinese, with emphasis on their costumes; presented by Elizabeth Gilman, Baltimore, in 1938. 11 watercolors in portfolio.

(7) *Wang Hsu-kao Collection.* News photographs of the ceremonies commemorating the return of the French Special Concessions in Tientsin on June 5, 1943. Presented by Wang Hsu-kao, mayor of Tientsin under the Nanking puppet regime (1940-45), and received by transfer in 1947. Approximately 200 photoprints.

(8) *Wu-Liang Temple Collection.* Rubbings of the stone carvings of the Wu-Liang Temple. Purchased from Kegan Paul of London in 1951. Approximately 50 rubbings.

(9) *Wang Ching-wei Collection.* Photographs of official functions, receptions, and conferences, involving Wang Ching-wei (1883-1944), who headed the Executive Yuan of the Nanking puppet regime. Compiled by the Japanese Ministry of Foreign Affairs on the occasion of his state visit to Japan in 1941. 50 photoprints.

(10) *Lo Collection.* Exhibit photographs of Japanese activities in China during the Sino-Japanese war (1937-45); assembled by Dr. T. Y. Lo, Director of the Chinese Military Pictorial Service. Presented by him through Elaine Gendream of Washington, D.C., in 1945-1946. 288 photographs in 16 portfolios.

(11) *White Brothers Visual Units Collection.* Photographs of Chinese architecture, people, and daily life in 1929; taken by Herbert C. White and J. Henry White of St. Helena, California. Received as copyright deposits in 1931-1932. Approximately 220 mounted photoprints.

(12) *McCoy Collection.* Photographs and other illustrative materials relating to the military career of Maj. Gen. Frank R. McCoy; presented by him in 1951. Approximately 600 photoprints and reproductions and 15 glass-lantern slides (3½" x 4"). Contains photocopies of Oriental arts, archaeological objects in the museum of Port Arthur, plus an album of Harbin (1932-33), Manchuria.

(13) *Manchurian Motion Picture Production Collection.* Photographs of the studio's activities beginning in 1939. Approximately 50 photoprints.

(14) *Pauley Mission Collection.* Photographs made during the Edwin A. Pauley Mission's visit to Manchuria in June 1946, to investigate the removal and destruction of Japanese industrial installations by the Soviet occupation forces. Approximately 100 photoprints in album.

(15) *Gamble Collection.* Photographs and photocopies of missionaries and Chinese daily life made in the 1860s and 1870s; collected by William Gamble (1830-86) and presented by his heirs in 1938. 46 cartes-de-visite and 4 cabinet portraits.

(16) *Northeast Asia Collection.* Japanese photographs of archaeological sites, sculptures, agricultural activities, street scenes and the like, in China, Korea, Manchuria, and Mongolia. Issued in Japan and received by transfer in 1947. Approximately 400 photoprints in 3 albums.

(17) *American National Red Cross Collection.* Original photographic negatives and photoprints of the American Red Cross covering the period 1900-30. Approximately 62,000 glass-plate negatives, including some photographs relating to relief work in Siberia and Manchuria in 1919-20.

(18) *Carpenter Collection.* An album of photographs with title *China: Book 2, (1915-1935).* Shrines and memorials, United States legation, army barracks, etc., at Peking; and various scenes of Mukden, Hankow, Tientsin, and Shanghai. Approximately 130 photographs with brief handwritten captions. Originally collected by Frank G. Carpenter.

(19) *Genthe Collection.* Photo negatives with accompanying proofs and prints which constitute virtually the entire life work of Arnold Genthe (1869-1942). Approximately 20,000 glass plates and film negatives, including his famous series on Chinatown in San Francisco (ca. 1896-1900).

COLLECTIONS ON JAPAN

(1) *Murray Collection.* Original Japanese brush drawings and water colors of objects and people, presumably made in 1878; presented by Mrs. David Murray of New Brunswick, New Jersey, in 1909. Approximately 50 items.

(2) *Uchiyama Collection.* Photographs of Japanese army maneuvers in 1898; received by transfer in 1947 from Japan. Originally, they were located at the library of the Japanese Army General Staff Headquarters. Approximately 50 photoprints in album.

(3) *Matsuzaki Collection.* Photographs of Japanese manufactures, possibly relating to the Japanese exhibit at the United States Centennial Exhibition held in Philadelphia in 1876. 104 photoprints.

(4) *Turner Collection.* See above item 2 under Chinese Collections.

(5) *Kurile Islands Exploration Collection.* Original photographs of villages, terrain, harbors, native groups, camp activities, etc., on the Kurile Islands in 1891-1892. Approximately 100 photoprints.

(6) *Nazi Collection.* Photographs and other pictures confiscated in Germany after World War II. Approximately 100,000 items, including a small number of photoprints relating to Japan.

(7) *Noble Collection.* Photographs, portraits, postcards, and photoprints of Russian and Japanese delegates attending the peace conference at Portsmouth, New Hampshire, in August 1905; assembled by Edmund Noble, a correspondent for the Boston *Herald.* Approximately 60 photoprints and postcards.

(8) *Pershing Collection.* Photographs and pictures relating to the private life and military career of Gen. John J. Pershing, including his early life and experiences in Japan and the Philippines. Approximately 12,500 items.

(9) *Chadbourne Collection.* Original 19th-century Japanese woodcuts, printed in colors, representing Americans and Europeans and their way of life in Japan in the 1850s. There are 188 prints in 10 portfolios. Included are 6 Nagasaki-e (prints produced before 1853); and a few prints directly relating to Perry's expedition to Japan (1853-1854).

(10) *Campbell Collection.* Original drawings by Daniel Campbell while staying in Japan in 1867. 22 drawings.

(11) *Von Siebold Collection.* Photocopies of prints and photos from a German exhibition on the life and time of Philipp Franz von Siebold, 1796-1866, a German explorer who was in Japan from 1823-29, and 1859-1862). Approximately 250 items.

(12) *Hobson Collection.* Varied portraits and photographs relating to the career of Adm. Richmond P. Hobson, U.S. Navy, from 1890-1936. Approximately 125 photoprints, including some materials on Japan.

(13) *Tokyo Dai-Shin-Sai Gaho Collection.* Chromolithographs of fire and destruction in Tokyo caused by the earthquake of 1923. 14 prints.

(14) *Japanese Board of Tourist Industry Collection.* Stock public-relations photographs of Japanese cities, daily life, scenery, industries, and recreation, issued by the Japanese Board of Tourist Industry in the second decade of the 20th century. Approximately 150 photoprints.

(15) *Yokohama Specie Bank Collection.* Photographs of the building, offices, and banking operations from 1900-1915. Approximately 60 photoprints in album.

(16) *Noyes Collection.* Japanese war prints, color woodcuts, and caricatures concerning the Sino-Japanese War (1894-1895) and the Russo-

Japanese War (1904-1905), which were collected by Crosby N. Noyes. There are 118 woodcuts plus 6 small prints.

(17) *Kanji Collection.* 50 photographs dealing with Japanese soldiers in action in China, mostly 1930-1940; transferred from the U.S. Department of Defense in 1953.

COLLECTIONS ON KOREA

(1) *Janse Collection.* See item 3 under Chinese Collections above.

(2) *Leach Collection.* Original watercolor drawings of Korean figures; collected by Dr. Philip Leach in 1934; 50 watercolors in portfolios.

(3) *Genthe Collection.* See item 4 under Japanese Collections above.

(4) *Korean Collection.* Photographs taken by the Japanese military around 1900. Approximately 128 photoprints in album.

(5) *Mitchell Collection.* Photographs assembled by Gen. William Mitchell (1879-1936), numbering 6,978 items in 33 albums and about 100 nitrate-base film negatives; also contains some photographs of Korea from 1919-1924.

COLLECTIONS ON OUTER MONGOLIA

(1) *Yudin Collection.* Pencil, pen-and-ink, and watercolor drawings collected by G. V. Yudin of 19th-century Siberia and Mongolia. Approximately 333 sketches and drawings mounted in large albums.

The following are general or small collections relating to East Asia:

CHINA

(1) *Franklin Ohlinger Collection.* Lot 10,254. 20 photos of China and Korea around the 1890s.

(2) *John Barrett Collection.* Lot 9,027. 71 photos of Chinese and Manchurian people around the turn of the century.

(3) *Miscellaneous Office of War Information (OWI) Pictures.* Lot 1,814. Contains materials relating to "China road under construction."

(4) *Miscellaneous lot:* photographs of Chinese ceramics and other antiquities of Han and Sung dynasties found in northern Indo-China. Approximately 200 photos assembled by Olov R. T. Janse in 1947. Lot 2846.

(5) *Photographs* concerning the war activities of the Far Eastern peoples, 1940-1945. Lot 3472. 16 photos.

(6) *Genthe Collection.* Lot 4964. Photocopies of ancient and modern Chinese and Japanese paintings, collected by Arnold Genthe. Approximately 75 photographs.

(7) *Chinese Nationalist Party (Kuomintang) posters,* ca. 1923. Lot 8535. 14 posters.

(8) *Paul S. Reinsch Collection.* Paul Reinsch, U.S. Minister China, 1913-1919. Lot 10560. 29 photographs.

(9) *George G. Bain Collection.* Approximately 300 news photos of China, ca. 1905-1926.

JAPAN

(1) *Set of reproductions of Japanese works of art.* Lot 2865. 20 plates individually published by various museums.

(2) *Miscellaneous collection of postcard photographs* concerning Japan. Lot 3691. Approximately 200 photos from the 1930s.

(3) *J. D. Batchelder Collection.* Lot 8648. 50 hand-colored photos in album, ca. 1890.

(4) *A series of photographs* presenting the art of Japan. Lot 2618. Approximately 300 photos presented by the Japanese government, possibly in 1920.

(5) *Collection of miscellaneous items* concerning the Orient, 1735-1895. Lot 3225. Contains engravings of Japanese princes, etc., approximately 100 prints.

(6) *Hiroshige Collection.* Lot 4318. Book of original color woodcuts under title *Series of fifty-three stations of Tokaido.* 53 prints made in 1830-1850(?).

(7) *Reproductions of Oriental art, 1930-1935(?).* Lot 5672. Two portfolios titled "A Collection of masterpieces by Hokusai (1780-1844)." 80 reproductions of photographs.

(8) *Album* with binder's title *The Russo-Japanese War* published by K. Ogawa. Lot 6074. Approximately 250 reproductions of photographs made around 1905-1906.

(9) *The Japanese army, 1935.* Lot 6342. Approximately 500 reproductions of photographs in 1935.

(10) *William Howard Taft and his party* in Hawaii, Japan, and the Philippines. Lot 8637. 54 photographs taken by Burr McIntosh in 1905.

(11) *Identification pictures* of Japanese naval vessels issued in 1943 by the U.S. Navy. Lot 2406. 75 plates.

(12) *Small lot of photographs* of Japanese war criminals 1945-1946. Lot 2084. 25 snapshots taken by Aubrey St. Kenworthy.

(13) *Buddhist statues* in the Horyuji temple at Nara. Lot 6379. 51 photos taken by Denjiro Hasegawa in 1950.

(14) *Carl A. Spaatz Collection.* Lot 7587. Aerial views of Japan, 1945. 150 photos in 3 small albums.

(15) *Occupation of Tsinan, China,* by the Japanese Army in 1928. Lot 11488. 161 photos.

(16) *Battle scenes of the Boxer uprising, 1900.* Lot 10,959. 5 Japanese lithographic collections.

KOREA, TIBET, AND MONGOLIA

(1) *Frank G. Carpenter Collection.* Lot 5806. Album of photographs with title *Korea, Manchuria, Book 1* (1910-20?). Approximately 125 photos.

(2) *William E. Warne Collection.* Lot 10446. 525 color slides on Korea made in 1956-59.

(3) *Scenes in Tibet.* Lot 4673. 25 photos made on the Ernst Shafer expedition to Tibet in 1930-1933.

(4) *Mongolian Ardyn Gar Urlag.* Lot 9288. 84 reproductions of photos, drawings, etc., of Mongolian handicraft, ca. 1850-1940.

(5) *Ira C. Eaker Collection.* Lot 10417. 75 photos in album relating to the 20th American Air Force's operations in Japan, China, etc.

(6) *Sven Hedin Institute Collection* (unprocessed). Approximately 3,000 photoprints of Tibet by the German Scientific Expedition, ca. 1938.

4.   For still pictures, no fees are required; and no equipment is available. Materials not copyrighted or restricted may be copied by the LC Photoduplication Service at a fixed fee. Photographic copies, photostats, microfilms, slides, and blue-line prints are frequently utilized for copying purposes. The facilities may not be used by high school students; undergraduate college students must provide a letter from an instructor endorsing their project.

The best reference tool available for collections of prints, photos, and posters is Paul Vandervilt, *Guide to the Special Collections of Prints and Photographs in the Library of Congress* (LC, 1955). However, it is badly outdated. For further information pertaining to the division's holdings on East Asia, contact the reference specialists of the division.

F7 Marine Corps Still Photographic Archives (Museum and Historical Center) USMC

1.   a. *Washington Navy Yard Building 58*
9th and M Streets, SE
Washington, D.C. 20374
433-3634

  b. 10:00 A.M.-4:00 P.M.   Monday-Friday

  c. Visitors are encouraged to telephone ahead to ensure that the appropriate personnel and the required records are available.

  d. Brig. Gen. E. H. Simmons (ret.), Director of Marine Corps History and Museums
Lt. Col. W. V. Bjork, Head, Support Branch
Gunnery Sgt. W. K. Judge, Head, Still Photographic Archives

2.   The Marine Corps Still Photographic Archives currently contain over 500,000 negatives and transparencies. The Archives do not contain classified or restricted material, and all records are considered public domain.

3.   WORLD WAR II ERA COLLECTION

Photographic coverage of the Marine Corps activities during World War II represents about half of the entire photo collection. This comprehensive documentation highlights various aspects of training, recruiting, transportation, equipment, weapons, aviation, medical care, and logistics in relation to Marine Corps participation in the war. Combat photographs of the major battles in the Pacific are abundant, including combat scenes from Guadalcanal, Bouganville, Cape Gloucester, Saipan, Tarawa, Pelelieu, Iwo Jima, and Okinawa. Most of this collection is in black and white; however, some color photos are available.

KOREAN WAR ERA COLLECTION

The coverage of Marine Corps air/ground operations and other activities during the Korean War is substantial. Especially extensive is coverage of events subsequent to the Inchon landing in September 1950. This group contains views of early helicopter operations as well as the hardships of cold-weather warfare.

Photographs of camps, airfields, frontline areas, equipment, and training of other United States troops by the Marines during the Korean War are fairly comprehensive. Mostly in black and white, a small number of color prints are also available.

In addition, the Archives contain a large number of photos pertaining to the Vietnam War and current activities of the U.S. Marine Corps.

Approximately 16,000 Marine Corps photographic records depicting scenes prior to World War II have been transferred to the National Archives and Records Service for permanent retention.

Finally, it should be pointed out that over 6.7 million feet of film is deposited with the Marine Corps' Moton Picture/Video Tape Archives, Quantico, Virginia.

4.   b. An appointment is not required; however, visitors are advised to telephone ahead to ensure access to the desired materials.

c. The archives do not have the necessary facilities to reproduce the material in its files. All photo work is done at a Marine Corps photo lab; however, requests for photoreproduction can be processed through the archives. Mass printing is not authorized for sale to the public, and reproductions are limited to three copies for each item. A fee is charged for this service.

5.   The Still Photographic Archives maintain a photo reference library which is open to the public from 10:00 A.M. to 4:00 P.M. on week days. Identification of each item is based on the use of conventional 5 x 8 index cards, filed by major subject. Each card contains a sample print, caption information, and the negative number. The archives also maintain research and reference materials, including a cross-index of names identifying the records of over 32,000 individuals on index cards which are filed alphabetically.

National Air and Space Museum Library (Smithsonian Institution) Photo Collection See entry A31.

**National Anthropological Archives (Smithsonian Institution—
National Museum of Natural History) Photo Collections** See entry B7.

**F8 National Archives and Records Service (NARS)   (General Services
Administration) (GSA)—Audiovisual Archives Division**

1. a. *8th Street and Pennsylvania Avenue, NW
        (Entrance from Pennsylvania Avenue only)
        Washington, D.C. 20408
        523-3267 (Motion Picture and Sound Recordings); 523-3054 (Still Pic-
        ture); and 523-3236 (Division as a whole).*

    b. 8:45 A.M.-5:00 P.M.   Monday-Friday

    c. Open to the public. Users must obtain a pass ("researcher identification
        card") issued by the NARS to work in this branch. It can be obtained
        from the Central Research staff in Room 200B. There are no general
        restrictions on the use of materials, though some items may require
        special permission from the originating agency or donor.

    d. James Moore, Director
        William Murphy, Chief, Motion Picture and Sound-Recording Branch
        Joe Thomas, Chief, Still-Picture Branch

2.   Many fascinating items are contained in the various record groups.
        Altogether, the NARS hold nearly 6 million still pictures and about
        100,000 reels of motion-picture films including an undetermined number
        of items on East Asia. Undoubtedly, this is one of the most comprehen-
        sive depositories of films and still pictures on East Asia in Washington,
        D.C.

3.   The following description of the NARS' motion- and still-picture collec-
        tions is based partly on the *Guide to the National Archives of the United
        States* (1974), and partly on the card catalogs maintained by the Motion
        Picture and Sound-Recording Branch and the Still-Picture Branch of
        the NARS. Film and still-picture holdings will be discussed separately
        by record-group number.

MOTION PCTURES

RG 18: *Records of the Army Air Forces* include among 5,828 reels of
films: "China Crisis: The Story of the Fourteenth Air Force" (1945);
the Lytton Commission investigation in Manchuria (1932); "Army
Air Forces—Pacific" (1946); and "New Guinea and China Campaigns"
1942-1945. In addition, 33 items of outtakes, information films, newsreels, and documentaries are included in this record group, covering
among other things supply missions in the China-Burma-India theater
of operation; and bomb damage in Okinawa, Tokyo, Yokohama, and
Nagasaki.
RG 22: *Records of the Fish and Wildlife Service* include one of the 13
reels filmed between 1915-1937 entitled "Romance of Pearl Culture in
Japan" (1922) showing how pearls were cultivated at the pearl fisheries
owned by Mr. K. Mikimoto on the Bay of Ise.

RG 33: *Records of the Federal Extension Service* include among 89 reels: "Soybeans at Home—Manchuria" (1928), 2 reels; "Persimmon Harvesting and Storage in China" (1928); and "Naturalized Plant Immigration" (1929) showing plants imported from Manchuria and China. Also, the collection contains "Holding the Japanese Beetle" (1926); and "Beware the Japanese Beetle" (1934) showing the damages it causes and methods to control infestation.

RG 56: *General Records of the Department of the Treasury* contain mostly incentive films used in connection with defense and Victory bond promotional drives by the Savings Bonds Division. They include: "The Price of Freedom" (1942); "What Makes a Battle" (1944), which has many scenes of combat between Japanese troops and U.S. Marines; "My Japan" (ca. 1943) designed to stimulate war-bond purchases; and "Iwo Jima" (1945).

RG 59: *General Records of the Department of State* have 2 films on China, 1 on Japan, and 8 on Korea, mostly dealing with the Korean war and the U.N. involvement in the conflict. The 2 films on China cover the Chinese war efforts against Japan during World War II, while "Japanese Peace Treaty and Conference" (1951) documents the signing of the Japanese peace treaty at San Francisco in September 1951.

RG 80: *General Records of the Department of the Navy* contain films (7,168 reels) made or collected by the Navy and used in training during World War II relating to kamikaze attacks; the battles of Midway and the Marianas; the invasion of the Solomon Islands, Eniwetock, Saipan, and Guam; preparations for the invasion of the Ryukyu islands; bombing raids over Japan; and Japan and the Japanese people. Also, the collection contains the Navy's Pacific engagements and landings during World War II and the Korean war; the Japanese surrender ceremonies; the Allied Occupation of Japan; and returning Japanese prisoners of war.

RG 107: *Office of the Secretary of War* record group contains films (191 reels) produced by the Bureau of Public Relations during World War II. Included are "Japanese Surrender and American Occupation—Tokyo" (1945); "Mission to Manchuria" (1945); "Japanese Surrender Activities" (1945); and "The American Flag Over Tokyo" (1945).

RG 111: *Records of the Office of the Chief Signal Officer* have, among 15,597 reels produced from 1909 to 1954, a number covering various aspects of World War II in all theaters of operations including the Japanese invasion of China, 1937; the dropping of the atom bombs; the Cairo, Teheran, Yalta, Quebec, and San Francisco conferences; and Allied military governments in Germany and Japan. Films relating to the Korean War cover various aspects of the conflict and the armistice negotiations. In addition, some films made in Japan are included in the RG 111. Altogether there are 63 titles on East Asia (i.e., 25 titles on China, 14 on Korea, and 24 on Japan); they can be identified in the card catalog located at the branch.

RG 127: *Records of the U.S. Marine Corps* contain 21 reels of film produced during World War II, including "With the Marines at Tarawa" (1944); "Mud and Soldiers"—Japanese footage edited by the U.S. Marine Corps (ca. 1943); and "Bulletin on the Okinawa Operation" (1945).

RG 131: *Records of the Office of Alien Property* contain films (36 reels) produced in the 1930s including "World Cruise" of the Hamburg-

American Line that shows Japanese gardens, pearls, street scenes of Yokohama, the Buddha at Kamakura, Mount Fuji, Shanghai, Peking, Korea, etc. Also a few Japanese feature films are included in the record group.

RG 170: "Records of the Bureau of Narcotics and Dangerous Drugs" contain 14 reels of film relating to drug traffic and the enforcement of narcotics laws in China and the United States in 1928-37.

RG 200: *National Archives Gift Collection* has over 13,000 reels, including newsreels, 1919-67; "The March of Time," 1939-51; World War II films, 1940-45; Ford Collection, 1914-56; Harmon Foundation Collection, 1930-51; League of Nations collection, 1920-46 (56 reels); and other educational and documentary films, 1915-67. An undetermined number of newsreels as well as films on East Asia are found in this collection. At least 6 titles on China, including "Inside China Today" (1944); 4 on Japan and 5 on Korea can be identified in the card catalogs.

RG 208: *Records of the Office of War Information* include 661 reels of informational, propaganda, and documentary films covering various aspects of World War II; they depict the Allied peoples, their customs, and their contributions to the war effort; and the Axis powers and their conduct of the war, military strength, and ambitions. At least 6 titles relating to the United States war effort against Japan in the Pacific, plus 6 newsreels on China can be readily identified in the card catalogs. A film, narrated in Chinese, shows memorial services held in Chungking, China, honoring President Franklin D. Roosevelt in 1945.

RG 210: *Records of the Office of Strategic Services* contain 24 reels of film depicting the industry and people of Honolulu, Hawaii, prior to the Japanese attack on December 7, 1941. Produced in the years 1942-45, they include films describing the social structure and behavioral patterns of the Japanese as well as the natural resources of Japan. Also, RG 226 contains a number of unclassified OSS films on Japan and China.

RG 238: *National Archives Collection of World War II—War Crimes Records* include 76 reels of film used as evidence at the war-crimes trials of Axis leaders before the International Military Tribunal, Nuremberg, 1945-46, and before the International Military Tribunal for the Far East, Tokyo, 1946-48. A Japanese film entitled "Japan in Time of Emergency" (1933) is included in the collection.

RG 242: *National Archives Collection of Foreign Records Seized,* 1941- , contains films (2,224 reels) seized from the Axis powers include Japanese documentaries and newsreels, 1932-45, relating to the fishing industry, travel in Japan, the invasion of China, and many aspects of the war in the Pacific from 1941 to 1945. At least 18 newsreels and 5 propaganda films (c.g., "Kōdō Nippon," "Tōyō no Gaika," etc.) can be identified in the card catalogs. Some Russian and North Korean films concerning the 38th parallel in 1950 and of American prisoners of war at Pyongyang are also included in this collection. There are, in addition, Chinese Communist anti-Chiang Kai-shek propaganda films made after 1945.

RG 286: *Records of the Agency for International Development* contain a film entitled "Strength for Peace: A Report on the Mutual Defense Assistance Program" (ca. 1955) that covers the United States involvement in East Asia in the early 1950s.

RG 306: *Records of the United States Information Agency (USIA)* contain documentaries (368 reels) produced or acquired by the USIA for distribution abroad, concerning many aspects of life in the United States, United States foreign relations, cultural exchanges, trade, etc. On March 24, 1977, a major collection acquired by the USIA (581 reels) was deposited with the NARS. Included are films (negatives, masters, and prints) of the "Formosa News" (1950-1951), "Korean News" (1950-1952), and "Liberty News" (1960-1968) newsreel series produced and/or distributed by the USIA in Taiwan and South Korea. The films are in the Korean and Chinese languages. English scripts for the Liberty News series are also included.

RG 342: *Records of U.S. Air Force Commands, Activities, and Organization* contain 4,370 reels of film made or collected by the Air Force, including an undetermined number of films on Allied bombing missions in the Pacific area; the effects of bombing raids on Japan, including the bombing of Hiroshima and Nagasaki (19 reels); the surrender of Japan; and the customs, religion, industry, and Allied occupation of Japan. The collection also includes some captured Japanese films relating to preparation for the Pearl Harbor attack and World War II combat; and films on aerial aspects of the Korean combat operation and truce-signing ceremonies in 1953.

STILL PICTURES

The still-picture collection has no central, general catalog as does the film collection at the NARS.

RG 18: *Records of the Army Air Force* include 446-495 individual photographs relating to aviation in World War I; and bombing squadrons in World War II with an undetermined number of pictures on East Asia.

RG 19: *Records of the Bureau of Ships* contain several negatives showing the construction of river gunboats in China.

RG 22: *Records of the Fish and Wildlife Service* consist of 20-25 items containing photographs relating to a cruise of the *Albatross* to North and South America, 1887-91, including scenes of Chinese fishing villages on the California coast during the 1880s.

RG 26: *Records of the U.S. Coast Guard* include some 50-100 photographs of Japanese merchant vessels, 1937-41.

RG 37: *Records of the Hydrographic Office* contain 181 photographs of lighthouses, lightships, and harbors in Uruguay and Japan, 1877-1937.

RG 38: *Records of the Office of the Chief of Naval Operations* include an aerial mosaic of Nanking, made in China, in 1929, and an undetermined number of photos of coastal formations of the Japanese mandated islands (the Marshall, Caroline, and Mariana islands).

RG 59: *Records of the Department of State* contain many photographs relating to East Asia among its collection of over 70,000. Included are photos of the members of "Le Congress de Pekin," 1901, the signing of the Russo-Japanese peace treaty of 1905, and pictures of the Japanese internees during World War II and Vice President Richard M. Nixon's tour of the Far East in 1953.

RG 77: *Records of the Office of the Chief of Engineers* contain an undetermined number of photos of troops and scenes in China during the China Relief Expedition, 1900-1901.

RG 80: *General Records of the Department of Navy,* by far the most extensive collection, have more than 250,000 photographs taken by the Japanese Navy during World War II, including the Japanese surrender ceremonies aboard the U.S.S. *Missouri* in September 1945.

RG 111: *Records of the Office of the Chief Signal Officer* contain approximately 885 items relating to East Asia. Included are about 388 photos relating to the Chinese Boxer Rebellion, 1900-1901, and the Japanese capture of the German treaty port of Tsingtao, China, in 1914; approximately 377 photos of U.S. forces in China after the Boxer Rebellion to the 1930s; and about 120 photos relating to the Sino-Japanese War, 1937-1945.

RG 127: *Records of the U.S. Marine Corps* include an undetermined number of photos of artworks such as Japanese paintings on silk showing Japanese impressions of the U.S. Marines commanded by Commodore Matthew C. Perry in the 1850s and some scenes of China in the twentieth century.

RG 131: *Records of the Office of Alien Property* contain an unspecified number of photographs pertaining to Japanese property seized during World War II; this material is restricted for use by the general public.

RG 151: *Records of the Bureau of Foreign and Domestic Commerce* include photos relating to the Bureau's operations abroad (including China and Japan) from 1899-1939. The exact number of photos on East Asia cannot be ascertained.

RG 165: *Records of the War Department General and Special Staffs* include photos of United States and foreign troops in China during the Boxer Rebellion; photos of German, Russian, and Japanese military equipment and Japanese activities, 1921-45, that were collected by the Intelligence Division; and photos relating to the Russo-Japanese War of 1904-05.

RG 200: *National Archives Gift Collection* contains approximately 60 photographs relating to the Korean Punitive Expedition undertaken under the command of Commodore C. R. Percy Rodgers in 1871.

RG 208: *Records of the Office of War Information* include among the 206,100 photographs some 3,000-5,000 photos relating to East Asia, mostly produced during World War II.

RG 210: *Records of the War Relocation Authority* include approximately 12,600 photographs of Japanese property in the United States before the evacuation by the WRA.

RG 226: *Records of the Office of Strategic Services* contain 228 photographs relating to the industrial development of China, Japan, and the Philippines prior to World War II (1919-1940).

RG 238: *National Archives Collection of World War II War Crimes Records* includes about 2,000 photos of the courtrooms, judges, counsels, witnesses, and defendants involved in the International Military Tribunal for the Far East, 1946-48.

RG 242: *National Archives Collection of Foreign Records Seized* includes some 323,797 photographs (many relating to Japan) of World War I as well as the activities of the Axis powers and their leaders in World War II.

RG 306: *Records of the USIA* include several thousand photos on East Asia under various subject headings. Many of them were used in connection with news activities of the agency's Information Center Service from 1948 to the mid-1960s.

RG 331: *Records of the Allied Operational and Occupational Headquarters, WW II* contain about 31 photographs and graphs prepared by the General Headquarters, Supreme Commander for the Allied Powers, relating to the prison population of Japan, population changes in Japan, food imports, and other subjects, from 1940-45.

RG 342: *Records of U.S. Air Force Commands, Activities and Organizations* include 25-30 volumes of photos documenting all Air Force activities in Germany and Japan following World War II (1945-1959).

4. a. Individual screening devices for both 16-mm and 35-mm films are available in the motion-picture research room.

   b. Researchers should make reservations at least one day in advance.

   c. All services are without charge except reproducing services described in 4d below.

   d. The division can provide researchers with reproduction services for both still and motion pictures, provided the films are not restricted by copyright laws or otherwise limited. There is a schedule of fees charged for these services. Government-produced or distributed films which are still in circulation can also be rented or purchased from the National Audiovisual Center (General Services Administration) in Capitol Heights, Maryland.

5. The division does not have published finding aids. However, several mimeographed caption lists and preliminary inventories are available. Though incomplete and outdated, they are useful in identifying the record groups with films on East Asia. The card catalogs located in the division are also helpful in locating films and still pictures relating to East Asia.

   Other available aids include: Mayfield S. Bray and William T. Murphy, *Motion Pictures in the Audiovisual Archives Division of the National Archives* (1972); Mayfield S. Bray, *Still Pictures in the Audiovisual Archives Division of the National Archives* (1972); and Mayfield S. Bray and William T. Murphy, *Audiovisual Records in the National Archives Relating to World War II* (ca. 1970). Copies of these titles can be obtained, while the supply lasts, free upon request.

F9 National Audiovisual Center (General Services Administration)

1. a. *Washington, D.C. 20409*
   Physical locations: Capitol Heights, Md.
   (301) 763-1896

   b. 8:00 A.M.-4:30 P.M.   Monday-Friday

   c. Open to the public.

   d. John H. McLean, Director

2-3.   The National Audiovisual Center was established in 1969: (1) to serve as the central clearinghouse for all United States government-produced audiovisual materials; and (2) to make federally produced audiovisual materials available to the public through distribution services (i.e., sales, rental, and loan referrals). The center's audiovisual materials cover a variety of subjects (e.g., medicine, education, aviation and space technology, vocational training, and environmental sciences). Many are designed for general use; however, some are designed for specific training or instructional programs. In order to increase the effectiveness of these audiovisual programs, many are accompanied by printed materials such as teacher manuals, student workbooks, or scripts.

Currently, the center maintains over 9,000 titles of audiovisual materials (mostly 16-mm motion pictures) for sale and/or rental. The center's holdings on East Asia include approximately 12 films dealing with the United States' involvement in World War II in the Pacific and over 24 films pertaining to the Korean War. These films were produced mostly in the 1940s and 1950s by the military branches of the United States.

4.   a. No screening facilities are available on the premises. However, preview prior to purchase is available for 16-mm motion pictures.

b. Open to the public free of charge.

c-d. The Center maintains a list of prices for over 9,000 items available for sale and/or rental.

5.   The Center maintains a master data file on over 20,000 audiovisual materials produced by the United States government; the file is constantly updated. At the same time, the Center has published a catalog entitled *Reference List of U.S. Government Produced Audiovisual Materials, 1978,* which can be purchased for $5.75 from the Superintendent of Documents, U.S. Government Printing Office, Washington, D.C. 20402. A brochure entitled *National Audiovisual Center, Services to the Public* is available free on request. For further information about the availability of the federally produced audiovisual materials for sale, rental, or loan, write to the center or call (301) 763-1896.

National Geographic Society Library See entry A32.

F10 Naval Historical Center (Navy Department)—Curator Branch—Photographic Section

1.   a. *Washington Navy Yard, Building 76*
Washington, D.C. 20374
433-2765

b. 7:30 A.M.-4:30 P.M.   Monday-Friday

c. Researchers should call for an appointment to use the collection.

d. Capt. J. H. B. Smith, Head, Curator Branch, Department of Navy
Charles Haberlein, Jr., Head of the Photographic Section

2.   The Naval Historical Center's Photographic Section has been the Navy's primary repository for pictorial materials of historic interest. It holds more than 200,000 selected historic photographs spanning the entire period of United States naval history; they are readily available through the use of a comprehensive subject card index.

3.   These unclassified photographs are largely of naval ships and Asian scenes in the 1900-1940 period. There are a modest number of photos of other years. Most Navy photographs of the post-1940 period are deposited with the National Archives and the Naval Photographic Center (see entry F11). Although its file on the Korean War is rather weak, fairly good files exist on the following actions and campaigns of WW II: the Pearl Harbor attack, Midway, Guadalcanal and Central Solomons, and Leyte Gulf.

4.   Reproductions of most Naval Historical Center photographs are handled by the Naval Photographic Center and the Navy Office of Information. For further information, contact R. A. Carlisle at 697-6752.

5.   Copies of a brochure entitled *Photographic Section, Naval Historical Center: A Brief Description* can be obtained free on request.

F11 Naval Photographic Center (Navy Department)

1.   a. *Naval District Washington, Building 168*
Anacostia, D.C. 20374
433-2168/2169 (Still)
433-2115 (Motion)
433-2711 (Production Control Office)

    b. 7:15 A.M.-3:45 P.M.   Monday-Friday

    c. Researchers must call for an appointment.

    d. Jack Carter, Head, Library Division
Carl Carlson, Head, Film Depository Division

2-3.   The Center's photo collection consists of approximately 750,000 black-and-white and color photographs, about 1,000 of which relate to the U.S. Navy's activities in Japan, South Korea, and Okinawa. In addition, the collection covers a number of nonmilitary subjects, such as street scenes, parades, customs, and the countryside. Virtually all of the collection is unclassified. The Center also holds negatives for most of the photos in the Naval Historical Center's photo collection (see entry F10).

    The Film Depository Division holds about 50-60 rolls of film on Okinawa, mostly World War II vintage (e.g., "Aerials of Bombardment of Okinawa; Naha Town, and Invasion Fleet"); 200-300 rolls (350-400 feet each) on Japan since the 1950s (e.g., "Color Story of Japan"); about 10 titles on South Korea (e.g., "Supplements to 'This is Korea' "); and about 5 titles on China (e.g., "Scenes in Northern China"). In addition to United States naval activities in East Asia, the films cover other nonmilitary subjects and scenes in Japan, China, and Korea.

4. c. For extensive searches of the holdings or other research service, the Film Depository Division charges an hourly fee.

   d. There are copies of some still pictures available for sale. Copies of other photos can be ordered through:

   > Chief of Information
   > Department of the Navy (OI-22)
   > Room 2d340, Pentagon
   > Washington, D.C. 20350
   > (202) 697-0866

5. Unpublished indexes for both the still- and motion-picture collections are available. For still pictures, the Center maintains a card-drawer file arranged by subject and by class of ships and aircraft. A geographic file and a personality file are also maintained for reference.

F12 Peace Corps (ACTION) Photograph Collection

1. a. *Paramount Building, Room 305*
      1735 Eye Street, NW
      Washington, D.C. 20525
      254-7524

   b. 8:30 A.M.-5:00 P.M.   Monday-Friday

   c. Open to the public; appointments recommended.

   d. Anne Bringsjord, Director of Photo Services

2-3. The collection consists of about 30,000 black-and-white photographs and 8,000 color slides primarily depicting the living and working experience of Peace Corps volunteers around the world. An indeterminate but sizable number of photos and slides on South Korea are included in the collection. Holdings are arranged by country.

4. The agency can supply a small number of prints to researchers without charge.

F13 Prince George's County Public Libraries

1. a. *Administrative Offices*
      6532 Adelphi Road
      Hyattsville, Md. 20782
      (301) 699-3500 (Films Service)

   b. 9:00 A.M.-6:00 P.M.   Monday-Friday (hours vary slightly for branches depending on the season).

   c. Any adult (18 years or over) with a Prince George's County Memorial Library borrower's card may borrow films free of charge. The same privilege is accorded to any adult with a borrower's card issued by a library participating in the Maryland Public Library Service Agreement. Nonresidents who do not otherwise qualify to borrow films may obtain full borrowing privileges (including films) by paying an annual non-resident fee of $5.00.

Use of the films is subject to certain restrictions: (1) films cannot be shown where admission is charged nor for fund-raising purposes; (2) they cannot be televised or duplicated in any way; and, (3) they are not for pre-college level classroom use.

Users may borrow a maximum of 4 titles (not to exceed 90 minutes running time), or 1 feature film per day. The loan period is overnight on weekdays (or 24 hours); and films borrowed on Friday or Saturday may be returned on the following Monday. Borrowers may pick up and return films to any of 18 different branches of the library or the administrative offices. Reservations must be made at the administrative offices at least 2 working days in advance.

2-3. The library's film collection consists of about 1,950 titles, both domestic and foreign, silent and sound. It includes about 35 titles of East Asian films: 28 Japanese feature films plus 2 Japanese documentaries; 4 documentaries on China; and 1 Taiwan film. The library has the largest collection of postwar Japanese feature films in the Washington area.

Among the available feature films are 28 classics of the Japanese cinema, including the following directed by Akira Kurosawa:

Drunken Angel (1948)	The Quiet Duel (1949)
Hidden Fortress (1958)	Rashomon (1950)
High and Low (1963)	Red Beard (1965)
I Live in Fear (1955)	Sugata Sanshiro (1943)
The Idiot (1951)	Seven Samurai (1954)
Ikiru (1952)	Throne of Blood (1957)
Lower Depths (1957)	Yojimbo (1961)
The Man Who Tread on the Tiger's Tail (1945)	

Those films produced under the direction of other eminent Japanese directors (e.g., Yasujiro Ōzu, Junji Kinoshita, Kenji Mizoguchi) include:

Autumn Afternoon (1962)	Princess Yang Kueifei (1955)
Double Suicide (1969)	The Tokyo Story (1953)
I Was Born, But (1932)	24 Eyes (1954)
Late Spring (1949)	Ugetsu Monogatari (1953)
Life of Haru (1952)	Utamaro and His 5 Women (1946)

In addition the library contains 2 documentaries on Japan: *Japanese* and *Japanese Boy*.

The library's film holdings on China consist of 4 documentaries: *China '71* (1971); *A Hole in the Bamboo Curtain* (1972); *Battle of China* (1944); and *The Roots of Madness* (1967). In addition, there is 1 film from Taiwan entitled *The Family of Free China*. No Korean film is available.

4. a. Borrowers must find their own 16-mm sound projectors; the library does not provide film projectors.

b. Reservations must be made (at least 2 working days in advance) through the administrative offices of the library. Reservations for popular feature films should be made one or two months in advance.

5. The library publishes an annual *Film Catalog* which is for sale at all branches.

Senate Historical Office See entry K28.

F14 State Department Collection

1.   a. *Bureau of Public Affairs, Office of Public Communication*
State Department Building, Room 4827A
2201 C Street, NW
Washington, D.C. 20520
632-9437/8203

     b. 8:45 A.M.-5:30 P.M. Monday-Friday

     c. Open to researchers by appointment. Call ahead to arrange a visit.

     d. Cheryl Tucker, Film Officer

2-3.   The collection contains approximately 2,000 color slides and 350 black-and-white photographs, including about 20 pictures on the PRC, 20 on Japan, and 15 on South Korea. The Office of Public Communication also has a 4-part film entitled *The History of U.S. Foreign Relations* (30 minutes in length for each part). These films can be borrowed without charge from distributors located nationwide. For further information, call Cheryl Tucker (632-9437).

4.   Reproduction services are available. Limited photographic prints can be ordered without charge.

Note: The State Department's Audio-Visual Services Division (Room B-258) has approximately 5,700 mounted black-and-white photographs dating from 1933-1957. It also maintains over 100,000 negatives, covering embassies and other State Department facilities abroad and ceremonies, conferences, treaty signings, visits by foreign dignitaries, and other functions within the State Department. For further information, contact Thomas L. Williams, Jr. (632-1634).

U.S.-China People's Friendship Association (Washington, D.C., Chapter) Film Library See entry H45.

United Nations Information Center Film Collection See entry A40.

F15 University of Maryland East Asia Collection

1.   a. *McKeldin Library*
University of Maryland
College Park, Md. 20742
(301) 454-2819/5459

     b. 9:00 A.M.-5:00 P.M. Monday-Friday

    c. Open to researchers.

    d. Frank Joseph Shulman, Head

2-3.   The East Asia Collection contains more than 100 albums of published and unpublished photographs which formerly belonged to the "Kaigun-kan" (a reference library/museum attached to the Japanese Ministry of Navy in the pre-1945 period). These albums were confiscated during the Allied Occupation of Japan (1945-1952) by the Civil Censorship Detachment/Civil Intelligence Section of SCAP. Subsequently, they were acquired by the University of Maryland as part of its "Gordon W. Prange Collection" of publications and unpublished materials from the Allied Occupation of Japan.

    Altogether more than several thousand published and unpublished photographs are included in the collection. Many deal with the Sino-Japanese War (1894-1895), the Russo-Japanese War, (1904-1905), and various aspects of Japanese shipbuilding, naval training, and other related activities. None, however, touches on Japan's campaigns in the Pacific in the 1940s against the United States, although some photos cover the Sino-Japanese undeclared war (1937-1945).

    In addition, the collection contains an album with numerous photographs relating to the life and career of Adm. Heihachiro Togo (1846-1934), who was the commander-in-chief of the Japanese fleet which annihilated Russia's Baltic Fleet off the coast of Japan during the Russo-Japanese War. Also included in the collection is an album of photographs of various graduating classes of the Edajima Naval Academy (Hiroshima Prefecture). Photographs of Prince Takamatsu no Miya Nobuhito (1905-) who graduated from the Academy in 1924 are contained in the album.

4.   While no reservations are required, appointments are recommended. Copies of the photographs are not available; however, arrangements can be made for reproduction of the photographs.

5.   Although these albums are uncataloged, a brief annotated list of the albums is available at the East Asia Collection.

University of Maryland Undergraduate Library See entry A42.

Washington Post **Photographic Collection** See entry N16.

Washington Star **Library** See entry N17.

G Data Banks

Entry Form for Data Banks (G)

1. General Information
   a. *Address; telephone number(s)*
   b. Hours of service
   c. Conditions of access (including fees charged for information retrieval)
   d. Name/title of director and key staff members

2. Description of data files (hard-data and bibliographic-reference)

3. Bibliographic aids facilitating use of storage media

Agency for International Development (AID)—Development Information Center See entry A2.

Agency for International Development (AID) Economic and Social Data Bank See entry K1.

AGRICOLA See entry A41.

Agriculture Department—Documentation Center See entry K2.

G1 Agriculture Department—Foreign Development and Competition Division

1. a. *500 12th Street, SW*
      Washington, D.C. 20250
      447-8824

   b. 8:30 A.M.-5:00 P.M.   Monday-Friday

    c. The data base is maintained primarily for internal use; appointments are required.

    d. Dr. Joseph Willett, Director
Marge Bever, Special Assistant for International Data (447-2623)

2.   The division maintains a computerized data base which contains a USDA-compiled index of world agricultural production (1950-present); data on international grain-crop acreage and yields; international trade data compiled by the United Nations (1967-present); trade and production data compiled by the United Nations Food and Agricultural Organization (FAO), 1961-1974; and U.S. Agency for International Development Population data, by country (1950-present).

American Psychological Association—Psychological Information Services (PsycINFO) See entry H11.

Brookings Institution Social Science Computational Center See entry M5.

Bureau of Standards—Standard Reference Data System See entry K5.

Center for Naval Analyses Computer Center See entry M9.

G2 Census Bureau—Demographic Data-Retrieval System (DDRS)

1.   a. *Population Division*
U.S. Bureau of the Census
Scuderi Building
4235 28th Ave.
Marlow Heights, Md. 20031
Mail: U.S. Department of Commerce, Bureau of the Census,
    Washington, D.C. 20233
763-2834

    b. 8:30 A.M.-5:00 P.M.   Monday-Friday

    c. Open to researchers by appointment.

    d. Martha A. Bargar, Chief

    The Demographic Data-Retrieval System comprises a collection of selected demographic statistics that have been indexed and stored for automated retrieval. These data include tabular statistics that relate primarily to the years 1965 and after, and to adjustments and projections of that data. The purpose of the DDRS is to provide the rapid retrieval of data for research in demography.

More specifically, the DDRS consists of statstical data (95 percent) and bibliographic references (5 percent) to data or to articles containing demographic data relating mostly to the developing countries of the world. The data tables are microfilmed from original sources, cross-coded according to country, date of data, and specific demographic subject variables. Over 34,000 data tables comprise the base for the DDRS. Data are from published censuses and official government statistical periodicals, demographic and fertility surveys, and select United Nations unpublished papers. Geographic areas include countries of Latin America, Asia (except the PRC and Mongolia), Africa, and Oceania.

3.   Questions about the DDRS and requests for demographic data may be obtained free of charge through Martha Bargar.

Commerce Department, National Bureau of Standards—Standard Reference Data System See entry K5.

Commerce Department—National Technical Information Service (NTIS) "NTISearch" See entry K5.

G3 Defense Documentation Center (Department of Defense)

1. a. *Cameron Station, Building 5*
    Alexandria, Va. 22314
    (202) 274-7633 (Document Information)
    (202) 274-6881 (Public Affairs)

    b. 7:30 A.M.-4:00 P.M.   Monday-Friday

    c. Restricted to Department of Defense (DOD) personnel and authorized staff members of research organizations under DOD contract or grant.

    d. Hubert E. Sauter, Administrator

2.   The Defense Documentation Center (DDC) is a computerized repository for over 1.2 million research reports (both classified and unclassified) produced under the auspices of the Department of Defense. Virtually all formal research results funded by DOD are deposited here. The focus of the collection is on the physical sciences, technology, and engineering as they relate to national defense and military affairs. Some social science research on international affairs (including East Asia) is also included. The bibliographic data base is on computer tape, whereas full research reports are recorded on microfiche. Unclassified reports in the data base are available to the public through the National Technical Information Service (see entry K5).

3.   DDC distributes an unclassified biweekly *Technical Abstracts Bulletin* of recent acquisitions to registered users on DOD contracts. No published bibliographies of DDC holdings are available to the public.

G4 Educational Resources Information Center (ERIC)

1.   a. *Dissemination and Improvement Practice*
      Division of Information Resources
      National Institute of Education
      U.S. Department of Health, Education and Welfare
      1200 19th Street, NW
      Washington, D.C. 20208
      254-7934 (Information)
      254-5500 (Central ERIC)

   b. 8:00 A.M.-4:30 P.M.   Monday-Friday

   c. Various fee schedules exist for the different services of the clearinghouses (ERIC) and for other institutions or computer systems which allow access to ERIC data bases.

   d. Robert Chesney, Head

2.   ERIC is a national information system for education which is composed of Central ERIC and 16 subject-oriented clearinghouses. Together they abstract, index, catalog, and annotate materials dealing with almost every aspect of education. These result in a data base (by authors, subject matters, and institutions) which may be searched manually as well as by computer. As of October 1978, over 300,000 items (including journal articles and research papers) were stored in the ERIC data retrieval system including 1,311 items on Japan; 1,741 on China; 280 on Korea; and 8 on Taiwan.

At present the Central ERIC and three of the 16 clearinghouses are located in the Washington area: those on higher education (296-2597), teacher education (293-7280), and languages and linguistics (703/528-4312). Each of the 16 clearinghouses publishes books, reports, and bibliographies on its subject category every year. The following will be of assistance to researchers in working with ERIC data bases:

> *Resources in Education* (RIE) (a monthly index);
> *Current Index to Journals in Education* (monthly index);
> *Thesaurus of ERIC Descriptors;* and
> *ERIC Identifiers: Term Posting and Statistics for Research in Education.*

Researchers may obtain access to ERIC by computer almost anywhere in the United States and some foreign countries (including Japan and Hong Kong). Various fee schedules exist for the use of the ERIC data bases through the clearinghouses or other computer systems which allow access to ERIC. For further information, researchers should contact the National Institute for Education, Educational Reference Center, Educational Resource Division of the U.S. Department of Health, Education, and Welfare, which is located at 1832 M Street, NW, Room 705, Washington, D.C. 20208 (254-7934) or a local ERIC clearinghouse.

3.   NIE has published a number of handbooks and pamphlets, including *Survey of ERIC Data Base Search Services* (1978) by Elizabeth Pugh et al., *Directory of ERIC Collections in the Washington, D.C. Area: 1976, Directory of ERIC Microfiche Collections* (Arranged by Geographic Locations) (1978), and *How to Use ERIC* (1978).

Energy Department—World Energy Data System (WENDS)
See entry K9.

Energy Information Administration Clearinghouse (Energy Department) See entry K9.

Health, Education, and Welfare Department—Alcohol, Drug Abuse, and Mental Health Administration (ADAMHA): National Clearinghouse for Alcohol Information; National Clearinghouse for Drug Abuse Information; and National Clearinghouse for Mental Health Information See entry K14.

Institute for Defense Analysis Computer Facility See entry M22.

G5 International Bank for Reconstruction and Development (World Bank)—Data System

1. a. *1818 H Street, NW*
   Washington, D.C. 20433
   477-3951

   b. 9:00 A.M.-5:00 P.M.   Monday-Friday

   c. Arrangements for visits should be made in advance. Copies of magnetic tapes are available to private users (e.g., universities, research organizations, individual researchers) upon request at little or no cost.

   d. Helen Hughes, Director, Economic Analysis and Projections Department
      Robert A. McPheeters, Jr., Data System Advisor

2-3. The World Bank maintains a variety of socio-economic data in machine-readable form, including the following data bases which can be of interest to East Asian specialists: (1) "Socio-Economic Data Bank" contains time series on a wide range of macro-level social and economic indicators, by country (transcribed from the Bank's *Trade Tables, World Economic and Social Indicators,* and *World Bank Atlas*); (2) "External Debt (or Debtor-Reporting) Data System" covers data on public borrowing, foreign debts, and balance of payments, by country (transcribed mostly from the Bank's *World Debt Tables*); (3) "Capital Markets Data System" contains data on transactions in international capital markets (transcribed from the Bank's quarterly *Borrowing in International Cap-*

ital Markets); (4) "Commodities and Commodity Prices Data System" consists of time series of data published in the annual *Commodity Trade and Price Trends;* and, (5) "Metals and Minerals Data Base" contains data drawn from various international and national governmental sources.

G6 International Monetary Fund (IMF)—Data Fund

1.　a. *700 19th Street, NW*
Washington, D.C. 20431
477-3207

　　b. 9:00 A.M.-5:00 P.M.　Monday-Friday

　　c. Arrangements for visits should be made in advance. Copies of the Data Fund's magnetic tapes can be subscribed to on an annual basis (i.e., $400 per year for universities and $1,000 for other). Each subscription consists of 12 monthly tapes containing the data published in the 4 major publications of the IMF listed below.

　　d. Werner Dannemann, Director, Bureau of Statistics
Robert L. Kline, Chief, Data Fund Division

2-3.　　The bureau has a computer system, called "Data Fund," which makes the data contained in the following IMF publications available in machine-readable form (e.g., statistics from East Asian countries include Japan, South Korea, and Taiwan. Occasionally data from the PRC can be found):

International Financial Statistics (monthly) is a standard source of comparable country statistics on exchange rates, international reserves, money and credit, external trade, prices and production, balance of payments, government finance, and national accounts. The computer tapes contain approximately 16,000 time series with data reported since 1948.

Direction of Trade (monthly) contains each member country's direction of trade with comparative data for the corresponding period of the previous year. The computer tapes contain approximately 42,000 time series reported in this monthly publication.

Balance of Payments Yearbook is a compilation of over 100 countries' balance of payments statistics reported to the IMF. Beginning with volume 29 (1965), the annual issue brings together in 1 volume the data released in 12 monthly issues as data become available. The computer tapes contain about 39,000 time series published in this publication.

Government Finance Statistics Yearbook (GFS) is a compilation of comparable statistics on government finances. It provides classifications of the detail of government revenues, grants, expenditures, lending, financing, and debts. Information is also given on the institutional units of government and the account through which they operate. The magnetic tapes contain approximately 16,500 annual time series of data reported in the GFS.

International Trade Commission—"East-West Trade Statistics Monitoring System" See entry K18.

Joint Publications Research Service—*TRANSDEX* See entry K20.

Library of Congress   MARC; SCORPIO; National Referral Center See entry A30, Division of Science and Technology.

National Audiovisual Center (General Services Administration) See entry F9.

National Library of Medicine Data Bases See entry A34.

G7 **National Space Science Data Center (National Aeronautics and Space Administration)**

1.   a. *Goddard Space Flight Center, Building 26*
        Greenbelt, Md. 20771
        (301) 982-6695

      b. 8:00 A.M.-4:30 P.M.   Monday-Friday

      c. Open to researchers by appointment.

      d. James I. Vette, Director

2.   The Space Science Data Center maintains 9 million feet of microfilm and 64,000 magnetic tapes (computerized). Bibliographic information, substantive reports, technical data, and other materials on space programs of the United States and certain foreign countries, such as Japan, can be found here. For example, "Orbit information" for the Japanese satellite EXOS-A ("Kayoko") launched in the spring of 1978 is stored in the data base. Officials at the Data Center expect to receive more "scientific information" from Japan in the near future. "Orbit information" for "Shinsei" (launched in 1971), however, is not available at the Center nor is information on any one of the PRC's satellites.

3.   There is normally no charge for outside researchers to use the data bases at the Data Center. Brochures, including *Data and Distribution Services,* are available free on request. A highly informative *Report on Rocket and Satellite Information and Data Exchange* (1978) is also available from the Center. For further information, contact William E. Valente, Manager, Request Coordination, National Space Science Data Center ([301] 982-6695).

G8 *New York Times* Information Bank—Washington Office

1. a. *111 19th Street, NW*
      Arlington, Va. 22209
      (703) 243-7220

   b. 9:00 A.M.-5:00 P.M.   Monday-Friday

   c. Open to the public.

   d. David Cearnal, Regional Manager

2. This computerized data base contains over 1.5 million abstracts of news stories, editorials, and other pertinent items from the *New York Times* (since 1969) and more than 70 national and international periodicals (e.g., *Far Eastern Economic Review*). Researchers may utilize the Retail Service of the Information Bank, which can search the base for desired subjects for a fee. Abstracts are of 3-200 lines in length. For further information, call the Washington Office.

Smithsonian Science Information Exchange See entry K29.

SRI International Data Base See entry M32.

State Department—Foreign Affairs Document and Reference Center (FADRC) System See entry K30.

State Department Foreign Affairs Research Documentation Center See entry K30.

Transportation Department—"TRISNET" See entry A39.

Treasury Department—The Developing Countries Data Bank See entry K32.

U.S.D.A. Technical Information Systems See entry A41.

G9 United Nations Environment Program International Referral System (UNEP/IRS)

1. a. *U.S. National Focal Point*
      UNEP/IRS (PM-213)
      U.S. Environmental Protection Agency

401 M Street, SW (Room 2902)
Washington, D.C. 20460
755-1836/1838

b. 9:00 A.M.-5:00 P.M. Monday-Friday

c. Open to the public.

d. Carol Alexander, Director

2. UNEP/IRS, an independent agency of the United Nations (established in 1972), is a computerized data base of environmental information for over 80 participating U.N. members (e.g., the U.S., China, and Japan). The purpose of the UNEP/IRS is to link users to sources of environmental information and to facilitate the transfer and use of environmental information on a global basis. Over 7,000 sources of information are registered throughout the world. Individual countries establish "national focal points" to collect pertinent information and data sources which in turn are listed in the IRS central directory. The U.S. National Focal Point—the U.S. International Environmental Referral Center—began its operation in October 1975. Referral services are provided free of charge and are available to all interested organizations and individuals. Information is available in 26 categories (e.g., pollution, energy resources, fresh water, land use and misuse, nonrenewable resources, etc.).

3. Copies of *United Nations Environmental Program/International Referral System General Information* as well as *UNEP/IRS: Policy* and *User's Manual* are available free on request. For further information, contact Charlene S. Sayers (755-1836), who is Source Coordinator for the U.S. International Environmental Referral Center.

ORGANIZATIONS

H Associations (Academic, Cultural, and Professional)

Entry Form for Associations (H)

1. *Address; telephone number(s)*
2. Founding date
3. Chief official and title
4. Staff
5. Number of members
6. Program description
7. Sections or divisions
8. Library
9. Conventions/meetings
10. Publications
11. Affiliated organizations

H1 American Association for the Advancement of Science (AAAS)

1. *1776 Massachusetts Avenue, NW*
   Washington, D.C. 20036
   467-4400

2. 1848

3. Kenneth E. Boulding, President
   William D. Carey, Executive Officer, AAAS

4. The AAAS has about 160 staff members in its main office in Washington, D.C.

5. The Association's membership numbers about 129,000 including 365 in Japan, 37 in Taiwan, 37 in South Korea, and 2 in the People's Republic of China. It has nearly 300 affiliated societies and academies.

6.   The Association is the nation's largest scientific society. The objectives of the AAAS are to further the work of scientists, to facilitate cooperation among them, to improve the effectiveness of science in the promotion of human welfare, and to increase public understanding and appreciation of the importance and promise of the methods of science in human progress.

Its Office of International Science (OIS) has developed a network of organizations designed to facilitate contacts between AAAS members and scientists abroad. In Washington, the office also sponsors a series of informal activities designed to encourage the exchange of information between scientists and administrators in government agencies, professional associations, and foreign embassies.

8.   The association has a small library for staff use.

9.   The AAS holds annual meetings at which as many as 1,000 papers may be given. It has also sponsored special meetings, such as the "Conference on Legal and Scientific Uncertainties of Weather Modification" (1976). As an associate member of the Pacific Science Association (PSA), AAAS sent its delegation to participate in the Third Inter-Congress of the PSA which was held in Bali, Indonesia, in July 1977.

10.   The AAAS publishes the weekly magazine *Science,* symposium volumes, bibliographies, and books on special topics. It also sells annual meeting tapes containing special lectures delivered at these meetings (e.g., "Science and People's Republic of China"). For further information, see *Catalog: Periodicals, Books, Tapes, and Reprints 1977-1978* (AAAS, 1977); the catalog is published annually.

H2 American Association of Colleges for Teacher Education (AACTE)

1.   *1 Dupont Circle, NW Suite 610*
       Washington, D.C. 20036
       293-2450

2.   1948

3.   Dr. Edward C. Pomeroy, Executive Director

4.   The association has a staff of 31.

5.   The AACTE membership consists of 789 colleges and universities in the United States.

6-7.   The primary emphasis of the association is on teacher education, but its International Section deals with all areas of educational development. Three basic programs in the international area are: (1) an internship program—educators from abroad are placed as administrative interns in member institutions; (2) an arrangement with the U.S. Agency for International Development to recruit specialists for overseas projects, such as the Korean Educational Development Institute in Seoul which is designed to improve and enhance the educational system in South Korea as well as to create more effective and efficient educational programs; and, (3) study abroad for teachers—the National Education Association and

AACTE cosponsor study abroad programs for teachers, including an Annual Shipboard Conference in the United States dealing with international issues.

9. In addition to its own annual convention, AACTE participates in the annual conventions of the International Council on Education for Teaching, "The World Assembly," which is held yearly in various locations throughout the world. [In 1979 it will be held in East Asia.]

10. The Association publishes the *AACTE Bulletin,* a monthly newsletter about events relevant to educators, and the quarterly *Journal of Teacher Education.*

11. AACTE is a fiscal agent and cosponsor of the ERIC Clearinghouse on Teacher Education. In addition, it operates the secretariat and provides leadership support for the International Council on Education for Teaching (ICET).

H3 American Association of Museums (AAM)

1. *1055 Thomas Jefferson Street, NW (Suite 428)*
   Washington, D.C. 20007
   338-5300

2. 1906

3. Lawrence L. Reger, Director

4. The Washington office has a staff of 17.

5. About 5,600 members; 1,100 institutions and 4,500 individuals.

6. AAM is dedicated to promote the goals of museums as cultural, educational, and scientific resources in the United States and Canada and to foster continued improvement of the museum profession. The Association sponsors seminars and provides professional services, including accreditation and federal representation for members.

7. The AAM coordinates its activities closely with the International Council of Museums (ICOM) through the ICOM Committee of the Association, which is housed in the same suite. The Committee is headed by Thomas Messer, vice chairman of the AAM, and is coordinated by Maria Papageorge (338-5300). The ICOM Committee administers an international exchange program of museum curators. Approximately 15 to 20 foreign curators visit the United States under the program, including representatives from Japan and South Korea. The ICOM headquarters is located in Paris, France.

8. AAM has a small reference library that contains about 1,500 volumes on art and art history. On-site use of the library can be arranged through the AAM office.

9. AAM's annual meeting is held in different parts of the United States.

10. AAM's *Museum News* (bimonthly) occasionally carries articles on foreign museums.

H4 American Association of University Women (AAUW)

1. *2401 Virginia Avenue, NW*
   Washington, D.C. 20037
   785-7700

2. 1882

3. Dr. Helen B. Wolfe, Executive Director

4. The office has a staff of 86 including 26 professional staff members.

5. AAUW membership numbers approximately 190,000 nationwide.

6. AAUW is the largest and oldest national organization for the advancement of women. It is dedicated to promote understanding and friendship among university women, to encourage international cooperation, to further the development of education, and to encourage the full application of members' skills to cultural and community affairs.

   The AAUW Educational Foundation offers fellowships to American women and to women from abroad. AAUW International Fellowships, which number about 49 per year, are awarded to outstanding women in foreign countries to pursue advanced study in the United States and to return to their home countries to give service and leadership. Past and present recipients of the fellowships include women from 80 nations abroad, including Japan, Korea, and Taiwan.

8. The association has a small library with an emphasis on women's studies. It may be used by scholars through prior arrangements with the AAUW office.

9. The association sponsors AAUW United Nations Seminars annually. A recent seminar on "Disarmament and Human Rights" was held in San Francisco on March 11, 1978. In addition, the AAUW sponsors a number of other conferences and seminars, such as the Pacific Basin Conference: "East Meets West: Culturally Conditioned Views of the Role of Women," which was held at the East-West Center, Honolulu, Hawaii, from February 28-March 5, 1977. It was jointly sponsored by the AAUW, the International Federation of University Women, and the East-West Cultural Learning Institute. About 144 participants from 18 different countries of the Pacific Basin attended the conference.

10. In addition to *Graduate Women* (bimonthly), the association publishes a number of other pamphlets and reports, such as the proceedings of the *Pacific Basin Conference East Meets West: Culturally Conditioned Views of the Role of Women* (1977), *U.S. Food Policies: A Primer* by J. David Edwards (1977), and an occasional newsletter entitled *United Nations Issues.*

11. AAUW members also belong to the International Federation of University Women (Geneva, Switzerland) which links women's organizations in 54 different countries (e.g., Japan, South Korea, etc.).

H5 American Bar Association—Governmental Relations Office

1. *1800 M Street, N.W.*
   Washington, D.C. 20036
   331-2200

2. 1878

3. Herbert E. Hoffman, Director
   Government Relations Office

4. The Governmental Relations Office has a staff of about 25, 5 of whom are lawyers.

5. The ABA has over 222,000 members nationwide (about 50 percent of all American attorneys belong).

6. The American Bar Association is the national organization of the legal profession. Its objectives are twofold: professional improvement and public service, including a wide range of activities to improve the administration of civil and criminal justice and the availability of legal services to the public.

7. ABA's International Law Section (staffed in the ABA's main office—1155 East 60th Street, Chicago, Illinois 60637) has about 30 committees, including a Far Eastern Law committee (Chairman: E. Charles Routh, Seattle, Washington), an International Human Rights Committee, and a Law of the Sea Committee. These committees work on various topics relating to East Asia. Another active committee within the ABA is the Joint Committee on International Legal Exchanges (ILEX) which consists of members from 11 of the ABA's substantive sections. This committee is chaired by Charles R. Norberg (Washington, D.C.), who is assisted by staff director Kathrine L. Ebert (Washington office). ILEX carries out a number of exchange and training programs with approximately 40 foreign countries including Japan, South Korea, China, and Taiwan. Each year at least one or two Japanese lawyers come to the United States under the auspices of the National Personnel Authority of Japan. The United States itinerary for these Japanese Government Fellows is prepared by ILEX. ILEX also handles programs for several United Nations Fellows each year.

8. The Washington office has a small, specialized library with about 2,000 volumes, including ABA and state bar publications and material dealing with Congress. Outsiders may use the library with the prior permission of the librarian.

9. The annual convention of the ABA is held in August and its midyear meeting in February. The International Law Section holds its spring meeting in Washington, D.C., concurrent with the spring meeting of the American Society of International Law (see entry H12). Occasional seminars called "National Institutes" are held in various parts of the United States (e.g., the National Institute on Japan and East Asia was held in Seattle, Washington, in April 1977).

10.   The ABA publishes a number of periodicals, such as the *International Law News* (quarterly), *International Lawyer* (quarterly), and *American Bar Association Journal* (monthly). The ABA also publishes a series of books based on its National Institutes, including 3 of particular interest: *Current Legal Aspects of Doing Business in the Far East* (1972); *Current Legal Aspects of Doing Business With Sino-Soviet Nations* (1973); and *Current Legal Aspects of Doing Business in Japan and East Asia* (1978).

H6 American Council on Education

1.   *1 Dupont Circle*
        Washington, D.C. 20036
        833-4700

2.   1918

3.   J. W. Peltason, President

4.   The office has a staff of 195, including about 75 professionals.

5.   Approximately 1,500 universities and colleges plus educational associations.

6-7.   The Council's international programs are administered by three separate units: (1) The Division of International Educational Relations fosters improved relations between educational institutions and the federal government and aims to increase the funding of federal programs for international education; (2) the Overseas Liaison Committee promotes linkages between American institutions of higher education and those in developing countries; and, (3) the Council for the International Exchange of Scholars administers for the U.S. International Communication Agency with supervision from the Board of Foreign Scholarships the senior scholars program under the provisions of the Fulbright-Hays Act. (For details, see entry J5.)

8.   ACE has a reference library (total holdings 3,500) which is available for on-site use by educational researchers. The collection is strong in the history of higher education, educational management, and finance.

10.   ACE has published a number of books and reports, including *International Handbook of Universities* (1974); *World List 1975-1976* (1976)—a directory covering more than 6,000 universities in 146 countries; and *International Directory for Educational Liaison* (1973).

H7 American Film Institute

1.   *John F. Kennedy Center for the Performing Arts*
        2700 F Street, NW
        Washington, D.C. 20566
        828-4000

2. 1967

3. George Stevens, Jr., Director

4. The AFL has a staff of about 70 members in Washington, D.C.

5. Over 90,000 members in the United States and abroad.

6. AFI is an organization created by the National Endowment for the Arts to conduct interrelated programs to preserve the heritage and advance the art of film and television in the United States. It preserves and catalogs motion pictures, operates a conservatory to train film makers, offers National Education Services programs, helps institutions nationwide to present classic film programs, and provides grants to independent film makers. The Institute also shows series of East Asian films, especially those of Japan.

7. The Theater Programming section (Michael Webb, Director) has files with information about films that AFI has shown, including an East Asian film series (e.g., "Kenji Mizoguchi," "Changing Images of China," etc.). The National Education Service (Sam Grogg, Director) handles library and information service, research and curriculum development, and international educational liaison with teachers in the field of cinema and television.

8. AFI has a reference library with total holdings of about 1,200 volumes, mostly on films, television, and the performing arts. Currently, the library subscribes to over 130 journals. Its clipping files contain materials on Japan, China, and Korea. It also maintains a "Theater File" series that deals with information on films shown by the AFI. The AFI Archives, comprising over 14,000 films, is located at the Library of Congress (Motion Picture, Broadcasting, and Recorded-Sound Division). On-site use of AFI library is possible with prior arrangements with the office. The Library is open from 9:00 A.M.-5:00 P.M., Monday through Friday.

9. The Institute conducts several workshops annually at its Center for Advanced Film Studies (Beverly Hills, California), including (1) a workshop on film making for teachers and producers; (2) a summer institute for the college teachers of humanities with interest in film (funded by the Rockefeller Foundation); (3) a workshop on documentaries. In addition, AFI offers 6 seminars per year on films for the local colleges (e.g., "Rediscovery Course," "Third World Series,") in Washington, D.C.

10. In cooperation with UNESCO, AFI has published *The Education of the Film-Maker: An International View* (Paris: UNESCO, 1975), which contains a chapter on Japan. Currently the Institute is engaged in a major publishing venture, the *American Film Institute Catalog of Feature Films in the U.S. 1893-1970*. So far volumes on the 1920s and the 1960s have been published. This comprehensive encyclopedia of movies in America contains information about East Asian films shown in the United States. In addition, AFI publishes *American Film* 10 times a

year, featuring occasional articles dealing with East Asian films. It also publishes *Factfile,* a series designed to provide reference information on films and television; the November 1977 issue dealt with the "Third World Cinema."

11. AFI is an associate member of CILECT (Centre International de Liaison des Ecoles de Cinéma et de Télévision in Brussels); and a member of the International Federation of Film Archivists.

H8 American Historical Association (AHA)

1. *400 A Street, S.E.*
   Washington, D.C. 20003
   544-2422

2. Organized in 1884; and incorporated by Congress in 1889.

3. John Hope Franklin, President
   Mack Thompson, Executive Director

4. The main office has about 20 staff members.

5. The AHA membership numbers about 15,000.

6. The AHA is a nonprofit, professional organization which endeavors to encourage and improve the quality of teaching and research in history and to promote the status and rights of historians at home and abroad. The association also attempts to enhance employment opportunities for historians through the *Employment Information Bulletin* and *Careers for Students of History.* Among the AHA prizes for historical research is the John K. Fairbank Prize in East Asian History which is offered in odd numbered years for an outstanding book on the history of China, Vietnam, Mongolia, Chinese Central Asia, Manchuria, Korea, or Japan (since the year 1800).

7. The AHA's Standing Committee on International Historical Activities has contact with Asian historians, often through work on the quinquennial Congress of the International Committee of Historical Sciences.

9. The association holds an annual meeting in late December; and the site varies (e.g., 1979 site: New York; 1980, Washington, D.C.).

10. *The American Historical Review* appears five times a year. One or more main articles on East Asian topics usually can be expected annually. In addition, reviews of books on pertinent subjects are included in every issue. The association publishes a valuable bibliography on current periodical literature on individual countries and regions. Entitled *Recently Published Articles,* it is published three times per year and cites over 15,000 references annually, including many from journals published abroad. The AHA also publishes a pamphlet series which includes titles on East Asian topics.

H9 American National Red Cross

1. *17th and D Streets, NW*
    Washington, D.C. 20006
    737-8300

2. 1881

3. Frank Stanton, Chairman
    George M. Elsey, President

4. It has a staff of over 500 in the Washington, D.C., area.

6. The Red Cross is a largely voluntary organization dedicated to the prevention and alleviation of human suffering caused by natural calamities or man-made disasters in the United States and abroad. The American Red Cross takes part in the League of Red Cross Societies, a worldwide federation, and in the International Committee of the Red Cross. Through these international bodies, it interacts with Red Cross societies of East Asian countries (e.g., Japan, South Korea).

7. The Office of International Services normally coordinates international activities for the American Red Cross. Dorothy Taaffe is Director of the Office (857-3591).

8. The National Headquarters Library has a number of resources in addition to its extensive archival and vertical file material (see entry B1). Among the items of potential interest to East Asian specialists are:
    American Red Cross Annual Reports 1900-1977 (bound vols.): These reports include information about financial and relief works provided by the American Red Cross around the world. There is no general index, but information can be found chronologically (e.g., the 1924 report includes information concerning relief work done in Japan in the aftermath of the 1923 earthquake in the Tokyo area);
    The History of the American National Red Cross (monograph series, 49 vols.): This series of monographs contains information pertaining to the activities of the American Red Cross prior to 1946. Among the volumes of interest to East Asia specialists are: *The American Red Cross During WW II in the Pacific Theater* (vol. 14); *The American Red Cross in China, Burma, and India 1942-46* (vol. 15); *Report of the China Famine Relief* (American Red Cross October 1920-September 1921); and *The Report of the American Red Cross Commission to China* (1929).
    In addition, the following periodical holdings of the library may also be of interest to East Asia students: *Red Cross Courier*, 1922-51; and *The American Red Cross Magazine*, 1912-20. These periodicals contain several listings on China, Japan, and Korea. *The International Review of the Red Cross* of the International Committee of the Red Cross can also be useful to researchers.
    The library is open to researchers from 8:30 A.M. to 4:45 P.M. Monday through Friday. Edna Moon is the librarian (857-3491); and

Rudy Clemen (857-3647) and Leon Gilbert (857-3459) handle collections on international affairs. Interlibrary loan and photocopying services are available.

9. The International Conference of the Red Cross meets once every 4 years at different sites around the world. In 1977 the conference was held in Bucharest, Rumania.

10. Point 8 above.

11. It is a member of the International Committee of the Red Cross and the League of Red Cross Societies.

H10 American Political Science Association (APSA)

1. *1527 New Hampshire Avenue, NW*
   Washington, D.C. 20036
   483-2512

2. 1903

3. Evron Kirkpatrick, Executive Director
   Walter E. Beach, Assistant Director

4. The APSA's main office has a staff of about 20.

5. The association has more than 17,000 dues-paying members, a majority of whom come from the academic community.

6. The APSA is a nonprofit, professional and scholarly organization which seeks to promote and improve the study and teaching of political science. Many APSA members specialize in international politics, comparative government and politics, and related fields. The association endeavors to realize its objectives largely through publications and conferences. In addition, it provides various services to members, including a job referral service.

9. The APSA hosts annual conferences, normally in early September, that include some panels dealing with aspects of East Asian politics and diplomacy. The annual convention also serves as a meeting place for those seeking jobs in the field and potential employers.

10. The *American Political Science Review* (quarterly) carries articles and book reviews in the field of East Asian studies. The *P S* , a quarterly news journal published by the APSA, carries newsworthy items not only from the United States but also from abroad. The APSA also publishes teaching materials and biographical directories.

H11 American Psychological Association (APA)

1. *1200 17th Street, NW*
   Washington, D.C. 20036
   833-7600

2.   1925

3.   Dr. M. Brewster Smith, President
     Dr. Charles A. Kiesler, Executive Officer

4.   Altogether about 200 professional, administrative, and supportive staff members are employed by the APA's central office.

5.   Nationwide, the association has more than 46,000 dues-paying members, representing most of the qualified psychologists in the United States.

6.   The APA's purpose is to advance psychology as a science, as a profession, and as a means of promoting human welfare. Specifically, it endeavors to promote research in psychology, improve the qualifications and competence of psychologists through high standards of ethical conduct, education, and achievement, and disseminate psychological knowledge through meetings and publications.

8.   The APA has a small research library which contains about 800 books on psychology, JSAS documents on microfiches, and bound volumes of the 18 journals APA has published. Other journals retained are primarily titles included in *Psychological Abstracts*. The library is available to scholars for on-site use by appointment. APA's Psychological Information Services' (PsycINFO) data base contains records published in the *Psychological Abstracts* journal (1967 to present). Each year PsychINFO scans materials from over 950 periodicals worldwide and about 1,500 books, technical reports, and monographs. The materials selected for inclusion in the data base are original, published contributions to the field of psychology. As of the beginning of 1978, 242,395 records were stored in the data base with annual additions of 25,000-27,000. For further information, call Lois Granick, Manager, PsychINFO Section.

9.   The APA holds annual conventions in different cities. It has also been an active participant in international psychological conferences (e.g., International Association of Applied Psychology, International Union of Psychological Science, etc.).

10. The APA publishes 18 psychological journals and a monthly newspaper. In addition, it produces *Psychological Abstracts* (monthly) which compiles summaries of the world's scientific literature in psychology and related disciplines. Triennial cumulative indexes to *Psychological Abstracts* are available for 1969-1971, 1972-1974, and 1975-1977.

H12 American Society of International Law

1.   *2223 Massachusetts Avenue, NW*
     Washington, D.C. 20008
     265-4313

2.   1906

3.   C. Clyde Ferguson, Jr., President
     Seymour J. Rubin, Executive Vice President and Executive Director

4. The office has a staff of 21.

5. There are approximately 5,600 members, including lawyers, educators, diplomats, government officials, and students in about 100 different countries.

6. The society is devoted to fostering the study of international law and seeks to encourage a greater role for law in international relations. Its programs include the organization of study groups on such topics as the problems of expanding trade with Communist China, the improvement of international trade, direct-broadcast satellites, the law of the seas, international environmental control, global energy management, and many others.

8. The society has a small library with emphasis on periodicals and books on international law.

9. An annual meeting is held in Washington, D.C., every April.

10. In addition to its quarterly journal, *American Journal of International Law,* the Society publishes a quarterly newsletter; bimonthly *International Legal Materials;* and the proceedings of its annual meeting, as well as books and occasional papers.

H13 American Sociological Association (ASA)

1. *1722 N Street, NW*
   Washington, D.C. 20036
   833-3410

2. 1905

3. Dr. Hubert M. Blalock, President
   Dr. Russell R. Dynes, Executive Officer

4. There are about 18 staff members in the ASA office.

5. 14,100 members nationwide.

6. The ASA was established in 1905 to further research and teaching in sociology. Membership includes scholars, professional social workers, and others, many of whom have research interests in or related to East Asia.

7. The Committee on World Sociology, chaired by David Wiley (Michigan State University), oversees various liaison groups for different regions of the world, including a liaison group for East Asia. The group's principal purpose is to develop a network of specialists having contacts in East Asian countries. The group is thus in a position to put scholars interested in East Asia in contact with other sociologists in the United States and abroad.

9. The annual convention of the ASA sometimes has sessions specifically dealing with East Asia. More often, the conventions are organized along topical, rather than geographic, lines; and papers relating to East Asia are likely to be scattered among various topical areas.

10. The official journal of the ASA is the *American Sociological Review* (bimonthly), which carries occasional articles relating to East Asia. In addition, the association publishes a number of other journals including *Contemporary Sociology: A Journal of Reviews* (bimonthly) devoted to extensive book reviews; *The American Sociologist* (quarterly); and *ASA FOOTNOTE* (9 times a year).

11. The ASA is a member of the International Sociological Association (ISA). The ISA has an executive committee and various research committees, on which American and East Asian sociologists often serve.

H14 Amnesty International, USA—Washington Office

1. *6 E Street, SE*
   Washington, D.C. 20003
   544-0200

2. Founded in London in 1961, the Washington Office was established in 1976.

3. Stephaine Grant, Director, Washington Office

4. The office has 5 paid staff members.

5. The organization has over 70,000 members in the United States.

6. Amnesty International is a worldwide human rights movement which works for the release of men and women imprisoned anywhere for their beliefs, color, ethnic origin, language, or religion, provided they have neither used nor advocated violence. Members of Amnesty International are divided into groups; each group is assigned to work for the release of three prisoners of conscience, whose rights and interests the group endeavors to defend. The group writes letters to the prisoners' countries, visit these countries' embassies, and works for the release—and, if desired, the emigration—of these prisoners. Members of the association disseminate information concerning their work through a variety of channels, including public talks and discussions.

9. The organization's working groups hold frequent meetings. Interested scholars should contact the local office to ascertain which groups may be working with prisoners in the East Asian countries.

10. The London and New York offices publish and distribute to members a bimonthly newsletter, *Amnesty Action,* and a seminannual bulletin entitled *Matchbox Quarterly.* Also available from the New York office are the organization's annual report and other publications, such as *Report of an Amnesty International Mission to the Republic of Korea, 27 March-9 April 1975* (1977).

H15 Arms Control Association (ACA)

1. *11 Dupont Circle, NW (Suite 900)*
   Washington, D.C. 20036
   797-6450

2. 1971

3. William H. Kincade, Executive Director

4. The office has 3 full-time staff members plus 1 student intern.

5. 600 members nationwide.

6. The Arms Control Association is a nonprofit, nonpartisan organization dedicated to promoting public understanding of the need for effective arms control and disarmament. It also seeks to promote world peace through a reduction of international tensions. Under a cooperative agreement, the ACA participates in a number of joint ventures with the Carnegie Endowment for International Peace.

9. The Association has sponsored special conferences on topics relating to disarmament and arms control. In September 1977, the ACA cosponsored with the Carnegie Endowment a conference at Talloires, France, on priorities for the U.N. Special Session on Disarmament in May-June 1978. The proceedings of the 1977 conference were published under the auspices of the Carnegie Endowment for International Peace: *Opportunities for Disarmament: A Preview of the 1978 United Nations Special Session on Disarmament* edited by Jane M. O. Sharp (1978).

10. *Arms Control Today* is the monthly newsletter published by ACA. It carries occasional articles on East Asian affairs such as "Chinese Modernization and U.S. Arms Sales" (September 1977).

H16 Asia Foundation—Washington Office

1. *2301 E Street, NW*
    Washington, D.C. 20037
    223-5268

2. 1954

3. Allen C. Choate, Representative, Washington, D.C.
    (Main office is located in San Francisco, California).

4. The Washington office has a staff of 2.

5. The function of the foundation's Washington office is to serve as a liaison with the government and the university research centers in the nation's capital. Requests for specific information should be directed to the foundation's main office: 550 Kearny Street, San Francisco, California 94108.

6. The Asia Foundation is a publicly supported, nonprofit, private organization headquartered in San Francisco. The foundation's goals are to help Asians develop human resources and institutions needed for open, just, and self-reliant societies; to facilitate regional cooperation among Asians; and to contribute to understanding between the peoples of Asia and the United States.
    The Asia Foundation receives funds for its programs from both the United States government and the private sector. It specializes in small

and medium-size grants (approximately 600 per year) to finance local projects in Asia, to provide training for Asians at home or abroad, or to make available specialized skills.

Most programs and projects financed in recent years are in the following fields: education; rural and urban community affairs; law and public administration; regional cooperation for Asian development; management, manpower, and the economic development; and publications, libraries, and the media. Its grant programs are complemented by the distribution of American books and journals to academic centers in Asia. Approximately 1 million books and journals are donated annually under the program; and more than 13 million books and journals have been sent to Asia under the *Books for Asia* program.

In addition, the Foundation awards grants to many leading professional societies in the United States to strengthen bonds with comparable groups in Asia. This support enables Asians to receive memberships in American societies and subscriptions to professional journals, to attend important conferences in the United States, or to complete and publish research papers.

The foundation periodically sponsors or cosponsors special programs, exhibits, workshops and symposia that help to develop American appreciation and understanding of Asian society, art, and culture. Support is also furnished by the foundation to certain private American organizations which provide orientation and related services to Asian visitors.

10.   The foundation publishes *The Asian Student* (a weekly newspaper) which is distributed to over 25,000 Asian students studying in the United States (free of charge) as well as to 5,000 other subscribers. Other publications of the foundation include: *Program Bulletin* (quarterly); *The Asia Foundation News* (bimonthly); *Asian Student Orientation Handbook;* and occasional papers on developmental and social change in Asian countries.

H17 Asia Society—Washington Center

1.   *1776 Massachusetts Avenue, NW*
        Washington, D.C. 20036
        234-4894

2.   1956 (The society's main office is located in New York City.)

3.   Robert W. Barnett, Director, Washington Center

4.   The Washington Center has a staff of 3.

5.   The society has over 2,300 members on the United States.

6.   The Asia Society is a nonprofit, nonpolitical, tax-exempt educational organization dedicated to the promotion of American understanding of Asia as well as meaningful trans-Pacific discourse. It is concerned with both the traditional arts and humanities and with contemporary social, political, economic, and cultural issues. Under the direction of Robert W. Barnett, former deputy assistant secretary of state for East Asian and Pacific Affairs, the society's Washington center has developed a program

of off-the-record sessions at which knowledgeable and influential Asians meet with small groups of Americans drawn from Washington's foreign affairs community. The Washington center also distributes a monthly calendar of lectures and other programs in the Washington area sponsored by the center, embassies, universities, country committees, and other groups concerned with Asia. Some 300-400 such events are held each year.

9. In addition to the occasional "off-the-record" sessions mentioned above, the Washington center serves as the secretariat for the annual "Williamsburg" conferences. These meetings, held on both sides of the Pacific, bring togther leading Americans and Asians to consider issues of common concern to the people of the Pacific region.

10. The principal publication of the society's Washington Center is the monthly *Calendar of Events* which lists important lectures and cultural events scheduled in the Washington area by various organizations concerned with Asia. It is indispensable for anyone wishing to keep abreast with the Asia-related cultural events in the Washington area. In addition to lectures, exhibitions, the monthly newsletter also carries information about various educational programs such as instruction in Asian languages, music, and dance sponsored by cultural organizations in the Washington area. In order to receive a free copy of the newsletter, interested scholars should request the Washington office to place their names on the mailing list.

H18 Asian-American Free Labor Institute (AAFLI) (AFL-CIO)

1. *815 Sixteenth Street, NW*
   Washington, D.C. 20006
   737-3000

2. 1968

3. George Meany, President
   Morris Paladino, Executive Director

4. The Institute has about 35 staff members.

6. The AAFLI was organized in 1968 to promote free labor unionism in Asia and to train Asian labor leaders in trade union techniques, basic economics, and democratic principles. To meet the educational needs of Asian trade unions, AAFLI has sponsored hundreds of educational projects in many countries of Asia, including seminars, workshops, and educational conferences.

   Through close cooperation with the host country's trade union, AAFLI helps plan and organize educational projects, and provides technical assistance in the form of audiovisual equipment and lectures from AFL-CIO affiliates. The Institute also helps unions in Asian countries to develop social and economic projects, such as credit unions and workers' health clinics to promote the welfare of union workers.

To provide Asian trade unionists with a broader exposure to trade union techniques and theories, AAFLI supports several programs which allow Asian labor leaders to visit and study in the United States for a semester at Harvard University and the University of Wisconsin. Frequently, the institute also provides international travel assistance to Asian trade unionists who plan to attend international labor conferences. The Federation of Korean Trade Unions (FKTU) has been an active participant and beneficiary of the AAFLI programs since 1968. More than 66 seminars sponsored by the AAFLI were held in South Korea from 1974 to 1976, drawing more than 4,100 participants. The FKTU has also received technical and financial assistance from the AAFLI in developing urgently needed trade union projects in South Korea, such as labor health clinics and mobile education units.

8.   The institute does not have its own library, but uses the AFL-CIO library which is housed in the same building. (See entry A4.)

9.   Through close cooperation with AFL-CIO affiliates, AAFLI has been able to tap the resources of some of America's major labor organizations. Under "Union-to-Union" programs, American trade union leaders and their Asian counterparts join in international conferences. A consortium of American unions in the metal trades attracted 24 union leaders from Japan, South Korea, Malaysia, and the Philippines to a conference on health and safety problems from workers in the electronics industry in Manila in 1975. In 1976, an Asian regional conference for transport workers was jointly sponsored by the International Transport Workers Federation and the Brotherhood of Railway and Airline Clerks. Twenty-three leaders from transport unions in Singapore, Thailand, Japan, Indonesia, and Malaysia attended the Singapore conference. In addition, AAFLI set up arrangements for Asian trade union leaders to attend the biennial AFL-CIO convention while the AFL-CIO's International Department has arranged annually for a AFL-CIO delegation's visit to Japan, Korea, and other Asian countries. In March 1978, an AFL-CIO delegation attended the 10th annual conference of the Japanese Confederation of Labor ("Dōmei") and exchanged views with the Dōmei leaders on the international economic situation, domestic economic conditions, and other economic and political developments that affected the union workers' interests. The delegation also held talks with the leaders of the General Council of Japanese Trade Unions ("Sōhyō"), the Federation of Independent Unions of Japan ("Chūritsu Rōren"), and the National Federation of Industrial Organizations ("Shinsanbetsu").

For further information about the AFL-CIO's International Department's activities, call or write to James Ellenberger, Director, International Department, AFL-CIO (637-5036).

10.   The AAFLI has published over 50 different pamphlets, manuals, and books for its own programs as well as those of cooperating unions. These publications have appeared in Bengali, English, Korean, Indonesian, Thai, and Turkish. Recent publications include: *Building Unions in Asia—Unique Task*; and *Asia: A Study in Emerging Unions*. The in-

stitute also publishes a monthly *Newsletter* which contains reports on projects and activities supported by the AAFLI. Copies of *Asian-American Free Labor Institute Progress Report 1977* are available free on request.

11.   American Federation of Labor—Congress of Industrial Organizations (AFL-CIO).

H19 Association of Asian-American Chambers of Commerce

1.   *769 National Press Building*
14th and F Streets, NW
Washington, D.C. 20045
Mail: P.O. Box 1933, Washington, D.C. 20013
638-7171

2.   1962

3.   Bernard B. Blazes, Acting President
K. Nakatsukasa, Executive Secretary
Dr. Edward von Rothkirch, Co-Executive Secretary

4.   The office has a staff of 6.

5.   The association's membership consists of 2,800 institutional and individual members here and in Asia.

6.   The primary objective of the association is to promote trade, tourism, and cultural relations between North American and non-Communist Asian countries by discussing problems of common concern with the business leaders of these Asian countries.

8.   The association has a small reference library with about 800 volumes on trade, business, and United States-East Asian relations. Outside researchers may use it by making prior arrangements with the office.

9.   Annual meeting is held alternately in the United States and Asia.

10.   *Asian-American Journal of Commerce* (quarterly) is published by the association. The association also publishes its newsletters 8 times a year.

H20 Carnegie Endowment for International Peace—Washington Office

1.   *11 Dupont Circle, NW*
Washington, D.C. 20036
797-6400

2.   1910

3.   Thomas L. Hughes, President

4.   Executive board and standing committee members plus program officers number about 45. There is an additional staff of 25.

6-7.   The Carnegie Endowment seeks to promote international peace by conducting its own programs of research, investigation, discussion, publication, and training in such fields as arms control, pre-crisis fact-finding, international law and organization, and United States foreign policy.

  The Carnegie Endowment for International Peace administers the International Law Program which is headed by Thomas M. Franck. "Face-to-Face," sponsored jointly by the Carnegie Endowment and the American Foreign Service Association, is a program designed to bring together government officials and private individuals to discuss foreign policy issues. The Arms Control Division is headed by William H. Kincade, the current director of the independent Arms Control Association (see entry H15).

9.   Periodic and irregular meetings are sponsored by the Washington office; scholars should check with each unit for details and accessibility.

10.   The Carnegie Endowment has recently sponsored or published the following books relating to East Asia: *China, Oil, and Asia: Conflict Ahead?* (1977) by Selig S. Harrison; and *Japan in Southeast Asia* (1976) by Raul S. Manglapus. In addition, it has produced a color videotape cassette entitled "Focus on China" as a part of its Focus Television Programs.

11.   The Carnegie Endowment cooperates with a number of organizations, such as the Arms Control Association, German Marshall Fund of the United States, and the American Foreign Service Association.

H21 Chinese Opera Society of Washington, D.C.

1.   *c/o Dr. George Yang*
  6625 Marywood Road
  Bethesda, Md. 20903
  (301) 686-1638 (Bertland Mao)

2.   1974

3.   Dr. Stanley Chuang, President
  Bertland Mao, Vice President

4.   The Opera Society's membership numbers about 50.

6.   The Chinese Opera Society of Washington, D.C., is a nonprofit organization established in 1974 to provide opportunities for nonprofessionals to perform the art of Chinese opera before American audiences in the hope of promoting cultural understanding between Americans and Chinese.

  The society performs at least twice a year; 3 of its most recent productions were *White Serpent* (presented at the University of Maryland auditorium in September 1977); and *Conqueror of Daechu* and *Butterfly Fantasy* (at the same auditorium in June 1978).

9.   The society holds weekly practices. For further information, call Bertland Mao (301/686-1638).

10. The society does not issue a publication of its own; however, it has videotapes of its productions and performances (e.g., *White Serpent*). For further information call Bertland Mao (686-1638).

H22 Chinese-English Translation Assistance Group (CETA)

1. *9811 Connecticut Avenue*
   Kensington, Md. 20795
   (301) 946-7007

2. 1971

3. J. Mathias, Executive Secretary

4. CETA has a staff of 3 plus several part-time volunteers.

6. CETA is a voluntary association of language specialists from United States government agencies (e.g. State, Commerce, Defense, National Science Foundation, Library of Congress, etc.) and some 70 universities and institutions in the United States and abroad. One of CETA's major functions is to serve as a clearinghouse for information relating to dictionary building, machine translation, and computer application to Chinese-language study that would be of interest to scholars working on China.

   Currently CETA's principal project is improvement of a computer-stored and printed Chinese-English dictionary of over 100,000 general terms. Efforts are also underway to enlarge and refine existing companion collections of more than 10,000 colloquial expressions and of over 500,000 scientific and technical terms.

9. Occasionally, CETA sponsors China seminars. For instance, it sponsored a seminar on "The Climate for Communication and Exchange with China," which was held at the Foreign Service Institute of the U.S. State Department on February 20, 1978. CETA-sponsored conferences are open to the public. For further information, call (301) 946-7007.

10. CETA's recent publications include: *Compilation of Chinese Dictionaries in All Languages* (New Haven: Yale University Far Eastern Publication, 1974). Copies of *CETA Bulletin* (irregular) may be obtained free upon request.

H23 Committee for a Free China

1. *1101 Connecticut Ave., NW (Suite 705)*
   Washington, D.C. 20036
   457-0867

2. 1972

3. Dr. Walter H. Judd, President
   Dr. Charles A. Moser, Treasurer

4.   The committee's policies are made by the 16-member Board of Directors.

5.   The committee's activities are supported by about 30,000 members and contributors.

6.   The committee is concerned with the gathering and dissemination of information relating to China and Taiwan and hopes to promote freedom and human rights for the Chinese people. Many of its supporters were formerly members of the Committee of One Million on U.S.-China Relations which opposed United Nations representation for the People's Republic of China. It is concerned with the future of United States relations with Peking and Taipei.

9.   The committee sponsors seminars and conference on China. For example, it sponsored a conference on "The United States and China after MAO" in cooperation with 21 other organizations on November 30, 1976.

10. The committee publishes *China Report* (several times a year). Occasionally, it also publishes conference reports, such as *The United States and China After Mao: A Summary* (1976) and *Source Book: The United States and China after Mao* (1976).

East Asian Ethnic Churches and Religious Organizations For a list of East Asian ethnic churches and religious organizations in the Washington area, see Appendix III.

East Asian Ethnic Organizations, and Social Recreational Clubs For a list, see Appendix IV.

H24 East-West Trade Council

1.   *1700 Pennsylvania Avenue, NW (Suite 670)*
     Washington, D.C. 20006
     393-6240

2.   1972

3.   Max N. Berry, Executive Director

4.   The council has 4 staff members.

5.   There are currently about 400 members, including representatives of American business, trade associations, government agencies, and educational institutions interested in East-West trade.

6.   The East-West Trade Council is a nonprofit organization financed solely by membership dues and contributions. It is the oldest United States trade association specializing in East-West trade. The council works closely with officials of the executive and legislative branches of the

federal government and with foreign governments and business leaders to broaden and improve trade relations between the United States and the Communist countries, including the People's Republic of China.

9. EWTC sponsors frequent symposia on East-West trade and other meetings relating to trip reports by delegations returning from Communist countries. Information about these meetings and symposia can be obtained from the office of the EWTC.

10. *The East-West Trade Council Newsletter* is published twice a month; it is available to anyone on a subscription basis.

H25 Foreign Student Service Council of Greater Washington (FSSC)

1. *1623 Belmont Street, NW*
   Washington, D.C. 20009
   232-4979

2. 1957

3. James W. Symington, Chairman, Board of Directors

4. The office has a staff of 4 plus volunteers and interns.

6. The FSSC is a nonprofit educational community service organization devoted exclusively to the needs of university foreign students (local and transient). Its programs are designed to supplement the on-campus experience of students and to achieve better understanding of American life. Its staff and volunteers provide home hospitality, sightseeing, seminars, and other services. Two weeks advance notice (plus $2.00 registration fee) is required for home hospitality; and the foreign student needs to provide such relevant information as his or her university, degrees sought, major field of interest, time, date, and means of arrival in Washington. More than 6,000 foreign students are the beneficiaries of services provided by FSSC every year.

9. FSSC conducts periodic seminars for selected foreign students on the United States government and current affairs.

H26 Ikebana International, Inc.—Washington, D.C., Chapter

1. *P.O. Box 9663*
   Washington, D.C. 20016
   (703) 536-9275

2. 1956 in Washington, D.C.

3. Betty Taylor, President

5. The Washington Chapter membership numbers about 400.

6. Ikebana International is a nonprofit cultural organization which seeks to promote an appreciation for the Japanese art of flower arrangement. The

Washington chapter sponsors Ikebana exhibitions and demonstrations as well as lectures on Japanese flower arrangement by such internationally recognized Ikebana masters as Meikof Kasuya, the headmaster of the Ichiyo School of Ikebana in Japan.

9. Monthly workshops plus 3 program meetings are held annually.

10. A quarterly *Ikebana* (published by Ikebana International, Inc., Tokyo, Japan) is distributed to the membership.

11. Ikebana International, Inc., Tokyo, Japan.

H27 International Student House

1. *1825 R Street, NW*
   Washington, D.C. 20009
   232-4007

2. 1936

3. Jerrold Scoutt, Jr., President
   Paul Feys, Executive Director

4. ISH office has a staff of 4.

5. 400 members.

6. International Student House is a private, nonprofit organization dedicated to the promotion of international understanding and goodwill by way of providing residences to international students studying at local universities. As of April 1978, there were 60 resident students including 3 Japanese, 3 Korean, and 1 Chinese. Scholars and researchers from foreign countries may also apply for residence while doing research in Washington, D.C. International Student House facilities are frequently utilized by other civic organizations for seminars, conferences, and cultural exhibits. *ISH Monthly Calendar of Events* lists the schedule of forthcoming meetings.

H28 International Visitors Information Service (IVIS)

1. *801 19th Street, NW*
   Washington, D.C. 20006
   872-8747

2. 1961

3. Nancy S. McCloskey, Executive Director

4. The office has a staff of 6, including the executive director.

6. IVIS is a private, nonprofit community organization that offers a diversified program of services to international visitors to the Washington Metropolitan Area. Seventy-eight local organizations sharing the concern

for the welfare of international visitors join with IVIS to form the IVIS Council, and its programs are operated with the support of over 1,200 volunteers living in the Washington area.

IVIS multilingual volunteers and staff at the Information and Reception Center (open from 9:00 A.M.-5:00 P.M. Monday through Friday) provide visitors with a variety of information pertaining to sightseeing, accommodations, restaurants, bilingual medical assistance, and religious services. The IVIS also maintains an information center at Union Station in Washington, D.C., and at Dulles International Airport (open from 12:00 noon to 8:00 P.M., 7 days a week).

IVIS also provides the following programs free of charge: (1) "IVIS Language Bank program" provides telephone language assistance in more than 45 languages, 7 days a week, 24 hours a day (call 872-8747); (2) "home hospitality program" arranges for visitors to visit briefly with host families to get acquainted with American family life; (3) multilingual "escort service" provides non-English speaking visitors with escorting services for sightseeing, shopping, professional, or medical appointments; and, (4) "international conference service program" provides an experienced corps of multilingual volunteers to assist at international conferences in the Washington area with registration, information, interpreting, and escorts. Requests for visits with the host family and multilingual escort service must be made in person in the IVIS office at least 48 hours in advance.

Periodically, IVIS also assists with group projects which require special planning and coordination. For example, on 3 occasions, IVIS has arranged the Washington program of visiting delegations from the People's Republic of China at the request of the National Committee on U.S.-China Relations, Inc. More recently, Chinese-speaking IVIS volunteers provided language assistance to the Wushu Martial Arts Troupe and accompanied them on sight-seeing excursions as well as home visits.

10. Recent IVIS publications include: *Organizations Serving International Visitors in the National Capital Area* (1973); and *Traveler Information Needs* (prepared for U.S. Department of Transportation, 1977). Copies of IVIS brochures are available free upon request.

11. Meridian House International is its parent organization (entry H34).

H29 Japan-America Society of Washington

1. *1302 18th Street, NW (Suite 704)*
    Washington, D.C. 20036
    223-1772

2. 1957

3. U. Alexis Johnson, President
    Arthur R. Dornheim, Executive Secretary

4. The Washington office has 2 staff members.

5. About 900 individual and 25 corporate members.

6. The Japan-America Society of Washington was established in 1957 by Americans and Japanese who desired to promote better understanding of each other's culture and way of life. It is a nonprofit, nonpolitical organization dedicated to broad cultural and educational objectives. The society's programs include lectures, films, other cultural events and social meetings, and a Japanese-language training program. It sponsors each spring a community-wide Japan Bazaar and festival. The society has the support of both the Japanese Embassy and the U.S. Department of State.

8. The society has a small library containing about 600 volumes with emphasis on Japanese culture, reference works, and dictionaries. Borrowing privileges are available to members only; however, researchers may use the facilities by appointment.

9. The society's annual meeting is normally held in October.

10. The *Bulletin of the Japan-America Society of Washington* is published by the society from 6 to 8 times per year.

H30 Japan Foundation—Washington Office

1. *Suite 430, Watergate Office Building*
   600 New Hampshire Avenue, NW
   Washington, D.C. 20037
   965-4313

2. 1972

3. Hidemi Kon, President
   Masaki Kodama, Director, Washington Office

4. The Washington office has a staff of 5. (The foundation's main headquarters is located in Tokyo.)

6. The Japan Foundation was established by the Japanese government in 1972 as a special corporation with the objective of promoting international cultural exchanges and mutual understanding between Japan and other countries. In order to attain these objectives, the foundation operates the following programs: (1) an exchange of scholars, writers, artists, and other professionals; (2) support for Japanese studies and language programs; (3) assistance to performing arts and cultural exhibitions; (4) the preparation and distribution of materials relating to Japanese culture abroad; and, (5) research, planning, and coordination of international cultural exchange programs. The foundation's operating budget for fiscal 1978 (excluding administrative expenditures) was about $14 million.

   For United States nationals, the Japan Foundation offers two types of fellowships: Professional Fellowships and Dissertation Fellowships. The number of Professional Fellowships available in 1979-1980 will be about 15 long-term fellowships and 5 for a shorter duration, whereas the dissertation fellowships available for the same fiscal year will be approximately 15.

   In addition to the fellowship programs, the foundation administers

Institutional Project Support Programs designed to assist in the study and understanding of Japanese culture and society in the United States. Any educational, cultural, or public affairs organization classified as a nonprofit institution is eligible to apply. The principal types of Institutional Project Support grants include: (1) visiting professorships—to enable Japanese professors and artists to teach or do research in American institutions of higher learning; (2) a staff expansion program for academic institutions in the United States; (3) a research program on Japan in the United States; (4) a conference/summer institute program; (5) an education-abroad program (e.g., language training in Japan); (6) a library support program; (7) a teaching-material program; and, (8) an audiovisual-material support program.

Awards are made once a year. Program announcements as well as application forms may be obtained from the Washington Office of the Japan Foundation or the nearest Consulate-General of Japan.

The foundation's operations in the United States are assisted by a 15-member American Advisory Committee, which is divided into 3 subcommittees: the Subcommittee for Professional Fellowships; the Subcommittee for Dissertation Fellowships; and the Subcommittee for Institutional Project Support Programs.

8. The Washington office has a small library which contains about 2,000 volumes (mostly Japanese-language materials), including *Nihon Bunkashi Taikei* (35 vols.); *Nihon Koten Bungaku Zenshū* (51 vols.); and Shogakkan (ed.), *Nihon no Rekishi* (32 vols.). It also has about 50 films and video cassettes on Japanese culture. On-site use of the library materials is available to serious scholars. Films (16 mm) and video cassettes may be borrowed without charge by academic institutions, museums, and public service groups. A listing of these films and cassettes is available on request.

9. The Japan Foundation sponsors monthly lectures on Japan in Washington, D.C. Among the guest lecturers have been Frank Gibney, Eleanor Kerkham, Nathaniel Thayer, Gerald L. Curtis, Robert Scalapino, and Ezra Vogel. The monthly lectures are free and open to the public. For information about scheduled lectures, call 965-4313.

10. The foundation has an active publication program. Its principal organ is *The Japan Foundation Newsletter* (bimonthly) which carries useful information on the foundation activities as well as Japanese studies programs in the United States and abroad. It has also published an ongoing series of reference works such as *An Introductory Bibliography for Japanese Studies* and *Current Contents of Academic Journals in Japan*, and monographs on Japanese history, literature, arts and architecture, law, and economy.

H31 Japanese-American Citizens League (JACL)—Washington Office

1. *1730 Rhode Island Avenue, NW*
    Washington, D.C. 20036
    223-1240

2. 1930

3. Karl K. Nobuyuki, National Executive Director
    Ronald K. Ikejiri, Washington Representative

4. The Washington office has a staff of 2.

5. The league has approximately 31,000 members comprising 105 chapters, located from coast to coast.

6. JACL is primarily a national human and civil-rights organization devoted to advancing the welfare of persons of Japanese ancestry in the United States. The league serves its membership through representation of their interests at federal and state levels by way of conducting research and educational, cultural, and legislative programs and activities. It advocates equal employment opportunities for Japanese-Americans, the preservation of their cultural heritage, and the strengthening of bonds between the generations of Japanese-Americans.

    The JAL-JACL Cultural Heritage Fellowship program provides 8 weeks of study and travel in Japan (all expenses paid) for JACL members and their families. In addition, it also offers a JACL National Scholarship program for the league members and their families. Annually, 15 Freshman Scholarships and 4 Graduate/Collegiate Scholarships are awarded under the program.

9. JACL holds biennial national conventions. Its 26th Biennial Convention will be held in San Francisco in July 1980.

10. The league publishes a weekly *Pacific Citizen*. Copies of various brochures published by JACL, including *Better Americans in a Greater America*, are available free upon request.

H32 Korean Relief, Inc.

1. *1500 Franklin Street, NE*
    Washington, D.C. 20018
    Mail to: P.O. Box 2151, Washington, D.C. 20013
    526-4420

2. 1961

3. Rev. Aloysius Schwartz, Director
    William J. Vita, Managing Director

4. The Washington office has 4 staff members.

6. Korean Relief is a nonsectarian, nonprofit, philanthropic organization dedicated to the relief of orphans, the handicapped, and needy children in South Korea. Its activities are supported largely by contributions raised in the United States and partly by subsidies provided by the South Korean government. At present, its operations in South Korea involve the following: 3 boys' towns (2 in Pusan and 1 in Seoul); 2 girls' towns (1 in Seoul and the other in Pusan); a general hospital and tuberculosis sanitarium in Pusan; and several neighborhood dispensaries. Through

these programs, Korean Relief provides home care and educational programs to more than 3,000 Korean orphans and medical treatment to several hundred Koreans daily.

10. Copies of brochures entitled *Korean Relief Programs* and *Your Will . . . A Final Expression of Concern for the Poor and Needy* can be obtained free on request.

H33 Korean Scholarship Foundation in America

1. *P.O. Box 50005*
   F Street Station
   Washington, D.C. 20004
   (301) 460-8512

2. 1968

3. Dr. Yo Taik Song, President
   Dr. John D. Yun, Chairman, Board of Trustees

4. A 5-member Executive Council of the Board of Trustees administers the operations of the foundation.

6. The Korean Scholarship Foundation in America is a nonprofit, private organization, which was established in 1968 to provide financial assistance to the needy Korean or Korean-American students studying in the higher institutions of education in the United States. Annually, it provides about 10 scholarships to these students, each worth about $500. In addition to the scholarship program, the foundation is also dedicated to the promotion of cultural exchanges between the United States and the Republic of Korea. To achieve these basic objectives, the foundation sponsors fund-raising activities as well as cultural events, such as the tour of the Korean National Symphony Orchestra in the United States in January 1979.

10. The foundation publishes a semiannual *KSFA NEWS (Changhakhoe Hoebo)* in the Korean language. Complimentary copies can be obtained by writing to the foundation.

H34 Meridian House International (MHI)

1. *1630 Crescent Place, NW*
   Washington, D.C. 20009
   667-6800

2. 1960

3. Joseph John Jova, President

4. The MHI has a staff of 80.

6. Meridian House International is a nonprofit organization devoted to increasing international understanding and specializing in services to

international visitors to the United States. It endeavors to improve reception, orientation, and hospitality services for the visitors from abroad who arrive in the nation's capital each year and for those who travel throughout the United States.

In collaboration with other cultural organizations, such as the National Endowments for the Humanities and the Arts, MHI sponsors educational and cultural programs. Meridian House is currently sponsoring a national symposium on *Mexico Today*. In the spring of 1979 it will cosponsor an International Symposium on *Japan Today*.

Meridian House International also provides leadership, financial, and administrative services to:

(1) Visitor Program Service (VPS) designs and administers professional programs of study, observation, and travel throughout the United States for officially sponsored visitors from abroad. It also conducts seminars for the U.S. State Department and privately sponsored groups. VPS is located at 1776 Massachusetts Avenue, NW (452-0606).

(2) Washington International Center (WIC) conducts orientation programs and seminars on contemporary American society for United States government-sponsored grantees prior to their study at United States colleges and universities. The WIC staff is assisted by a corps of trained volunteers (332-1025).

(3) International Visitors Information Service (IVIS) assists tourists and official visitors to the nation's capital at 3 reception centers: 801 19th Street, NW; the National Visitors' Center; and Dulles International Airport. IVIS volunteers offer escort-interpreting, information, home hospitality, and language assistance in 48 languages. Programs for corporate visitors from abroad are also arranged (872-8747).

(4) The Hospitality and Information Service (THIS) assists foreign diplomats and their families in adapting to life in Washington. Volunteers welcome each newly arrived diplomatic family, and provide information, guidance, hospitality, and a variety of special activities to all levels of the diplomatic corps (232-3002).

Meridian House's Washington International Center conducts seminars once a month in cooperation with the Japanese Productivity Center. This program of training Japanese business leaders and technical scientists has been operating since 1950. Through this program, the Japanese people have an opportunity to travel throughout the United States and discuss their observations of American culture with economists, sociologists, and the like.

For the past 19 years, Washington International Center has also been holding an Annual Conference for Japanese Fulbright scholars.

H35 National Association for Foreign Students Affairs (NAFSA)

1. *1860 19th Street, NW*
   Washington, D.C. 20009
   462-4811

2. 1948

3. Cassandra Pyle, President (1978-79)
   Hugh M. Jenkins, Executive Vice President

4. The main office has 18 staff members.

5. NAFSA membership numbers about 2,600, one-half of which is institutional and the other half, individuals.

6. NAFSA was founded in 1948 with the cooperation of academic institutions and public and private agencies to further the knowledge and competence of persons concerned with international educational interchange in an effort to assure maximum benefits for individuals and institutions involved.

    The association serves as a source of professional training, as a guide to standards of performance, and as a spokesman for international educational exchange programs in governmental and educational circles. To achieve these ends, NAFSA provides professional training and information through national and regional conferences, workshops, publications, and consultations. It also supports research and developmental projects.

7. NAFSA has five major national commissions: Commission on Information Services; Commission on Liaison; Commission on Policy and Practice; Commission of Professional Development; and Commission on Representation.

8. The Association has a small library with an emphasis on international student affairs which may be used by researchers with prior arrangement with the office.

9. The national communications network of NAFSA operates through 12 geographic regions, which hold annual conferences as well as frequent workshops on specialized topics, such as credentials evaluation, immigration, and foreign-student affairs. As of 1978, there were over 203,000 foreign students studying in the United States, including 7,160 from Japan, 12,100 from Taiwan, and 3,630 from South Korea.

10. The *NAFSA Newsletter* is published monthly from October through June. In odd-numbered years, it also publishes *The NAFSA Directory*. In addition, it publishes a number of reference guides on foreign-student affairs, such as *Adviser's Manual of Federal Regulations Affecting Foreign Students and Scholars, A Guide to the Admission of Foreign Students,* and *A Guide for the Education of Foreign Students.* NAFSA also has several films on foreign-student organizations which may be loaned free of charge to educational institutions. At least 3 weeks advance notice is required.

H36 National Council for Community Services to International Visitors (COSERV)

1. *1630 Crescent Place, NW*
    Washington, D.C. 20009
    332-1028

2. 1961

3.   Robert A. Aylward, Executive Director

4.   The office has a staff of 4.

5.   The council's membership consists of 94 community organizations and about 39 national visitors' programming agencies.

6.   COSERV, a nonprofit organization, was established in 1961. Its purpose is to develop and coordinate services for visitors in the United States on short-term international exchange and training programs. COSERV seeks to encourage effective coordination between national agencies that send international visitors across the country and local organizations that receive these visitors in their communities.

9.   COSERV conducts annual regional conferences, triennial national conferences, and frequent seminars and workshops on topics relating to international visitors' service programs. Interested scholars should contact the COSERV office for further information.

10. In addition to its quarterly publication, *COSERV Newsletter Across the USA*, it has published *National Directory of Community Organizations Serving Short-Term International Visitors; Handbook for Communities Serving International Visitors;* and *Guide for Volunteer Hosts.*

11. Meridian House International.

H37   National Council for U.S.-China Trade

1.   *1050 17th Street, NW (Suite 350)*
     Washington, D.C. 20036
     331-0290

2.   1973

3.   John C. Brizendine, Chairman
     Christopher H. Phillips, President

4.   There are approximately 31 staff members in the Washington office and one representative in Hong Kong.

5.   Approximately 445 large and small United States firms are members.

6.   The council is a private, nonprofit organization (financed by membership dues) devoted to the promotion of trade with the People's Republic of China. It emphasizes practical assistance to United States firms interested in trading with China.
     Among its various functions, the council acts as host to Chinese trade officials visiting the United States; sponsors visits of commercial groups from China to United States firms and vice versa; represents the interests of companies involved in trade with the PRC to both American and Chinese authorities; serves as a contact point for reciprocal exhibitions in the two countries; and provides an extensive range of services related to doing business with China such as business advisory services (e.g., market evaluation and prospects) and comprehensive translation services in modern simplified Chinese. Brochures, reports, dialogue for slide

and film presentations, business cards, and other items have been translated for firms in a variety of fields.

The council has special rapport with China's foreign trade agencies. Its recognized counterpart in Peking is the China Council for the Promotion of International Trade (CCPIT).

8. The council has a reference library to serve the needs of its members. Included among the library's holdings are: a comprehensive collection of Chinese export catalogs; market studies on most aspects of China's economy; current files on all product areas relating to trade with the PRC; monthly Sino-U.S. trade statistics; and trip reports by visitors to China. Although its holdings may not exceed 500 volumes, its vertical file collection of clippings and papers is very extensive (i.e., 75 linear feet). On-site use of these materials by serious scholars may be arranged through the council.

9. The council sponsors conferences throughout the United States on the China trade for members and other businessmen, sometimes in cooperation with local, trade-oriented organizations. Recently, the council has organized national conferences on China's petroleum, agriculture, and mining and construction industries in Houston, Saint Louis, and Denver, respectively. Also, briefing sessions for trade delegations and orientation seminars for importers and participants in the Canton Trade Fair are frequently hosted by the council.

10. The council publishes *The China Business Review* (bimonthly). In addition, it has published a number of special reference materials relating to China, such as the *Directory of Foreign Trade Exhibitions in the PRC* (1977); *Directory of Scientific Research Institutes in the People's Republic of China* (1977); *Directory of US Importers of Chinese Products* (1977); and market surveys on *China's Petroleum, China's Agriculture,* and *China's Mining and Construction Industries.*

H38 National Education Association (NEA)

1. *1201 16th Street, NW*
    Washington, D.C. 20036
    833-4000

2. 1857

3. Terry Herndon, Executive Director (833-4303)

4. Professional, administrative, and support staff totals 600.

5. NEA membership consists of over 1.8 million teachers in the United States.

6-7. International programs of the association are coordinated by the Committee on International Relations (Braulio Alonso, Chairman, 833-4105). NEA maintains cooperative relationships with teachers' organizations around the world. The only East Asian country with which NEA maintains a close association is Japan. NEA has an annual exchange program with its Japanese counterpart, the Japan Teachers Union ("Nikkyōso").

11. NEA is an active member of the World Confederation of Organizations of the Teaching Profession.

H39 National Geographic Society

1. *17th and M Streets, NW*
   Washington, D.C. 20036
   857-7000

2. 1888

3. Robert E. Doyle, President

4. The Washington headquarters and the Membership Center Building in Gaithersburg, Md., have a staff of more than 2,000.

5. A total of 10,000,000 persons belong to the society.

6. The society sponsors expeditions and research in geography, natural history, archeology, astronomy, ethnology, and oceanography. It sends writers and photographers throughout the world and disseminates this information in magazines, maps, books, monographs, lectures, filmstrips, records, and media services. To encourage exploration, to promote scientific advances, and to recognize outstanding service to geography, the society presents medals, awards, and prizes for exceptional achievement. In Explorers Hall, at the society's headquarters, visitors can view exhibits and films on a variety of subjects. The hall is open free to the public from 9:00 A.M. to 6:00 P.M. Mondays through Fridays, 9:00 A.M. to 5:00 P.M. Saturdays and holidays, and 10:00 A.M. to 5:00 P.M. Sundays.

7. The maps and still-photo collections of the society are closed to outsiders.

8. The society's library is described in the Libraries section (see entry A32).

9. Weekly illustrated lectures on geography, science, and exploration are held from October to March at Constitution Hall. They are open to members only. For information and a schedule call 857-7700.

10. The society publishes the famous monthly *National Geographic* and *National Geographic WORLD;* the latter, a monthly magazine for childred 8 and older. Among dozens of other National Geographic publications are nature, history, and science books, an atlas of the world, "books for young explorers," 12- and 16-inch physical globes, and a mural map of the world. National Geographic articles published in 1977 and early 1978 of special interest to scholars included "Japan's Warriors of the Wind," April 1977; "Japan's Amazing Island Sea," December 1977; and "China's Incredible Find," April 1978.

H40 National Strategy Information Center, Inc. (NSIC)

1. *1730 Rhode Island Avenue, NW (Suite 601)*
   Washington, D.C. 20036
   296-6406

2.   1962

3.   Frank R. Barnett, President
      Sven Kraemer, Program Director

4.   NSIC Washington office has a staff of 4. (Its main headquarters are located in New York.)

6.   The National Strategy Information Center is a nonprofit, nonpartisan, tax-exempt organization established in 1962 to conduct educational programs in national security affairs. NSIC seeks to encourage civil-military partnerships in its educational efforts, for it believes that an informed public is vital to the survival of democratic political systems. NSIC carries out its program largely through sponsoring seminars, conferences, and publications.

9.   The center has also sponsored: (1) seminars and summer institutes on "National Security Education" for young scholars; (2) "policy workshops" on resource strategy, geopolitics, military reform, and comparative defense budgets; and, (3) "defense-innovation" conferences. For information concerning the NSIC schedule of events, contact the center's Washington office.

10.   NSIC publishes two important series: (1) Agenda Papers; and, (2) Strategy Papers. The first are short papers written to stimulate discussion of important United States domestic and foreign policy issues, whereas the Strategy Papers are monographs on foreign and defense policy issues. Among recent titles of value to East Asian specialists are: *The Sino-Soviet Confrontation: Implications for the Future* by Harold C. Hinton (1976); *The People's Liberation Army: Communist China's Armed Forces* by Angus Fraser (1973); and *The Asian Alliance: Japan and United States Policy* by Franz Michael and Gaston J. Sigur (1972).

H41 Overseas Writers

1.   *National Press Building (Room 1029)*
      14th and F Streets, NW
      Washington, D.C. 20045
      737-2934

2.   1921

3.   William Beecher, President

5.   The association has about 230 members.

6.   This is an organization of American and foreign correspondents with overseas experiences. The association can put researchers in touch with members currently working in the Washington area. For foreign correspondents from Japan, South Korea, and Taiwan, operating in the nation's capital, see Appendix 1. Most of their offices are located in the National Press Building.

10.   There is some overlapping of membership between this organization and the Department of State Correspondents Association, which is composed

of media representatives covering the United States Department of State (632-2454).

Potomac-Asia Communications, Inc. See entry N3.

H42 Society for International Development (SID)—Washington Office

1. *1346 Connecticut Avenue, NW*
   Washington, D.C. 20036
   296-3810

2. 1957

3. Robert Van Haefton, President, Washington Chapter.

5. The membership of the society now exceeds 6,000 in 134 countries and consists mainly of persons engaged in programs of global development. The Washington Chapter has a membership of about 1,000.

6. The SID is an international, nonprofit, educational and scientific organization. Its purpose is to provide a forum for the exchange of ideas, facts, and experiences among all persons professionally concerned with the vital problems of economic and social development in modernizing societies. The society has endorsed the strategy of the United Nations for the Second Development Decade and is committed to promoting its implementation. To advance its goals, the SID publishes a professional journal and a bimonthly survey, sponsors membership conferences dealing with a cluster of important issues, and seeks to foster intellectual cooperation among SID members. Since 1971, the SID's Washington chapter has sponsored a forum called "China Round Table" (See item 9 below).

9. Worldwide and regional membership conferences are held on an annual basis. The Washington chapter of the SID has sponsored "China Round Table" which meets once a month to discuss various topics relating to social, economic, and political developments of the People's Republic of China. It is chaired by Dr. Carroll K. Shaw. Usually, it meets at the Empress Restaurant, 1018 Vermont Avenue, NW, during the lunch hours (12:00-2:00 P.M.). Among the guest speakers has been former Japanese Ambassador to China, Heishiro Ogawa, whose topic was "New Developments in Sino-Japanese Relations." Scholars wishing to attend the monthly meeting should call (301) 598-6284.

10. The SID publishes *International Development Review* (quarterly) and *Survey of International Development* (bimonthly).

H43 Sumi-e Society of America, Inc.—Washington Area Chapter

1. *1341 Woodside Drive*
   McLean, Va. 22101
   (703) 893-4522

2. 1963 in New York

3. Resly Reis, National President
    Lilian Kyle and Shirley Kanode, Co-chairwomen, Washington Area Chapter

5. Total membership of the society is about 250 nationwide, 100 in the Washington area.

6. The Sumi-e Society is a nonprofit cultural organization dedicated to fostering and encouraging an appreciation of Oriental brush painting and the technique used in this art form, and to serving as a cultural bridge between East and West. The society sponsors exhibitions of *sumi-e* products at public and private galleries and furnishes information to individuals desiring to gain knowledge of this art. In addition to exhibitions (once or twice per year), the society's Washington Area Chapter sponsors workshops directed by notable Oriental brush painters from East Asia and the United States.

9. The society's annual meeting is usually held in the spring.

10. The *Sumi-e Notes* (quarterly) is published by the society's main headquarters in New York. For further information, call Ann O'Connell (703) 893-4522, the society's immediate past president.

H44 Tibet Society—Washington, D.C., Chapter

1. *3331 Buehler Court*
    Olney, Md. 20832

2. 1975

3. Dr. Robert J. Taylor, President
    William J. Lavery, Secretary-Treasurer (301) 344-7882

6. The Tibet Society is a nonprofit organization dedicated to the study and preservation of Tibetan civilization. The local chapter's activities consist of lectures, dinner meetings, field trips, and the like. Numerous Tibetan and Western scholars have been invited to speak to the local membership on such topics as Buddhism, Tibetan art, language, and culture. Local chapter members have taken field trips to the New York/New Jersey area to become acquainted with Tibetan resources there.

9. Frequent lectures and dinner meetings, plus annual events such as the celebration of the Tibetan New Year, receive special attention by local members.

10. *The Tibet Society Bulletin,* published once or twice annually is distributed to all members. Produced by the society's national headquarters, it is the first Western periodical devoted to Tibetan civilization.

11. The Washington, D.C., chapter is a part of the Tibet Society, Inc., Goodbody Hall 101, Indiana University, Bloomington, Indiana 47401.

H45 U.S.-China People's Friendship Association—Washington, D.C., Chapter

1. *11402 Newport Mill Road*
   Wheaton, Md. 20902
   (301) 434-7459
   Mail to: P.O. Box 40503 Palisades Station, Washington, D.C. 20016

2. 1972

3. Mary Chandler, Coordinator   *(301) 946-8048*

4. Approximately 350 in the Washington area.

6. The association is an organization dedicated to the improvement of relations and communications between the United States and the People's Republic of China. To do this, it sponsors seminars, panel discussions, lectures, and films. In addition, it also organizes group tours of the PRC in cooperation with the PRC Liaison Office in Washington and China International Travel Service. Several different types of tours (ranging from 14 days to 45 days) are available for those interested in visiting China. It has a good working relationship with the PRC in arranging group tours for the Americans.

8. It has a film library which contains about 12 Chinese films plus additional films readily available from its sister chapters for loan. Anyone interested in renting the films should contact Joe Weichbrodt (301) 434-7459. Also, a large number of slides produced by the association members who have visited the PRC are available.

10. The national organization's newsletter, *New China*, is distributed among the local chapter members 4 times per year.

11. The national office of U.S.-China People's Friendship Association is located at 635 South Westlake Avenue, Los Angeles, California 90057.

H46 United States-Japan Trade Council

1. *1000 Connecticut Avenue, NW*
   Washington, D.C. 20036
   296-5633

2. 1957

3. Robert Angel, Director

4. Staff of 13.

6. The United States-Japan Trade Council is a nonprofit research and publications organization, funded by the Japanese Ministry of Foreign Affairs and registered with the U.S. Department of Justice as an agent of the government of Japan. As such, it works closely with the Embassy of Japan. Among other things, the council is interested in fostering

better trade relations between the United States and Japan; it advises the Japanese Ministry of Foreign Affairs as well as Japanese business-men on the political and economic situation in the United States; and it disseminates information and data relating to U.S.-Japan trade rela-tions through its publications. The council also sponsors seminars and conferences to promote the above-mentioned objectives.

8. The council has a research library with emphasis on the collection of materials in the field of economics, finance, and trade. The total hold-ings of the library number around 1,000 titles in 4,000 volumes (mostly in English). The library subscribes to numerous Japanese and English periodicals, including airmail editions of 4 daily Japanese newspapers and several Japanese trade and financial journals. On-site use of the materials with the permission of the council is possible for researchers from 9:00 A.M. to 5:30 P.M. weekdays.

9. The council publishes a number of regular and occasional publications such as: *Trade Roundout* (bimonthly); *The Japan-U.S. Trade Council Report* (twice per week); and *Report on Agriculture* (irregular) and other ad hoc issues. It also publishes a monthly bulletin entitled *Japan Economic Survey* which is circulated among 6,000 to 8,000 organiza-tions and individuals in the United States.

10. See point 6 above.

United States Strategic Institute See entry N12.

H47 Washington Institute of Foreign Affairs

1. *613 15th Street, NW*
   Washington, D.C. 20005
   737-5932

2. 1961

3. Loy W. Henderson, Chairman of the Board
   Lyman L. Lemnitzer, President

5. There are about 180 resident and 50 nonresident members in the Wash-ington area. Membership consists of individuals who have experience in international affairs in various capacities, whether diplomatic, military, intelligence, business, or academic.

6-9. The purpose of the institute is to promote greater knowledge and under-standing of international affairs among its members and other American and foreign officials and leaders who are engaged in international activi-ties. The institute encourages creative thinking on current and long-term problems in the field of foreign affairs.
   The institute's principal activity centers around regular meetings fea-turing prominent speakers on foreign affairs. The sessions are closed to nonmembers and are considered off-the-record.

10.   Copies of *The Washington Institute of Foreign Affairs* (a directory) is
        available free on request.

H48 World Federalists Association (WFA)

1.   *1011 Arlington Blvd. (Suite W219)*
        Arlington, Va. 22209
        (703) 524-2141

2.   1947

3.   Norman Cousins, President

4.   The office has a staff of 6.

5.   Approximately 8,500.

6.   WFA is a tax-exempt educational organization whose long-range goal is
        to establish a "limited world government" with adequate power to
        handle specific global problems (e.g., war, resources, the distribution of
        food, and the use of the seas). Among the issues studied by the Associa-
        tion are the problems of the arms race and the law of the sea.

7.   The WFA has an observer at the United Nations with nongovernmental
        organization status.

10.   The association publishes a quarterly journal, *World Federalist News-
        letter*.

11.   WFA is affiliated with the World Association of World Federalists.

H49 World Peace Through Law Center (WPTLC)

1.   *1000 Connecticut Avenue, NW (Suite 800)*
        Washington, D.C. 20036
        466-5420, 466-5428

2.   1957; established originally as Special Committee of the American Bar
        Association.

3.   Charles S. Rhyne, President

4.   The staff consists of 5 administrative and support members plus several
        interns and other part-time workers.

5.   Approximately 150,000 members worldwide.

6.   WPTLC was established in 1957 to work for the establishment of an
        effective and just world legal order. The center is the first worldwide
        effort to mobilize resources of the 1 million judges, lawyers, law pro-
        fessors, and law students of the nations of the world for the establish-
        ment of an effective international legal order. It is a nonpolitical, non-
        profit organization that sponsors research on a variety of topics.

7. WPTLC has a number of sections. Of particular interest to scholars are the sections on Intellectual Property: Patents, Trademarks and Copyrights; Law and Computer Technology and Human Rights; and International Legal Education.

9. The 1979 conference (held biennially) will take place in Madrid, Spain.

10. Publications of the WPTLC include the *World Legal Directory*, a computerized list of the worldwide directory of the legal profession; the *World Jurist* (bimonthly newsletter); and the *World Law Review* (proceedings of the biennial WPTLC conferences); and other special publications on current developments in international law.

11. The center is affiliated with the following: (1) the World Association of Judges; (2) the World Association of Lawyers; (3) the World Association of Law Professors; and, (4) the World Association of Law Students. These organizations have members from East Asian countries.

H50 World Population Society (WPS)

1. *1337 Connecticut Avenue*
   Washington, D.C. 20036
   833-2440

2. 1973

3. Philander P. Claxton, Jr., President

4. A 5-member executive committee of the society and 2 staff members run the Washington Office.

5. The society has about 1,100 members in over 60 different countries.

6. The WPS was organized in 1973 to help solve global population problems. Its basic objective is to encourage multidisciplinary approaches to population problems. The society's projects are geared to promote key recommendations of the World Population Plan of Action which was adopted by the U.N. World Population Conference in Bucharest in 1974.

8. It does not have its own library, but has arrangements with the Population Reference Bureau's library which is located in the same building.

9. The WPS sponsors international conferences, symposia, and workshops related to action programs to advance the World Population Plan of Action. For example, it hosted "The WPS International Population Conference" in Washington in February 1974; a similar meeting with the theme of "Since Bucharest" in Washington, D.C., in November 1975; and still a third, "Fulfillment of the World Population Plan of Action," in 1976. An international population conference was held in Manila, the Philippines, in the summer of 1978.

J Cultural Exchange Organizations

Entry Form for Cultural Exchange Organizations (J)

1. *Address; telephone number(s)*
2. Founding date
3. Chief official and title
4. Staff
5. Budget and its source
6. Affiliation with other organizations
7. Program or description
8. Publications

J1 Academic Travel Abroad, Inc. (ATA)

1. *1346 Connecticut Avenue, NW (Suite 423)*
   Washington, D.C. 20036
   223-2484

2. 1950

3. David Parry, Executive Director

4. There are 13 full-time staff members handling "tour operations," and 40 part-time employees, mostly tour directors.

5. Revenues come from the various tours ATA conducts.

7. ATA organizes educational and study tours for groups only. Travel accommodations, educational programs, and itinerary are arranged for both colleges and secondary schools, museums, and professional organizations. For example, ATA has assisted the Smithsonian Associates Travel Program in organizing its overseas educational tours, including tours to Japan. ATA is willing to assist groups interested in study-travel to any East Asian country.

J2 American Council of Young Political Leaders (ACYPL)

1. *North Lobby*
    918 16th Street, NW
    Washington, D.C. 20006
    (202) 466-7420

2. 1966

3. H. Joseph Farmer, Executive Director

4. The ACYPL has a staff of 4.

5. The ACYPL operations were once supported solely by private sources (i.e., foundation grants and corporate contributions); however, it currently receives most of its funding from the U.S. International Communication Agency (formerly the Bureau of Educational and Cultural Affairs of the Department of State).

6. Affiliated with the Atlantic Association of Young Political Leaders and the Atlantic Council of the United States.

7. The ACYPL was established to help prepare the future political leadership of the United States to deal more effectively with foreign policy problems. It seeks to provide opportunities for young American politicians to gain insight into the vital area of international affairs by providing exchange programs, conferences, seminars, study tours, and bilateral and multilateral meetings with young leaders from other countries.

    With regard to East Asia, the ACYPL has developed a program with Japan which involves exchange visits and seminars. The ACYPL also cosponsored with the National Committee on U.S.-China Relations, Inc., a delegation of young United States politicians for a study tour of the People's Republic of China in May 1977.

8. Copies of *The American Council of Young Political Leaders* may be obtained free upon request.

J3 American Council on International Sports (ACIS)

1. *817 23rd Street, NW*
    Washington, D.C. 20052
    676-7246/7247

2. 1976

3. Dr. Carl A. Troester, Jr., Executive Director

4. It has a staff of 2.

5. The council's programs are supported by grants from the U.S. State Department, the American Revolution Bicentennial Administration, and program participants.

6. ACIS cooperates with the U.S. State Department, the U.S. Olympic Committee, UNESCO, the International Council on Health, Physical Education, and Recreation (ICHPER) and other sports federations.

7.   ACIS administers a large number of physical education programs. ACIS aims primarily to promote exchanges of people, information, and sport skills between the United States and other countries. At present there are no exchange programs with East Asian nations. Indirectly, however, it interacts with East Asia through its participation in the ICHPER whose 83-member nations include Japan, South Korea, and Taiwan.

8.   An informational brochure is available on request.

Asia Foundation See entry H16.

J4 Committee on Scholarly Communication with the People's Republic of China (CSCPRC) (National Academy of Sciences)

1.   *2100 Pennsylvania Avenue, NW*
(Mailing Address: National Academy of Sciences, 2101 Constitution Avenue)
Washington, D.C. 20418
389-6683

2.   1966

3.   CSCPRC has a staff of 12.

4.   Lewis Branscomb, Chairman
Dr. Mary Brown Bullock, Staff Director

6.   The committee was formed in 1966 by the American Council of Learned Societies, the National Academy of Sciences, and the Social Science Research Council. Members of the CSCPRC represent a broad range of fields in the natural sciences, social sciences, and humanities. The CSCPRC staff operates from within the Commission on International Relations of the National Academy of Sciences.

7.   The CSCPRC negotiates a yearly exchange program involving an average of 6 groups each way with the Chinese Scientific and Technical Association (STAPRC). The CSCPRC chooses topics of interest to American scholars and proposes these to the STAPRC, which likewise suggests topics to the CSCPRC. The CSCPRC hosts Chinese groups in the United States, just as the STAPRC hosts American groups visiting China under the exchange program.

    The CSCPRC has created 8 disciplinary panels to assist in selecting topics of relevance and interest to the American scholarly community. These panels cover the atmospheric and earth sciences, mathematics and physical sciences, engineering sciences, biomedical sciences, agricultural sciences, social sciences, humanities, and China studies. The chairman of each panel is a member of the CSCPRC. The other 3 members are respected scholars in their field who have an interest in and knowledge of scholarly communication with China.

    The CSCPRC meets in June to choose a slate of proposals for the following year based on the recommendations of the panels. Interested scholars are invited to send their suggestions to the staff no later than the end of April. Ideas received in previous years are automatically reconsidered. The panels review suggestions received by the CSCPRC and seek new suggestions from colleagues in the field.

Delegation members are chosen on the basis of scholarly merit, institutional diversity, and geographical distribution. An attempt is made to include younger scholars and minorities. Final approval rests with the Executive Committee. Scholars who have been to China within the previous five years are generally excluded from the delegation unless their presence is deemed important for continuity in successive visits within a given field. Approximately 12 to 15 members constitute a delegation, and 6 delegations are sent each year. For its own use and for the use of others interested in scholarly communication with individuals and organizations in China, the CSCPRC maintains a small library of materials such as trip reports, abstracts, Chinese journals, press reports, and other information pertinent to scholarly activities in China. These materials are available for on-site use during working hours (9:00 A.M.-5:00 P.M.) Monday through Friday. Approximately 70 periodicals plus over 200 titles are available at the library.

Occasional "wrap-up meetings" (or trip-report meetings) are held under the CSCPRC's auspices. These meetings are open to the public.

8. The CSCPRC endeavors to publish the trip reports of its delegations. Some reports have been published directly through the Printing and Publishing Office of the National Academy of Sciences, while others have been printed by outside publishers. Some recent reports include: *Acupuncture Anesthesia in the People's Republic of China* (1976); *Solid State Physics in the People's Republic of China* (1976); *Insect Control in the People's Republic of China* (1975); *Oral Contraceptives and Steroid Chemistry in the People's Republic of China* (1977); *Wheat Studies in the People's Republic of China* (1977); and *Rural Small-Scale Industry in the People's Republic of China* (1977). A complete list of CSCPRC reports is available from the Washington office.

In addition to the trip reports, the CSCPRC issues free of charge a bimonthly publication, *China Exchange Newsletter,* which covers scholarly exchange activities with China and a bibliography of recent works on China.

J5 Council for International Exchange of Scholars (CIES)

1. *11 Dupont Circle, NW*
Washington, D.C. 20036
833-4950

2. 1947

3. Charles Blitzer, Chairman
Adolph Y. Wilburn, Director

4. CIES staff consists of about 50 professional and support members.

6. American Council on Education

7.   CIES is a private, nonprofit organization which facilitates the international exchange of scholars between the United States and foreign countries by administering government fellowship programs. Under contract with International Communication Agency, it administers the postdoctoral and professorial division of the Fulbright-Hays Mutual Educational and Cultural Exchange program in cooperation with international educational agencies abroad. The council screens American candidates and awards grants for lectureships and research abroad; it also makes institutional arrangements in the United States for visiting Fulbright scholars who have been chosen under the program by their national agencies. In addition, each grantee must be approved by the Board of Foreign Scholarships, a 12-member board appointed by the president of the United States to supervise and provide policy guidance for the Fulbright-Hays program. Approximately 500 American scholars are sent abroad each year, while about the same number of foreign scholars come to the United States. For years, Japan, Korea, and Taiwan have been active participants in the program.

8.   A number of informational brochures about the Fulbright-Hays Mutual Educational Exchange Program administered by the CIES are available free on request. They include *General Information Fulbright-Hays Awards for University Lecturing and Postdoctoral Research Abroad,* and *Council for International Exchange of Scholars: Programs, Activities, Organization.* CIES announcements on lecturing and research opportunities abroad are issued each spring. Interested scholars should write to the CIES for the brochures and applications.

J6 Experiment in International Living (EIL)

1.   *1346 Connecticut Avenue, NW, Suite 802*
      Washington, D.C. 20036
      872-1330

2.   1932

3.   Kathy Spaar, Regional Representative, Washington Office

4.   The Washington office has a staff of 3; however, the total staff for EIL including the headquarters office in Brattleboro, Vermont, and several regional offices, numbers over 120.

5.   The organization derives its income from participants' fees, gifts, foundation grants, endowment revenue, and government contracts. The annual budget exceeds $5 million.

6.   The EIL is a member of such organizations as the U.S. National Commission for UNESCO, the Society for International Development, the Council on International Educational Exchange, the National Association for Foreign Student Affairs, the Association of World Colleges and Universities, and the National Council for Community Services to International Visitors. In addition, it cooperates closely with such organizations as AFS International Scholarships, ACTION/Peace Corps, the National Association of Independent Schools, CARE, the International

Christian Youth Exchange, the National 4-H Foundation, Partners of the Alliance, and the World University Service.

7. EIL is a private, nonprofit, educational organization which specializes in international home-stay exchange programs, travel from and into this country, and cross-cultural education programs. It operates a number of exchange programs designed to meet the needs of both American and foreign students. For example, its "Summer Abroad Program" offers opportunities for American high school and college students to experiment with a 3- to 4-week home-stay in the host country. Each year, about 1,200 students visit 35 countries under this program (25 percent of them on scholarships sponsored by various educational and community groups in the United States). It also handles the "Academic Study Abroad Program" for high school and college students with emphasis on independent study and field work.

For foreign students and visitors, EIL operates: (1) "International Students of English Program"—8 weeks of study at Dominican College in San Francisco plus 3 weeks home-stay; (2) "Learn English in the USA Program"—a 10-week study program plus 3 weeks of home-stay; and (3) "International High School Program"—5 to 10 months of study plus home-stay in the United States. Under these programs, approximately 500 Japanese students come to the United States annually, while a much smaller number of American students go to Japan (e.g., 18 in 1977). An extensive language-training program is offered by EIL's School for International Training (Brattleboro, Vermont).

8. EIL brochures describing various summer programs are available free on request.

J7 Institute of International Education—Washington, D.C., Office

1. *11 Dupont Circle (Suite 200)*
    Washington, D.C. 20036
    483-0001

2. 1919

3. Peter D. Pelham, Vice President for Government Affairs

4. The IIE's Washington Office is staffed by about 25 professional and staff members.

6. Institute of International Education, New York.

7. The IIE was established in 1919 to promote international understanding and cooperation through the exchange of students and scholars. It is the largest and most active American educational exchange agency, and its activities are worldwide and serve all segments of higher education.

IIE administers student-exchange programs with over 120 countries and provides services to technical-assistance programs abroad. Each year approximately 10,000 individuals study outside their homelands under programs directly administered by the IIE. Among these programs, IIE is in charge of the Fulbright-Hays Mutual Educational and Cultural

Exchange Act for the United States and foreign graduate students. Over 370 American students were selected by the IIE under the program in 1976, while it supervised nearly 2,000 foreign students (or recipients of the Fulbright-Hays awards) who had come to the United States under the program in the same year. The IIE also supervised several hundred foreign students visiting the United States to study English. Another important program administered by the IIE is the "International Visitors Program." Each year, over 500 distinguished guests from abroad come to the United States under the auspices of the International Communication Agency (U.S.). Japan, South Korea, and Taiwan have been active participants in all of the exchange programs mentioned above. Finally, the IIE also administers programs for foreign governments and universities. It has, for example, supervised the graduate academic programs of 115 fellows sent to the United States under the Republic of China's Ministry of Defense program in 1976. It also supervised several trainees (agricultural and rural development) sent by the South Korean government in the same year. In addition, the institute provided administrative services to 13 American agricultural specialists and consultants assigned to the Office of Rural Development/Crop Improvement Research Center in Suweon, Korea.

8. A number of informational brochures about exchange programs administered by the IIE are available free on request. They include *International Visitors Program; IIE Services to Overseas Technical Assistance Programs; Sponsored Projects, 1976; Education: A Global Commitment* (for corporations); and *IIE Publications*. The institute has also published a number of reference books, handbooks, and directories for students and scholars interested in international exchange programs (e.g., *International Educational Exchange: A Bibliography; Scholarships and Fellowships for Foreign Study: A Selected Bibliography; Handbook on International Study for U.S. Nationals,* 2 volumes; *U.S. College-Sponsored Programs Abroad;* and *Teaching Abroad*).

Japan Foundation See entry H30.

Japan-U.S. Friendship Commission See entry K19.

Korean Scholarship Foundation in America See entry H33.

J8 National 4-H Council

1. *7100 Connecticut Avenue, NW*
   Washington, D.C. 20015
   656-9000

2. Organized in 1976 and fully operative on February 1, 1977, the National 4-H Council merges the National 4-H Service Committee (Chicago) and the National 4-H Foundation (Washington, D.C.)

3. Grant A. Shrum, Executive Director
    Melvin J. Thompson, Director, International Division

4. The Washington office has a staff of 167 including about 30 professionals.

5. Total 4-H budget figures are unavailable. However, its International Division works with over 1 million dollars per year.

6. The 4-H youth program is a branch of the Cooperative Extension Service of the U.S. Department of Agriculture and state Land-Grant Universities.

7. National 4-H Council administers a number of international exchange programs, the oldest of which is the International 4-H Youth Exchange (IFYE). IFYE exchange programs (i.e., IFYE Ambassador, IFYE Caravan and IFYE Representative) are designed to provide an educational cross-cultural experience, to increase international understanding, to give emphasis to the value of 4-H and similar programs, and to assist in the development of youth programs throughout the world. Participants live and work with host families while actively participating in the youth programs of the host countries. During 1977, for example, young men and women from 35 countries were exchanged with young Americans through the IFYE programs—the majority spending 6 weeks to 5 months living with families in their host country. Each year nearly 2,000 families around the world provide a home for the participants who are between 16 and 25 years of age with 4-H backgrounds or other youth organization experiences. Japan, South Korea, and Taiwan are active participants in the IFYE programs.

    Other 4-H international exchange and training programs include the International Youth Development Project (YDP), the Professional Rural Youth Leader Exchange (PRYLE), International Extension 4-H Travel Seminars, and exchange programs with the Soviet Union and Hungary.

    National 4-H Council also has a cooperative program of international youth exchanges with the Labo International Exchange Foundation of Japan. Since 1972, more than 3,000 Japanese youngsters and 430 adults have participated in home-stay visits in the United States and Canada. During the same period, over 1,300 American and Canadian 4-H members and accompanying adults have stayed in Labo homes in Japan.

8. Among many 4-H brochures and publications, the following are most informative on its international programs: *International Intrigue* (1974); *World Atlas of 4-H* (1970); and *Handbook of National 4-H Council Programs and Services* (1977).

J9 Sister Cities International (The Town Affiliation Association of the U.S., Inc.)

1. *1625 Eye Street, NW (Suite 424-26)*
    Washington, D.C. 20006
    293-5504

2. 1956

3. Betty Wilson, President, Board of Directors
   Thomas W. Gittins, Executive Vice President

4. The SCI's main office has a staff of 10.

5. Sister Cities International is totally a private effort. The national organization receives support from the International Communication Agency, from member cities in the United States, from the Agency for International Development, and from private foundations and corporations.

6. SCI is the principal program of the Town Affiliation Association of the United States, Inc.

7. SCI is a tax-exempt, nonprofit organization established to further international cooperation and understanding through Sister City affiliations between cities in the United States and those in foreign countries. Under the program, 640 United States cities are affiliated with 847 cities in 78 foreign countries, including 131 cities in Japan, 12 in South Korea, and 8 in Taiwan. In Tokyo, Japan, the Japan Municipal League for International Friendship encourages Japanese Sister Cities.

   Under the program, cities and their citizens exchange goods, ideas, and people in a wide variety of cultural, youth, educational, professional, and technical-assistance projects.

   The SCI's Washington office provides technical as well as administrative support to United States cities interested in establishing affiliations with foreign cities. It also serves as the information center for the participating cities.

8. The SCI publishes a bimonthly newsletter, *Sister City News,* as well as a number of frequently revised materials relating to the program: *Your Community in World Affairs; Sister Cities by State and Country; National Directory of Sister Cities in the United States; Fund Raising and Transportation in Sister City Projects;* and others.

K United States Government Agencies

Entry Form for United States Government Agencies   (K)

1. General Information
    a. *Address; telephone number(s)*
    b. Conditions of access
    c. Name/title of director and heads of relevant divisions

2. Agency's programs and research activities
    a. In-house research
    b. Contract research
    c. Research grants
    d. Employment of outside consultants
    e. International exchange programs

3. Agency libraries and reference facilities

4. Agency's publications and records

5. Detailed description of relevant divisions

K1 Agency for International Development (AID)

1. a. *State Department Building*
        320 21st Street, NW
        Washington, D.C. 20523
        655-4000 (Information)
        632-1850 (Freedom-of-Information and Public Inquiries)

    b. Not open to the public without appointment or prior approval.

2. AID administers the foreign-assistance programs of the United States
    with emphasis on development assistance to less-developed countries.
    Specifically, the agency endeavors to help the less-developed countries
    (LDC) of the Third World increase their economic productivity and

promote economic and political stability by way of loans, grants, and technical-assistance programs. AID-sponsored development programs encompass many fields, such as agriculture, nutrition, population planning, health care, education, housing, and development planning.

Since 1962, AID has administered extensive research programs under contract. AID-funded research projects have been designed either to enhance the ability of the recipient countries to handle specific problems or to contribute directly to solutions. Many research projects relating to South Korea and Taiwan have been funded in the past; however, the number is rapidly dwindling as AID operations in these countries are either completed (Taiwan) or being phased out (South Korea).

3. See Libraries section (entry A2).

4. The internal records and unpublished reports of the AID bureaus and offices are periodically turned over to the agency's Communications and Records Management Division for storage in the Washington Federal Records Center, Suitland, Maryland. These records may become available to researchers by contacting AID Freedom-of-Information Officer, Arnold Dadian (632-1850), who maintains shelflist indexes of such documents. After a request has been made for specific documents, they are retrieved from storage, reviewed for declassification, and then made available to the researchers. The time required for processing such requests depends on the amount of materials involved. Only when these documents are transferred to the National Archives and Records Service do the agency's materials become readily accessible to a researcher. In addition to the Freedom-of-Information Officer, the AID Records Management staff (632-8518) and the originating agency office keep a shelflist index of the stored documents.

The Office of Development Information is located in the New State Department Building (formerly titled the "AID Reference Center") and maintains the agency's research studies, published and unpublished, classified and unclassified, as well as program reports and project files.

AID publications include: *A.I.D. Research and Development Abstracts,* which contain information on AID-funded studies as well as how to purchase a copy of any study listed; and *Food Production and Nutrition* (1976), volume 1 of a projected multivolume series entitled *Research Literature for Development.* AID-funded research projects are listed in *Current Technical Service Contracts and Grants* (semiannual index). Copies of these publications can be obtained from the Bureau for Development Support (235-8936). AID also publishes *Fiscal Year Submission to the Congress* (annual budget); and two periodicals: *AGENDA* (a monthly bulletin) containing short articles and news notes on topics relating to international development; and *Front Lines* (weekly), an internal agency newsletter. Copies of these publications can be obtained from the Office of Public Affairs (632-8628). Also available from the bureau is AID brochure, *AID's Challenge in an Interdependent World* (1977). The agency has also compiled *AID Bibliography Series,* consisting of 28 subject bibliographies on development-related fields. Copies are available in the Office of Development Information (632-9345).

5.   BUREAU FOR ASIA
     John F. Sullivan, Assistant Administrator
     632-9223

AID operations in East Asia are not extensive. South Korea and Taiwan are the only East Asian countries that have had AID missions. Currently, only South Korea receives AID assistance, which is steadily declining. Within the next few years (probably by 1981), the AID mission and its representatives in Korea are expected to complete their operations and will close down their offices in Korea, largely because of South Korea's economic development and growth.

Besides South Korea, other countries that the bureau is concerned with include: the Philippines, Malaysia, Thailand, India, Bangladesh, Pakistan, Sri Lanka, Afghanistan, and Nepal. AID country-desk officers in the Bureau of Asia are a primary source of information pertaining to United States aid programs, the operations of the AID field missions, current economic conditions, and development activities in the countries of their specialization. They can provide researchers with unclassified agency materials such as "working documents," "program evaluation studies," and *Development Assistance Program* (DAP) field reports from USAID missions. The desk officer can also arrange appointments with specialists knowledgeable about a particular country's development projects and activities.

The AID country desk officer for South Korea is:

Donald Melville (632-9844)
Office of Development Planning
Donald D. Cohen, Director (632-9044)

In the Office of Development Planning, the chief of the research and evaluation staff, Robert Meehan, is the best contact for information on research pertinent to East Asia. This office reviews and approves research proposals from within the agency and from outside researchers. It administers funds for research directly relevant to AID operational programs. Insofar as research on South Korea is concerned, relatively little work is funded by this office, largely because the AID programs in South Korea are being phased out.

BUREAU FOR PROGRAM AND POLICY COORDINATION
Alexander Shakow, Assistant Administrator
632-9482
Eric Griffel, Asian Coordinator
632-3017

Various functional offices within this bureau, such as the Office of Development Program Review and Evaluation (632-8594), provide policy recommendations, and conduct foreign-aid effectiveness analyses and program reviews for the AID administrator. In the bureau, the official to contact for Korea is Michael Stack (632-9110), who is knowledgeable about current AID operations in the country.

Office of Program Information and Analysis Services
  Statistics and Report Division
  Economic and Social Data Bank (ESDB)
1735 North Lynn Street, 6th floor
Pomponio Plaza, Rosslyn
Arlington, Va. 22209
(703) 235-9836

The Statistics and Report Division maintains a computerized Economic and Social Data Bank (ESDB), which derives its data from various sources including the United Nations, the World Bank, and individual national government agencies, including AID. Relevant economic data on Asia can be obtained from computer runs through the ESDB.

The division also publishes several unclassified statistical publications that may be of interest to East Asian specialists. The annually updated *U.S. Overseas Loans and Grants, and Assistance from International Organizations: Obligations and Loan Authorizations, July 1, 1945,* contains statistical tables for Asian countries, including Japan, South Korea, and Taiwan. It lists United States economic and military assistance for the periods 1946-1948, 1949-1952, 1953-1961, 1962-1969, and annually since 1970, with a supplement listing major international lending institutions that offered aid to these countries. It has also published the highly informative *Asia Economic Growth Trends (1977); Selected Economic Data for the Less Developed Countries;* and periodically updated *Food and Total Agricultural Production in Less Developed Countries, 1950–.* (The source for the statistics used are derived from the U.S. Department of Agriculture.

The staff can assist researchers in obtaining desired statistical information and data on Asia from the ESDB and other sources.

BUREAU OF DEVELOPMENT SUPPORT
632-8558

This bureau provides technical expertise and support to USAID field missions throughout the world. Its offices are organized along functional lines; and each office administers AID contract research projects in its field of specialization. Usually, each office has one or more staff members with technical expertise in Asian aspects of the functional specialization. Unless otherwise noted, the offices listed below are located in the Rosslyn Plaza Building, 1601 Kent Street, Arlington, Virginia 22209.

Office of Agriculture   (703) 235-8945
Office of Development Administration   (703) 235-9024
Office of Education   (703) 235-9015
Office of Energy   (703) 235-1720
Office of Engineering   (703) 235-9827
Office of Health   (703) 235-8929
Office of Nutrition   (703) 235-8927
Office of Population   (703) 235-8117
Office of International Training   (703) 235-1853
Office of Rural Development and Development Administration
    (703) 235-8918

Office of Science and Technology   (703) 235-9046

Office of Title XII Coordination   (703) 235-9054   (This office administers programs for "prevention of famine" and "freedom from hunger.")

Office of Urban Development   (703) 235-8902.

BUREAU OF PRIVATE AND DEVELOPMENT COOPERATION
(Newly created as a result of reorganization, it has jurisdiction over several offices listed below.)
632-8558

Office of Reimbursable Development Programs
Robert B. Brougham, Regional Program Officer for Asia
632-7937

This office administers and arranges many types of assistance programs, such as technical and training services that any "friendly" foreign country or nongovernmental organization (including voluntary groups) may request, provided that they can pay for them. Its services are not restricted to former U.S.-aid recipient nations or countries of a certain economic status (e.g., "less-developed countries"). "Target countries" for this AID assistance program include any nation that can afford it. In Asia, such assistance is currently given to South Korea, the Philippines, Thailand, and Malaysia.

Office of Food-for-Peace
Pomponio Plaza, Room 549
1735 North Lynn Street
Arlington, Virginia 22209
(703) 235-9220

This office administers United States food-aid programs with funds provided by the U.S. Department of Agriculture. Currently, the office is administering a "Title I concessional agreement" food-aid program in South Korea. The program is based on an agreement signed in July 1977, which authorizes the sale of agricultural commodities (including 460,000 tons of wheat worth $43.8 million) to South Korea with long-term credits. In addition, the office has been administering a bilateral Textile Agreement with Korea since 1971. For further information on these programs in South Korea and other Asian countries, contact Albert Mercker (235-9238) or the treaty section of the Department of State. The office issues an *Annual Report to the President* which contains pertinent statistics for Asia.

Office of United States Foreign Disaster Assistance
Ann C. Martindell, Director
632-8924

This office serves as the United States national coordinating center for public and private relief activities in case of natural disasters in Asia and around the world. It publishes an annual report entitled *Foreign Disaster Emergency Relief.*

Office of Labor Affairs
Dale E. Good, Director
632-3662

The office serves as the principal AID/State Department unit for liaison with the AFL-CIO and its Asian activities (see entry H18).

Office of American Schools and Hospitals Abroad
235-9190

The main objective of this office is to promote better understanding between the United States and various foreign countries. It has assisted in the establishment of a Presbyterian medical center in Chunju, South Korea, and is planning to establish a polio rehabilitation center in Taiwan.

Office of Private and Voluntary Organizations
632-9206

This office acts as the liaison between private voluntary organizations (PVO) and the government of the country to which it is offering assistance. Some of these PVO's include: CARE; Asia Foundation; Catholic Relief Services; and International Voluntary Services. The office also provides consulting service to the PVOs.

Office of Women in Development
Arvonne Fraser, Coordinator
632-3992

This office conducts research and awards contracts on women in the development process, primarily from a regional and broader comparative perspective. Some studies on women's roles in South Korea have been funded by the office. For further information, call the coordinator's office.

Office of Public Affairs
Arnold Dadian, Freedom-of-Information Officer
632-1850

This unit is most cooperative in helping outside researchers gain access to classified AID documents. An estimated 95 percent of the materials requested under the Freedom-of-Information Act have been released to researchers. Such materials may be examined by outside scholars in the staff's office. The office can also provide assistance to researchers in obtaining shelflist indexes to the inactive agency records currently stored in the Washington Federal Records Center, Suitland, Md.

K2 Agriculture Department (USDA)

1. a. *Independence Avenue between 12th and 14th Streets, SW*
    Washington, D.C. 20250
    447-2791 (Information)

    b. Department offices are open to the public; however, appointments are recommended.

2. Various divisions of the U.S. Department of Agriculture collect information and conduct research on agriculture and related matters in East Asia. Most research is done in-house; but some is done by outside scholars under contract.

3. See U.S.D.A. Technical Information Systems (entry A41).

4. Most of the important research documents and reports of the Foreign Agricultural Service and the Economic Research Service branches are accessible to outside researchers. There is, however, no centralized USDA records-management system; internal records of each branch remain in the unit's files until they are forwarded to the National Archives. Bibliographies and other publications of the USDA are described below together with the originating agency.

5. ECONOMICS, STATISTICS AND COOPERATIVE SERVICE (ESCS)

    500 12th Street, NW

    Foreign Demand and Competition Division
    Centrally Planned Countries
    Wade Gregory, Acting Program Leader (447-8106)
    Charles Y. Liu, Project Leader for Current Situation, People's Republic of China and North Korean Agriculture (447-8380)

    This unit monitors the current agricultural situation in the PRC and North Korea. Results of in-house research, including notebooks on current work, are ordinarily open to scholars. However, the staff makes it clear that they do not conduct a great deal of research. A statistical clerk maintains historical and current information which might be of interest to researchers.

    Developing Countries Program Area
    Wade Gregory, Program Leader (447-8106)
    John B. Parker, Jr., Country Analyst for South Korea (447-8107)
    Amjad H. Gill, Country Analyst for Taiwan (447-8107)

    This unit monitors South Korean and Taiwanese agricultural production, trade, changes in policy and government programs which would influence United States agricultural exports to both countries. Production statistics are available from a wide selection of official books published in English as well as Korean and Chinese which are kept in the office. Statistical tables are tabulated on the countries' agricultural trade over the last 20 years for use in trade projections.
      ESCS has a Research Agreement with Michigan State University for a study of Korean agriculture. The study, initiated in September 1977, includes two main objectives: (1) the analysis of South Korea's import needs for agricultural products and the likely U.S. share of the market in the future; and, (2) the modification of a previously developed model of the Korean agricultural sector for use by ESCS. The agreement draws on studies conducted by Michigan State University during the period 1971-1977 under the sponsorship of the USAID. Principal contacts are David Culver in ESCS and Michael Abkin at Michigan State.

Developed Countries Program Area
Reed Friend, Program Leader (447-6809)
William Coyle, Country Analyst for Japan (447-6809)

This office monitors Japanese agricultural production and trade. Special attention is given to economic and political developments that would affect U.S. agricultural exports to Japan.

ESCS has published several studies recently which may be of interest to East Asian scholars: *Impact of a Resale Price Increase on Japan's Wheat Imports* (February 1977) by Bruce Greenshields; and *Japan: Production and Imports of Food, An Analysis of the Welfare Cost of Production* (November 1977) by Malcom Bale and Bruce Greenshields.

Also under contract with ESCS: *A Simulation Model for Assessing the Ingredient Composition of Formula Feed in Japan* (September 1977) by the Boston Consulting Group, Tokyo, Japan; and *Japanese Wheat Import and Pricing Policies* (May 1978) by the Japan Flour Millers Association, Tokyo, Japan.

ESCS also publishes:

The Agricultural Situation of Asia (annually in the spring), with sections on Japan, North and South Korea, and Taiwan. This publication reviews relevant developments and the outlook for agricultural trade and production in each of the countries.

The Agricultural Situation in the People's Republic of China (annually) reviews the past year and projects the outlook for the coming year.

Foreign Agricultural Trade of the United States (monthly) includes contributed articles from country analysts.

Analysts also submit articles for publication in *Foreign Agriculture* published by the Foreign Agricultural Service.

Copies of these publications can be obtained from the units concerned or from the ESCS Publications Unit (447-7255). The Publications Unit maintains a comprehensive card index of ESCS foreign economic research publications, most of which are available at the National Agricultural Library.

National Economic Analysis Division
Agricultural History Branch
Wayne Rasmussen, Supervisory Historian   447-8183

Documentation Center
Gerald Ogden, Supervisor
Cynthia M. Kenyon, Director   447-2474

The Agricultural History Branch maintains a vertical file containing a limited collection of USDA press releases, articles and documents dealing with agricultural economics and food programs related to East Asia. It also maintains a bibliographic card index of books and articles on agricultural history (domestic and foreign) with East Asian country divisions.

The Documentation Center of the Agricultural History Branch maintains a computerized bibliographic data base on agricultural economics (primarily books, articles, and papers authored by American agricultural economists). The data base is a component part of the Department library's AGRICOLA system (see entry A41), and can be used by researchers without charge through the library's terminals.

FOREIGN AGRICULTURAL SERVICE (FAS)

USDA, South Building, 14th Street and Independence Avenue, SW

The FAS along with the ESCS are the two main branches of the USDA which monitor agricultural and economic developments in East Asia. Basically, the FAS is commodity oriented, whereas the ESCS is country or regionally oriented. Both branches work closely together. In addition to the information and data supplied by the Census Bureau of the U.S. Commerce Department, the FAS also derives information from the 65 key agricultural attaché posts (attached to the United States embassies and consulates) around the world, which gather current information on agricultural production, market conditions, trade and agricultural policies of each country. Currently, in East Asia, United States agricultural attachés are stationed in Japan, South Korea, and Taiwan. (An "agricultural representative" is stationed in the PRC.) Their dispatches are supplemented by the findings of USDA agricultural marketing specialists and economists who analyze various data in Washington. The agricultural attachés' reports, which are generally unclassified, can be obtained by outside researchers from the FAS Communications, Reports, and Records Office (447-6135).

Foreign Commodity Analysis
Brice Meeker, Director   447-7233

Staff agricultural economists of this office analyze world agricultural commodities from the standpoint of production, supply, trade, marketing, price, and consumption. The office is divided into separate units by agricultural commodity group and includes: Cotton Division (447-6271); Dairy, Livestock, and Poultry Division (447-7217); Fruit and Vegetable Division (447-5330); Grain and Feed Division (447-6219); Oilseeds and Products Division (447-7037); Sugar and Tropical Products Division (447-3423); and Tobacco Division (447-3000). Although the scope of each division's analysis is global, each has staff members who are knowledgeable about East Asian commodities.

FAS publications relevant to East Asian specialists include: *Foreign Agriculture* (weekly) which contains articles on international agricultural and food-related subjects (an annual index for the preceding year is published); *Foreign Agriculture Circular* (published periodically) which generally carries data on the principal commodities traded in international markets (e.g., coffee, sugar, cocoa, fruits, livestock, etc.); *Weekly Roundup of World Food Production and Trade,* a regular news release; and *U.S. Foreign Agricultural Trade Statistics Report* (annual). Occasionally, *Special Issues* are published under *Foreign Agriculture;* generally, they focus on a particular country or region rather than primary commodities.

Copies of these publications can be obtained from the FAS Information Division (447-3448). FAS Foreign Information Publications Section (447-7937) maintains copies of all FAS publications issued since 1951.

INTERNATIONAL DEVELOPMENT STAFF (IDS)

USDA, South Building, 14th Street and Independence Avenue, SW
William A. Faught, Director   447-7393

The International Development Staff provides technical assistance advisers for agricultural development projects sponsored by the U.S. Agency for International Development, the World Bank, and the U.N. Food and Agriculture Organization. It also coordinates agricultural training programs for foreign officials in the U.S. USDA/USAID Reports and Technical Inquiries Group (447-2893) of the IDS provides technical information to U.S. field missions engaged in agricultural assistance programs abroad, including East Asia. IDS is also responsible for the USDA participation in the U.S.-Japan Cooperative Science Program since 1961, which involves joint studies in various fields including agriculture. Its reference collection, consisting of various monographs, IDS studies, a vertical file of the U.S. field mission reports by country, and other miscellaneous reports, is available to outside researchers.

OFFICE OF THE GENERAL SALES MANAGER (OGSM)

USDA, South Building, 14th Street and Independence Avenue, SW
Kelly M. Harrison, General Sales Manager   447-2612

This office administers, in cooperation with the U.S. Agency for International Development, the "P.L. 480 program" and other foreign grains sales. It also keeps track of the foreign sales of private United States agricultural commodity exporters. Its publications include an annual report entitled *Food for Peace,* which contains statistical data on United States food aid to East Asian countries; and *U.S. Export Sales,* a weekly statistical bulletin summarizing the commercial sales of private U.S. food exporters.

SCIENCE AND EDUCATION ADMINISTRATION

Hyattsville, Maryland

James M. Nieling, Acting Director   (301) 436-8309

This office (formerly known as Agricultural Research Service) participates on behalf of the USDA in the "U.S.-Japan Cooperative Program in Natural Resources" (UJNR). The cooperative program which was established in 1964 covers a broad spectrum, including forestry, seismology, marine sciences and resources, forestry and fire research, etc. For further information, contact Dr. Chester R. Benjamin (301/436-8308). Copies of *Second Five-Year Report of the U.S.-Japan Cooperative Program in Natural Resources, 1969-1974* are available upon request from Dr. Benjamin's office.

K3 Arms Control and Disarmament Agency (ACDA)

1. a. *U.S. Department of State*
   320 21st Street, NW
   Washington, D.C. 20451
   632-9504/9505 (Public Affairs)

   b. The agency's offices are not open to the public; researchers should call first for an appointment.

2. ACDA's primary function is to advise the president, the secretary of state, and Congress on arms-control matters. Both in-house and contract research are undertaken to acquire scientific, economic, political, military, and technological information and data needed in formulating the arms-control and disarmament policy of the United States. Agency announcements of research opportunities are published in the *Commerce Business Daily*, U.S. Department of Commerce. In addition, unsolicited but pertinent research proposals will be considered by the agency's Contract Office (632-0451). For further information, contact Evalyn W. Dexter (235-8248). Although the agency's primary interest centers on the SALT and other arms-limitation negotiations with the Soviet Union, it also monitors arms buildups and the flow of the arms trade in the other regions of the world. Edward T. Fei (632-8659) is an ACDA arms transfer specialist for East Asia, whereas Dean F. Rust (632-7905) is an East Asia specialist in the agency's Non-Proliferation Bureau. Both can help researchers by referring them to other experts in the Departments of State and Defense as well as by providing them with factual information.

3. ACDA Library (Room 804, 1700 North Lynn Street, Arlington, Virginia 22209) contains a collection of the agency's publications and unclassified contract-research reports. The library's general-reference materials (i.e., 8,000 volumes) include a small number of titles on the arms trade, nuclear nonproliferation and other arms-related topics on major regions of the world, including East Asia. The library is open from 9:00 A.M.-4:45 P.M., Monday through Friday. Scholars should contact the librarian (235-9550) for permission to use the facilities, which are located in a restricted building.

4. ACDA publications include *Documents on Disarmament* (an annual compilation of documents on arms-control and disarmament developments); *Arms Control Report* (an annual report to the Congress); *World Military Expenditures and Arms Transfers, 1965-1974* (updated annually); and *Arms Control and Disarmament Agreements: Tests and History of Negotiations* (1977). Copies of these publications can be obtained from the Office of Public Affairs (632-0392).

   The agency's unclassified reports resulting from research sponsored by ACDA are sent to more than 180 public and university libraries nationwide and are available to the public for a nominal charge. For further information, see *ACDA External Research Reports* (irregular); and *Official Publications of the United States Arms Control and Disarmament Agency*.

The agency's internal records, including classified research reports, are maintained by the Office of Administration's Communications Services section (632-866/0931). Access to these classified records is possible only through Freedom-of-Information Act procedures. The person to contact is Charles Oleszycki (632-0760), ACDA's Freedom of Information officer.

K4 Central Intelligence Agency (CIA)

1. a. *Langley, Virginia*
      (703) 351-1100 (Information)
      (703) 351-7676 (Public Affairs)
      Mail: Washington, D.C. 20505

   b. Closed to anyone without a security clearance or an appointment arranged in advance. The agency occasionally schedules tours for large groups (100-500 persons) from academic, business, and other private organizations. For further information, contact the Public Affairs Office.

2. At time, the CIA funds contract research for technical studies and for aspects of methodology and model-building. The agency also hires outside foreign-area specialists as consultants for regional studies. Inquiries for research opportunities and contracts should be referred to James King (351-7848), the agency's Coordinator for Academic Relations and External Analytical Support.

3. The CIA Library (351-7848) and its facilities and resources (e.g., books, maps, film collections) are not accessible to outside researchers. As a result, no detailed descriptions of these resources are possible; a few general remarks, however, may be helpful. First, the library contains unclassified as well as classified materials. Second, its holdings on East Asia are substantial; and unclassified materials may be obtained through interlibrary loans. The library's unclassified book holdings are indexed in the computerized Ohio College Library Catalog (OCLC), Columbus, Ohio. As for the map collection, classified maps are inaccessible for outside researchers; however, the CIA's unclassified map holdings are duplicated by the map collections of the Library of Congress (see entry E3) and the Interior Department's Geological Survey (see entry E2). Films of the agency include documentaries, newsreels, and features, mostly from the World War II period and after.

4. The CIA publishes a number of unclassified publications, including a semiannual *National Basic Intelligence Factbook* which contains political, economic, and military data on foreign countries; *Chiefs of State and Cabinet Members of Foreign Governments* (monthly); *Economic Indicators* (weekly); *International Energy Biweekly Statistical Review*; *International Oil Developments Statistical Survey*; *Communist Aid to the Less Developed Countries of the Free World* (annual); and other special studies. These publications are released to the public through the Library of Congress Exchange and Gift Division's "Documents Expediting Project" (426-5253). The Documents Expediting Project staff will distribute the "CIA Reference Aid series" on an annual subscription basis.

For a subscription fee of $225 per year, subscribers will receive a copy of every publication the project staff will receive for the forthcoming year from the CIA plus a copy of any back issue still on hand. A card index to all CIA publications received since the inception of the project in 1973 is maintained by the project staff at the Library of Congress (LC). A copy of each CIA publication is also entered into the LC's main collection. Copies of the publications may be purchased through the LC's Photoduplication Service (426-5640). Local Washington-area libraries subscribing to the "CIA Reference Aid series" include those of the University of Maryland, the American University, and George Mason University. Copies of the *National Basic Intelligence Fact Book* as well as unclassified CIA-produced maps of foreign countries can be purchased at U.S. Government Printing Office bookstores.

As for the internal records of the CIA, they are classified and may be accessible only through Freedom-of-Information Act procedures. The agency's Information and Privacy Coordinator Gene Wilson (351-7486) handles FOI requests. The documents released through FOI Act requests are listed in the *Declassified Documents Quarterly Catalog* published by the Carrollton Press of Arlington, Virginia (see entry N5).

K5 Commerce Department

1. a. *14th Street and Constitution Avenue, NW*
      Washington, D.C. 20230
      377-2000 (Information)

   b. Open to the public

2. The United States Department of Commerce provides a wide variety of services and programs to the American business community including research for the increased use of science and technology in the development of the United States economy. Most research is conducted in-house; however, some divisions of the department occasionally utilize outside scholars on research contracts or as consultants. Various functional subunits of the department which deal with East Asia are described below under point 5.

3. For the Department of Commerce's main library and the libraries of various branches, see "Libraries" section (entries A9, A10, A11, A12, and A13).

4. Each major unit of the Department of Commerce has its own records-management office which stores internal records until they are transferred to the National Archives. Ivy Parr (377-3630), Chief of the department's Records-Management Division, can direct scholars to appropriate records-management offices and provide assistance in gaining access to retired documents. Access to classified documents of the Department of Commerce can be possible only through the Freedom-of-Information Act procedures. Such requests should be routed through Carolyn Wong, Head of the Central Reference and Records Inspection Facility (377-5659), Information Management Division, in the Office of Organization and Management Systems.

The Commerce Department publishes a biweekly magazine entitled *Commerce America* which contains reports on foreign and domestic business conditions and developments. A semi-annual issue of the magazine covers the world-trade outlook, with a section devoted to East Asian coverage. It also publishes *Commerce Business Daily*. The department's major publications are listed in an annual *Commerce Publications Catalog and Index*. These publications and bibliographies are discussed together with their originating offices below.

5. **INDUSTRY AND TRADE ADMINISTRATION (ITA)**

Frank A. Weil, Assistant Secretary   377-2867

The primary function of the Industry and Trade Administration (formerly the Domestic and International Business Administration) is to promote the growth of U.S. industry, to strengthen the international commercial position of the United States, and to stimulate the expansion of United States exports.

BUREAU OF INTERNATIONAL ECONOMIC POLICY AND RESEARCH (BIEPR)   377-3022

This bureau is responsible for the research, analysis, and formulation of international economic and commercial policies and programs relating to trade, finance, and investment. The staff initiates and reviews research on developments affecting United States trade and commercial interests abroad, including East Asia.

Office of Country Affairs   377-3695

Country specialists in the Office of Country Affairs monitor trade and economic trends and developments abroad, including East Asia. The Japan Staff within the Industrialized Nations Division studies and coordinates the department's policy position on bilateral economic and commercial relations with Japan, and monitors developments relating to the items covered by various United States-Japanese agreements (e.g., U.S.-Japanese Trade Communique of January 13, 1978). Either Deane Black (377-5279) or Chadwick Johnson (377-5145) can provide researchers with recent information and data on United States-Japanese trade relations. The Japan Staff also serves as de facto secretariat for the Joint United States-Japan Trade Facilitation Committee (TFC) which was established in September 1977. Developments in South Korea and Taiwan are monitored by the staff of the Developing Nations Division. James Johnston (377-2954) is quite knowledgeable about United States trade and commercial relations with South Korea and Taiwan. These desk officers constitute an East Asian specialist's primary contact and referral point within the Department of Commerce.

Office of International Economic Research   377-5638

This unit conducts research on international economic policy issues, sector analysis, export projections, and worldwide trade developments and trends. It publishes a number of studies on foreign trade and the international economy. As part of its "Staff Economic Report" series, the office has published: *U.S. Trade with Developing Economies: The*

Growing Importance of Manufactured Goods (1975); *Capital Requirements of the Non-OPEC Less Developed Countries* (1976); *Selected Basic Reference on Trade Barriers and International Trade Flows* (1976); and *Survey of Current International Economic Research* (an annotated bibliography). The office also publishes various statistical series such as *International Economic Indicators* (quarterly); *Market Shares Reports* (annual); *Overseas Business Reports*; and *Trends in U.S. Foreign Trade* (monthly) containing East Asian data by country and commodity.

There are two reference facilities operated by the unit, both of which are open to the public: World Trade Reference Room (377-4855) and U.S. Foreign Trade Reference Room (377-2185). The former contains a collection of the official trade-statistics publications of every foreign government in the world (with holdings normally dating back 4 years), while the latter holds detailed Bureau of the Census statistics on United States foreign trade back to 1940.

Office of International Trade Policy 377-5327

This office is responsible for the development and implementation of the department's position on international trade policy, including tariffs, import quotas, international commodity agreements, and trade negotiations and agreements. The office prepares progress reports on multilateral trade negotiations in the department's biweekly journal, *Commerce America*.

BUREAU OF EAST-WEST TRADE (BEWT) 377-5251

This bureau coordinates policies and programs for trade with the Communist countries. It analyzes problems peculiar to East-West trade, and studies the market potential for United States business in these Communist countries.

Office of East-West Country Affairs
PRC Affairs Division
William W. Clarke, Director 377-3583

All activities of the Industry and Trade Administration involving the PRC, Outer Mongolia, and North Korea (and to a lesser extent Vietnam-Cambodia) are handled by this division of BEWT. The division compiles, maintains, and disseminates the department's information about PRC trade and related economic subjects. Its functions are primarily to promote trade and regulate exports with Communist countries.

BEWT receives and processes the trade statistics provided by the Bureau of the Census of the Department of Commerce. Computer runs are printed monthly, quarterly, and annually, detailing commodities exported to and imported from the PRC. In addition, BEWT receives annual statistics from the 14 leading industrial nations (including Japan) and Belgium and Luxembourg regarding their trade with the PRC.

As no formal diplomatic relations existed between the United States and the PRC until December 31, 1978, trade negotiations were previously handled by the National Council for U.S.-China Trade (see entry H37). This private, nonprofit organization has the most up-to-date information pertaining to U.S.-PRC trade.

The PRC Division also participates in the East-West Trade Advisory Committee which is comprised of private businessmen, scholars, and government officials. The committee meetings are open to the public and serve as a forum for the exchange of ideas between BEWT, United States business and academic representatives. The agenda and date for each meeting are announced in the *Federal Register* (see entry N9). For further information, contact Gary Teske (377-4422).

In addition to these meetings, this division conducts seminars for businessmen interested in trade with the PRC. These seminars are held frequently and are open to the public. For the schedule of the forthcoming seminars, contact Martha Avery (377-3583).

The international trade specialists of this division will be willing to lecture for any organization located in the United States on topics relating to business with Communist China.

The BEWT statistical data bases are kept in the Office of East-West Policy and Planning (377-2456). This computerized trade information is the most extensive not only in the Washington area, but also in the entire United States (data are available from 1971 to the present). Scholars may have access to computer print-outs of this office. For further information, contact Robert Teal (377-5097).

The PRC Affairs Division distributes without charge a large number of publications and information sheets, including those of other government agencies. Some of its recent publications include: *Selected Trade and Economic Data of the Centrally Planned Economies* (1978); and *U.S. Trade Status with Communist Countries*. The division's staff also contributes to the United States Congress' *Joint Economic Committee Compendium* of research papers and reports concerning the economy of the PRC. It is issued on a 3-year rotating basis with similar compendia on the USSR and Eastern Europe published in the other years. A new volume on the PRC published in November 1978, is available through the GPO. For further information, contact John Hardt of the Library of Congress (426-5789), who is the editor of the volume.

Copies of an information brochure entitled *An Introduction to the Bureau of East-West Trade* (May 1976) are available free upon request.

BUREAU OF EXPORT DEVELOPMENT   377-5261

This bureau bears chief responsibility for developing and implementing the department's export expansion programs. It provides United States business firms with counseling, marketing information services, and sales-promotional assistance programs abroad. It manages export promotion and export expansion facilities, such as trade fairs and trade centers in foreign countries, and dispatches trade missions to promote United States exports to foreign countries (excepting the Communist countries).

Office of International Marketing
Richard Garnitz, Director   377-4231

This unit's primary function is to help United States business sell its goods in international markets by providing commercial, economic, and marketing information on export prospects and methods of marketing goods, and other export development activities. It manages export-promotion and export-expansion facilities, such as trade fairs and trade centers in key foreign cities (e.g., Tokyo, Taipei, etc.). Robert Kelly (377-5401), Country Market Manager for East Asia (e.g., South Korea, Taiwan, etc.) and Raymond Eiselt (377-2896), Country Market Manager for Japan are quite knowledgeable about United States trade relations with East Asian countries and can assist researchers in obtaining the bureau's recent publications pertaining to East Asia. These include: *Global Market Surveys* (in-depth foreign-market research reports covering 20-30 of the best foreign markets for selected United States products) and *Overseas Business Reports* covering specific countries or areas with economic and marketing data, laws, import, export and exchange regulations, and trade statistics. As part of this series, *Marketing in Japan* (April 1978) and *Marketing in Korea* (March 1977) have been published. In addition, the bureau publishes *Country Market Survey* on foreign markets; *International Marketing Events;* and *Index to Foreign Market Reports* which identifies reports received monthly from the United States Foreign Service (i.e., United States embassies and consulates) abroad concerning the host country's production trends and market potential.

The Office of Export Development (377-5131) maintains an Export Information Reference Room (377-2997) which contains a vertical file on a number of foreign countries, including South Korea. Most of the materials in the Korean file are studies conducted by the World Bank and the Asia Development Bank on economic projects and market reports. It is open to the public. For further information, contact Betty W. Patrick (377-2997), who is in charge of the reference room.

The Bureau of Export Development also compiles *World Traders Data Reports,* containing detailed commercial information (or "credit reports") on individual foreign firms. These reports are prepared by the United States embassies and consulates abroad to provide guidelines on the reliability of the foreign firms doing business with United States corporations. Profiles of major East Asian firms doing business with the United States can be obtained by contacting the Office of International Marketing (377-4231).

BUREAU OF ECONOMIC ANALYSIS   523-0777 (Information)

Tower Building
14th and K Streets, NW
Washington, D.C. 20230

This bureau monitors the "economic accounts" of the United States, including the nation's balance of payments. Its monthly journal, *Survey of Current Business,* publishes economic data relating to East Asia. The bureau's Reference Room (523-0595) contains copies of BEA periodicals and staff papers.

International Investment Division   523-0660/0661

This unit measures direct United States investment abroad and analyzes the economic impact of multinational corporations. It receives confidential quarterly reports from United States corporations with foreign investments; and publishes aggregated annual statistics of United States investment abroad, including East Asia, by country and region in *Survey* of *Current Business*. In addition, it has published *U.S. Direct Investment Abroad* for the years 1966-1977, which contains various data relating to United States investment overseas. Also useful is the division's publication entitled *Revised Data Series on U.S. Direct Investment Abroad, 1966-1974* (1976), which contains information and data on net capital outflows, reinvestment earnings, fees, and royalties. The Division's *Special Survey of U.S. Multinational Companies, 1970* (1972) covers the activities of United States multinational corporations and their foreign affiliates from 1966-1970.

The unit's raw data is transferred to computer tapes for storage. Outside researchers can have limited access to the tapes on a commercial basis. For further information, contact the division's Data Retrieval and Analysis Branch (523-0981).

Balance of Payment Division   523-0620

This division of the Bureau of Economic Analysis prepares current statistics and analyses of the balance of international payments (quarterly) and the international investment position of the United States (annually). The results are published quarterly in the issues of *Survey of Current Business*.

BUREAU OF THE CENSUS   (301) 763-7662 (Information)
Suitland Road and Silver Hill Road
Suitland, Maryland
(Mail: Department of Commerce
        Washington, D.C. 20233)

The Census Bureau is a general-purpose statistical agency which collects, tabulates, and publishes various statistical data on the people and economies of the United States and foreign countries. The bureau produces a considerable amount of East Asian demographic and foreign-trade statistics, as described below.

Foreign Trade Division   (301) 763-5342
Federal Office Building 3
Suitland, Maryland

On the basis of information obtained primarily from Shipper's Export Declarations and Customs entries, this division compiles detailed statistical data on the quantity and value of United States foreign trade, by commodity and country of destination or origin. This data is published in a series of monthly publications such as: *U.S. Export; U.S. General Imports; Highlights of U.S. Export and Import Trade; U.S. Waterborne Exports and General Imports,* and *U.S. Airborne Exports and General Imports.* Contents of these publications are briefly described in *Guide to Foreign Trade Statistics*. Most of the unit's published statistical tabulations are available also in microform and computer tape. For reference information on United States-East Asian trade relations for the past 5 years, contact the division's Trade Information Branch (763-5140).

Foreign Demographic Analysis Division (FDAD)
711   14th Street, NW, Room 705
Washington, D.C. 20230
Dr. John Aird, Chief   376-7692

This division studies population, manpower, economics, and statistical reporting systems of foreign countries, particularly Communist countries (e.g., the PRC). Some of the unit's research is computerized, namely population projections and gross value of industrial output statistics. For the division's noncomputerized data, see FDAD Library (entry A12). Recent FDAD publications include: *Non-Agricultural Employment in Mainland China* (1965); *Estimate and Projection of the Population of Mainland China 1953-1986* (1968); *Population Estimate for the Provinces of the People's Republic of China, 1953-1974* (1974); *Provincial Industrial Output in the People's Republic of China: 1949-75* (1976); and *Provinces of the People's Republic of China: A Political and Economic Bibliography* (1976).

Computer runs of population and gross values of industrial-output data can be obtained without charge. Contact Dr. Aird (376-7692) for further information.

Population Division   (301) 763-2870
International Demographic Statistics Staff
Scuderi Building
4235   28th Avenue
Marlow Heights, Maryland 20031

This unit compiles and evaluates a wide variety of current demographic data of the developing countries on the basis of official census and other statistical publications. It publishes a biannual *World Population* which contains statistics for total population and vital rates (e.g., births, deaths, growth rates, etc.) by country from 1950 to 1977. A "Country Demographic Profiles" series provides more detailed statistics for individual countries. *Country Demographic Profiles: Republic of China* was published in February 1978; and a similar volume on *Republic of Korea* was published in the summer of 1978. The unit also publishes occasional "International Research Documents," focusing on methodology and other specialized topics in the demographic studies.

The unit's International Demographic Data Center (763-2834) maintains extensive foreign population data (microfilmed) and can supply researchers with hard-copy demographic statistics on East Asian countries dating back to about 1955.

MARITIME ADMINISTRATION
Main Commerce Building

Office of International Activities   377-5685

This office manages United States maritime relations with foreign countries including East Asian governments. The staff can discuss the administration's work relating to East Asia, such as the shipment of grains and other commodities, trade studies, and participation in bilateral and multilateral conferences with East Asian nations.

Office of Trade Studies and Statistics   377-4578

This office compiles statistics on United States seaborne trade with East Asia and on East Asian merchant shipping, by country. Data is available to scholars in hard copy or computer print-outs. In addition, copies of its annual publications containing East Asian data can be obtained. These include *Merchant Fleets of the World; A Statistical Analysis of the World's Merchant Fleets; New Ship Construction;* and *Essential U.S. Trade Routes.*

NATIONAL OCEANIC AND ATMOSPHERIC ADMINISTRATION
(NOAA)   (301) 443-8910 (Information)
Washington Science Center
6010 Executive Boulevard
Rockville, Maryland 20852

Office of Oceanic and Atmospheric Sciences
International Relations Section   (301) 443-8761

The International Relations staff can refer researchers to NOAA's climatological, meteorological, oceanographic, and marine resources and other research centers for reference materials and data pertaining to East Asia. Dr. Nels Johnson is especially knowledgeable about NOAA's international programs.

National Ocean (Coast and Geodetic) Survey   (301) 443-8204

This unit handles world mapping and surveying for the Federal Aviation Administration (Department of Transportation) and the NOAA fleet, which visits East Asia.

Library and Information Services Division   (301) 443-8330 (Reference)

NOAA's library holdings on atmospheric and earth sciences, oceanography, hydrology, and fisheries are housed in several library centers throughout the Washington area. Inquiries regarding collection contents as well as center locations are handled by the division personnel.

National Marine Fisheries Service   634-7283

Office of the Assistant Director for International Fisheries
International Analysis and Services Division   (634-7267/7307)
Page Building No. 2, 3300 Whitehaven Street, NW
Washington, D.C. 20235

The International Analysis and Services Division collects extensive data on East Asian fishing and related subjects, including the economics of fishing, trade, marketing, government regulations and policies, and international disputes. These data are gathered from foreign government publications and trade journals, as well as from those of the United States government. The files are arranged by country and subject (including photographs and maps).

PATENTS AND TRADEMARK OFFICE   (703) 557-3080
Crystal Plaza Building 3
2021 Jefferson Davis Highway
Arlington, Virginia 22202
Mail: Washington, D.C. 20231

Office of Legislation and International Affairs   (703) 557-3065
Crystal Plaza Building 6

This office collects materials on foreign patent and trademark laws and regulations from around the world. The staff can provide reference information relating to the PRC, Japan, South Korea, and Taiwan. The office's own small library has a few holdings pertaining to East Asia; however, the Patent Office Scientific Library has extensive materials on Japan. It is described in the Libraries section (entry A13). The Office of Micrographic Systems (703-557-0410) maintains an extensive collection of microfilmed Japanese patent specification texts (in the vernacular language) covering the years 1969-1978. Over 40,000 Japanese patent texts are microfilmed annually. For further information, contact Kent Hughes (557-0410).

NATIONAL BUREAU OF STANDARDS (NBS)   (301) 921-1000
Gaithersburg, Maryland (Mail: Washington, D.C. 20234)
Edward L. Brady, Associate Director for Information Programs
(301) 921-3641

Office of International Relations
Steffen Peiser, Chief   (301) 921-2463

NBS has continuous on-going contacts with East Asian countries. NBS has participated in the "U.S.-Japan Cooperative Science Program" (since 1961) as well as the "U.S.-Japan Science Cooperative Program for Natural Resources" (since 1964). The bureau's responsibility involves not only an exchange of information with Japan, but also joint studies on technical work such as "earthquake prediction research." For South Korea, the bureau has provided a wide range of technical assistance, especially in connection with the establishment of the Korea Standards Research Institute (KSRI) in Seoul in 1975. The bureau has provided standard reference data as well as training for the KSRI personnel. Chang O. Kim of the NBS serves as coordinator for the United States-South Korea program (301-921-3889). With the PRC, the bureau has no formal exchange program. Nevertheless, informal contact and exchange visits between NBS personnel and their Chinese counterparts take place occasionally.

The Standard Reference Data System (921-2467) in the associate director's office coordinates the work of the four divisions of the NBS: Institute of Applied Technology; Institute for Basic Standards; Institute of Materials Research; and the Institute of Computer Sciences and Technology. The primary focus of the NSRDS is on the physical and chemical properties of well-characterized materials or systems. An effort is made to assess the accuracy of data reported in the primary research literature and to prepare compilations of critically evaluated data which will serve as reliable and convenient standards for the scientific and technical community. Copies of *National Standard Reference Data System Publication List, 1964-1977* are available free on request. An information brochure, *National Bureau of Standards at a Glance,* can also be obtained without charge on request.

National Technical Information Service (NTIS)   (703) 321-8500
5285 Port Royal Road
Springfield, Virginia 22161

NTIS Information Center and Bookstore
425   13th Street, NW, Suite 620
Washington, D.C. 20004
Mary Sutton, Manager   724-3374

NTIS is the central outlet for the public sale of government-sponsored research, development engineering reports and similar analyses prepared by federal agencies, their contractors or grantees, or by special study groups. NTIS also sells machine-processable data files. NTIS currently offers over 1 million titles for sale (covering projects from 1947), including about 150,000 titles of foreign origin. About 70,000 new titles are added annually.

Using the agency's on-line computer search service (NTISearch), more than 500,000 federally sponsored research reports published since 1964 can be located. Additional information on ongoing and recently terminated research projects, compiled by the Smithsonian Science Information Exchange (see entry K29), are also available. Tools for searching the NTIS titles include the new *Subject Guide to the NTIS Information Collection* with annual revisions and 3-4 year cumulations and the *Abstract Newsletter,* currently for 26 different subjects. *The Government Reports Announcements and Index* (biweekly) is another useful reference tool for the NTIS customers. In addition, over 1,000 *Published Searches* on various topics are available from computer searches already conducted by the NTIS. For a fee, researchers can request on-line searches for topics of interest to them that have not been covered by the *Published Searches.* The NTIS Bibliographic Data File (on magnetic tape) includes unpublished research summaries and can be leased by outside researchers.

NTIS publications of interest to East Asian specialists include: *Foreign Broadcast Information Service (FBIS) Daily Foreign Press and Radio Translations* (volume 1: the *People's Republic of China;* and volume 4: *Asia and Pacific*); Joint Publications Research Service (JPRS) translations and abstracts on the People's Republic of China, North Korea, and Japan; *Foreign Markets Reports; Foreign Market Airgrams;* and other monthly foreign-trade data.

In addition, NTIS has published numerous government-funded research reports on East Asia, including the following titles published in 1976: *Current Practice of the PRC with regard to International Law; Implications of China's Prospective Petroleum Development; The U.S./ Japan Military Alliance: Japanese Perceptions and the Prospective Impact of Evolving U.S. Military Doctrine and Technologies; Japan's Foreign Policy: Metamorphosis in Asia;* and *The Future of U.S. Military Commitments to Japan and Korea.*

K6 Congress

1. a. *The Capitol*
Washington, D.C. 20510
224-3121

   b. The galleries of the Senate and the House of Representatives, as well as most committee hearings are open to the public.

2. The legislative work is done largely by standing committees of both houses of Congress. (There are 15 in the Senate, and 22 in the House.) Those committees and subcommittees with active interest in East Asian affairs are listed below. Staff members of these committees are not only knowledgeable about the legislative process, but also willing to confer with scholars interested in the committees' operations. The *Congressional Record* contains a "Daily Digest" section which lists announcements of forthcoming committee activities including locations and subject matter. In addition, a schedule of congressional activities appears in the *Washington Post*.

   The Congressional Research Service (see entry K7) serves as the principal research organ for both houses of Congress. East Asian specialists in CRS's Foreign Affairs and Defense Division can help qualified researchers on recent or forthcoming congressional activities pertaining to East Asian affairs.

3. The Library of Congress is described in the Libraries section (see entry A30).

4. The *Congressional Record,* which is published daily while Congress is in session, prints the proceedings of the Senate and House of Representatives. Committee publications such as transcripts of hearings, special reports, and other documents are available from the office of each committee's staff. These publications can be purchased at Government Printing Office bookstores (see entry N9). In addition, they are available at the federal depository libraries. Researchers may request the committee staff to place their names on the committee's mailing list to receive free copies.

   The Government Printing Office (GPO) regularly issues subject-bibliographies of congressional publications on foreign affairs, United States intelligence activities, and other topics which can be obtained without charge at GPO bookstores.

STANDING COMMITTEES OF THE SENATE

Agriculture, Nutrition, and Forestry   224-2035
Russell Senate Office Building, Room 324
This committee specializes in matters relating to food, nutrition, and hunger, both in the United States and abroad. It has a subcommittee on Foreign Agricultural Policy.

Appropriations   224-3471
Dirksen Senate Office Building, Room 1235
The committee deals with appropriations for all governmental programs. Its Subcommittee on Foreign Operations reviews appropriations for foreign-assistance programs.

Armed Services   224-3871
Russell Senate Office Building, Room 212
This committee has jurisdiction over matters relating to the national military establishment, including military space activities, intelligence, arms control, and military research and development.

Banking, Housing, and Urban Affairs   224-7391
Dirksen Senate Office Building, Room 5300
The committee has jurisdiction over financial matters (other than appropriations and taxes), international economic affairs as they affect United States monetary policy, credit and financial institutions, economic growth, and urban affairs.

Commerce, Science and Transportation   224-4971
Dirksen Senate Office Building, Room 5202
The committee is concerned with interstate and foreign commerce, science and technology, transportation, communication, and consumer affairs.

Energy and Natural Resources   224-4971
Dirksen Senate Office Building, Room 3106
This committee specializes in matters relating to energy policy, regulation, conservation, research and development, and the distribution and utilization of natural resources.

Finance   224-4515
Dirksen Senate Office Building, Room 2227
The committee has jurisdiction over revenues and tax matters in general, and customs, tariffs, import quotas, and Social Security.

Foreign Relations   224-4651
Dirksen Senate Office Building, Room 4229
The committee specializes in matters relating to foreign relations, the diplomatic service, the United Nations and international monetary organizations, and foreign loans. It has a number of important subcommittees including those on East Asia and Pacific Affairs, Foreign Assistance, Foreign Economic Policy, International Operations, and Arms Control, Oceans, and International Environment.

Judiciary   224-5225
Dirksen Senate Office Building, Room 2226
The committee's jurisdiction includes civil liberties, immigration and naturalization, bankruptcy, mutiny, espionage, counterfeiting, and the United States judicial system.

Human Resources   224-5375
Dirksen Senate Office Building, Room 4230
The committee deals with education, labor, health, and the public welfare.

STANDING COMMITTEES OF THE HOUSE OF
REPRESENTATIVES
(No description is provided for committees whose interests coincide with Senate committees bearing the same or a similar name.)

Agriculture   225-2171
Longworth House Office Building, Room 1301

Appropriations   225-2771
The Capitol, Room H-218
Includes a Subcommittee on Foreign Operations.

Armed Services
Rayburn House Office Building, Room 2120
Includes a Subcommittee on Intelligence and Military Application of Nuclear Energy.

Banking, Currency, and Housing   225-4247
Rayburn House Office Building, Room 2129
The committee studies and reviews financial matters other than taxes and appropriations, including economic and price stabilization, valuation and devaluation of the dollar, international finance, international financial and monetary organizations, private and public housing, and the federal deposit insurance and reserve system. It has a Subcommittee on International Development Institutions and Finance; and a Subcommittee on International Trade, Investment, and Monetary Policy.

Education and Labor   225-4527
Rayburn House Office Building, Room 2170

International Relations   225-5021
Rayburn House Office Building, Room 2170
Formerly known as the Foreign Affairs Committee, this committee contains a number of important subcommittees including those on: Asian and Pacific Affairs; International Development; International Economic Policy and Trade; International Operations; International Organizations; and Security and Scientific Affairs.

Interstate and Foreign Commerce   225-2927
Rayburn House Office Building, Room 2125
The committee's jurisdiction includes matters pertaining to interstate and foreign commerce, communications, travel and tourism, and public health.

Judiciary   225-3951
Rayburn House Office Building, Room 2137

Merchant Marine and Fisheries   225-4047
Longworth House Office Building, Room 1334
This committee deals with matters involving the merchant marine, navigation and pilotage laws, international fishing agreements, and conservation of fisheries and wildlife.

Science and Technology   225-6375
Rayburn House Office Building, Room 2321
The committee is concerned with scientific and astronautical research and development, environmental and energy research (except nuclear energy), domestic and international scientific planning, analysis, and cooperation.

Ways and Means   225-3625
Longworth House Office Building, Room 1102
In addition to revenues and taxation in general, the committee is also concerned with reciprocal trade agreements, customs, and the transportation of dutiable goods.

JOINT COMMITTEES OF THE CONGRESS

Economic 224-5171
Dirksen Senate Office Building, Room G-133
This committee is concerned with economic growth, fiscal policy, and international economics. It has a subcommittee on International Economics.

Note: In addition, various Select and Special committees of both houses of Congress, such as the Senate's Select Committee on Intelligence (224-1700), the House Permanent Select Committee on Intelligence (225-4121), the House Select Committee on Ethics (225-8461), and the Senate Select Committee on Ethics (224-2981), will occasionally deal with East Asian-related matters (e.g., the Tong Sun Park case).

K7 Congressional Research Service (CRS)

1. a. *Library of Congress Building*
    10 1st Street, SE
    Washington, D.C. 20540
    426-5700

    b. Not open to the public.

    c. Gilbert Gude, Director

2. The sole function of the CRS is to provide reference and research assistance to members of Congress and congressional committees. The funds appropriated for the CRS do not provide for the publication of the research projects for public consumption. The services are rendered solely for the members of Congress; and the research products are the property of the congressional member or committee which requested them. Another member of Congress or committee can obtain these materials only through specific arrangements by which CRS receives approval of the member or committee which requested the product. Periodically, some CRS research studies are read into the *Congressional Record* or published in a congressional committee report.

    The Foreign Affairs and National Defense Division (William Whitson, Chief) prepares research reports, background studies, and other materials on major regions of the world, including East Asia. Although most research projects are undertaken directly upon request by a congressional committee or congressman, sometimes the staff can initiate projects that may be of current concern in Congress. Within this division, there are a number of research teams including an East Asia/Pacific team. The type of research performed by the team includes: (1) major analytical research on topics and issues such as human rights in East Asian countries, normalization of Sino-American diplomatic relations, United States troop withdrawal from South Korea, trade problems with Japan, etc.; and, (2) oral briefings of the most recent developments in East Asia for congressional staff members.

3. See Library of Congress (entry A30).

4.   CRS *Issue Briefs* review major policy topics, summarizing the pertinent legislative history, and providing bibliographies for further reading. *CRS Review* (a monthly digest of CRS activities) is sent to each member of Congress. In addition reports on public policy issues, known as *Multilithed Report Series,* are compiled for the members of Congress.

   The CRS also indexes recent periodical articles on public policy issues (including foreign affairs, by country) from about 1,500 journals. This "Bibliographic Citation" file is accessible to researchers in machine-readable format through the SCORPIO data base located in the Library of Congress (see entry A30).

K8   Defense Department (DOD)

1.   a.   *The Pentagon*
         Washington, D.C. 20301
         545-6700 (Information)
         697-9312 (Public Affairs)

   b.   Closed to those without security clearance or an appointment arranged in advance.

2.   The Department of Defense (DOD) and its major components—the Departments of the Army, Navy, and Air Force—have divisions which support some external research. Most of the work done for DOD is on a contract basis. For details see point 5 below.

3.   See Army Library (entry A7) and Navy Department Library (entry A36).

4.   Each major subunit of DOD controls its own internal records until they are transferred to the National Archives. DOD's Records Management Branch (695-0970) can refer outside researchers to individual records-control sections within the department. Freedom-of-Information Act requests for the records of the Office of the Secretary of Defense and the Joint Chiefs of Staff are processed by the Directorate for Freedom-of-Information and Security Review (697-4325) in the Office of the Assistant Secretary of Defense for Public Affairs. The Directorate can refer researchers to appropriate Freedom-of-Information officers in other DOD branches.

   Virtually all research reports from DOD contracts (both classified and unclassified) are deposited with the Defense Documentation Center (DDC) (see entry G3). Unclassified research reports are available at the National Technical Information Service, whereas the classified ones remain inaccessible to outside researchers. Some of the DOD-prepared data on the armed forces of East Asian countries and United States military assistance to East Asia can be found in *Foreign Military Sales and Military Assistance Facts* (annual) published by DOD's Defense Security Assistance Agency. Free copies are available upon request.

5. OFFICE OF THE ASSISTANT SECRETARY OF DEFENSE FOR
    INTERNATIONAL SECURITY AFFAIRS (ISA)
    Michael Armacost, Deputy Assistant Secretary of Defense for ISA (East
    Asia, Pacific, and Inter-American Affairs)
    Directorate, East Asia and Pacific Region   695-4175
    Brig. Gen. T. C. Pinckney, Director

This office develops and coordinates DOD policies and research in the
fields of international political-military and economic affairs. It studies
general problems of international security as well as arms control and
disarmament questions; administration of overseas military assistance
programs; arms sales to foreign powers; and provides policy guidance
for United States military missions abroad and for United States representatives to international organizations and conferences. The office is
also responsible for negotiating and monitoring agreements with foreign
governments with regard to equipment, facilities, operating rights, and
the status of forces.

The ISA administers an extensive external research program with
emphasis on identifying and analyzing alternative defense policies to
cope with international problems likely to affect the security of the
United States. Research for ISA is performed by various federal contract
research centers (e.g., Institute for Defense Analyses), other private
nonprofit research organizations and university-based research centers.
Research proposals are accepted from these and other research organizations if they meet ISA requirements.

ISA does not issue any recurring research publications. Nor does it
compile a comprehensive bibliography of its unclassified research on
East Asia that is available to the public. Interested researchers may contact the staff assistant to the Deputy Assistant Secretary for ISA for a
description of research done on selected subjects and for assistance in
gaining access to such materials. Many of the unclassified research
reports funded by this office can be purchased through the National
Technical Information Service (see entry K5). An example of the
published work found by ISA is Thomas W. Robinson's *The Sino-
Soviet Border Situation, 1969-1975: Military, Diplomatic, and Political
Maneuvering*. Part 2 of *U.S. Security Interests on the Sino-Soviet Periph-
ery* (Croton-on-Hudson, N.Y.: Hudson Institute, 1976).

DEFENSE ADVANCED RESEARCH
    PROJECTS AGENCY (DARPA)
Administrative Office   694-3032
Architect Building, Room 802
1400 Wilson Boulevard
Arlington, Va. 22209

To supplement the research programs of the 3 military services, **DARPA**
conducts research in such fields as strategic technology, tactical technology, nuclear monitoring, materials sciences, information processing
techniques, and cybernetics technology. Research related to foreign and
national security affairs is carried out at both the basic and exploratory
research levels and is administered by the DARPA's Cybernetic Technology Office (694-1303).

The Cybernetic Technology Office places emphasis on the development of a prototype crisis early-warning system; development of prototype systems for defining and measuring United States national interests abroad; development of quantitative methods for assessing and forecasting strategic threat situations; development and application of advanced analytic and computerized approaches to strategic planning and forecasting in short- to long-run periods. Most of the research conducted in these areas is unclassified, and results are published frequently in professional journals. For information concerning research proposals, write to: the Director of Defense Advanced Research Project Agency. Copies of the agency's brochure, *Defense Advanced Research Projects Agency,* are available upon request.

DEFENSE INTELLIGENCE AGENCY (DIA)
697-7072 (Information)
Deputy Director for Intelligence Research
    Eastern Division   692-5909
    Freedom-of-Information Service   692-5766

DIA coordinates intelligence-gathering activities of the three United States military intelligence services: The Army's Assistant Chief of Staff for Intelligence (ACSI), the Office of Naval Intelligence (ONI), and the Air Force Intelligence Service (AFIS). From United States embassies throughout the world, including East Asia, defense attachés from the United States armed forces provide DIA analysts with information on military capabilities, personnel, deployments, equipment, political roles, as well as biographic data on leading members of the officer corps of each country's armed forces. Information and data so gathered remain classified. DIA also conducts extensive research on major foreign powers. However, its work is classified and no inventory of its research is available. Although most agency research is done in-house, qualified outside specialists are hired on contract to undertake research on major foreign powers, including the PRC.
    The DIA Reference Library (692-5311) is closed to outside researchers.

OFFICE OF THE SECRETARY OF DEFENSE (OSD)
Public Affairs
Philip A. Farris, Staff Assistant for Public Correspondence   697-6462

Because of the sensitive nature of DOD operations and activities, it is difficult to obtain information about the major divisions of the Defense Department. For this reason, scholars should contact Mr. Farris who can assist them in locating the divisions and personnel most appropriate for making further inquiries. He can also provide general information about DOD.

Historian's Office
Alfred Goldberg, Historian   697-4216/4217

This office conducts and prepares historical studies of the Department of Defense. It maintains a reference file of unclassified materials such as DOD publications and press clippings relating to the structural evolution of the department and the military services. It also maintains a small number of inactive DOD documents. Some of the works under preparation by the Historian's Office include a multivolume history of the Office of the Secretary of Defense, a volume on the organizational evolution of the DOD since 1947, a study of the United States military assistance program and NATO, 1948-1951, and a 2-volume history of United States prisoners of war in Indochina. Reference assistance to scholars is provided by the staff of this office which is accessible to outside scholars on an appointment basis.

DEFENSE SECURITY ASSISTANCE AGENCY   695-3291
Directorate for Operations
East Asia Division   697-7080

The East Asia Division administers United States military assistance programs (MAP) in East Asia. The agency issues an unclassified *Foreign Military Sales and Military Assistance Facts* (annual), which contains statistical data on United States military assistance programs as well as arms sales by country for the last 10 years. Copies of the publication may be obtained without charge from Stanley Stack, Director of the Data Management Division (697-3574).

NATIONAL SECURITY AGENCY (NSA)   (301) 688-6524
    (Information)
Fort George G. Meade, Md. 20755

Along with the Central Intelligence Agency (CIA) and Defense Intelligence Agency (DIA), NSA is one of the "Big Three" of the United States intelligence community. It conducts highly technical intelligence-gathering activities worldwide; however, its organizational structure remains classified.

OFFICE OF THE SECRETARY OF THE JOINT CHIEFS OF STAFF
Historical Division   697-3088
Documents Division   695-5363

The Historical Division is responsible for the compilation of the histories of the Joint Chiefs of Staff (JCS) and for special background studies. Most of its work is classified. However, Chief Historian Robert J. Watson and his staff can assist scholars in identifying and locating JCS documents.

The Documents Division reviews internal records for release through the National Archives and processes Freedom-of-Information Act requests for JCS documents. Normally, a 20-year schedule for declassification of the JCS documents is in effect. As a result, most of the JCS documents relating to World War II and the immediate postwar period are available at the National Archives and Records Service. For further information on the available JCS documents, contact William Cunliffe (523-3340) in the National Archives Modern Military Records Branch.

DEPARTMENT OF THE ARMY   697-2352 (Public Information)
Office Deputy Chief of Staff for Operations and Plans
Politico-Military Division   697-6850

This office supports foreign affairs research through contract with Foreign Area Studies, The American University, Washington, D.C. (see entry M3), for the preparation of area handbooks for various foreign countries. The 109 area handbooks published so far are available at the Government Printing Office bookstores, the U.S. Army Publications Center, and National Technical Information Center.

In addition, the office also carries out research on various international issues affecting United States security interests in major regions of the world, including East Asia. Occasionally, it hires outside specialists to perform contract research on important security issues. An example of such work is *The Maintenance of U.S. Forces in Korea* (unclassified) by a research team of the Stanford Research Institute headed by William M. Carpenter and Young C. Kim in 1975.

THE ADJUTANT GENERAL   695-0163
Records Management Division (Administrative Management Directorate)
S. J. Pomrenze, Chief
Forrestal Building, Room GA084
1000 Independence Avenue, SW
Washington, D.C. 20314

The Records Management Division and its branches can provide valuable assistance to scholars seeking access to the U.S. Army historical records. It administers a number of programs, grants clearance, and access to classified materials, determines what has been declassified, and helps the National Archives and Records Service in processing Army documents and records.

CHIEF OF PUBLIC AFFAIRS
697-2352 (Public information inquiries)
697-2351 (Public Information Division—News)

The Public Information Division handles Freedom-of-Information requests. The staff can also provide scholars with general information and directions for the various subunits of the Army.

CENTER OF MILITARY HISTORY   693-5002
Forrestal Building, Room 6A015
1000 Independence Avenue, SW
Washington, D.C. 20314
Brig. Gen. James L. Collins, Jr., Chief of Military History
Dr. Maurice Matloff, Chief Historian

The Center of Military History conducts historical studies on the U.S. Army. Most of its research is done by the staff. The Center has published a number of U.S. Army historical studies, including the *United States Army in World War II, United States Army in the Korean War,* and an *Army Lineage* series. Copies of *Publications of the U.S. Army Center of Military History* can be obtained without charge upon request.

The Center of Military History's reference library contains a large collection of Army publications, regulations, and directories. Among its holdings (totaling about 35,000 volumes), one can find about 300-400 volumes on East Asia, including the following: *South Korean Interim Government Activities* (34 volumes); *Summation of Nonmilitary Activities in Japan and Korea* (1945-1948) (35 volumes); *Summation of Military Government Activities in Korea* (1945-1947) (34 volumes); and *Monthly Summary of Operations—S.W. Pacific Area* (WW II period) 20 volumes).

Staff historians will assist researchers in locating U.S. Army source materials in the National Archives as well as in the Army Military History Institute at Carlisle Barracks, Carlisle, Pennsylvania 17013.

For the archival resources located at the Center, see entry B3 in the Archives section of this guide.

DEPARTMENT OF THE NAVY (AND THE MARINE CORPS)
697-4627 (Public Information)
The Pentagon
Washington, D.C. 20350

OFFICE OF NAVAL INTELLIGENCE
Rear Adm. Donald P. Harvey, Director   695-3944

Because of the nature of the sources used, most of the office's work is classified. Its primary function is to monitor major developments in the naval programs of foreign powers. Researchers seeking specific information should write a letter of inquiry to the office, explaining precisely what information they want and requesting advice on how to get it. Also scholars should cite the Freedom-of-Information Act as it pertains to their cases. The informative book *Naval Intelligence Command* (1975) and an organizational chart are available free on request. An unclassified "History of Naval Intelligence" is under preparation by Capt. Lyman Packard.

NAVAL HISTORICAL CENTER   433-2210/2364
Washington Navy Yard, Building 220
9th and M Streets, SE
Washington, D.C. 20374
Rear Adm. J. D. H. Kane, Jr., Director
William J. Morgan, Head, Historical Research Branch
Capt. J. H. B. Smith, Head, Curator Branch
Comdr. T. A. Damon, Director, Navy Memorial Museum
Dr. Dean C. Allard, Director, Operational Archives Branch

The Naval Historical Center is entrusted with the task of conducting research, writing, and publication programs in the field of U.S. Naval history. In addition to a library (entry A36), archives (entry B9), museum (entry C12), and still-pictures collection (entry F10), it provides a number of other reference services to naval officials, researchers, and the general public.

The Center has published many titles of potential interest to East Asian specialists, including the multivolume *Dictionary of American Naval Fighting Ships;* a periodically updated *United States Naval History: A Bibliography; U.S. Naval History Sources in the Washington Area and Suggested Research Subjects* (1970) by Dean C. Allard and Betty Bern; *Pearl Harbor: Why, How, Fleet Salvage and Final Appraisal* (1968) by Vice Adm. Homer N. Wallin; *United States Administration of the Trust Territories of the Pacific Islands* (1957), 3 volumes, by Comdr. Dorothy E. Richard; and *Bulletins of the Intelligence Center, Pacific Ocean Area Joint Intelligence Center, Pacific Ocean Area and the Commander in Chief Pacific and Pacific Ocean Area, 1942-1946* (41 microfilm reels). Copies of *Naval History Division Publications in Print* can be obtained free on request.

MARINE CORPS HISTORY AND MUSEUM DIVISION
433-3534 (Information)
433-3483 (Reference)
Washington Navy Yard, Building 58
9th and M Streets, SE
Washington, D.C. 20374
Brig. Gen. E. H. Simmons, Director of Marine Corps History and
Museums
Henry I. Shaw, Jr., Chief Historian

This division handles research, writing, archival, and museum programs related to the study of the history of the United States Marine Corps. Its publications are described in the *Marine Corps Historical Publications Catalog,* which is periodically updated and available from the division. The publications relating to East Asia include: *The United States Marines in North China, 1945 to 1949* (1968); *One Hundred Eighty Landings of the United States Marines 1800-1934* (1934); *History of the U.S. Marine Corps Operations in World War II* (Vol. 5: *China and Japan*); *U.S. Marine Operations in Korea,* 5 vols.; and *The United States Marines in the Occupation of Japan* (1969) by Henry I. Shaw, Jr. Free copies of *Marine Corps Historical Publications Catalog* are available on request.

Note: Archives, personal papers, oral history, and still-photo collections as well as the reference library of the Marine Corps Historical Center are described in the appropriate sections of this guide.

DEPARTMENT OF THE AIR FORCE
695-5554 (Public Information)

DIRECTORATE OF ADMINISTRATION
Documentation Systems Division
Documentation Information and Services Branch
M. Kip Ward, Chief   695-4992

This branch handles researchers' requests for information based on the Freedom-of-Information Act. The staff can also be helpful in locating desired research materials within the Department of the Air Force.

OFFICE OF INFORMATION
Magazine and Book Branch   697-4065
Security Review Branch   697-3222

Scholars seeking access to Air Force records in the National Archives
and other depositories must obtain prior clearance through this branch.
The staff can assist researchers in locating the materials needed and in
obtaining limited clearance. However, all research involving classified
materials must be reviewed by the Security Review Branch within the
Office of Information.

OFFICE OF AIR FORCE HISTORY
Forrestal Building, Room 8EO82
1000 Independence Avenue, SW
Washington, D.C. 20314
Maj. Gen. John W. Huston, Chief   693-7399
Dr. Stanley L. Falk, Chief Historian

Staff historians of this office will assist researchers in locating Air Force
records. The majority of the Air Force's official archives is located at the
Albert F. Simpson Historical Research Center, Maxwell Air Force Base
in Alabama. Another major collection is maintained by the National
Archives in Suitland, Maryland. Records of the Air Corps and Army
Air Forces Central Correspondence files, the Air Corps Library, and
other collections dating from 1907 to 1954 are located in Suitland as
are Air Force records after 1954. The office has published a number of
titles, including: *United States Air Force History: A Guide to Documentary Sources* (1973) compiled by Lawrence J. Paszek and *United
States Air Force History: An Annotated Bibliography* (1971) by Mary
Ann Cresswell and Carl Berger. Copies of these publications can be
obtained without charge on request.

NATIONAL DEFENSE UNIVERSITY
693-1076 (Public Affairs)
Fort Lesley J. McNair
4th and P Streets, SW
Washington, D.C. 20319

The National Defense University conducts an annual 10-month course
of concentrated study on national security for about 140 senior United
States military officers and civilian government officials. Issue-oriented
East Asian area seminars and lectures are an integral part of the core
courses offered at the university. Students may take East Asian area
studies as an elective. Most lectures and seminars are conducted by the
specialists (both within and outside the government) invited by the
university. The annual course guide and syllabus on East Asian studies
may be obtained from the National Defense University's Chief of Staff
(693-8318) or from the Director of East Asian Studies.

The National Defense University Library (693-8437) has a collection
of English-language literature on East Asian history, economics, politics,
and international relations. The East Asian collection consists mostly of
post-1960 imprints and numbers approximately 2,000 volumes. The
library is not open to the public, but outside researchers may use the
facilities with prior permission of the Director of the Library (693-8437).

K9 Energy Department (DOE)

1. a. *Forrestal Building*
    1000 Independence Avenue, SW
    Washington, D.C. 20545
    252-5000 (Information)

    Note: Various offices of the newly created Department of Energy are scattered throughout the Washington area as of the spring of 1979. However, they are scheduled to be consolidated at the Forrestal Building (which houses DOE's headquarters) in the near future. Inevitably, locations and telephone numbers of many of the offices listed below will become out-of-date shortly. When the phone numbers listed below become inoperative, contact the DOE information operator (252-5000) for new addresses and phone numbers of the offices concerned.

    b. Access to some offices is restricted. Researchers should arrange appointments in advance.

2. Many units of the Energy Department conduct research in the field of energy development, conservation, and management. Most of the research is done by the in-house staff, but some outside research firms are contracted to carry out specific projects for the DOE. For details, see point 5 below.

3. Each major DOE agency has a small specialized reference library designed specifically for staff use.

4. Because of the relative newness of the Department (established on October 1, 1977) both its publication program and internal record-management system are still in the embryonic stage. Copies of the following publications are available on request from the Office of Public Affairs (252-5466): *The National Energy Plan* (1977); *U.S. Department of Energy Organization and Functions: Fact Book* (1978); and U.S. Department of Energy, Energy Information Administration, *Annual Report to Congress*. Those wishing to receive DOE's highly informative *Monthly Energy Review* may subscribe at $50 per year through the National Technical Information Service, Commerce Department (see entry K5).

    Any request for access to classified materials of the Department based on the Freedom-of-Information Act should be directed to the Freedom-of-Information officer in the Office of Public Affairs (252-5466).

5. ASSISTANT SECRETARY FOR INTERNATIONAL AFFAIRS
    252-5800
    Harry E. Bergold, Jr.

    The Assistant Secretary for International Affairs is responsible for the department's international energy policy, and his office monitors world energy price and supply trends and technological developments. In addition, this office is responsible for the development of the DOE's policy positions on nuclear nonproliferation and nuclear fuel issues. It also handles international cooperative energy programs with foreign governments and international organizations.

Bureau of International Programs   252-5921
Holsey G. Handyside, Deputy Assistant Secretary for International Programs

Office of International Programs   252-6140
Dr. Jack Vanderryn, Director

A desk officer (Bill Carter, 252-6144) in the Office of International programs monitors energy research and development activities and technology transfers, including nuclear energy, in East Asia. His data derive from the reports of DOE field representative in Tokyo as well as from the United States Department of State materials. Both classified and unclassified documents are interfiled in his office and are not accessible to outside researchers. However, he will be willing to confer with scholars and refer them to appropriate branches and personnel within the Department. For information on South Korea, researchers should also consult with Diana Gulbinowicz (252-6153) in the Office of International Programs.

Office of Nuclear Affairs   252-6175
Hal Bengelsdorf, Director

This office monitors the development and use of nuclear power for energy, in the United States and abroad, including aspects specified in the bilateral and multilateral agreements signed by the United States and foreign governments. Currently, the United States has cooperative agreements with Japan, South Korea, and Taiwan. Of these, the most extensive is the United States-Japanese agreement for cooperation in the civil uses of atomic energy, signed in 1955 and amended several times subsequently. There are 12 U.S.-built or licensed nuclear power reactors operating in Japan and an additional 10 U.S.-licensed power reactors are under construction. In 1969, a technical exchange agreement on fast breeder reactors between the United States and Japan was signed. This agreement has provided for exchanges in the following areas: reactor physics, nuclear safety, fuels and materials, and sodium technology. In 1976 the agreement was expanded to include the exchange of information on plant experience and component development. Cooperation under the fast reactor exchange has included reciprocal visits and the exchange of technical reports between the United States and Japan. In addition, over the years, the United States has provided not only enriched uranium but also plutonium to Japan.

The Office of Nuclear Affairs also monitors nuclear fuel export transactions as well as matters relating to nuclear nonproliferation. Copies of "International Cooperation in Energy R & D" (1977) can be obtained free upon request.

Bureau of International Trade and Resources   252-5918
Peter Borre, Deputy Assistant Secretary for International Trade and Resources

Staff analysts in the Office of Trade and Resources within the bureau monitor oil production, consumption, imports and exports in East Asia, whereas another unit in the bureau, the Office of Industry Operations, keeps track of the U.S. oil companies' operations and activities in the various regions of the world, including East Asia.

Bureau of International Policy Development   252-5915
Sarah Jackson, Deputy Assistant Secretary for International
  Policy Development

Staff members in the Office of Special Regions Policy within the bureau
are involved in the formulation of DOE's policies toward foreign countries. Barbara Allen (252-6380) is a Japan specialist covering U.S.-
Japanese bilateral relations, while Robert Ichord (252-6380) is responsible for the study of U.S.-Asian/Pacific relations and North-South relations. Those desiring information and data relating to East Asian
countries will find Ichord particularly helpful.

The Office of Less Developed Countries (LDC) Programs within the
bureau has developed a computerized "World Energy Data System"
(WENDS) in cooperation with the ARGONNE National Laboratory
(Argonne, Illinois). The WENDS contains energy-related data on 53
foreign countries, including the PRC, Japan, South Korea, and Taiwan.
More specifically, it has two different types of data bases: country data
and technology data. The country data deals with information pertaining to indigenous energy policy, production and consumption, and supply and demand of energy resources in each of the 53 countries covered. The technology data, on the other hand, deals with 9 specific categories of energy information, including solar, nuclear, and geothermal
energy development programs of the foreign countries. The computerized data system is not accessible to outside researchers. For further information, contact Martha Strong (376-9842).

Bureau for International Energy Research   252-5890
A. Denny Ellerman, Deputy Assistant Secretary for International
  Energy Research

Within the bureau, staff members in the Office of Current Assessments
monitor East Asian energy research developments relating to oil, gas,
coal, and nuclear energy. Their data base includes United States intelligence sources. The unit publishes an unclassified and periodically updated report on *The Role of Foreign Governments in the Energy Industries* which contains a chapter on Japan (but nothing on the PRC, South
Korea, and Taiwan).

Another unit of the bureau, the Office of Market Analysis, monitors
energy market developments in OECD countries (which include Japan)
and non-OPEC developing countries, including the PRC, South Korea,
and Taiwan. Its primary focus is on the supply and demand of energy
in these countries. For further information, contact Dr. Harman Frans-
sen (252-5893) who is the director of the Office of Market Analysis.

ENERGY INFORMATION ADMINISTRATION (EIA)

The EIA is responsible for collecting, processing, and publishing data on
energy resources and reserves, the financial status of energy-producing
companies, production, demand, consumption, and the supply of energy
here and abroad. The EIA is also responsible for analyzing long-term
energy trends in the United States and abroad.

Bureau of Energy Data   566-9698
Office of Energy Data and Interpretation
Division of Interfuel, Nuclear, and Other Energy Resources Statistics
International Statistics Branch   566-6545

The International Statistics Branch maintains an extensive collection of foreign publications, including those from Japan, South Korea, and Taiwan, which are largely statistical yearbooks containing data on each country's energy production and consumption, imports and exports, etc. This specialized collection is filed not only by country, but also by energy commodity (e.g., coal, gas, oil, nuclear, etc.). It is located in the International Statistics Branch Documentation Center and may be consulted by outside researchers. For further information, contact Patricia Bush (566-6590).

The branch's staff prepares and updates energy statistical surveys of foreign countries that include the PRC, Japan, South Korea, and Taiwan. This data may be made accessible to researchers through arrangements with the office.

Bureau of Applied Analysis
Office of Integrative Analysis   566-9705
International Energy Analysis Division   566-9387

The International Energy Analysis Division is engaged in economic forecasting and modeling by utilizing various computerized programs. Its computer files include United Nations data on world energy consumption from 1950-1975 and DOE profiles of foreign countries' nuclear plants and capacity, including Japan, South Korea, and Taiwan. Computer printouts will be available to researchers upon request. For further information, contact W. Calvin Kilgore (566-9397), who is the division director.

ENERGY INFORMATION ADMINISTRATION
    CLEARINGHOUSE   634-5641
Thomas Daugherty, Director

The clearinghouse distributes several EIA publications of potential interest to East Asia specialists, including *International Petroleum Annual* which reports data on oil production, consumption, trade, and prices by country; *World Natural Gas, Annual;* an annual *World Petroleum Production* report on OPEC member nations; and *Monthly Energy Review* with statistics based on published CIA data.

K10 Environmental Protection Agency (EPA)

1. a. *Waterside Mall*
        401 M Street, SW
        Washington, D.C. 20460
        755-2673

    b. Open to researchers; however, appointments are recommended.

2. The agency's Office of International Activities (OIA) (755-2780) coordinates various international programs designed to maximize international cooperation in coping with environmental pollution problems.

   Bilateral Programs: The OIA's bilateral activities range from exchanging environmental documents to supplying emergency expertise and supervising foreign-based research. As of May 1978, the only East Asian country with which the United States had a bilateral agreement was Japan. On the basis of the United States-Japan Environmental Agreement signed in August 1975, the United States-Japan Joint Planning and Coordinating Committee meets once a year, alternately in Japan and the United States. In addition, annual meetings are also held for each of the 13 bilateral projects (e.g., waste water, solid waste, air pollution, etc.) established by the agreement. Persons interested in United States-Asian exchange programs should contact Kirk Maconaughay (755-0523/8712). Some reference material, such as *Quality of the Environment in Japan* (1977), is available through Maconaughay's office.

   U.S. International Referral Center (755-1836) maintains a collection of miscellaneous foreign environmental documents acquired by EPA from 1972-1976 through bilateral information-exchange programs. The collection may be examined by outside researchers through prior arrangement with the office. Cataloged by country, a national index is available. The Center can also provide researchers with an international directory of environmental information available in the more than 70 participant countries of the United Nations Environment Program–International Referral System. Information concerning sources of East Asian environmental information by country can be obtained from the EPA's U.S. International Environmental Referral Center.

4. The EPA library (755-0308) contains over 10,000 books and 180,000 documents with emphasis on air, water and noise pollution, ecological matters, and antipollution programs. The library also receives over 500 periodicals, including several from East Asia. The library issues a quarterly *EPA Reports Bibliography* which can be purchased at the Commerce Department's National Technical Information Center (NTIS).

K11 Export-Import Bank of the United States (Eximbank)

1. a. *811 Vermont Avenue, NW*
      Washington, D.C. 20571
      566-2117

   b. Open to the public; however, internal records are restricted.

2. The "Eximbank" is an independent agency of the United States government which provides loans, guarantees, and insurance to help finance the sale of American goods and services abroad. The bank's staff works closely with the Department of State and the Department of Commerce in assessing the ability of specific foreign buyers to pay for United States imports. Although individual country loan records and assessments are confidential, staff members will gladly discuss general questions with scholars.

The bank's Policy Analysis Staff (566-8861) conducts research on internat.ɔnal economic developments which could affect the bank and its programs. Research areas include methodologies for economic analysis and reviews of bank programs, export financing patterns, and programs in the United States and abroad, trends in individual industries and commodities worldwide, domestic and international capital-market developments, and fluctuations in interest rates, prices, and other economic indicators. These studies are also considered confidential.

For many years, Japan, South Korea, and Taiwan have been active customers of the Eximbank. The bank's recent transactions with these East Asian countries have been as follows: Japan—Bank of Tokyo secured a loan of $75 million for United States cotton to be spun and processed (October 31, 1977); South Korea—Korea Development Bank obtained a loan of $44 million for purchasing overhead cranes and machine tools (April 17, 1978); and Taiwan—Taiwan Power Company received a loan of $194 million to import United States nuclear fuel (April 17, 1978).

4. Virtually all of the bank's loan-project files, research reports, and other internal records are considered confidential. Scholars may gain access to them only through Freedom-of-Information Act processes. Most of Eximbank's internal records (1934-present) are under the custody of the Administration Division (566-8815). A computerized index is being developed for records pertaining to the bank's active loan projects. For further information, contact Helen Wall, Manager of Records and Central Files (566-8815).

Eximbank publications are distributed by the Public Affairs Office (566-8881). Included are *Annual Report*; *Report to the U.S. Congress on Export Credit Competition and the Export-Import Bank of the United States* (semiannual); *Eximbank Record* (monthly newsletter); *Eximbank—Export Financing for: American Exporters, Overseas Buyers, Banks* (1978); and *A Businessman's Guide to the Cooperative Financing Facility* (1978). Also available are copies of *Press Releases* for the past two years. The older ones are loosely bound, filed both chronologically and geographically, and are available to the public.

K12 Federal Reserve Board

1. a. *20th Street and Constitution Avenue, NW*
    Washington, D.C. 20551
    452-3204 (Public Affairs Office)
    452-3684 (Freedom-of-Information Office)

    b. Open to the public; however, appointments are recommended.

2. The Federal Reserve System serves as the central bank of the United States. The System's Board of Governors oversees the operations of the 12 Federal Reserve Banks, their 25 branches, and other facilities located nationwide. Its Division of International Finance monitors international economic matters affecting United States monetary policy (e.g., foreign-exchange market developments, changes in the balance of payments, economic and financial developments abroad, etc.). In addition, the

division collects and analyzes information and data relating to the activities of United States banks abroad and for foreign banks in the United States.

The division's policy analysis and basic research activities are carried out largely by a staff of economists who are organized into 7 different sections. However, the division occasionally hires university professors and outside economists for various consulting roles. Scholars are frequently invited to lead or participate in staff seminars. For further information, contact the director of the Division of International Finance (452-3614).

The 7 functional sections of the division are as follows:

International Development Section (452-3771)
International Banking Section (452-3768)
U.S. International Transactions Section (452-3728)
Financial Market Section (452-3796)
World Payments and Economic Activity Section (452-3712)
International Trade and Financial Studies Section (452-3708)
Quantitative Studies Section (452-3540).

East Asian specialists should contact Robert F. Emery (452-3784), a staff economist specializing in East Asia in the International Development Section. He will be willing to confer with scholars interested in East Asian economic affairs.

3. The Federal Reserve Board Library is described in the Libraries section (entry A15).

4. From time to time, articles by staff members and statistical releases are published in the monthly *Federal Reserve Bulletin*. *Reports* and briefing papers selected for outside circulation and discussion are made available as "International Finance Discussion Papers" (e.g., *Asian Dollar Market* by Robert F. Emery). Copies may be obtained from the International Trade and Financial Studies Section (452-3708).

   Access to unpublished reports and other internal records, many of which are regarded as confidential, may be possible only through Freedom-of-Information Act procedures. Mrs. Rose Arnold (452-3684) is the Board's Freedom-of-Information officer.

K13 Foreign Claims Settlement Commission of the United States (FCSC)

1. a. *1111 20th Street, NW*
   Washington, D.C. 20579
   653-6166

   b. Open to the public.

2. The FCSC is an independent, quasijudicial agency within the Executive Branch of the United States government, which processes claims of United States nationals for losses suffered as a result of unfavorable action taken against them or their property by a foreign government. The commission has processed numerous claims filed by United States nationals for various damages resulting from military action during

World War II in specified areas of the European theater and in areas attacked and invaded by Japan, as well as claims against most Eastern European countries, the government of Cuba, and the People's Republic of China.

In the case of the Chinese Claims Program, the commission's mandate was to provide a record of losses for use in future negotiations with the PRC. The commission received and settled a total of 576 claims, rendering favorable decisions for 384 claims involving a total of $196,861,834 during 1969-1972.

The commission also supervised the operations of the Micronesian Claims Commission which administered the Micronesians' claims against Japan and the United States for damages arising out of hostilities between Japan and the United States during World War II as well as claims against the United States for losses arising after the various islands were secured by United States forces. From 1971 to 1976, the Micronesian Claims Commission processed about 11,000 claims awarding over $66 million to the Micronesian claimants.

The claims-files, which contain individual claims supporting background documentation, and the commission's rulings are stored in the Washington National Records Center in Suitland, Maryland. Researchers can examine these records by making arrangements with the Commission's library.

3. A small library (653-6152) contains volumes of the commission's decisions relating to claims against China, Eastern Europe, Cuba, and the Soviet Union as well as other claims programs. It maintains a card catalog for its holdings and a computer print-out index of the China claims.

4. The Commission publishes an *Annual Report to the Congress.*

K14 Health, Education, and Welfare Department (HEW)

1. a. *330 Independence Avenue, SW*
   Washington, D.C. 20201

   b. Open to the public.

2. The international programs administered by various branches of HEW, together with their publications and records, are described in sections 4-5 below.

3. See National Institute of Education—Educational Research Library (see entry A33) and National Library of Medicine (see entry A34).

4-5. EDUCATION DIVISION
   Office of Education—Division of International Education   245-9692
   Regional Office Building 3
   7th and D Streets, SW
   Washington, D.C. 20202

   The Division of International Education (DIE) plans and administers numerous training, institutional development, and research programs and services to expand and improve the international dimensions of education in the United States. DIE programs emphasize foreign language and area studies and the non-Western world. DIE is divided into 4 branches and a clearinghouse:

International Services and Research Branch (ISRB)   245-9425

ISRB conducts the long-standing programs of comparative studies on the educational systems of other countries. Some of the studies are done by staff specialists, others by outside specialists under contract. The Comparative Education Section (245-9425) has published a number of titles relating to East Asia. They include:

> *The Education of National Minorities in Communist China* (1970);
> *The Educational Revolution in China* (1972);
> *Education in Japan: A Century of Modern Development* (1975);
> and *Film Resources in Japan* (1975).

While the supply lasts, copies of the above and other CE publications may be obtained without charge from the ISRB.

International Studies Branch (ISB)   245-2356

This office administers NDEA Title VI and Fulbright-Hays programs for foreign-language and area studies. The following programs are available for East Asian specialists who are interested in conducting research abroad:

(1) *The Doctoral Dissertation Research Abroad Program* is designed to aid prospective teachers and scholars who wish to conduct original research in their area of specialization and to enhance their knowledge of the region, its people, and its language(s).

(2) *The Faculty Research Abroad Program* provides grants for research and study in foreign languages and area studies. It is designed to help U.S. institutions of higher education strengthen their faculty resources in foreign languages and area studies.

(3) *The Group Projects Abroad Program* provides grants to U.S. educational institutions for training, research, curriculum development, and/ or instructional materials preparation in international and intercultural studies.

(4) *The Advanced Language Training Program* awards are made to United States higher education institutions to provide intensive language training abroad in certain non-Western languages, including Chinese, Japanese, and Korean. For further information on these programs, contact either Shelley Laverty (245-2794) or Robert R. Dennis (245-9808).

In addition, the ISB also administers two domestic programs that can be of interest to East Asian specialists:

(1) *Foreign Language and Area Studies Fellowships Program* (NDEA Title VI program) offers fellowships for graduate students in foreign language and area studies. The fellowships program is administered by selected United States universities (NDEA area studies centers) to whom interested individuals should apply directly; and

(2) *Foreign Curriculum Consultant Program* provides experts from abroad to selected American educational institutions in planning and developing their curricula in foreign language and area studies.

International Exchange Branch (IEB)   245-2454

The Teacher Exchange Section (245-9700) administers two programs of interest to East Asian specialists:

The Seminars Abroad Program which provides opportunities for teachers and social studies curriculum specialists at the elementary, secondary, and college levels to participate in short-term seminars abroad.

The Teacher Exchange Program which provides opportunities for elementary and secondary school teachers and, in some cases, college faculty members (assistant professors and instructors) to teach abroad.

Ethnic Heritage Studies Branch (EHS)   245-2293

EHS provides grants to nonprofit educational institutions and organizations to promote ethnic heritage studies. Grants are for curriculum development or dissemination, training, and community activities. Grant guidelines and applications as well as the publication, *Ethnic Heritage Studies Program Grants 1974 through 1977,* are available from the EHS office.

DIE Clearinghouse   (245-7804)

This is a reference center which answers inquiries about activities that fall outside international educational programs and services administered by the Office of Education. These include student-exchange programs, regular academic-year-abroad programs, overseas employment, and programs of financial assistance to foreign students. Copies of "Study in Japan" are available free upon request. *Selected Programs and Services of the Division of International Education* and *Selected U.S. Office of Education Publications to Further International Education* are also available free upon request from the clearinghouse.

NATIONAL INSTITUTE OF EDUCATION (NIE)
Information and Communications Systems Division—Central ERIC
   Branch   254-5555
1200 19th Street, NW
Washington, D.C. 20208

In addition to limited international research in support of NIE's basic objectives and priorities, the institute participates in activities of the Center for Educational Research and Innovation of the Organization for Economic Cooperation and Development (OECD) which includes Japan. NIE is also participating in the proposed "Pacific Circle" which will include Japan, the United States, Canada, New Zealand, and Australia. These countries will exchange information about curricula materials and development, especially in the field of oceanography and trade. A preparatory meeting for the "Pacific Circle" was held in Tokyo in May 1978. For further information about NIE's international programs, contact Candice J. Sullivan (254-5680), coordinator of international activities.

The Information and Communications Division of NIE administers the computerized Educational Resources Information Center (ERIC) data bases. For details about ERIC, see the Data Bank section (entry G4). A free brochure describing the Educational Reference Center (and NIE's Proposals Clearinghouse) is available without charge on request.

PUBLIC HEALTH SERVICE
Office of the Assistant Secretary for Health
Office of International Health   (301) 443-4560
Parklawn Building
5600 Fishers Lane
Rockville, Maryland 20852

The Office of International Health (OIH) coordinates the overall international health activities of HEW. The office carries on research activities that provide background information for the appraisal of health-related matters in foreign countries and the evaluation of efforts directed toward the improvement of international health.

The OIH for Asia and the Western Pacific coordinates U.S.-Japan cooperative health programs, including activities carried out under the U.S.-Japan Cooperative Medical Science Program (with focus on health problems of Asia such as cholera, leprosy, tuberculosis, etc.); cooperation in cancer research under a bilateral Memorandum of Understanding on Cooperation in Cancer Research; and the U.S.-Japan Cooperative Science Program under which several basic biomedical studies are conducted. Other cooperative activities with Japan in the process of development are in vision research, health-statistics methodologies and consumer protection (foods and drugs). This office is also responsible for liaison with the Committee on Scholarly Communications with the People's Republic of China of the National Academy of Sciences (CSCPRC). The CSCPRC has assumed responsibility for exchanges with the PRC, and several exchanges in the health field have taken place in the past few years. Finally, the OIH also cooperates with the U.S. Agency for International Development (AID) in assisting South Korea, the Philippines, and Pakistan in public health.

The Office of International Health also serves as the program coordinator for United States participation in the World Health Organization (WHO) Regional Office for the Western Pacific.

ALCOHOL, DRUG ABUSE, AND MENTAL HEALTH
    ADMINISTRATION (ADAMHA)
International Activities Office   (301) 443-2600
Parklawn Building
5600 Fishers Lane
Rockville, Maryland 20852
Dr. Berkley C. Hathorne, International Activities Officer.

Within the Public Health Service, ADAMHA carries on extensive health-related research programs in many foreign countries, including those in East Asia. Social and behavioral science research on drug abuse and alcoholism has received a high priority in the research programs administered by 3 operating units of the ADAMHA: National Institute of Mental Health (NIMH); National Institute of Drug Abuse (NIDA); and National Institute on Alcohol Abuse and Alcoholism (NIAAA). ADAMHA's International Activities Office maintains contract-research project files and can provide assistance to researchers seeking access to pertinent sources of information from each of the 3 institutes.

For a summary of ADAMHA-funded research projects (listing the investigators, project, titles, amounts awarded, etc.), see *Alcohol, Drug Abuse, Mental Health, Research Grant Awards* (annual).

Of particular interest to East Asia specialists is the "Asian Pacific American Activities" program administered by the National Institute of Mental Health (NIMH). About $8 million in grants were awarded to some 30 Asian-American training and research projects from 1972 to 1978. Currently, this program is supporting the operation of the Asian-American Mental Health Research Center which is located at the University of Illinois, Chicago Circle, Chicago, Ill. For further information, contact Patrick Okura in the NIMH Office of International Mental Health (443-6458).

Each of the three institutes (NIMH, NIDA, and NIAA) has its own information clearinghouse, which is equipped with a computerized bibliographic data base containing translated abstracts of foreign-language books, periodical literature, and research reports in various languages, including Chinese, Japanese, and Korean. They also respond to inquiries for specific information on mental health, drug abuse, and alcoholism. Computer searches and other clearinghouse services are provided free of charge to qualified researchers. Contact:

National Clearinghouse for Mental Health Information
(301-443-4517);
National Clearinghouse for Drug Abuse Information
(301-443-6500);
National Clearinghouse for Alcohol Information   (301-948-4450).

NATIONAL INSTITUTES OF HEALTH (NIH)
John E. Fogarty International Center for Advanced Study in the
Health Sciences   (301) 496-1415
9000 Rockville Pike, Building 31, C Wing
Bethesda, Maryland 20014

NIH, one of the leading biomedical research facilities in the world, has broad international contacts with scientists abroad. Its international programs are coordinated by the Fogarty International Center, which administers international exchange and cooperative research programs, including the "U.S.-Japan Cooperative Science Agreement" of 1961 and "U.S.-Japan Cooperative Agreement" of 1965. The Center also provides postdoctoral fellowships and grants for research in the biomedical sciences.

International Cooperation and Geographic Studies (ICGS)
Dr. Joseph Quinn, Chief   496-5903

The Center's International Cooperation and Geographic Studies Branch publishes a number of important studies on foreign health systems, including the PRC. Some of the more recent titles on China include:

Medicine in Chinese Cultures: Comparative Studies of Health Care in Chinese and Other Societies (1975); by Arthur Kleinman et al.; *China Medicine As We Saw It* (1974) edited by Joseph R. Quinn; *Medicine and Public Health in the People's Republic of China* (1973) edited by Joseph R. Quinn; *Acupuncture Anesthesia in the People's Republic of China* (1975) by James Y. P. Chen; *Chinese Herbal Medicine* (1974) by C. P. Li; and *A Bibliography of Chinese Sources on Medicine and Public Health in the People's Republic of China, 1960-1970* (1973); and *Anticancer Agents Recently Developed in the People's Republic of China* (1974) by C. P. Li. Copies of these publications are available from the Government Printing Office (GPO).

Division of Research Grants   (301) 496-7381
Westwood Building
5333 Westbard Avenue
Bethesda, Maryland 20014

The division serves as the central research-fund granting agency for almost all divisions of HEW concerned with public health. Research proposals from American scholars interested in conducting overseas research in the health sciences are processed by this office. Announcements for research grants and application forms can be obtained by writing to the director of the division. For further information on research grants and fellowships, contact Dr. Carl Douglas (496-7211).

SOCIAL SECURITY ADMINISTRATION
Universal North Building, Room 705
1875 Connecticut Ave., NW
Washington, D.C. 20009
Office of External Affairs
Dr. Paul Fisher, Chief of International Staff
382-5025

The staff has professional contacts with social welfare administrators in Japan, South Korea, and Taiwan. Dr. Fisher has made several trips to South Korea and Taiwan in recent years to aid in efforts to streamline the operations of the social security systems. He is the East Asia specialists' best contact in the Social Security Administration. Copies of the following publications authored by Dr. Fisher are available free upon request: *Major Social Security Issues: Japan, 1972* (1973); and *Social Security and National Planning* (Taipei, July 1976).

Office of Research and Statistics
Comparative International Studies Staff (Room 322-B) 382-6698

The Comparative International Studies Staff studies social security systems of many foreign countries, including the PRC, Japan, South Korea, and Taiwan. A comprehensive outline of social security systems in some 130 nations is presented in *Social Security Programs Throughout the World* (periodically updated). This reference work is supplemented by *Social Security Bulletin* (monthly). In addition, occasional studies undertaken either by in-house staff or outside researchers under contract provide in-depth analysis of the social security systems in a specific country. Copies of these publications are available upon request from the office.

K15 Housing and Urban Development Department (HUD)

1 a. *451 7th Street, SW*
   Washington, D.C. 20410
   755-5111

   b. Open to the public.

2. In addition to the basic goal of supporting the domestic needs of housing
    and urban development, HUD is involved in international cooperative
    activities with foreign countries. Its international program is coordinated
    by the Office of International Affairs. Tila Maria de Hancock (755-
    7058), Assistant to the Secretary for International Affairs, is in charge
    of the overall operations of the office, which include a bilateral agree-
    ment with Japan in the field of housing and urban development.
        The Information and Technology Division (755-5770) of the Interna-
    tional Affairs Office maintains a foreign information retrieval system, a
    computerized bibliographic data base. The data are collected from for-
    eign materials and information coming into HUD through bilateral
    information exchanges and other channels. Entries in the information
    system are indexed by country, subject, and author. The staff will pro-
    vide searches of the data base for researchers without charge. For
    further information, contact Susan Judd (755-5770). At present, HUD
    has information-exchange programs with Japan, South Korea, and Tai-
    wan. With the PRC, there is no direct exchange of documents and infor-
    mation; however, information about the PRC is acquired through sec-
    ondary sources and other means.
        In addition, the office also provides arrangements for government
    officials and visitors from abroad to meet with their counterparts in
    Washington, D.C., and around the country. By far the largest number
    of visitors from East Asia are Japanese. Study tours for visiting foreign
    delegations are also arranged by HUD's Office of International Affairs.
    For further information, call or write to Tila Maria de Hancock (755-
    7058), Assistant to the Secretary for International Affairs, HUD.

3. The HUD library is described in the Libraries section (entry A23).

4. The Office of International Affairs publishes a number of valuable
    materials:
        HUD International Newsletter (formerly *HUD International Infor-
    mation Series*) contains information pertaining to foreign developments
    in housing technology and urban affairs, news of HUD's international
    activities, and a calendar of international events.
        HUD International Information Sources includes bibliographies and
    information sources abroad and at home. The *Foreign Accessions List*
    (quarterly), a list of foreign documents on housing and urban develop-
    ments which have been acquired by the HUD, is part of this series.
        HUD International Country Profiles covers a wide range of subjects.
    The June 1978 issue was devoted to "Urban Planning in the PRC" and
    was written by a member of the United States urban planning delegation
    that visited the PRC in 1977.

HUD International Review, a new quarterly journal, was published for the first time in 1978. Copies of these publications can be obtained without charge from the Information and Technology Division (755-5770).

K16 Interior Department

1. a. *18th and C Streets, NW*
      Washington, D.C. 20240
      343-3171 (Public Affairs)
      343-3170 (Information)

   b. Most offices are open to the public; however, appointments are recommended.

2. As the principal conservation agency of the United States, the Department of the Interior is responsible for the administration of nationally owned public lands and natural resources. The department carries on extensive in-house research relating to East Asia and occasionally hires outside scholars as consultants. For a description of the relevant divisions, see below.

3. See Interior Department—Natural Resources Library (entry A25) and Geological Survey Library (entry A17).

5. BUREAU OF MINES
   Columbia Plaza
   2401 E Street, NW
   Washington, D.C. 20241
   Office of International Data and Analysis   634-1168
   East Asian Area Office   634-1177
   K. P. Wang, Chief
   Edward Chin, East Asian Specialist

   The office is staffed by experts in East Asia mineralogy who can provide reference data and information pertaining to mineral resources, basic industry, industrial development, and metallurgy of East Asian countries. The staff has extensive source materials on East Asia, particularly China, and many "good connections" in East Asian countries. The staff performs all research, and supplements the flow of materials received in the office by occasional trips to East Asian countries.
   The annual performance of the mining industry in each East Asian country is reported in the "International Volume" of the *Minerals Yearbook,* one of a three-volume series. *Information Circulars* on individual countries are published on an ad hoc basis. Among the recent titles authored by the staff are: *The People's Republic of China: A New Industrial Power with a Strong Mineral Base* (1975) by K. P. Wang; *The Mineral Industry of Japan* (1974) by K. P. Wang; *Mineral Industries of the People's Republic of China* (1977) by K. P. Wang; and *Far East and South Asia* (1977) by K. P. Wang et al.

U.S. GEOLOGICAL SURVEY (USGS)
National Center   (703) 860-6118
12201 Sunrise Valley Drive
Reston, Virginia 22092

The U.S. Geological Survey plays an important role in the foreign assistance program, which includes the training of foreign geologists and hydrologists, both in their own countries and in the United States, and the development of geological and hydrological services of selected foreign countries. At the same time, staff members are engaged in a concerted effort with their foreign counterparts to obtain information on mineral and water resources in preparing comprehensive geological and resource maps of these less-developed countries. South Korea and Taiwan are actively involved in the assistance program. Studies are generally performed by the in-house staff, but specialists are occasionally recruited from universities or private industry. Furthermore, in support of the U.S. Antarctic Research Program, USGS personnel are associated with experts from 12 nations (including Japan) in mapping the earth-science research in Antarctica.

Finally, the Office of Earthquake Studies (860-6471) investigates earthquakes throughout the world and issues a quarterly progress report to the Department of State. Scholars interested in learning more about USGS international programs should contact the Office of International Geology (703) 860-6418.

The Geological Survey has published numerous technical studies on the geology, hydrology, and mineral resources of East Asian countries They are indexed in three reference publications: *Bibliography of Reports Resulting from U.S. Geological Survey Participation in the United States Technical Assistance Program, 1940-1967* (USGS Bulletin 1263); a supplement covering the years 1967-1974 (USGS Bulletin 1426); and an "open-file report" supplement covering the years 1975-1978. *USGS International Activities* (Professional Paper No. 975) can also be of interest to East Asian specialists.

HERITAGE CONSERVATION AND RECREATION SERVICE (HCRS)   343-5776
19th Street and Constitution Avenue, NW (Interior South)
Washington, D.C. 20240
Ernest A. Connally, Associate Director

The HCRS, National Park Service's Division of International Affairs and the U.S. Fish and Wildlife Service of the Interior Department together with the U.S. Forest Service of the Department of Agriculture have cosponsored the "U.S.-Japanese Natural Resources Panel on Conservation, Recreation and Parks." General meetings of the panel are held triennially when the United States delegations meet with their Japanese counterparts to discuss subjects of common interest such as urban recreation, park management, resource management, etc. Technical panel meetings are held annually to discuss problems and projects with the Japanese. The program is funded on a prorated basis, and each agency provides funds according to its involvement and interest. The last general panel meeting was held in Japan in November 1977 with the next scheduled for 1980 in the United States. A summary report of the 1977 meeting was written by Linda Van Karen (523-5260), Division of International Affairs, the National Park Service.

Office of Archaeology and Historical Preservation
343-5726
1100 L Street, NW
Washington, D.C. 20240
Jerry L. Rogers, Director

The archival reference materials of this office are arranged geographically, first by general area and then by specific country. The materials deal mainly with recreation, natural resources, and the wildlife of various countries and are in English and other languages.

U.S. FISH AND WILDLIFE SERVICE (FWS)
International Affairs Staff
Dr. Gerard Bertland, Chief   343-5188

Some work performed by the staff pertains to Japan, such as the administration (in cooperation with its Alaska Regional Office in Anchorage) of the U.S.-Japanese Treaty on Fish and Wildlife conservation. The Alaska representative is Dr. James Bartonek, 1813 D Street, Anchorage, Alaska 99501. There is also a binational technical panel to implement a U.S.-Japanese migratory-bird convention. The panel was established as part of the U.S.-Japan Cooperative Agreement for Natural Resources (UJNR).

NATIONAL PARK SERVICE—INTERNATIONAL PROGRAMS
Division of International Park Affairs   523-5260
1100 L Street, NW
Washington, D.C. 20290
Robert C. Milne, Chief

In cooperation with a number of other government agencies and the University of Michigan, the National Park Service sponsors an annual International Seminar on National Parks in the late summer. The NPS also provides training programs for representatives from foreign countries in park management and conservation. It has also been actively involved in the operation of the U.S.-Japan Panel on National Parks which meets once a year.

At present, the Interior Department has no plans for similar programs or panels with the PRC, South Korea, or Taiwan.

K17 International Communication Agency (ICA)

1. a. *1750 Pennsylvania Avenue, NW*
      Washington, D.C. 20547
      724-9843 (Information)

   b. Agency offices (except for the library) are open to the public; call in advance for hours and arrangements to see the agency's personnel.

2.　　On April 1, 1978, the former U.S. Information Agency was reorganized into the International Communication Agency (ICA) by merging with the former Bureau of Educational and Cultural Affairs of the U.S. Department of State. The ICA is entrusted with the task of promoting mutual understanding between the people of the United States and the people of other countries by way of disseminating cultural information about the United States to foreign audiences through a variety of communications media and by way of sponsoring the broadest possible exchange of people and ideas between the United States and foreign countries. The ICA conducts both in-house and contract research on international communications and cultural exchanges. Outside scholars and specialists are hired as consultants.

3.　　The ICA Library is described in the Libraries section (see entry A26).

4.　　The ICA produces a number of publications, research reports, films, and tapes. Almost all of these products are unclassified. Two of the most widely circulated ICA publications are *Problems of Communism* (bimonthly) and *America Illustrated* (in foreign languages). The ICA Documents Index System (DIS), a computerized list of ICA documents (i.e., classified, declassified, unclassified), is managed by agency Archivist Raymond Harvey (724-9372). DIS read-outs can itemize message communications, internal memoranda, country assessments, and research reports by date, subject, or geographic area of the world. Researchers wishing to gain access to this print-out and/or the documents listed on it should contact the Office of Assistant Director for Public Information (724-9103).

5.　　OFFICE OF ASSISTANT DIRECTOR (EAST ASIA AND PACIFIC)
Morton S. Smith, Assistant Director　724-9174
Robert L. Nichols, Deputy Director　724-9172

As the key East Asian units of ICA, this office oversees the agency's programs in East Asia and coordinates the activities between ICA field offices in East Asia and the agency's media production teams in Washington, D.C., (e.g., Broadcasting, Press and Publications, Motion Pictures and Television, etc.). Country-desk officers for Japan and Korea (724-9346), the PRC, Taiwan, Hong Kong, Singapore (724-9196) are accessible and willing to discuss with scholars ICA programs in these countries.

OFFICE OF ASSISTANT DIRECTOR (BROADCASTING)
R. Peter Straus, Assistant Director
East Asia and Pacific Division
Fred A. Coffey, Jr., Director
HEW Building, Room 2137
330 Independence Avenue, SW
Washington, D.C. 20201
755-4840

This division produces the Voice of America (VOA) shortwave daily radio broadcasts to East Asia (see entry N15): 8½ hours in Mandarin Chinese, and 1½ hours in Korean. It also produces tapes of newscasts and commentaries to East Asian radio stations through USICA field offices. A considerable amount of "raw materials" accumulated for possible inclusion in VOA broadcasts (e.g., tapes of historically significant events, ceremonies, interviews, and speeches relating to East Asia) are retained in VOA's Program Documentation Staff Tape Library (755-4643). VOA broadcast tapes, however, are seldom kept longer than three months. Information concerning the content of VOA broadcast programming is published in its daily *Content Report*, which lists program titles and indicates in-house sources. A brief quarterly VOA *Broadcast Schedule* lists broadcasts for pertinent languages. On-site use of these materials can be arranged through the VOA Public Information Office, Room 2137 of the HEW Building (755-4744).

PRESS AND PUBLICATIONS SERVICE (formerly Office of Assistant Director for Press and Publications)
Charles R. Beecham, Assistant Director
1776 Pennsylvania Avenue, NW
Washington, D.C. 20547
724-9712

The Publications Division of this service (724-9718) publishes periodicals for dissemination in East Asia: *Economic Impact* (quarterly); *Horizons U.S.A.* (quarterly); *Dialogue* (quarterly); and *Problems of Communism* (bimonthly). They are distributed to East Asia in English only.

The Press Division's East Asia and Pacific Branch (724-9744) provides daily teletype news service to the East Asian news media with emphasis on White House press briefings, addresses of United States leaders, and background information on United States domestic and foreign policies. Outside scholars are occasionally commissioned to write commentaries on current issues in U.S.-East Asian relations. The contents of the Press Division's teletype news coverage are indexed by *Text Catalog* (regularly updated), which is available in the division's reading room (Room 402).

OFFICE OF ASSISTANT DIRECTOR (MOTION PICTURES AND TELEVISION)
Robert Gordon, Program Affairs Officer—East Asia and Pacific
Patrick Henry Building
601 D Street, NW, Room 2116
Washington, D.C. 20547
376-7794/7793

This unit produces ICA's film series on aspects of United States society thought to be of interest to East Asian audiences. It also videotapes television interviews with United States government officials on topics relating to U.S.-East Asian relations for distribution by ICA field offices in East Asia. The motion pictures and videotapes currently used by the ICA may be viewed in the unit's two screening rooms. An *Active ICA/ IMV Films and Television Programs Master Catalog* (updated biannually) is available upon request from the office. Copies of inactive items are stored in ICA's New York City film archives and may be ordered for screening in the Washington office.

OFFICE OF ASSISTANT DIRECTOR (INFORMATION
CENTERS) (ICS)
Howard W. Hardy, Acting Director
1717 H Street, NW
Washington, D.C. 20547
632-6700

This office provides logistical support to ICA information centers in
East Asia. It supplies books for information libraries, art collections,
and other materials for traveling exhibits, and speakers for ICA-spon-
sored seminars and conferences in East Asia.

OFFICE OF POLICY AND PLANS

Washington Foreign Press Center
Walter Kohl, Director
202 National Press Building
529 14th Street, NW
Washington, D.C. 20045
724-1643

ICA's Washington Foreign Press Center provides various information
services to foreign media representatives stationed in Washington (e.g.,
ICA and commercial wire services teletype outlets, radio tie lines to the
Department of State and the Department of Defense press briefings,
etc.). The Center also maintains a regularly updated directory of foreign
correspondents assigned to Washington. Copies are available on request.

OFFICE OF RESEARCH (IOR)   724-9545
Harold Engle, Acting Director

This unit conducts research on East Asian attitudes, media habits, and
reactions to ICA programs. Besides its in-house research in this field,
this unit also contracts outside scholars for research and employs consultants. Field data are usually obtained through contract research.

Three divisions within the Office of Research analyze East Asian field
data; The Media Research Division (724-9590) evaluates the impact of
ICA information programs on East Asian audiences (by country) and
compiles an on-going series of "program evaluation studies." The Atti-
tude and Audience Research Division (724-9036) handles public opinion
surveys of East Asians' attitudes toward various domestic and international issues and publishes country studies and trend analyses. The
same unit also produces "influence-structure studies" which deal with
changes in the political power structures of East Asian nations. Finally,
the Foreign Information Research Division (724-9289) analyzes Communist activities on a worldwide basis.

The Office of Research distributes its research reports to 45 depository
libraries in the United States, including the Library of Congress. A list
of these depositories is available. The office also produces two indexes:
Research in ICA: On-Going Programs and Planned Projects and *Research Reports Issued* (both are available on request).

OFFICE OF EDUCATIONAL AND CULTURAL AFFAIRS
632-2464

The International Communication Agency now administers United States educational and cultural exchange programs. Until March 1978, these programs were administered by the Department of State's Bureau of Educational and Cultural Affairs. These programs are designed to give people of other countries a better sense of life in the United States and enables Americans to acquire a more accurate perception of other cultures. The exchange programs include:

(1) *Academic Program:* Under the Fulbright-Hays Mutual Educational and Cultural Exchange Act (see entry J7), the office administers in co-operation with the Institute of International Education the annual exchange of approximately 1,750 United States and foreign predoctoral students and 1,000 professors and senior researchers. The program is operated under the supervision of a 12-member Board of Foreign Scholarship appointed by the president of the United States. Japan, South Korea, and Taiwan have been active participants in the program.
(2) *Foreign Leaders Program:* Invitations are extended annually by United States chiefs of diplomatic missions abroad to about 2,000 foreign leaders in government, labor, the mass media, science, education and other fields to visit their counterparts in the United States. Assisting in the work of planning these visits are more than 100,000 American volunteers and 90 community organizations, many of which are members of the National Council for Community Services to International Visitors (COSERV) (see entry H36).
(3) *Performing Arts Program:* Qualified artists and performing groups are assisted in arranging private tours in other countries. Through workshops and seminars, they are encouraged to develop professional relationships with their counterparts.
(4) *Athletic Program:* Through continued contacts with national and international sports and physical education groups, ICA fosters and facilitates international exchanges in this field.
(5) *Grants-in-Aid Program:* ICA extends financial assistance to private United States organizations which complement government programs in enhancing mutual understanding between Americans and the people of other countries.
(6) *East-West Center:* ICA serves a liaison function with the Center for Cultural and Technical Interchange between East and West (or "East-West Center") in Hawaii. This autonomous institution of learning for Americans and for the people of South Asia and the Pacific is designed to promote better understanding through cooperative programs of research, study, and training.
For further information on the above-mentioned programs, contact Donald Ferguson (724-9080).

OFFICE OF ASSISTANT DIRECTOR (PUBLIC INFORMATION)
Directorate for Programs

This unit administers the voluntary speakers programs. Annually, about 200 American experts in a wide variety of fields travel overseas to participate in transnational dialogues with fellow experts abroad. For further information, contact Harold Schneidman (724-9349).

K18 International Trade Commission (ITC)
(formerly, U.S. Tariff Commission)

1. a. *701 E Street, NW*
        Washington, D.C. 20436
        523-0173

    b. Open to the public.

    The U.S. International Trade Commission is an independent agency that advises the president and Congress on tariff and trade matters. The commission investigates the effects of imports of specific foreign commodities on domestic United States agriculture and industry. The commission also conducts research in the fields of tariffs, international trade, and commercial policy.

    An important program of the Office of Economic Research is known as the "East-West Trade Statistics Monitoring System" (Magdolna Kornis, 724-0074). This system in accordance with the Trade Act of 1974 makes systematic analyses of trade data supplied by the Department of Commerce's Bureau of East-West Trade. The system functions to provide advice to the ITC, Congress, and the president on trade developments with the nonmarket economy (Communist) countries. The latter include the People's Republic of China, the Mongolian People's Republic and, at a later date, possibly North Korea, pending trade developments. This advice appears regularly in quarterly reports. Computer runs are printed monthly as well as quarterly and are available to researchers.

4. The Director of Administration (523-0287) has custody over the inactive internal records. The commission's secretary, Kenneth Mason (523-0161), serves as the Freedom-of-Information Officer for the ITC.

5. The Commission publishes a number of important reports, including *Operation of the Trade Agreement Program* (annual report); and *Quarterly Report to the Congress and the East-West Foreign Trade Board on Trade Between the U.S. and Non-Market Economies*. The Office of Economic Research publishes occasional special reports on such topics as *Implications for U.S. Trade of Granting Most-Favored Nation Treatment to the PRC*.

K19 Japan-United States Friendship Commission

1. a. *1875 Connecticut Avenue, NW, Suite 709*
        Washington, D.C. 20009
        673-5295

    b. Open to the public from 9:00 A.M.-5:00 P.M.   Monday-Friday

    c. John W. Hall, Chairman
        Francis B. Tenny, Executive Director

2.   The Japan-United States Friendship Commission was estabilshed by the United States Congress in 1975 (P.L. 94-118). Income from a United States government Trust Fund of $30,000,000 (in dollars and yen combined) is available for the promotion of scholarly, cultural, and artistic activities between Japan and the United States. The fund originates from part of the Japanese government's repayments for immediate postwar American assistance to Japan, and for United States facilities built on Okinawa and turned over to Japan in 1972.

The fund and the program are administered by a commission of 18 Americans representing the fields of scholarship, the mass media, business, the Congress, and the Executive Branch of the United States government. As an independent agency of the United States government, it is accountable to Congress and the president.

Requests for grant support from the institutions will be considered by the commission under the following 4 project areas:

(1) *Japanese Studies* (for Americans): The commission will consider a broad range of proposals for support of Japanese studies programs for American educational institutions, but will not entertain applications from individuals directly. All grants will be made or entrusted to universities or other organizations which will also be responsible for such individual selections as may be required.

Support available in this category includes: (a) post-graduate training of specialists in Japanese studies; (b) scholarly research and publications about Japan; (c) intensive Japanese-language study programs; (d) major collections of Japanese books and publications by appropriate American libraries; (e) professional schools (e.g., law, business, journalism, etc.); and (f) elementary, secondary, and teacher-education programs, including curriculum development.

(2) *American Studies* (for Japanese): The commission will consider proposals from Japanese universities or other organizations for support of teaching, research, seminars, publications, and library collections on American history and civilization, and on the economic, social, and political institutions of the United States. Proposals from Japanese institutions will be evaluated by professionals from Japan and the United States.

(3) *The Arts* (for both Americans and Japanese): The commission will support opportunities for American and Japanese individuals of creative talent and achievement in the visual, performing, and literary arts to study or to perform in the traditional and modern art forms of the partner country. The commission will also consider applications from educational and artistic organizations for training and apprenticeship programs in the arts of the other country. Performing arts tours, which lack a viable commercial base, may be also funded.

(4) *Cultural Communication and Public Affairs* (for the United States): The commission will consider proposals from organizations promising a national or major regional impact for programs in: (a) museums and fine arts education, including exhibitions of art and artifacts; (b) educational television; (c) opportunities for Japanese participation in American intellectual activities, including conferences and seminars, publications, transactions, and joint research with American counterparts on common socio-economic-political problems; and (4) opportunities for

American organizations in the fields of political, social, economic, mass media, and public affairs, to develop on-going exchange relationships with their Japanese counterparts.

Grants for regular programs of the commission will normally be awarded in October and April. Specific proposals should be received by September 1 or March 1. All grants (about $2 million per year) made by the commission will be listed in the commission's annual report of activities. Inquiries from American or Japanese organizations or individuals should be directed to the executive director of the commission.

4. Copies of the *Annual Report of the Japan-United States Friendship Commission* are available free upon request. Also available are copies of *Japan-United States Friendship Commission: Announcement of Programs, 1977-1978*.

K20 Joint Publications Research Service (JPRS)

1. a. *1000 North Glebe Road*
   Arlington, Va. 22201
   (703) 841-1050

   b. Researchers should call for appointments with the staff or information concerning access to the reading room.

2. JPRS publishes translations of foreign-language materials on a number of subjects. It provides this translation support as a service of common concern for various United States government agencies and departments. Included are a series of translations of East Asian material on various topics:

    The PRC: political, sociological, economic, military, scientific, agricultural, and technological information.
    Japan: political, economic, sociological, military, scientific, and technological developments.
    Mongolia: political, governmental, sociological, economic, and technical developments.
    N. Korea: political, economic, sociological, military, and governmental affairs.
    Translations on South and East Asia: political, sociological, economic, military, and governmental affairs (contain information on South Korea and other Asian countries).

    Problemy Dal'nego Vostoka ("Problems of the Far East"): A Soviet quarterly specializing in Far Eastern affairs which carries articles written by Soviet experts on political, economic, scientific, and technological aspects of life in China and other Asian countries.

    JPRS is in almost constant need of persons capable of translating and abstracting Chinese, Japanese, and Korean language material. The work is performed at home on a contractual basis; compensation is based on the translator's skills. Interested scholars should contact JPRS at the address above.

3. The JPRS reading room contains some hard-bound copies of its publications for the period from October 1973 through June 1975. Those published since 1975 are on microfiche; a reader is available. Tables of contents pages for JPRS publications since 1965 are on file here, arranged by geographic area and report title. Reports are also available at the Library of Congress.

4. Except for copyrighted material, which only government agencies receive, JPRS publications are sold by the National Technical Information Service, United States Department of Commerce (see entry K5). JPRS does not index its own publications; however, the Microphoto Division of Bell and Howell (Old Mansfield Road, Wooster, Ohio 44691) issues such an index entitled *TRANSDEX*. This monthly index is arranged by author, subject, country, and original course.

Note: Materials on East Asia are also found in the following worldwide reports published by JPRS:

Translations on Narcotics and Dangerous Drugs;
Translations on Environmental Quality;
Translations on Law of the Sea;
Translations on Telecommunications Policy, Research and Development; and
World Epidemiology Review.

K21 Justice Department

1. a. *Constitution Avenue and 10th Street, NW*
Washington, D.C. 20530
737-8200

b. Some departmental agencies, such as the Federal Bureau of Investigation (FBI) are closed to the public. Researchers should check with individual offices for their hours and regulations.

4. For access to the Justice Department's restricted internal records, contact the department's Freedom-of-Information office (739-3184).

5. CRIMINAL DIVISION
Foreign Agents Registration Unit   739-3154

All foreign agents (including lobbyists, but excluding diplomats and commercial agents) as well as representatives of foreign political parties are required to register with this unit and to provide it with a detailed description of their activities and sources of support. They must also file a copy of any material they disseminate in this country. These records are accessible to researchers at the:

Public Office   739-2332
Federal Triangle Building
315   9th Street (at D Street), NW
Washington, D.C. 20530

Xeroxed copies of the records may be obtained at cost. *The Annual Report of the Attorney General* provides a list of foreign agents registered with this unit. Also available at the Public Office are 120 case histories (1956-present) of foreign espionage agents.

Other branches of the Criminal Division with international responsibilities include the Governmental Regulation and Labor Section (739-3761), which handles treaties, extradition, and immigration matters; and the Internal Security Section's Statutory Unit, an enforcement agency (739-3936).

FEDERAL BUREAU OF INVESTIGATION (FBI)
J. Edgar Hoover Building
Pennsylvania Avenue between 9th and 10th Streets, NW
Washington, D.C. 20535

The FBI is responsible for domestic counterespionage and counterintelligence investigations as well as over 200 federal statutes dealing with criminal and domestic security investigations. The bureau operates under the Department of Justice guidelines for domestic intelligence operations, a copy of which can be obtained from the department on request. The FBI's internal records are classified. However, the Freedom-of-Information Act may enable researchers to obtain information on past official investigations conducted by the FBI. Requests should be sent to the director of the FBI. The FBI's Public Affairs Office (324-5352) provides reference and other assistance to scholars.

IMMIGRATION AND NATURALIZATION SERVICE   376-8490
425 I Street, NW
Washington, D.C. 20536

The Statistical Branch of this division monitors East Asian immigration into the United States. It has current monthly computer print-outs of immigration figures for the United States. The unit can also provide detailed immigration figures by quarter of year, country of origin, age, sex, and occupation. The branch's library contains a substantial collection of historical literature and statistical data. The *Annual Report* of the Commissioner of Immigration and Naturalization contains various statistical tables pertaining to current and past immigrants to the United States.

DRUG ENFORCEMENT ADMINISTRATION (DEA)
1405 I Street, NW
Washington, D.C. 20537
633-1249 (Public Affairs)

This agency has jurisdiction over the investigation and enforcement of matters involving illicit drug trafficking. Most agency files are classified; however, researchers may be able to obtain some restricted information under the Freedom-of-Information Act. The DEA's quarterly magazine, *Drug Enforcement*, features articles relating to international activities.

K22 Labor Department

1. **a.** *New Department of Labor Building*
   200 Constitution Avenue, NW
   Washington, D.C. 20210
   523-6666

   b. Department offices are open to the public.

2. The East Asia-related functions of the Labor Department bureaus are described below (point 5).

3. The Labor Department Library is described in the Libraries section (entry A29).

4. Foreign labor statistics, compiled by the Department's Bureau of Labor Statistics, are contained in the Bureau's *Handbook of Labor Statistics*. The Bureau also issues quarterly releases on the Department of State cost-of-living indexes and living quarters allowances in foreign cities.

5. BUREAU OF LABOR STATISTICS
   Division of Foreign Labor Statistics and Trade
   John Chandler, Chief   523-9291

   A wide range of research on labor forces, employment, unemployment, compensation, and productivity in developed countries such as Japan is conducted by this division. The division receives statistical publications and other materials on labor development from United States embassies and consulates, international organizations, and national statistical offices. It also monitors changes in imports, output, and employment in order to evaluate the relationship between foreign trade and domestic employment.

   The facilities offered to government and private researchers include: (1) current periodicals and other reference materials on principal labor statistics; (2) publications and releases prepared by the division staff members; and, (3) limited consultation provided by experienced staff members in the field of international labor statistics.

   The division publishes a *Handbook of Labor Statistics* which includes foreign labor statistics usually in comparison with the United States. The tables compiled are concerned primarily with developed countries (e.g., Japan). "The Foreign Labor Statistical Reports" released by the bureau cover a variety of international comparative figures, mainly of the Western industrial countries plus Japan. The tables contain statistical data and information difficult to find elsewhere.

   The Bureau of Labor Statistics also maintains a collection of foreign publications received from various countries. Some of the material is in the original foreign language (e.g., Japanese), but most items have English texts.

BUREAU OF INTERNATIONAL LABOR AFFAIRS
Office of Foreign Economic Research
Harry Gilman, Director   523-7597

This office conducts external and in-house programs of applied research to evaluate the effects of United States international trade and investment policies on United States employment. Its areas of research include evaluations of costs and benefits of trade liberalization on employment; the effects of direct foreign investment and the transfer of technology by United States firms to foreign countries on wages and employment of United States workers; and evaluation of the Trade Adjustment Assistance Program.

The office requests that interested scholars submit research proposals. The Request for Proposals (RFP), outlining specific topics of interest to the bureau, are announced in the *Commerce Business Daily* (published by the United States Department of Commerce). In recent years, many universities, economic consulting firms, and individual scholars have been awarded contracts. A file of completed research projects is maintained by the office and is available to interested researchers on request.

OFFICE OF FOREIGN LABOR AFFAIRS
Dan Lazorchick, Director   523-7571

East Asia staff in this office are the Labor Department's primary specialists on U.S.-East Asian labor relations and East Asian trade-unionism. They serve as the department's liaison with labor attachés in United States embassies in East Asian countries and also with American labor organizations interested in East Asia. They are accessible to private researchers and will make available unclassified materials.

OFFICE OF POLICY AND PROGRAM DEVELOPMENT
Gerald Holmes, Director   523-6234

This office is publishing two new publications series: *Country Labor Profiles;* and *Monographs on International Labor Affairs.* The files maintained by the office are primarily for the use of the staff and not designed for the use of outside researchers. However, interested scholars should contact Glenn Halm, who handles East Asian labor affairs in the office.

K23 National Endowment for the Humanities (NEH)

1. a. *806 15th Street, NW*
      Washington, D.C. 20506
      724-0386 (Public Affairs Office)

   b. 9:00 A.M.-5:30 P.M.   Monday-Friday
      Open to the public.

2.   The National Endowment for the Humanities (NEH) has no program specifically designed for the support of East Asian-related projects. However, through its Division of Fellowships and its Division of Re-

search Grants, the Humanities Endowment does support research projects and individual study dealing with foreign areas and cultures beyond research or study by degree candidates working toward their degrees.

According to the act which established the NEH the humanities include, but are not limited to, the following fields: history, philosophy, languages, literature, linguistics, archaeology, jurisprudence, history and criticism of the arts, ethics, comparative religion, and those aspects of the social sciences employing historical or philosophical approaches. This last category includes cultural anthropology, sociology, political theory, international relations, and other subjects concerned with questions of value and not with quantitative matters. In fiscal year 1977, NEH granted over $1.3 million for 42 East Asian-related projects.

The Division of Fellowships awards support to individual humanists in their work as scholars, teachers, and interpreters of the humanities. Examples of projects receiving grants under various categories (for fiscal 1977) are as follows:

Fellowships for Independent Study and Research
"The *Fang-shih* of Medieval China and His Role in the Development of Narrative"
"Chinese *Yueh-fu* Poetry"
"Sino-Korean Relations, 1885-1894"
"Confucian Statecraft in Transition: The Rise of Li Hung-chang, 1853-1875"

Summer Stipends
"The Royal Navy and the Imperial Japanese Navy, 1936-1945"
"Investigation of Source Materials Concerning the Chinese Buddhist Philosopher Paramartha"
"The Intellectual Biography of a Modern Chinese Poet: Wen I-to (1899-1946)"

Summer Seminars for College Teachers
"The History of China, 1600-1975"
"Comparative Approaches to Order and Authority in Modern Japanese Political Development"

For further information about these and other fellowship programs, inquiries should be addressed to Division of Fellowships (724-0238).

The Division of Research Grants funds collaborative projects and work on research tools, collections, translations, editing, and similar undertakings aimed at building up the materials and resources necessary for conducting humanistic research in the United States. Examples of projects receiving grants under various categories for fiscal 1977 were:

General Research (collaborative efforts)
"Preparation of the *Cambridge History of China,* Volumes XII and XIII."
"New Light on the Study of Chinese Secret Societies."

Research Tools
"Toishan Glossary and Grammar."

Editing
"The Post-1949 Writings of Mao Tse-Tung."

Research Collections
"The Allied Occupation of Japan, 1945-1952: Processing and Preserving Materials."

Translations (into English)
"A Translation of the *Wen Xuan* (Literary Selections)."
"Medieval Japanese Law: Central Government Decrees, 1336-1573."

For further information about these and other research programs, contact Division of Research Grants (724-0226).

Information on application procedures and deadlines is available in the publications noted below.

4.   The NEH *Program Announcement* brochure, issued annually, is most useful to scholars. It lists and describes the activities of the 4 basic divisions of NEH (Research Grants, Fellowships, Education Programs, and Public Programs) and provides details about application procedures and deadlines. A more detailed publication on each of the divisions is also available.

The *Annual Report* describes NEH's programs and activities, and lists all grant recipients and amounts awarded during a particular fiscal year.

These and other publications of NEH are available free on request from its Public Affairs Office.

K24 National Science Foundation (NSF)

1. a. *1800 G Street, NW*
Washington, D.C. 20550
632-7970

b. 8:30 A.M.-5:00 P.M.   Monday-Friday.

c. Richard C. Atkinson, Director

2. a-d. NSF is the sole agency of the federal government for which the support of basic research is the principal mission. According to its 1976 annual report, the foundation dispersed over $677 million for basic and applied research programs in 6 major areas of research: (1) mathematical and physical sciences and engineering; (2) astronomical, atmospheric, earth and ocean sciences; (3) biological, behavioral, and social sciences; (4) science education; (5) research applied to national needs; and, (6) scientific, technological, and international affairs. Although most of the funds are for the study of the natural and life sciences and technology, a small number of projects relating to East Asian countries are funded. Support is provided in the form of research grants and contracts. Scientists perform consultative services for the NSF, though seldom in the social sciences.

e. (1) *United States-Japan Cooperative Science Program:* The purpose of this program is to increase the effectiveness of the interaction between American and Japanese scientific communities. To achieve this objective, the NSF supports seminars, research visits of United States scientists who spend 6 to 12 months with a Japanese host institution, and cooperative research projects under the program. The cooperative program is jointly administered by the NSF's Division of International Programs (INT/NSF) and by the Japan Society for the Promotion of Science (JSPS) [Nihon Gakujutsu Shinkōkai] in Japan. The program is not intended to function as a primary source of research funds (e.g., salary, equipment); basic financial support should be available from funding sources other than INT/NSF and JSPS. INT/NSF will consider requests only for supplemental support (e.g., international travel costs for short research visits to Japan, the shipment of materials, etc.) needed to expand a domestic United States project into a bilateral one.

Proposals are considered in all recognized branches of science and technology. NSF does not fund projects in clinical medicine, the arts and humanities, business, or social work. The United States proposal may be submitted by academic institutions, governmental labs, private and public scientific organizations, and by unaffiliated individual scientists. The United States scientist must be a citizen or permanent resident of the United States and must hold a doctoral degree or have equivalent professional experience. Annually, about 20 cooperative projects and 20 seminars are funded by INT/NSF and JSPS under the program. For further information, telephone 632-5782 or write to Stephen R. Mosier, United States-Japan Cooperative Science Program, Division of International Programs, National Science Foundation.

(2) *U.S.-Republic of China Cooperative Science Program:* The U.S.-R.O.C. Cooperative Science Program was established in 1969 (1) to increase the contacts and cooperation between scientists and the scientific communities of the two countries; (2) to provide more frequent opportunities for the exchange of scientific information, ideas, and techniques; (3) to attack problems of common concerns; and, (4) to utilize special facilities available in both countries. The scope of cooperation encompasses all recognized branches of science, including the social sciences.

Under the program INT/NSF and its counterpart in Taiwan (National Science Council) supports: (1) the exchange of scientists, including short-term, intermediate-term, and long-term visitors; (2) cooperative research; and (3) seminars. INT/NSF will give special consideration to those American scientists who wish to collaborate with Chinese scientists at one of the 6 research centers in Taiwan (e.g., the Mathematics Research Center, the Agricultural Research Center at National Taiwan University, etc.) or with Chinese scientists working in departments of other institutions which have active graduate programs. Applicants must have possessed a doctoral degree or its equivalent for at least 5 years, and must be a citizen or a permanent member of the American scientific community. Annually, about 15 cooperative projects, 2 seminars, and 6 short-term visits are funded under the program. For further information, telephone 632-5782 or write to Dr. James A. Holt, Division of International Programs, National Science Foundation.

(3) *U.S.-Republic of Korea Cooperative Science Program:* The purpose of the U.S.-Republic of Korea Cooperative Science Program is to increase the effectiveness of the interaction of the United States and Korean scientific communities. To achieve this objective, the program supports (1) research visits of United States scientists who spend 6 months to 12 months with a Korean host institution; (2) short-term

visits necessary to develop cooperative research projects; and (3) cooperative research projects. Guidelines for these proposals are available from the Division of International Programs, NSF.

U.S. and Korean scientists may submit applications to the program for approval of their proposals when special benefits can be expected from collaboration—sharing of unusual facilities and research environments, joining of complementary skills in experimentation and theoretical analysis, combined use of resources in solving problems of common concern, and similar unique combinations of talents and resources. The U.S.-R.O.K. program is jointly administered by NSF in the United States and by the Korea Science and Engineering Foundation (KOSEF) in Korea. Proposed cooperation under this program should be of clearcut benefit to both sides. Concurrent submission of proposals by the United States principal investigator to NSF and by the Korean investigator to KOSEF is required for cooperative research projects. Such proposals are assessed independently by both executive agencies and require joint approval to be included under the program. The program was begun in 1976 and 4 projects and 1 conference in biochemical engineering were approved in the first year.

For further information, telephone 632-5782 or write to Dr. James A. Holt, U.S.-R.O.K. Cooperative Science Program, Division of International Programs, National Science Foundation.

4.   The NSF administers the Special Foreign Currency Science Information Program (SFCSI), under which original foreign-language materials are translated into English by foreign contractors and made available to scientists in this country. Since 1959, over 1 million pages of materials have been translated under the program. Translations from the SFCSI Program are announced in the *Government Reports Announcements/Index* and *Weekly Government Abstracts* published by the National Technical Information Service (NTIS), United States Department of Commerce. NTIS also publishes the SFCSI *List of Translations in Process* annually. In addition, it produces periodically annotated bibliographies entitled *Translations from the Scientific Literature;* the first volume covering 1960-1973 was published in 1974; the second volume covering 1974-1975 appeared in June 1976; and the latest one covering 1976-1977 was issued in 1978.

Among many NSF publications, the following may be of interest to East Asia specialists: *The United States-Japan Cooperative Science Program (1961-1976) Report on the Third Five Years—1971-1976* (1977); *United States-Republic of China Cooperative Science Program, July 1, 1976 through June 30, 1977* (1978); *Summary of Active Awards and Completed Projects of the Division of Policy Research and Analysis* (January 1978); *Program Announcement for Extramural Research (Fiscal Year 1978)* (Division of Policy Research and Analysis, November 1977); and *Division of Social Sciences Grant List* (annual). Copies of the following are free upon request: *NSF Organizational Directory; U.S.-East Asia Cooperative Science Program: Guidelines for Proposal Submission* (mimeo); *A Selected List of Major Fellowship Opportunities and Aids to Advanced Education for United States Citizens;* and *A Selected List of Major Fellowship Opportunities and Aids to Advanced Education for Foreign Nationals.*

For information, inquiries, and discussion of informal research proposals, scholars should contact the appropriate individual in charge of the specific programs which may be in the fields of the scholars' interest. All formal research proposals, requests for application forms, and questions about application procedures should be directed to the Central Processing Section, NSF, Washington, D.C. 20550. (632-5728)

5. NSF operates through 7 basic branches, known as directorates. Here, however, some of the more important directorates for East Asianists will be described briefly.

(1) The Directorate for Scientific, Technological, and International Affairs (STIA) [Harvey Averch, Assistant Director—254-3020] has 4 divisions, each of which may have programs of some relevance for East Asian specialists.

(a) Division of International Programs (INT)
Dr. Bodo Bartocha, Director   632-5798
Latin America and Pacific Section
J. E. O'Connell, Section Head   632-5806
Stephen R. Mosier, Program Manager, U.S.-Japan Programs
Dr. James A. Hold, Program Manager, U.S.-Republic of China and
    U.S.-East Asia Programs   632-5782
This office should be the first point of contact for researchers interested in East Asia. As mentioned in section 2 above, NSF has a number of cooperative science programs with East Asian countries, such as Japan, South Korea, and Taiwan.

(b) Division of Science Resources Studies (SRS)
Dr. Charles E. Falk, Director   634-4634
2000 L Street, NW, Washington, D.C. 20550
This division sponsors studies of the scientific (both human and capital) resources of foreign countries. It has a library of reference materials on this subject.

(c) Division of Policy Research and Analysis
Alden S. Bean, Director   632-5990
This division sponsors research relating to the environment, energy and resources, the socioeconomic effects of science and technology, and innovation processes (industrial and technological). At least 6 research projects recently funded by the division were related to Japan.

(2) Another branch of the NSF which interacts with East Asian scientists is: Directorate for Astronomical, Atmospheric, Earth, and Ocean Sciences (AAEO), John B. Slaughter, Assistant Director (632-7300). Its Division of Polar Programs (DPP) (Edward P. Todd, Director, 632-4024) is actively involved in research on the Antarctic region, where American and Japanese scientists are engaged in a cooperative project called "dry valley drilling" with New Zealand.

(3) It may be useful for East Asian specialists with expertise in the social sciences to check with the Directorate for Biological, Behavioral, and Social Sciences (BBS), Eloise E. Clark, Assistant Director (632-7867). BBS's Division of Social Sciences supports a number of basic re-

search projects in economics, geography and regional science, law, political science, sociology, history, and the philosophy of science. Over 300 research projects (including some involving doctoral dissertation research) are funded annually. Some of these deal with East Asian countries.

An important contractor of the NSF is:
The Fellowship Office, National Research Council
National Academy of Sciences
2101 Constitution Avenue, NW
Washington, D.C. 20418
The Program Director for Graduate and Post-Graduate Programs
(282-7154) is Dr. Thomas S. Quarles.

The Fellowship Office administers the graduate and postdoctoral fellowships for the National Science Foundation. Three different types of graduate and postgraduate fellowship programs are offered annually.

(a) *Graduate Fellowships:* The NSF awards approximately 550 new 3-year graduate fellowships annually to individuals who have demonstrated ability and special aptitude for advanced training in the sciences. These fellowships are awarded for study leading to master's and doctoral degrees in the mathematical, physical, medical, biological, engineering and social sciences, and in the history and philosophy of sciences.

(b) *Grants for Improving Doctoral Dissertation Research:* Under this program, grants are awarded in support of doctoral dissertation research in the environmental, behavioral, neural, and social sciences in order to improve the overall quality of dissertation research in these sciences. Grants will be awarded for periods up to 24 months.

(c) *National Needs Postdoctoral Fellowships:* The NSF instituted this program in 1978 to strengthen personnel resources for scientists in the United States. Each applicant must present a plan of scientific research and study which relates to a national need or problem in the sciences. (Excluded are clinical programs, as well as proposals in education, business, history, social work, or public health.) The usual tenure of a postdoctoral fellowship is 9 or 12 months.

K25 National Security Council (NSC)

1. a. *Old Executive Office Building*
   17th Street and Pennsylvania Avenue, NW
   Washington, D.C. 20506
   395-3400

   b. No public access except by appointment.

2. National Security Council staff members including the council's East Asian specialists Nick Platt (395-3345) and Michel Oksenberg (395-3044) are not available to outside researchers for obvious reasons relating to national security. The NSC occasionally hires outside scholars as consultants on an *ad hoc* basis.

4.   Access to most National Security Council documents is restricted to authorized government officials. However, through Freedom-of-Information Act (FOI) procedures, access to the council's documents may be possible. Maj. Robert M. Kimmit (395-4970) or Dr. Beverly Zweiben (395-3116) should be contacted for FOI-related inquiries. Periodically, the Council provides the Military Archives Division—Modern Military Branch of the National Archives (see entry B8) with an updated, computer print-out list of documents which have been wholly or partially declassified by the NSC. Although no formal NSC record group has been established by the National Archives, copies of many of these declassified NSC records (1947-present) are available at the Modern Military Branch of the National Archives. A complete index to NSC policy papers (1-177) issued from 1947-1953 is also available at the Modern Military Branch. Another important repository for NSC documents is the presidential library system.

Finally, President Carter's Executive Order 12065, issued on July 3, 1978 has instituted a "20-year rule" in declassifying United States government documents. The Executive Order does not apply to documents from foreign governments which may be withheld for 30 years. For details of Executive Order 12065, see *Federal Register,* July 3, 1978, Part IV.

K26 Overseas Private Investment Corporation (OPIC)

1. a. *Board of Trade Building*
      1129 20th Street, NW
      Washington, D.C. 20527
      632-1804

    b. Open to the public; however, appointments are recommended.

2.   OPIC was organized in 1971 to provide United States businessmen interested in investing overseas with the following services: (1) to insure the contributions of United States private investors against certain political risks of expropriation, currency inconvertibility, and war, revolution, and insurrection in developing countries; and (2) to provide financial assistance (e.g., project loans and loan guaranties) and investment counseling to United States investors. By facilitating the participation of private investors in the economic and social development of some 90 less developed, friendly countries, OPIC programs complement the development assistance programs administered by the U.S. Agency for International Development (AID) which assist the governments of such countries. Since 1971, OPIC has been very active in insuring and financing United States private investors in South Korea and Taiwan. Arvin Kramish (632-9646) in OPIC's Insurance Department (632-8990) and Brooks H. Browne (254-3227) in the Finance Department (632-8544) monitor business conditions and the investment climate in East Asia. These officials can be contacted for further information on OPIC operations in East Asia, particularly South Korea and Taiwan which have attracted investments from many American firms.

3. OPIC's library (632-9329) has various holdings relating to international business, economy, and investment, including reports from several United States corporations with investments in East Asia, publications of United States government agencies (e.g., State, Commerce, Treasury, Agriculture, etc.), World Bank/International Monetary Fund studies collections of foreign-country data, and other documents. There are also records documenting OPIC's involvement in overseas investment disputes and settlements. The library is open to researchers from 8:45 A.M. to 5:30 P.M., Monday through Friday.

4. OPIC's internal records, such as claims settlement files as well as information submitted by United States firms operating in East Asia, are considered confidential and are not available to outside researchers. OPIC's Freedom-of-Information officer is Robert Jordan (632-1854), Director of Public Affairs.

5. The agency publishes an *Annual Report* and a bimonthly newsletter entitled *Topics*. Copies of these publications are available free on request.

K27 Peace Corps (ACTION)

1. a. *806 Connecticut Avenue, NW*
        Washington, D.C. 20525
        254-7526 (Communications)

    b. 8:30 A.M.-5:15 P.M.   Open to the public; however, appointments are recommended.

2. ACTION's Office of International Operations administers the agency's overseas programs. The only country desk dealing with East Asia is the Korean/Thailand desk in the Office of International Operations. The desk officer provides liaison between field volunteers and the Washington headquarters. Currently, there are 6 projects operated by the Peace Corps in South Korea, including Disease Control, Disease Eradication, Rehabilitation, English-language teaching, and vocational education. Researchers should contact the Korea/Thailand desk (254-8870) for information concerning the agency's Korea programs.

    The Evaluation Division (254-7983; toll free 800-424-8580) of the Office of Policy and Planning is responsible for assessments of Peace Corps programs abroad. Rick William, Evaluation Coordinator, maintains an annually updated bibliography of evaluations. Geographic, linguistic, and programmatic specialists are hired as consultants and occasionally private research contractors are used by this division.

3. The ACTION Library is described in the Libraries section (entry A1).

4. The agency publishes *Program and Training Journal,* which contains background and country-training information for Peace Corps volunteers. For information about the operational records of the Peace Corps, contact John Nolan (254-8105) who serves as the Peace Corps' Freedom-of-Information officer.

K28 Senate Historical Office

1. a. *Office of the Secretary*
       Senate Historical Office
       United States Senate
       Washington, D.C. 20510
       224-6900

    b. 9:00 A.M.-5:00 P.M.   Monday-Friday.   Open to the public.

    c. Richard A. Baker, Senate Historian
       Donald A. Ritchie, Associate Historian

2. The office aims to provide bibliographic and research assistance to scholars, especially historians and political scientists. It seeks to aid researchers in gaining access to primary source materials created by the Senate and its members over the past 190 years. It serves as a clearinghouse for Senate-related research activities.

4. Currently, the staff of the Senate Historical Office is preparing several research aids of potential value to researchers studying United States policies, relations, and attitudes toward East Asian countries. Current publications include: *The United States Senate Historical Bibliography* (1974) by Richard A. Baker which focuses on the institutional development of the United States Senate as well as biographies and collected writings of 200 former senators; and a newsletter, *Senate History*. Available to researchers is information soon to be published in "Catalog of Collections of Senators' Papers," a computer-based catalog of senators' papers with information on the scope, location, and accessibility of the collections; and "Checklist of Unpublished Hearings," a list of transcripts of previously inaccessible, closed-door executive session records of various Senate committees, including the Senate Committee on Foreign Relations.

5. The office does not have a library, but administers an extensive collection of Senate-related photographs. It aims to collect pictures of all men and women who have served in the Senate. For further information, contact John O. Hamilton, photo-historian. The office has also begun an oral history project to tape-record the recollections of retiring senior staff members.

K29 Smithsonian Institution

1. a. *Headquarters*
       1000 Jefferson Drive, SW
       Washington, D.C. 20560
       628-4422

    b. Museums and galleries are open to the public seven days a week (except Christmas Day), the libraries are open Mondays through Fridays; however, an appointment is required for the administrative offices.

2. The Smithsonian Institution conducts research, publishes the results of studies, explorations, and investigations, and preserves for study and reference over 65-million items of scientific, cultural, and historical interest. In addition, it maintains various exhibits representative of the arts, technology, aeronautics and space exploration, and American natural history. It also participates in the international exchange of learned publications and engages in programs of education and national and international cooperative research and training.

3. The libraries and archives of the Smithsonian Institution are listed in this guide under the names of the appropriate galleries and museums. The name index of this guide, under Smithsonian Institution, lists the museums and galleries affiliated with the Institution.

4. The monthly *Smithsonian* magazine covers news and activities of the Institution and carries many articles on subjects of general interest, including some on East Asia.

5. The Smithsonian Institution administers a large number of national collections, museums, art galleries, archives, laboratories, and even the National Zoological Park. Since many of these and their programs are described elsewhere in the guide, only divisions not covered in other sections are detailed below.

SMITHSONIAN SCIENCE INFORMATION EXCHANGE (SSIE)
381-4211
1730 M Street, NW (Suite 300)
Washington, D.C. 20036
Hours: 9:00 A.M.-5:00 P.M.   Monday-Friday
Dr. David F. Hersey, Director
Ann Riodan, Chief of the Social Sciences Branch
Rhoda Goldman, Chief of the Behavioral Sciences Branch

SSIE is a clearinghouse of information on research in progress. Annually, it collects, indexes, stores, and retrieves information on approximately 125,000 government and nongovernment research projects in the life, physical, and social sciences. About 80 percent of the listed projects are funded by the federal government. Research projects of some state government agencies, private foundations, universities, and nonprofit research organizations make up the rest.

Each Notice of Research Project (NRP) contains information on the supporting organization's name and address; the grant, contract, or agency control number assigned to the project; the project title; the name and address of the performing organization; the name and specialty or departmental affiliation of the researcher(s); the duration and level of funding; and usually a 200-word description of the research project.

For a fee, the staff can search the current and historical files of NRPs that cover the present as well as the two previous fiscal years. Other services available include pre-designed research-information packages in subject areas of current interest; dissemination of selective ongoing-research information on a monthly or a quarterly basis; and compilations and tabulations of specific data desired.

The *SSIE Science Newsletter* appears 10 times per year, updating information about the SSIE data base.

INTERNATIONAL EXCHANGE SERVICE   381-5311
1111 North Capitol Street, NE
Washington, D.C. 20002
John E. Estes, Director

Through the International Exchange Service, governmental and private institutions in the United States exchange publications with organizations in other countries. This includes the exchange of official United States publications with foreign countries, including Japan, South Korea, and Taiwan. Full sets of United States government publications and series (i.e., *Congressional Record* and *Federal Register*) are sent to Japan, South Korea, and Taiwan. Incoming publications from these countries go to the Library of Congress, the National Library of Medicine, the National Agricultural Library, and the like. Before 1969, there was no exchange of publications between the United States and the People's Republic of China. At present, there is a limited exchange.

By 1981, however, the IES will phase out its role in the exchange of official government publications, which will then be assumed by the Government Printing Office. Nevertheless, the international exchange of scientific and literary publications among academic and other learned institutions will continue as a program of the Smithsonian under the IES.

SMITHSONIAN ASSOCIATES   381-6264

The Smithsonian Institution offers the National Associates, Resident Associates, and Contributing Membership programs for individuals interested in participating in various activities of the Institution. An information and reception center is located for the Associates in the Smithsonian Institution Building ("The Castle"). Smithsonian Associates can participate in lectures at 1000 Jefferson Drive, SW, Washington, D.C., sponsored by the Smithsonian Institution, such as "The Arts of Edo" by Jane Griffin (May 1978) and "The Art of Japan" by Roger Pineau (June 1977). They can also participate in the Smithsonian Associates Travel Program, which offers group tours of foreign countries, including Japan. These tours are educational and cultural in nature and are led by experts in the countries visited. At present, no tours are offered to the PRC, South Korea, or Taiwan. Scholars interested in participating in tours sponsored by the Smithsonian Associates should contact:

Smithsonian Associates Travel Program
Arts and Industry Building
Washington, D.C. 20560
(381-5635)

For visitors to Washington, D.C., the Smithsonian Institution also offers an instant reference service for events and exhibits of current interest—Dial-a-Museum, 737-8811.

DWIGHT D. EISENHOWER INSTITUTE FOR HISTORICAL
    RESEARCH   381-5453/5518
National Museum of History and Technology
Constitution Avenue at 14th Street, NW (Room 4601)
Washington, D.C. 20560
Dr. Forrest C. Pogue, Director

Hours: 9:00 A.M.-5:00 P.M.   Monday-Friday

The Eisenhower Institute was established in 1975 to serve as a center for scholarly research in the field of military history with emphasis on the meaning of war, its effect on civilization, and the role of the armed forces in the maintenance of peace and security in society. The institute sponsors, supports, and participates in scholarly seminars, conferences, and publications relating to military history. For example, in August 1975, the institute sponsored a conference of the "Commission Internationale d'Histore Militaire" at the Smithsonian Institution with delegates coming from 26 countries. More recently the institute cosponsored with the American Committee for the History of the Second World War a conference on "Americans as Proconsuls: U.S. Military Government in Germany and Japan, 1944-52," which was held at the Smithsonian Institution's Carmichael Auditorium on May 21-22, 1977. The conference was also supported by the Douglas MacArthur Memorial Library (Norfolk, Virginia) and the George C. Marshall Research Library (Lexington, Virginia). The Eisenhower Institute also serves as a clearinghouse for American and foreign scholars desiring access to documents on military history located in Washington, D.C., and at other locations in the United States and abroad.

K30 State Department

1. a. *2201 C Street, NW*
      Washington, D.C. 20520
      655-4000 (Information)
      632-9606 (Bureau of Public Affairs)
      632-0772 (Freedom-of-Information Staff)

   b. Access to the Department of State building is restricted. Appointments with department officials should be made in advance.

2. As the principal organ of the United States government in the conduct of foreign relations, the Department of State has active, sustaining interests in the affairs and developments of East Asia. To fulfill its task effectively, the department conducts a great deal of research in foreign affairs, including East Asia. Both the Bureau of East Asian and Pacific Affairs and the Bureau of Intelligence and Research utilize East Asia-oriented contract research and hire outside scholars as consultants. Department officials are usually willing to talk with individual researchers within the limits imposed by security regulations.

3. The Department of State Library is described in the Libraries section (entry A38).

4. In addition to the *Foreign Relations of the United States* series, the Department publishes the weekly *Department of State Bulletin;* a *Background Notes* series of general information fact sheets, by country (updated every two years); *Gist,* a series of 1-page information sheets on current international issues; and a monthly *Department of State Newsletter.*

   Other useful department publications include: *Biographic Register* of Department of State officials (classified since 1974); *Key Officers of Foreign Service Posts—Guide for Business Representatives* (formerly

Foreign Service List); *Diplomatic List* and *Employees of Diplomatic Missions* (quarterly lists of the foreign diplomats in Washington); *Foreign Consular Officers in the United States* (annual); and *Lists of Visits of Presidents of the United States to Foreign Countries, 1789-1976;* and *Lists of Visits of Foreign Chiefs of State and Heads of State* and *Heads of Government, 1789-1976.*

In addition, the department issues a variety of special public releases, including "discussion papers," special reports, information pamphlets, policy statements, speeches, news conferences, and other items. To be placed on the department's mailing list, contact the Bureau of Public Affairs' Office of Plans and Management (632-9859). Other publications are discussed below under their originating office.

For bibliographies, see *Major Publications of the Department of State: An Annotated Bibliography* (revised edition, 1977), and 3 successive issues of *Publications of the Department of State* covering the periods, 1929-1952, 1953-1957, and 1958-1960.

Finally, the department's internal classified records (e.g., dispatches, telegrams, and other messages between the department and its diplomatic posts abroad, inter- and intra-office memoranda, policy papers and studies, etc.) are filed in the Bureau of Administration's Foreign Affairs Document and Reference Center (FADRC). Eventually, these documents are forwarded to the National Archives, where they become accessible to researchers.

Normally, they are declassified up to the latest year for which the department's official *Foreign Relations of the United States* has been completed (1949 as of 1978). Access to more recent records is possible only through Freedom-of-Information Act procedures. For further information, contact Barbara Ennis, Director, Freedom-of-Information staff (632-0772).

5. BUREAU OF EAST ASIAN AND PACIFIC AFFAIRS (EA/P)
632-9596
Assistant Secretary Richard Holbrook

This bureau coordinates and supervises United States diplomatic activities in East Asia. The bureau's country-desk officers serve as an East Asian specialists' initial contact in the Department of State. As time permits, with prior arrangement, they will confer with researchers and will provide information on current developments in the East Asian countries under their responsibility. They will also make available unclassified documents or publications which may be useful to the researchers. Directors of the relevant East Asian country desk staff are as follows:

Republic of China (Room 5310), Harvey Feldman, Director (632-7710)
Japan (Room 4210), Nicholas Platt, Director (632-3152)
Korea (Room 6317), Robert Rich, Director (632-0780)
People's Republic of China and Mongolia Affairs (Room 4318A), Harry E. T. Thayer, Director (632-6300)

In addition to these country offices, the bureau has 3 other important offices. The Office of Economic Policy (632-4835) handles general economic relations and activities including aid, trade, and commodities and commercial affairs in the region. The office of Regional Affairs (632-2343) handles political-military activities, U.N., refugee, labor and other related affairs relating to East Asia. Finally, the Office of Public Affairs (632-2538) assists with public inquiries, prepares congressional testimony and works with the press and other media representatives. The Public Affairs Office will also assist in arranging appointments with the bureau's personnel.

The bureau regularly publishes *Background Notes* (or "Country Notes") on each of the countries in East Asia as well as transcripts of public statements and congressional testimony.

BUREAU OF INTELLIGENCE AND RESEARCH (INR)
Harold H. Saunders, Director
632-0342
Office of Research and Analysis for East Asia and Pacific
Herbert Horowitz, Director
632-1338

As the principal research arm of the Department of State on East Asian affairs, this office prepares a large number of research papers and memoranda each year, ranging from 1-page current intelligence analyses to more lengthy research papers and memoranda. Its primary clientele are high-level officials of the Department of State and other government agencies. Research subjects encompass the full range of Northeast and Southeast Asian policy issues. In terms of scope, these studies are primarily short- and mid-term in range. Virtually all of the office's work is classified.

Office of External Research (INR/XR)
E. Raymond Platig, Director (632-1342)
Edward G. Griffin, Senior Program Officer for East Asia and Pacific (632-3968)

The Office of External Research serves as the Department of State's primary linkage-point with private scholars. It administers the department's contract-research program to meet the department's needs for timely research assistance from the private sector. The office also hires outside scholars as consultants. In addition, it invites periodically selected East Asian scholars to participate with government officials in conferences, colloquia, roundtable discussions, and ambassadorial briefings.

The office also serves as the staff secretariat for the government-wide Inter-Agency Committee on Foreign Affairs Research (IC/FAR). In this capacity, the Office of External Research functions as a coordinating point as well as an information clearinghouse for federally funded research on foreign affairs.

The unit also publishes a quarterly and annual computerized inventory of *Government-Supported Research Projects on Foreign Affairs* (unclassified). *Foreign Affairs Research: A Directory of Government Resources* (revised edition, 1977) is available for qualified researchers.

The Office of External Research also administers the Foreign Affairs Research Documentation Center (703/235-9420). This facility, which is located at 1800 North Kent Street, Arlington, Virginia 22209, collects and disseminates both government-supported research and unpublished research papers by individual scholars in the private sector. Its collection consists of over 15,000 recently completed studies on foreign affairs and related subjects. These research papers are held for 5 years, after which they are discarded. Scholars may borrow Department of State funded research papers from the center. Other papers, however, must be obtained directly from the individual author or sponsoring government agency.

Papers available on East Asia and Pacific Area at the documentation center can be found in a monthly acquisition list entitled *Foreign Affairs Research Papers Available.* In addition, *Special Foreign Affairs Research Papers Available* (annual) series includes a volume on East Asia and Pacific Area-related holdings. A 5-year (1971-1976) cumulative index of East Asian acquisitions is also available at the center which is open to the public.

Office of Economic Research and Analysis   632-2186
Michael E. C. Ely, Director

This office deals with international economic issues, including United States-East Asian economic relations. The Commodity and Developing Country Division (632-0453) is concerned with the North-South dialogue, commodity trade, and transportation. The Trade Investment and Payments Division (632-0090) supports research on, among other things, East Asian trade negotiations, balance-of-payments, foreign exchange and debt problems, and disputes involving private United States firms in East Asia. Scholars can obtain copies of *Communist Aid to the Less Developed Countries of the Free World* (annual)—an unclassified CIA publication—from the Communist Economic Relations Division (632-9128). Economic studies on individual East Asian countries and bilateral economic issues involving the United States are handled by the Regional Economic Division (632-9737). *Intelligence Report,* a classified publication for interagency use, is published occasionally by the Office of Economic Research and Analysis.

Office of Political-Military Affairs and Theatre Forces   632-2043
Robert H. Baraz, Director

International arms sales, national military production and military capabilities, nuclear capabilities, and potential international military confrontations are subjects carefully studied by this office. Its research frequently encompasses East Asia.

Office of Strategic Affairs   632-0222
Ross E. Cowey, Director

The research specialty of this office includes nuclear nonproliferation and technology transfer in East Asia.

Office of the Geographer   632-1428
Dr. Robert D. Hodgson, The Geographer

This office specializes in matters involving international boundaries, the law of the sea, and other related subjects. It publishes the *International Boundary Studies; Limits of the Sea* (irregular); and *Geographic Notes* which appears only if a significant change in an international boundary has occurred (e.g., emergence of a new state). It also publishes *Status of the World's Nations* (updated annually).

BUREAU OF ECONOMIC AND BUSINESS AFFAIRS (EB)
632-0396
Assistant Secretary Julius L. Katz

This bureau has overall responsibility for formulating and implementing United States foreign economic policy. It monitors economic developments and the policies of foreign countries, conducts bilateral and multilateral negotiations on economic issues, coordinates regional economic policies of the United States with other regional bureaus concerned. Unquestionably, many of its offices are involved in the formulation of United States economic policies toward East Asia in one form or another. As these offices are organized functionally rather than geographically, instead of attempting to describe the specific functions of each office involved, the titles of the offices and their telephone numbers are listed below, as the title of the office indicates the more important function of each office:

Office of Business Practices   632-9452
Office of Monetary Affairs   632-1114
Office of Development Finance   632-9426
Office of Investment Affairs   632-1128
Office of International Trade   632-2534
Office of East-West Trade   632-0964
> This office maintains liaison with the Department of Commerce on export-licensing of United States strategic materials to East Asia. It also prepares a *Battle Act* report (quadrennial) to the United States Congress.

Office of Fuels and Energy   632-1420
Office of International Commodities   632-7952
Office of Food Policy and Programs   632-3090
Office of Aviation (EB/TCA/OA)   632-0316
Office of International Communications Policy   632-3405
Office of Maritime Affairs   632-0704
Office of Commercial Affairs   632-8097

BUREAU OF POLITICO-MILITARY AFFAIRS (PM)   632-9022
Leslie H. Gelb, Director

This bureau is responsible for making recommendations in national security policy, military assistance, nuclear policy, and arms control and limitation. Virtually all of its work is classified. As it is functionally organized rather than geographically, with many divisions dealing with specific problems on a global scale, no attempt will be made to describe each office's structure and function. Instead, the titles and telephone numbers of the bureau's functional offices are listed below:

Office of International Security Policy (PM/ISP)   632-2056
Office of Nuclear Policy and Operations (PM/NPP)   632-1835
Office of Security Assistance and Sales (PM/SAS)   632-3882
Office of Munitions Control (Rosslyn, Virginia)   (703) 235-9755
Office of International Security Operations (PM/ISO)   632-1616
Office of Disarmament and Arms Control (PM/DCA)   632-1862.

BUREAU OF INTERNATIONAL ORGANIZATIONS AFFAIRS
(IO)   632-9600
Assistant Secretary Charles W. Maynes

This bureau coordinates and develops policy relating to United States participation in the United Nations and other international organizations. Activities of foreign delegations, including those from East Asia, and their attitudes toward United States policy positions within the United Nations system are closely monitored by staff members of several functional offices of the Bureau. These offices include: U.N. Political Affiairs (632-2392); International Economic Policy (632-2506); Human Rights Affairs (632-0572); U.N. Budget and Administration (632-3049); U.N. System Coordination (632-2752); International Conferences (632-0384); and U.N. Documents and Reference Staff (632-7992).

BUREAU OF OCEANS AND INTERNATIONAL ENVIRONMENTAL AND SCIENTIFIC AFFAIRS (OES)   632-1554

This bureau is responsible primarily for the formulation and implementation of United States foreign policy relating to oceans; fisheries; environmental, population, and nuclear problems; space energy; and the transfer of technology. In addition, it represents the United States in international negotiations and conferences pertaining to the area of its specialization and directs the department's Scientific/Technological and Fisheries Attaché programs. The functional offices of the bureau which interacts with East Asia countries include:

Office of Technology Policy and Space Affairs, Jacob Blackburn, Director   632-2432

Office of Bilateral and Multilateral Science and Technology Affairs, Robert C. Morris, Director   632-5329

Office of Environmental Affairs, Donald King, Director   632-9278

Office of Population Affairs, Luke Lee, Director   632-2232

Office of Non-Proliferation and Export Policy   632-3310

Office of Export and Import Control, Dixon Hoyle, Director 632-4101

Office of Energy Safeguard and Technology, John P. Boright, Director   632-3310

Office of Ocean Affairs, Morris D. Busby, Director   632-6491

Office of Fisheries Affairs, Larry Snead, Director   632-2009

Office of Marine Science and Technology Affairs, William L. Sullivan, Jr., Director   632-0853

BUREAU OF HUMAN RIGHTS AND HUMANITARIAN
AFFAIRS (HA)   632-0334
Patricia Derian, Assistant Secretary for Human Rights and Humanitarian Affairs

This bureau handles the Department of State's responsibilities for human rights, refugees, POWs, MIAs, and other humanitarian problems. It provides policy guidance on human rights and related matters to Department of State officials and works closely with other government agencies on this subject. It also coordinates the preparation of annual Department of State reports to Congress on the human-rights situation in every East Asian country which receives United States military or economic assistance. The bureau's staff maintains close contact with nongovernmental institutions and individuals interested in human-rights issues in the major regions of the world, including East Asia.

BUREAU OF PUBLIC AFFAIRS (PA)
Office of the Historian (PA/HO)
515 22nd Street, NW
Washington, D.C. 20520
632-9606
David F. Trask, Historian (632-1913)
John P. Glennon, Associate Historian, Asia, Africa and the Pacific (632-1984)
David W. Mabon, Asian and Pacific Group Chief (632-1910)

The primary function of the Historical Office is to prepare the Department of State's *Foreign Relations of the United States* series, which as of 1978 includes over 260 volumes covering the years 1861-1949. Thirty additional volumes covering the years 1950-1954 are currently in progress. The other major publications of the Historical Office include: *American Foreign Policy, 1950-1955: Basic Documents*, 2 vols; and *American Foreign Policy: Current Documents*, 12 annual vols., 1956 through 1967. These publications include a comprehensive record of important public statements, speeches, press releases, and other papers articulating the scope, goals, and implementation of United States foreign policy.

The Historical Office also provides information to the public on source materials for modern diplomatic history and on the history of the Department of State and the United States Foreign Service. Researchers interested in finding the department's past and present records and in gaining accessibility of the United States diplomatic records and source materials can get useful guidance from the staff.

The office has provided internships for undergraduate students and regularly employs a small number of professional historians on short-term contracts (i.e., 6-12 months). It has also provided other services to the academic community, such as guided tours of the Department's records facilities and discussion sessions.

Finally, the Historical Office publishes a bibliographic reference tool, *Major Publications of the Department of State: An Annotated Bibliography,* as well as occasional "Historical Studies" on various topics of United States diplomatic history.

Freedom-of-Information Staff (PA/FOI) 632-0772
Barbara Ennis, Director

This unit handles all the Freedom-of-Information Act-related requests for restricted Department of State records. Declassification-review requests are processed in cooperation with other units of the department (e.g., Foreign Affairs Document and Reference Center, regional bureaus, etc.). In 1976, nearly 500,000 pages of documents were reviewed, of which 353,000 pages were declassified and released to the public. These released documents can be examined in the unit's public-access reading room.

Office of Public Programs (PA/PP)
James Montgomery, Director   632-1433

This office organizes the department's Scholar-Diplomat Seminars, which bring scholars into the Department of State for 1 week of discussion sessions and participation in the work of either a geographic or functional bureau. Usually, there are two East Asian seminars per year. It also organizes Media-Diplomat Seminars and Executive-Diplomat Seminars with similar formats. In addition, this unit sponsors conferences and special briefings on United States foreign policy and also handles requests for department speakers from universities, business, and civic organizations. Information brochures are available free on request.

POLICY PLANNING STAFF (S/P)   632-2372
W. Anthony Lake, Director

The Policy Planning Staff is engaged in long-range planning, advising the Secretary of State with broad, global policy recommendations and perspectives independent from the policy lines of the geographic bureaus of the Department of State. The staff includes functional as well as area specialists, who are accessible to researchers. Most of its work is classified. The office sponsors an "Open Forum" luncheon-discussions series which serves as a forum for internal debate on policy issues among the department officials. No outsiders are allowed to participate. The staff publishes a classified magazine entitled *Open Forum.*

OFFICE OF THE LEGAL ADVISER   632-3039
Elizabeth G. Verville, Assistant Legal Adviser for East Asian and
Pacific Affairs

Inquiries concerning various aspects of international law and treaties are processed by the Office of the Legal Adviser. The staff can provide researchers with information on legal issues involving East Asian countries, including the status of treaties and other international agreements. Scholars may make arrangements to use the Office's Law Library (632-2628), which has a few legal reference works on East Asia.

The Office of Legal Adviser publishes a number of important serial titles on international law, including the *Digest of United States Practice in International Law* (annual); *Treaties in Force* (an annual list of all United States international agreements in force as of January 1 of each publication year); *United States Treaties and Other International Agreements* (1950-present). The office has also sponsored the publication of *Whiteman Digest of International Law* (15 vols.) by Marjorie M. Whiteman and a 13-volume *Treaties and Other International Agreements of the United States of America, 1776-1949.*

BUREAU OF ADMINISTRATION (A)   632-1492
Foreign Affairs Document and Reference Center (FADRC)
William H. Price, Director   632-0394

The center administers the central file of internal Department of State documents and records (e.g., cables, airgrams, memoranda, papers, reports, etc.) until such time as they are shipped to the National Archives. Records filed by FADRC since July 1973, have been computer-indexed. Access to FADRC materials (post-1949) is limited to department personnel. For the outsiders, access to the classified FADRC materials may be possible only through the Freedom-of-Information Act.

The center publishes very informative, unclassified *Country Fact Sheets*, regularly updated information fact sheets on foreign countries including the People's Republic of China, Japan, South Korea, Mongolia, North Korea, and Taiwan. Information and data covered in the publication include treaties and international agreements, military forces, foreign military purchases and military assistance programs, economic indicators, trade, United States assistance commitments, AID projects, educational, cultural and scientific exchange programs, United States private-investment levels, the foreign investment climate, United States citizen presence, and an annotated bibliography of the Department of State Library's periodical holdings on the countries covered.

FADRC also publishes a *Monthly Highlights Report,* which is classified and for internal use only.

FOREIGN SERVICE INSTITUTE (FSI)   (703) 235-8750
1400 Key Boulevard
Arlington, Va. 22209
Lawrence Dutton, Dean, School of Area Studies   235-8839
Hattie K. Colton, Assistant Dean and Chairperson, East Asian Studies 235-8842

Foreign Service personnel preparing to assume overseas assignments are given area and language training at the Foreign Service Institute, which is divided into three schools: School of Area Studies; School of Language Studies (703-235-8816); and School of Professional Studies (703-235-9779). The area studies courses make extensive use of guest lecturers, deriving about half of them from the nongovernment sector, mostly universities. These visiting lecturers are selected from a variety of institutions and disciplines on the basis of their professional reputations.

FSI is not a research center. Nevertheless, in a few areas, some research is carried out including individual papers prepared by the members of the Senior Seminar in Foreign Policy; occasional monographs written by Department of State Senior Fellows while assigned to a selected campus for an academic year; or new work in the field of language studies by the institute's language staff.

K31 Transportation Department (DOT)

1. a. *400 7th Street, SW*
   Washington, D.C. 20590
   426-4000

   b. Open to the public.

2. The Office of International Transportation Programs (426-4368) in the office of the Secretary is responsible for DOT's international cooperation program. The program involves research cooperation arrangements with about 25 foreign governments and international organizations. The only

research cooperation project currently in effect with East Asia is with Japan. It is administered by the International Cooperation Division (426-4398) of the Office of International Transportation Programs.

The International Transportation Division (755-7684) maintains files of foreign transportation data, which are supplied mostly by United States embassies abroad. Unclassified materials of the office will be available to qualified researchers.

DOT's Information Management Branch maintains, in conjunction with the Transportation Research Board of the National Academy of Science's National Research Council and many other organizations, an extensive data base known as TRISNET (Transportation Research Information Services Network). One of the components is the TRIS-ON-LINE base which includes a growing amount of international material. Presently, however, the amount of material dealing with East Asia is quite limited. The information includes abstracts of transportation literature, photocopies of reports, résumés of planned and ongoing research, references to numerical data bases and directories to transportation-related information centers. The system is accessible to outside researchers for a fee. It is also available at the Transportation Research Board of the National Research Council.

The Office of Systems Development and Technology can provide more information about TRISNET as well as the booklets entitled *TRISNET: A Network of Transportation Information Services and Activities* and *TRISNET: Directory to Transportation Research Information Service* (1976).

3. DOT Library is described in the Libraries section (entry A39).

5. OFFICE OF INTERNATIONAL TRANSPORTATION PROGRAMS
International Cooperation Division
Dr. Bernard Ramundo, Chief
426-4398

This division coordinates United States efforts on the bilateral agreement with Japan on transportation. In July 1969 a joint committee meeting was held in Tokyo that led to the creation of the "U.S.-Japan Transportation Research Panel (TRP)" as the principal forum for cooperation in transportation. Meetings are held annually, with the United States acting as host in alternate years. At the last meeting held in Tokyo, on December 5-12, 1977, the tenth in the series, urban transportation systems, offshore facilities, and railway systems were discussed. Exchange of information is an important part of these panel meetings. The desk officer to contact about the program is John Eymonerie (426-4398).

FEDERAL AVIATION ADMINISTRATION (FAA)   426-8521
800 Independence Avenue, SW
Washington, D.C. 20590

Office of International Aviation Affairs
Analysis and Evaluation Branch
426-3230/9366

Although the Office of International Transportation Programs coordinates much of the work involving other countries, this branch can provide research materials for East Asian specialists. General and statistical information-filebooks, mainly on aviation activities in various foreign countries, are maintained here. These filebooks, known as "Country Profiles," are well organized and informative, containing "Factual Data on Aviation Activities" and information on "International Aviation Relationships" for the PRC, Japan, South Korea, North Korea, Taiwan, and Hong Kong. Those wishing to use the "Country Profiles" should contact Jane Stolar (426-3230). In addition to the "Country Profiles," there is a separate set of files maintained for many countries, including those in East Asia. These files include interoffice/interdepartmental memos and correspondence as well as research papers (in-house and outside sources). Arrangements should be made with the office in advance to see these files.

There is also a small reference library designed primarily for the use of the staff with a focus on aviation (mostly nontechnical general literature).

K32 Treasury Department

1. **a.** *15th Street and Pennsylvania Avenue, NW*
   Washington, D.C. 20220
   566-2000
   566-2111 (Information)

   b. Visitors should arrange appointments in advance, for access to the building is restricted.

2. Most of the research is done by in-house staff economists, who prepare action-oriented memoranda designed for distribution within the department. For the department's research on international economy and finance, see point 5 below.

3. The Department of the Treasury Library contains a fairly comprehensive collection in the field of taxation and public finance, money and banking, international law, and economics. However, its holdings on East Asia are quite limited (i.e., 200 titles). The library issues a monthly review of current literature entitled *Treasury Notes*, which abstracts important new books and lists other books and periodical articles of interest to department employees. It is open to the public from 9:00 A.M.-5:30 P.M., Monday through Friday. For further information, call Anne E. Stewart, Librarian (566-2777/2778).

4. The following publications of the Office of the Assistant Secretary for International Affairs contain data on East Asian countries: *Report on Developing Countries External Debt and Debt Relief Provided by the United States* (annual); and *Annual Report of the National Advisory Council on International Monetary and Financial Policies*. In addition, the monthly *Treasury Bulletin* carries international financial statistics. Finally, the quarterly *Foreign Credits of the United States Government—Status of Active Foreign Credits of the United States Government* can be of interest to East Asian specialists.

   An OASIA compiled bibliography (called the "OASIA Clearing House") provides a selected listing of unpublished manuscripts in international economics as well as a list of unpublished in-house research papers. Copies of the list of unpublished in-house research papers are available upon request. If interested, call 964-5876, or write to: Department of the Treasury, Room 1001, Washington Building, Washington, D.C. 20220.

OFFICE OF THE ASSISTANT SECRETARY FOR INTERNATIONAL AFFAIRS (OASIA)   566-5363

Staff economists in the Office of the Assistant Secretary for International Affairs (OASIA) (566-5363) analyze international economic, financial, and monetary issues. OASIA's Office of the Deputy Assistant Secretary for Developing Nations (566-8243) oversees the operations of the Office of Developing Nations Finance (566-2373) as well as the Office of International Development Banks (566-8171). An East Asia coordinator within the Office of Developing Nations Finance (William McFadden, 566-5776) monitors East Asian monetary and financial conditions. The staff in this office is the best contact-point within the Treasury Department for information concerning balance-of-payments, debt levels, and general monetary, fiscal, and developmental conditions in East Asian countries. The Office of International Development Banks monitors the operations of the Asia Development Bank and makes recommendations for U.S. policy toward the bank. Contact Donald Sherk (566-8364) for further information.

OASIA's Office of East-West Economic Policy (Marjorie Searing, Director, 566-2611) provides data-collection services for the East-West Foreign Trade Board which monitors United States trade with non-market economy (Communist) countries in accordance with the Trade Act of 1974. The office helps prepare, together with the Department of Commerce, International Trade Commission, and others, the quarterly *East-West Foreign Trade Report*, which includes data on the PRC.

International Economic Analysis Staff   566-5828
John Karlick, Deputy Assistant Secretary for International Economic Analysis

The staff conducts research on various aspects of international financial, monetary, and economic problems. One of its current research projects focuses on the "model of the Japanese economy." The staff maintains a computerized data base called, "The Developing Countries Data Bank," which contains data (covering the period 1960-1975) on the national income, balance of payments, foreign debts, etc., of the developing countries of the world, including South Korea and Taiwan. Access to the data bank is limited, however, to government personnel.

L Foreign Government Agencies and International Organizations

Entry Form for International Organizations (L)

1. General information
   a. *Address; telephone number(s)*
   b. Hours of service
   c. Name/title of director

2. Description of services

3. Library

4. Publications

5. Description of relevant divisions

L1 Embassy of Japan

2520 Massachusetts Avenue, NW
Washington, D.C. 20008
234-2266

His Excellency Fumihiko Togo, Ambassador

Scholars wishing to see embassy personnel should contact the embassy in advance by letter or phone to arrange a meeting. The embassy building at the above address houses all but the Defense, Science and Visa sections which are located at:

Room 900, 600 New Hampshire Avenue, NW
Washington, D.C. 20037
234-2266

Researchers are advised to consult the latest *Diplomatic List* published by the United States Department of State for the names and addresses of the embassy staff.

Several sections of the embassy which may be important for the scholars interested in Japanese studies are as follows:

ECONOMIC SECTION
Koichiro Matsuura, Counselor

The Economic Section handles matters concerning economic and trade issues between Japan and the United States. The office is staffed not only by foreign service officers, but also by officials from various economy-related ministries in Japan such as the Ministry of International Trade and Industry, Construction, Economic Planning Agency, Welfare, Transportation, and Postal Affairs.

POLITICAL SECTION
Tatsuo Arima, Counselor

The Political Section is in charge of political and politico-military affairs, including Japanese-United States relations.

FINANCE SECTION
Nobuhiko Matsuno, Counselor

The Finance Section handles matters relating to budget, monetary affairs, and customs.

DEFENSE SECTION
Yutaka Tamura, Counselor

The Defense Section handles defense-related affairs and performs liaison work with the Pentagon.

SCIENCE SECTION
Kiichiro Nagara, Counselor

The Science Section handles scientific affairs including nuclear matters.

VISA SECTION

Those who intend to visit Japan must obtain a visa from the Visa Section or at one of the several Japanese consulates located in other parts of the United States (e.g., New York, Los Angeles, Hawaii).

INFORMATION SECTION
Yoshiko Karita, Counselor

The Information Section handles press, education, information, and cultural affairs for the embassy. In addition, it maintains a film collection consisting of about 100 titles of short documentaries which cover the agriculture, architecture, history, geography, sports, theater, industry, cities, and women of Japan. Classical Japanese arts such as Bunraku, Noh, Kabuki, Chanoyu, Ikebana, and gardens, are also included in the film collection. A title list of the films is available upon request by mail; borrowing, however, is in person only. These films are available in other parts of the United States where Japanese consulates are located. Reservations should be made as far in advance as possible. For television rights and purchase of copies, interested scholars should contact the Information Section of the Japanese Embassy.

L2 Embassy of the People's Republic of China

2300 Connecticut Avenue, NW
Washington, D.C. 20008
797-9000

His Excellency Tse-min Chai, Ambassador

Scholars should contact the appropriate staff member(s) in advance, by telephone or letter, to arrange a meeting. In general, the staff is very busy and has limited time for discussions or consultations with researchers. Effective as of January 1, 1979, official diplomatic relations were established between the PRC and the United States. Information on staff members of the PRC Embassy is available in the Department of State publication entitled *Diplomatic List* ("The Blue List").

CONSULAR AND VISA OFFICE   797-8909

Scholars who intend to visit the People's Republic of China as individuals, not as part of a group or on official scholarly exchanges, should write directly to China International Travel Service, Peking, People's Republic of China, for official Chinese approval and then apply for a visa at this office. Arrangements may also be made through major commercial airlines such as Pan American Airlines, Northwest Orient Airlines, Iran Airlines, Japan Airlines, Canadian-Pacific Airlines and the like. For further information call Mr. Li-teh Chi (797-8909).

CULTURAL AFFAIRS   797-8878

Scholars interested in purchasing Chinese official publications or in borrowing films for classroom use should contact Mr. Lung-huang Shih (797-8878). Several color films (35 mm) are available for educational purposes, provided that the borrowers pay for shipping and insurance. Two films "Handcraft and Arts" and "China Today" (1977) are currently available for classroom showing.

L3 Embassy of the Republic of Korea

2370 Massachusetts Avenue, NW
Washington, D.C. 20008
483-7383

His Excellency Yong Shik Kim, Ambassador

Scholars wishing to see embassy personnel should contact the appropriate staff member(s) by telephone or letter in advance to arrange a meeting. The most recent issue of the Department of State publication entitled *Diplomatic List* contains names and addresses of the current embassy staff.

Most offices of the ROK Embassy are housed in 2 buildings located in the same block of Massachusetts Avenue. The offices of the ambassador and ministers, as well as those of the political and economic affairs sections, are located in the main embassy building listed above. Scholars can contact the following officials as well as their staff located here:

Minister in charge of Economic Affairs: Yoon Sae Yang (234-4707)
Minister in charge of Political Affairs: Myung-Ho Oh (483-6797)
Political Counselor: Suk Kyu Kim (234-6924)
Economic Counselor: Hung Koo Kang (483-3122)

CONSULAR SECTION 483-7383
2320 Massachusetts Avenue, NW
Washington, D.C. 20008

Scholars wishing to visit South Korea should obtain a visa here or at one of the several Korean consulates located in other parts of the United States (e.g., New York, Chicago, Los Angeles). In addition to the Consular Section, several other offices (including those of military attachés) are located in this building.

Names and telephone numbers of the military and nonmilitary attachés are as follows:

Defense Attaché: Maj. Gen. Noh Young Park (483-1836)
Air Force Attaché: Col. Yong Chick Park (483-1836)
Navy Attaché: Capt. Son-Ho Park (483-1836)
Fishery Attaché: Han Mo Kim (483-9263)
Agricultural Attaché: Joong-Il Suh (483-1985)
Commercial Attaché: Eun Tak Lee (483-6589)
Education Attaché: Hee Kyu Park (332-7146)
Science Attaché: Kyung Mok Cho (483-1919)

OFFICE OF LOGISTICS SERVICE ATTACHÉ
Embassy of the Republic of Korea
2400 Wilson Boulevard
Arlington, Va. 22201
Chief: Brig. Gen. Jong Ye Choi (524-9274)

This office is in charge of purchasing defense material for the Ministry of National Defense (ROK).

KOREAN INFORMATION OFFICE
Embassy of the Republic of Korea
1414 22nd Street NW (Suite 101)
Washington, D.C. 20037
296-4256/4257
Chief: Su-Doc Kim

This office handles press and cultural affairs for the embassy. Among other functions, it provides to the public free materials on Korea and press releases, including the semimonthly *Korean Newsletter*. Scholars wishing to receive the newsletter and other official publications of the Republic of Korea should either call or write the Director of the Information Office. The office also has available for loan (free) about 30 documentaries and 10 feature films (e.g., "Choonhyang-jun") for classroom use and other educational purposes. A catalog of these films is under preparation and will be available in the near future. For further information, contact the Korean Information Office (296-4256).

L4 Food and Agriculture Organization (FAO) of the United Nations Liaison Office for North America

1. a. *1776 F Street, NW*
    Washington, D.C. 20437
    D. C. Kimmel, Director
    634-6215

    b. 8:00 A.M.-5:30 P.M.   Monday-Friday
    Open to the public.

2. The FAO is a specialized agency of the United Nations, which plays an increasingly important role in organizing technical and scientific assistance on a wide range of agricultural development problems. As the leading international agricultural organization, it works closely with other agencies, such as the United Nations Development Program (UNDP), the International Fund for Agriculture Development (IFAD), the World Bank (IBRD), and other regional development banks, in identifying and designing projects which will increase food production in the countries where the needs are greatest.

    FAO's Washington office serves essentially as a liaison office which coordinates FAO-administered programs in the United States and Canada. Among other responsibilities, it oversees the FAO scholarship program which brings in trainees nominated by the developing countries, including South Korea. Currently about 220 FAO scholarship recipients are receiving training in the United States, including 3 from South Korea.

3. FAO's Washington office maintains a reference library which contains a small collection of FAO documents and publications, including budgets and conference reports, FAO statistical yearbooks on world agricultural production and trade, fisheries, forest products, and other related subjects. In addition, the collection also includes FAO's international *Food and Agriculture Legislation* series, plus the *Monthly Bulletin of Agricultural and Economic Statistics, Ceres: FAO Review on Agriculture and Development* (bimonthly), and the Washington office's *Notes for North America*.

4. FAO has an extensive publication program with emphasis on food, nutrition, agriculture, forestry, and fisheries. Free copies of *FAO Books in Print* (annual) and *FAO Periodicals* are available on request.

L5 International Bank for Reconstruction and Development (IBRD) (World Bank)

1. a. *1818 H Street, NW*
    Washington, D.C. 20433
    477-1234

    b. Visitors should make an appointment to see bank officials.

    c. Robert S. McNamara, President

2.   IBRD (or World Bank) is a specialized agency of the United Nations which aims to assist the economic development of its members (129 nations). It provides financial and technical assistance for the economic development of the less-developed countries. In fiscal 1977, approximately $6 billion was loaned by the IBRD to finance a wide variety of projects in agriculture and rural development, education, electric power, industry, population planning, tourism, transportation, telecommunications, urban development, and water supply.

Japan, South Korea, and Taiwan have been active members of the World Bank in the postwar period.

IBRD carries out extensive research on various aspects of international economic problems. Outside scholars are frequently hired as consultants for such research projects. For details, see *World Bank Research Program: Abstracts of Current Studies (1977);* and *Use of Consultants by the World Bank and Its Borrowers (1974).*

3.   See the entry for "Joint Bank-Fund Library" (entry A28) in the Libraries section.

4.   All IBRD research reports and other working papers are filed in the Records Center of the Administrative Services Department (477-4356), which maintains an index of "Documentation Available to Staff."

IBRD has an extensive publication program including a number of periodical publications: (1) *World Bank Annual Report;* (2) *Summary Proceedings of the Annual Meeting;* (3) *Finance and Development* (quarterly); and a bimonthly newspaper entitled *Report.* In addition, several statistical reports prepared periodically by the bank staff will be of particular interest to East Asian specialists: (1) *World Economic and Social Indicators* (monthly); *World Debt Tables: External Public Debt of Developing Countries* (annual); *Commodity Trade and Price Trends* (annual); *World Bank Atlas* (annual); and *Borrowing in International Capital Markets* (quarterly).

IBRD also publishes the highly informative *World Bank Staff Working Papers* series. Some of the most recent titles include: *Alternative Development Strategies of Korea (1976-1990) in an Input-Output Dynamic Simulation Model* (March 1977); *Industrial Policy and Development in Korea* (August 1977); and *Korea's Experience with Export-Led Industrial Development* (1977).

Copies of many of these publications plus the *World Bank Catalog of Publications* can be obtained free upon request.

5.   East Asian and Pacific Regional Office
East Asia Division
B. David Loos, Director
477-4045

This office administers development assistance projects of the IBRD for East Asia. In recent years, its operations in South Korea have been most active, as it maintains only a supervising function over ongoing programs in Taiwan with no new programs. As a developed industrial country, Japan is not a recipient but an important donor nation for the IBRD programs. By the beginning of 1978, IBRD had loaned more than $2 billion to South Korea. In fiscal 1978 alone, the bank funded a $439-million loan for 6 projects involving irrigation, rural development, railroads, vocational training, and agricultural processing in South Korea.

To cooperate effectively with the South Korean government, various IBRD missions are dispatched regularly for frequent consultations between officials of the bank and the South Korean government. A large number of confidential economic reports and special studies are produced, including assessments of South Korean development requirements and priorities, policy recommendations, project appraisals, and loan evaluations. Many of the office's research publications are available, except those regarded as confidential.

L6 International Finance Corporation (IFC)

1. a. *1809 G Street, NW*
    Washington, D.C. 20433

    c. Judvhir Parmar, Vice President in Charge of East Asia
       Torstein Stephansen, Director, Department of Investments, Asia
       477-5035

2. IFC was established in 1956 as an affiliate of the World Bank to further economic development by encouraging the growth of private enterprises in 109 member countries, particularly in the less developed areas of the world. In East Asia, IFC operations are tapering off, as more countries of the region can finance their economic needs through commercial bank loans. The IFC has been inactive in Taiwan since 1976, while its investment activities and operations in South Korea have also tapered off. As of June 1977, IFC's investment commitments totaled $74 million in South Korea.

    From time to time, IFC hires outside consultants to perform specific tasks required, such as research and policy development.

4. Copies of the *International Finance Corporation Annual Report* can be obtained free upon request.

L7 International Monetary Fund (IMF)

1. a. *700   19th Street, NW*
    Washington, D.C. 20431
    477-7000

    b. Not open to the public. Visitors received on an appointment basis.

    c. J. de Larosidére, Managing Director

2. The IMF works to promote international monetary stability and the elimination of restrictive exchange practices among its 134 member nations, and it provides financial assistance to members in temporary

balance-of-payments difficulties. The fund's departments analyze international financial and economic conditions. East Asian activities are discussed below. Little contract research is funded, but the IMF maintains a pool of private international fiscal and central banking specialists to act as advisers to foreign governments.

3. See "Joint Bank-Fund Library" (entry A28) in the Libraries section.

4. Fund documents, reports, and other working papers—virtually all confidential—are filed in the Records Division of the IMF's Secretary Department, which maintains a cumulative list of international fund materials.

The IMF issues a broad range of periodical publications. The *Annual Report* of the Executive Directors reviews the fund's activities and surveys the world economy, with emphasis on balance-of-payments problems, exchange rates, international liquidity, and world trade. The *Annual Report on Exchange Restrictions* reviews developments in the field of exchange controls and restrictions, by country. *Summary Proceedings* is a record of the fund's annual meeting. The biweekly *IMF Survey* reports fund activities (including press releases, texts of communiques and major statements, SDR valuations, and exchange rates) within the context of developments in national economies and international finance. *Finance and Development,* a joint quarterly review of IMF/World Bank activities, is directed primarily toward a nontechnical audience. It contains articles dealing with problems of money and economic growth, national and international monetary policies, trade and exchange systems, economic development, and bank/fund development assistance. *Staff Papers* (4 issues per year) contains studies on monetary and financial problems prepared by members of the IMF staff.

Four major statistical periodicals are produced. The monthly *International Financial Statistics* contains data on exchange rates, international liquidity, money and banking, international trade, prices, production, government finance, interest rates, etc., by country and region. The monthly *Direction of Trade* provides data on imports and exports, by country, with comparative data for the corresponding period of the previous year. The *Government Finance Statistics Yearbook* provides data on revenues, expenditures, lending, financing, and the debt of central governments, and also indicates amounts represented by social-security funds and extra-budgetary operations. The *Balance of Payments Yearbook* (12 monthly and 1 annual issue) provides relevant statistics on member nations. Tapes relating to these statistical publications are available to subscribers.

Other publications include books on international liquidity, central banking, Asian economies, and legal aspects of the IMF, as well as *The International Monetary Fund, 1945-1965: Twenty Years of International Monetary Cooperation* (3 vols.) and *The International Monetary Fund, 1966-1971: The System Under Stress* (2 vols.); a pamphlet series on various aspects of the IMF and on subjects in its special fields of interest; and ad hoc official reports. *A Catalogue of Publications, 1946-1971* and a publications leaflet are available. Contact the IMF Publications Office or the Office of Information.

5. Asian Department
   Tun Thin, Director   477-2911

The principal operational wing of the IMF for East Asian affairs, the Asian Department, has a staff of some 41 professional economists (including 14 from Asia, of whom 5 are from East Asia) most of them assigned as country specialists in 5 geographic divisions. The department advises the fund's management and Executive Board on all matters concerning the economies and economic policies of East Asian countries, assists in the formulation of fund policies in relation to these countries and, along with other departments of the fund, provides technical assistance and financial advice. Staff teams make periodic trips to East Asian countries to collect data, analyze financial trends and policies, and hold policy consultations with national authorities responsible for economic affairs.

The department prepares an annual report on "recent economic developments" in each country of East Asia. It also produces highly confidential "staff reports" appraising economic conditions based on field consultations. These materials are not available to outside researchers. Asian Department staff members, however, are accessible to scholars.

Note: Scholars interested in obtaining visa and other information about Hong Kong, Macao, and Taiwan should contact the following offices:

(For Hong Kong)
Embassy of Great Britain
3100 Massachusetts Avenue, NW
Washington, D.C. 20008

(For Macao)
Embassy of Portugal
2125 Kalorama Road
Washington, D.C. 20008
483-7075

(For Taiwan)
Former Embassy of the Republic of China
2311 Massachusetts Avenue, NW
Washington, D.C. 20008
667-9000

M Research Centers, Academic Programs and Departments

Entry Form for Research Centers and Academic Programs and Departments (M)

1. *Address; telephone number(s)*
2. Founding date
3. Chief official and title
4. Staff; research and/or teaching personnel
5. Parental organizations
6. Principal fields of research and other activities
7. Library/special research facilities (including specialized collections and unique equipment; availability to nonmembers)
8. Recurring meetings sponsored by the center (open or closed)
9. Publications or other media of dissemination
10. Affiliated organizations

M1 Advanced International Studies Institute (AISI) (An Affiliate of the University of Miami)

1. *4330 East-West Highway*
   Bethesda, Md. 20014
   (301) 951-0818

2. 1978 (Successor to the Center for Advanced International Studies, Washington Research Division, University of Miami.)

3. Mose L. Harvey, Director

4. The institute has a staff of about 20 including 10 professional research analysts.

5. Affiliated with the University of Miami, Coral Gables, Florida, the institute assists in the graduate program in Soviet studies for the University of Miami.

6. AISI programs and activities are designed to disseminate knowledge affecting the international system in general and United States foreign policy in particular. Foremost among its research programs are: the Soviet Union and the People's Republic of China and their relations with each other, the United States, Eastern and Western Europe, Japan, and the Third World. Most research analysts at the institute are specialists in Soviet studies, who conduct nonclassified research for the government and private concerns and publish their findings on Soviet and international affairs.

7. The institute has a research library which contains over 50,000 volumes, mostly on Soviet studies. The FBIS collection is probably one of the most complete in the Washington area. JPRS publications and many Russian periodicals are among other holdings maintained by the library. On-site use of the library by serious researchers may be arranged through the office.

8. AISI sponsors numerous meetings and seminars on international affairs, many of them pertinent to China specialists. Outside experts from the government, business, and universities participate in seminars. Scholars wishing further information on the scheduled events of the institute should call (301) 951-0818.

9. AISI has an active publication program including monographs in international affairs, occasional papers, and periodicals (e.g., monthly *Soviet World Outlook*). Most monographs deal directly with the USSR; and the rest pertain to important regions of the world such as East Asia. An example of a recent monograph on East Asia is Morris Rothenberg's *Whither China: The View from the Kremlin* (1977). The institute also published Rothenburg's *Soviet Perceptions of the Chinese Succession* in its Occassional Papers series in 1975.

M2 American Enterprise Institute for Public Policy Research (AEI)

1. *1150 17th Street, NW*
   Washington, D.C. 20036
   862-5800

2. 1943

3. William J. Baroody, Jr., President
   Herman J. Schmidt, Chairman of the Board

4. The AEI staff consists of about 125 full-time members, including directors of various divisions, resident scholars, and fellows. Dr. Robert J. Pranger is currently the director of foreign and defense policy studies.

6. AEI is an independent, nonprofit, nonpartisan research and educational organization which does not itself take positions on policy issues. The institute studies national problems, fosters innovative research, identifies and presents varying points of view of policy issues, and develops options

for public policy. In domestic affairs, it works on government regulation, social security and retirement, health, energy and tax policies, and legislative analysis. AEI's foreign affairs and defense program brings together specialists from academic, business, and government circles to study international politics, defense policies, resources and technology, ethical-philosophical dimensions of international relations, and other related matters. Much of the institute's work will be of interest to East Asian specialists.

To broaden and strengthen its association within the academic community, as well as to contribute to the formulation of effective public policy, AEI disseminates information and research results broadly in cooperation with college and university libraries across the United States.

7. AEI has a small library designed for the use of its staff.

8. In order to discuss issues of unusual complexity, AEI sponsors numerous conferences, seminars, discussions, and debates annually. The proceedings of the conferences are published. Among recent AEI conferences topics have been "Japan-U.S. Assembly" in 1974 and 1975. In addition, the institute video-tapes a Public Policy Forum each month, bringing together leading exponents of varying viewpoints for discussion and question-and-answer sessions. These programs are aired on some 400 commercial and educational television stations (and cable-vision systems) and numerous radio stations nationwide. AEI also conducts graduate seminars for Washington area graduate students during the academic year. Finally, AEI has a "Discussion With . . ." series featuring scholars and other experts on major public policy issues.

9. The AEI has an extensive publication program. Of particular interest to East Asian specialists will be foreign affairs and defense studies which encompass major regions of the world. Some recent AEI titles which deal with East Asia are: *American Attitudes toward Japan, 1941-1975* (1975) by Sheila Johnson; *Asia and the Major Powers* (1972) by Robert A. Scalapino; *Asian Neutralism and U.S. Policy* (1975) by Sheldon W. Simon; *China's Scientific Policies* (1976) by Charles P. Ridley; *Japanese-American Relations* (1975) by Philip Caldwell et al.; *The Japanese Language in Contemporary Japan* (1977) by Andrew Miller; *Japan at the Polls: The House of Councillors Election of 1974* (1976) by Michael Blaker et al.; and, *Withdrawal of U.S. Troops from Korea?* (1977) by George McGovern and Richard G. Stillwell.

The annual list of *AEI Publications* is available free on request.

M3 American University—Foreign Area Studies (FAS)

1. *5010 Wisconsin Avenue, NW*
Washington, D.C. 20016
686-2769

2. In 1954 the Department of the Army began to produce Area Handbooks through a contract with the Human Relations Area Files (HRAF), New Haven, Connecticut; a Washington branch (WAHRAF) opened at American University in 1955. Three years later the university became the sole producer as the HRAF contract terminated.

3. William Evans-Smith, Director

4. FAS employs approximately 30 persons, some 18 of whom are professional researchers grouped into multidisciplinary teams. Another 12 staff members provide library, editorial, secretarial, and administrative services.

5. Foreign Area Studies is an integral part of American University, though located off campus and operates under a contract between the University and the Department of the Army.

6. FAS conducts the Area Handbook Program, preparing book-length studies about the social, economic, political, and military institutions— the people and society—of foreign countries. Aimed at the nonspecialist, with a stress on contemporary society, the books average about 350 pages and feature cartographic illustrations and tables. Annual usage of books exceeds 100,000 copies of the more than 100 titles in print. Countries of the Asia/Pacific area covered by these studies are: Afghanistan, Australia, Bangladesh, Burma, Ceylon, People's Republic of China, Republic of China, India, Indonesia, Japan, Khmer Republic, North Korea, South Korea, Laos, Malaysia, Mongolia, Nepal-Bhutan-Sikkim, Oceania, Pakistan, Philippines, Singapore, Thailand, South Vietnam, and North Vietnam. All are for sale by the Superintendent of Documents, U.S. Government Printing Office, Washington, D.C. 20402.

7. The FAS library is designed to meet the special research needs of its staff, and the holdings reflect an emphasis on current and reliable (secondary) sources of information on the nations covered in the books. Periodical subscriptions account for the major acquisitions. Some scholarly materials may be found here which are not readily available elsewhere in the area. The library can provide bibliographic assistance for its own and other Washington collections, has photoduplication services, and is open to qualified researchers who, if interested in using the facility, should call FAS for more information.

8. See point 6.

M4 Battelle Memorial Institute—Washington Operations

1. *2030 M Street, NW*
    Washington, D.C. 20036
    785-8400

2. 1925

3. Dr. Sherwood L. Fawcett, President
    George B. Johnson, Director, Washington Operations, and Vice President for Federal and International Sponsor Relations

4. The BMI Washington branch is staffed by 50-60 employees.

5. Main headquarters are located in Columbus, Ohio

6. The institute is one of the world's leading nonprofit scientific research development and educational organizations. It has 4 major research centers in the United States and Europe. Additionally, it has 4 sites for specialized research, as well as offices and correspondents in various parts of the world, including Tokyo and Taipei. Its staff of 6,300 scientists, engineers, and supporting specialists bring their skills and training in the physical, engineering, life, and social/behavioral sciences to bear on the problems and needs of contemporary society.

   The research conducted by Battelle extends from pure research to applied programs directed toward new products and processes. Its activities extend from nuclear research to oceanography; and from coal-gasification studies to sewage treatment; also included are environmental studies, programs and devices for improving health care, creative urban and area planning, and studies on land use. Much of the research (numbering over 3,000 projects per year) is supported by United States and foreign industrial companies, government agencies, and associations on a contract basis.

   The BMI has a close relationship with the Mitsubishi Corporation (Tokyo) which is an agent for Battelle. BMI has also helped establish the Korean Institute of Science and Technology (KIST) and has recently carried out a study on Taiwan's scientific infrastructure.

8. The BMI Washington branch sponsors various seminars and conferences. Participation in these meetings is limited to BMI clients and staff.

9. Several brochures and newsletters published by Battelle are free on request. Also, Battelle's annual bibliography, *Published Pages and Articles* (Battelle), may be obtained from the BMI's main office.

10. The Battelle Development Corporation and Scientific Advances, Inc. are affiliated with the BMI.

M5 Brookings Institution

1. *1775 Massachusetts Avenue, NW*
   Washington, D.C. 20036
   797-6000

2. 1927

3. Bruce K. MacLaury, President

4. The institution's 3 major research programs (Economic Studies, Governmental Studies, and Foreign Policy Studies) are conducted by a staff of about 35 senior fellows, 20 research associates, 25 research assistants, and a small number of consultants. About 45 additional staff members work for related programs, such as the Advanced Study Program, the Social Science Computation Center, and Publications.

6. The Brookings Institution is a private nonprofit organization devoted to research, education, and publication in economics, government, foreign policy, and the social sciences generally. Its principal purpose is to bring knowledge to bear on current and future public policy problems facing

the United States. It endeavors to serve as a bridge between scholarship and public policy, bringing new knowledge to the attention of policy makers and providing scholars with a better insight into complicated policy issues. The Advanced Study Program is designed to conduct seminars, conferences, and round-table discussions by drawing participants from government, academic, and business communities. Brookings is financed largely by endowment and by philanthropic foundations, corporations, and private individuals. Its funds are devoted to carrying out its own research and educational activities. Under the terms of its charter, it cannot conduct studies for private clients. However, it does undertake some unclassified government contract studies, reserving the right to publish its findings. The institution administers the following fellowship programs: Economic Policy Fellowships; Research Fellowships; Visiting Professor and Younger Scholar Programs; Guest Scholar Programs; and Federal Executive Fellowships.

7. The library of the Brookings Institution has about 55,000 volumes; however, its holdings on East Asia are relatively small—no more than 1,000 titles. They are for staff use only.

    The Social Science Computation Center (797-6180) has several computer data bases (mostly statistical data) and offers a number of computerized services. The center primarily serves the Brookings staff; however, it may also serve other nonprofit organizations, for a fee. Researchers wishing staff assistance should telephone before visiting the Center.

8. The institution does not sponsor regular meetings open to the public. Attendance at its meetings and conferences is strictly by invitation.

9. Brookings Institution has an active publication program. Its more recent publications are noted in its annual catalog, *Brookings Economics, Government, Foreign Policy Books* (1978), which lists a number of titles relating to East Asia. These include Richard E. Caves and Masu Uekusa, *Industrial Organization in Japan* (1976); Hugh Patrick and Henry Rosovsky (eds.), *Asia's New Giant: How the Japanese Economy Works* (1976); A. Doak Barnett, *China and the Major Powers in Asia* (1977); and Ralph N. Clough, *Deterrence and Defense in Korea: The Role of U.S. Forces* (1976).

M6 Center for Chinese Research Materials (CCRM) (Association of Research Libraries)

1. *1527 New Hampshire Avenue, NW*
    Washington, D.C. 20036
    387-7172

2. 1968

3. P. K. Yu, Director

4. The center has a staff of 6, including 2 senior researchers.

5. Association of Research Libraries.

6. The CCRM was established in 1968 to make available Chinese research materials, both current and historical, through its reproduction and publishing programs, and to provide bibliographic services. Materials reproduced by offset printing, microfilming, and xerographic copy-flow include newspapers, periodicals, monographs, government documents and archives, as well as research tools of value for scholarly work. Funded by grants from the Ford Foundation, the National Endowment for the Humanities, and the Mellon Foundation, the CCRM has also published from time to time books related to bibliographic control of Chinese research materials. The CCRM obtains original materials needed for reproduction through loan arrangements with libraries or private collections in the United States and abroad. The assembling of a serial title, many issues of which may be scattered over a number of locations, frequently requires extensive research. This time-consuming process, which many libraries cannot afford, has become common practice at CCRM. Thus, the CCRM is, in part, a publishing house, which also performs the functions of a reference service of a major research library.

7. The CCRM has a special collection of Chinese materials which number over 1,500 titles. Although the CCRM has no library or reading room facilities, serious scholars may use the materials on the premises.

9. Since its inception in May 1968, the CCRM has published more than 1,200 Chinese research materials in 8 broad categories: newspapers, periodicals, government publications, research aids, monographs, literature, newspaper supplements, and yearbooks. Subscribers to CCRM's publications include major universities and research centers in the United States and other academic centers and research libraries in many parts of the world.

    It is impossible to enumerate the large body of research material made available by the CCRM in the past years. The most significant titles produced by the center include: *North China Daily News* of Shanghai (1864-1951) on 298 reels of microfilm; *Hua-tzu jih-pao (The Chinese Mail)* of Hong Kong (1896-1940) on 81 reels; *Shen pao (Chinese Daily News)* of Shanghai (1872-1949) on 133 reels; *Shun-t'ien shih-pao (Peking Times)* of Peking (1901-1930) on 110 reels; *K'ang-chan wen-i (Literature of the War of Resistance)* of Chungking (1938-1946) in 4 volumes; and the *She-hui k'o-hsueh tsa-chih (Quarterly Review of Social Sciences)* of Peking and Nanking (1930-1948) in 10 volumes. As bibliographic tools, the CCRM has reproduced the *Jen-min jih-pao so-yin (Index to People's Daily)* from June 1948 to December 1971 in 24 volumes; *Ch'uan-kuo hsin shu-mu (National Bibliography)* from 1951-1966 in 20 volumes; and a reference tool entitled *A Chronology of Twentieth Century China, 1904-1949* in 6 volumes. For an annotated bibliography of CCRM's publications, see P. K. Yu (ed.), *Research Materials on Twentieth Century China: An Annotated List of CCRM Publications* (1975). For subsequent CCRM publications, scholars should consult recent issues of *Center for Chinese Research Materials Newsletter* (quarterly until the end of 1977; semiannually thereafter), distributed without charge to interested individuals.

10. Policy guidance for the CCRM's operation is provided by a 6-member advisory committee, equally served by faculty members and librarians, who are nominated by the Joint Committee on Contemporary China of

the American Council of Learned Societies (ACLS) and the Social Science Research Council (SSRC), and the Association of Research Libraries.

M7 Center for Defense Information (CDI)

1. *122 Maryland Avenue, NE*
   Washington, D.C. 20002
   543-0400

2. 1972

3. Rear Adm. (ret.) Gene R. La Rocque, Director

4. The CDI has a staff of 5 analysts, 5 administrative workers, and a few temporary interns.

5. The CDI's main field of research centers around United States military and foreign policy. Of interest to East Asian specialists are studies on Chinese and Japanese military capabilities and economic and political questions related to these countries. In conducting research on defense policy issues, the center seeks to present an alternative view to the Pentagon's.

7. The CDI library has about 1,500 volumes, which include government documents, Defense Department issuances, and recent congressional hearings on military and foreign policy issues. Fewer than 100 books deal with East Asia. However, the vertical file collection (e.g., newspaper clippings, magazine articles, and press releases) has several folders relating to China, Japan, and Korea. The library is open to the public from 9:00 A.M. to 5:00 P.M., Monday-Friday.

8. The center sponsors a series of occasional seminars on defense policy issues. Scholars should call for information and an invitation to these sessions, which are open and without cost.

9. The CDI publishes a short (8-12 pages) monthly newsletter entitled *The Defense Monitor* (10 times a year) which covers selected problems. Copies are available free on request. It also publishes articles and monographs, some of which deal with East Asia. Two of its most recent titles are *Current Issues in U.S. Defense Policy* edited by David T. Johnson and Barry R. Schneider (New York: Praeger, 1976); and Stefan H. Leader, *An Assessment of the Korean Military Situation* (CDI, 1977).

10. The CDI, the Center for International Policy, and the Center for National Security Studies are affiliated with the programs of the New York-based Fund for Peace.

M8 Center for International Policy (CIP)

1. *122 Maryland Avenue, NE*
   Washington, D.C. 20002
   544-6666

2. 1975

3.   Donald L. Ranard, Director

4.   The center has a staff of about 6 professional analysts and about 10 outside consultants.

5.   The CIP is an affiliate of the Fund for Peace (New York).

6.   The CIP is concerned about the erosion of democratic political systems around the world, particularly in countries where there is sizable United States involvement. The CIP is part of a nationwide effort to redirect United States foreign policy so that it will actively encourage justice, democracy, and human rights. Since 1975, the center has been actively involved in informing the press, the public, and government officials about the implications of United States foreign policy toward developing countries with special emphasis on the relationship of United States economic and military assistance to human rights.

7.   The CIP has a small library which may be used by serious researchers through prior arrangements with the center.

9.   The *International Policy Report,* the principal organ of the CIP, is published several times per year. It contains specific foreign policy issues researched by the center staff. The CIP also publicizes its findings on United States-aided governments that violate human rights in a concise annual survey entitled *Human Rights and the U.S. Foreign Assistance Program.*

10.   The CIP is affiliated with the Center for Defense Information and the Center for National Security Studies (all programs of the New York-based Fund for Peace).

M9 Center for Naval Analyses (CNA)

1.   *1401 Wilson Boulevard*
Arlington, Va. 22209
(703) 524-9400

2.   Created in 1962 by merging the Operations Evaluation Group (OEG) managed by the Massachusetts Institute of Technology with the Institute of Naval Studies.

3.   David B. Kassing, President

4.   The CNA staff consists of 165 professional analysts, 35 military personnel (from the Navy and Marine Corps) and another 200 technical support staff.

6.   CNA carries out research on contract for the Department of Defense with emphasis on a broad range of naval questions, including antisubmarine and submarine warfare, fleet air defense, and air warfare, naval communications, tactical development and evaluation, Navy resource analysis, and the development of new technology and weapons systems. The center also carries out nondefense research in such fields as international affairs, environmental and energy problems, and labor and manpower management.

7.   CNA has a library and a computer center restricted to staff use. To gain access to the Technical Reference Room, containing both classified and unclassified materials, outside researchers must have clearance and special permission from the Management Information Office. The same restrictions apply to the center's computer facilities.

9.   CNA publishes 2 indexes to its publications: 1 for classified work and the other for unclassified. The index for unclassified materials is available free on request. The most recent edition is *Index of Selected Publications (through December 1977),* issued in 1978. Requests for the publication should be addressed to the center's Management Information Office. All publications cleared for public release are available at CNA and at NTIS (see entry K5). An example of CNA's East Asian-related unclassified studies is: *Peking and the Problem of Japan, 1968-1972* (1972) by Abraham M. Halpern. Copies of the CNA Annual Report are available without charge on request.

M10 Center for U.S.—China Relations

1.   *422 C Street, NE*
        Washington, D.C. 20002
        547-0040

2.   1978

3.   Elaine Budd, Director

4.   The staff consists of 3 full-time researchers plus a few interns (mostly from the local universities).

5.   U.S.-China People's Friendship Association, whose headquarters are located at 635 S. Westlake Avenue (Room 202), Los Angeles, California 90057 (see also entry H45).

6.   The center is a research arm of the U.S.-China People's Friendship Association, whose major purpose is to improve relations and communications between the United States and the People's Republic of China. To do this, it seeks to educate Congress and the public on major issues relating to U.S.-PRC relations since 1949. The center's staff monitors developments in the United States Congress and other government agencies with regard to United States policy toward China; it scans scholarly journals as well as newspapers and magazines to monitor trends in United States public opinion toward the PRC; and it sponsors seminars and other conferences to educate the general public on U.S.-PRC relations.

7.   A reference library is planned in the near future. Eventually, the center plans to make its reference materials available to the general public.

9.   It plans to sponsor regional as well as local seminars on U.S.-PRC relations. Regional seminars are scheduled to be held in Chicago and Houston in 1979.

10. The center published a newsletter plus a book entitled "Americans Talk About U.S.-China Relations" in the fall of 1978. Under preparation is a background information booklet on Taiwan.

11. See point 5.

M11 EXOTECH Systems, Inc.

1. *1200 Quince Orchard Boulevard*
   Gaithersburg, Md. 20760

2. 1955

3. Libert Ehrman, President

4. The number of researchers varies, as most work is done on a contract basis; experts are brought in to carry out specific research projects of the EXOTECH.

6. The EXOTECH is a diversified firm, providing a full range of consulting, research, and engineering services in the social sciences, computer sciences, data processing, information-system design, government program evaluation, survey research, statistical-systems development, and electro-optical and hydromechanic technology. It has carried out many projects financed by AID, and other agencies of the United States government, the World Bank, the Export-Import Bank, and the governments and industries of other nations, including South Korea, Taiwan, and Japan. For example, it developed for Taiwan a central statistical system in the 1960s. It also developed in the same decade a national statistical system for South Korea involving an analysis of the organization and administration of data-processing operations. Currently, it is involved in projects relating to the construction of grain warehouses and farm machinery acquisition in South Korea.

7. The EXOTECH has a small library designed strictly for staff use only.

9. The EXOTECH has published a number of research reports, including: *Directory of Selected Scientific Institutions in Mainland China* (Hoover Institution Press, 1970); *Farm Mechanization Program for Korea* (1972); and *Statistical Publications in Korea: An Interim Report to the Government of the Republic of Korea* (1961).

M12 General Research Corporation (GRC)

1. *7655 Old Springhouse Road*
   McLean, Va. 22101
   (703) 893-5900

2. 1961

3. Joseph E. Hall, President
   Dr. John L. Allen, Head of East Coast Operations

4. There are 188 professional analysts and 65 support staff members in the McLean office.

6. The GRC carries out research in various fields, such as United States defense and foreign policy, energy, environment, economics, communications, and various scientific fields. The GRC's defense-related work is diversified within the major areas of systems technologies and operations management. The corporation is particularly interested in projects which involve electro-optical and radar sensors working in conjunction with modern high-speed, large scale computers. Its research ranges from the analysis of advanced concepts for ballistic missile defense to the assessment of high-energy lasers for defense of the field army and for spaceborne optic systems. In defense policy studies, the GRC's research activities cover the United States security interest in East Asia.

7. The GRC's library, containing nearly 30,000 books and pamphlets and about 350 current periodicals, is closed to the public. Library material of interest to East Asian specialists is available at the Defense Documentation Center (G3) and should be used there. Furthermore, all index cards for the library's holdings are sent in duplicate to the Army Library at the Pentagon (A7). Eugene Suto, director, and Patricia Wolf, assistant librarian, may be reached at extensions 418 or 419.

8. The GRC sponsors a number of meetings and seminars which may be of interest to East Asian specialists. However, they may be closed to outsiders. Those interested in further information should contact the organization directly.

9. The GRC's publications are not available to the public. All publications of potential interest to East Asian specialists are at the Defense Documentation Center. Scholars may telephone or write Eugene Suto about publications.

10. GRC is a subsidiary of Flow General, Inc.

M13 George Washington University—East Asian Languages and Literature Department

1. *Library Building, Room 613*
George Washington University
Washington, D.C. 20052
676-7263

2. 1971

3. Chung-wen Shih

4. The department has 3 full-time professors and 5 part-time instructors on the staff.

6. The department offers a broad range of courses in Chinese language, literature, linguistics, and a limited number of courses in the Japanese language. The department administers the undergraduate degree program

in Chinese language and literature (i.e., B.A. with a major in Chinese language and literature). In addition, it also offers an interdisciplinary M.A. program in East Asian Studies with concentration on Chinese language and literature.

8.   Lectures, films, and other events sponsored by the department are open to the public and announced in advance. Information about forthcoming activities may be obtained from the department office.

M14 George Washington University—East Asian Studies Program

1.   *School of Public and International Affairs (SPIA)*
George Washington University
Washington, D.C. 20052
678-6240

2.   1977

3.   Dr. William R. Johnson, Director

4.   Currently there are 11 professors offering courses in the program.

6.   The program for an M.A. in East Asian Studies is interdisciplinary and administered by the interdepartmental East Asian Studies Committee of the SPIA and the ISSS of George Washington University.

    Students with a social science focus (e.g., economics, history, geography, or political science) may complete either a 30-hour program, including a master's thesis, or a 36-hour program without the thesis. A special 2-semester Chinese-language course designed to enable students to read contemporary materials is essential. The program is designed for candidates preparing themselves for professional work in public life or those who already are in careers and wish to develop their expertise and credentials in East Asian Studies.

    The program also provides the option of a 30-hour Chinese language-and-literature concentration. This option is designed for students primarily interested in furthering their language skills and for preparing for advanced study in Chinese language and literature.

    For further information, see the entry for the Institute for Sino-Soviet Studies (M15).

M15 George Washington University—Institute for Sino-Soviet Studies (ISSS)

1.   *New Library Building, Suite 601*
22d and H Streets, NW
Washington, D.C. 20052
676-6340/6341

2.   1962

3.   Dr. Gaston Sigur, Director

4. Research and teaching staff of the institute number more than 20 full- and part-time faculty members in such disciplines as political science, history, economics, law, geography, and language and literature. Most members hold joint appointments with departments of the university.

5. The ISSS is an integral part of the School of Public and International Affairs of the George Washington University.

6. The institute seeks to develop and promote graduate teaching and research programs in Russian-Soviet, East European, East Asian studies. Though the ISSS is not a degree-granting division of the university, it offers programs of specialized graduate study and research within the School of Public and International Affairs. Courses are drawn from a variety of academic areas, and thus provide interdisciplinary studies of Soviet Russia, Eastern Europe, East Asia, and the Communist movement. Among the subjects taught by the staff are Sino-Soviet relations, economics and politics of Communist China, history, geography, political science, law, and the psychology of communism. The institute has developed a specialized research program through 2 research colloquia— East Asia, and Russia and Eastern Europe—which form a regular part of the curriculum. These research colloquia are interdisciplinary and interuniversity discussion groups which meet weekly and provide a unique vehicle for an exchange of views. The East Asia Colloquium (chaired by Dr. Harold C. Hinton) currently meets on Mondays from 1:00-3:00 P.M. The topics are related to research studies in progress by members or invited guests. Participants are members of the institute, selected advanced graduate students, experts from government, members of Congress and their staffs, and specialists from universities at home and abroad. The institute also encourages and supports relevant research by faculty members, visiting scholars, and associates. More information about this program may be obtained from the ISSS. In addition, fellowships, assistantships, and other financial assistance are available for qualified graduate students.

7. The ISSS library is separate from the main University Library in the Libraries section (entry A18). Some institute holdings are, however, included in the total figures for the George Washington University Library in the Libraries section, which contains these titles together. Of the more than 8,000 volumes currently located in the ISSS library, perhaps one-third relate to East Asian affairs. These titles are in both East Asian and Western languages. Most concentrations of materials are in the fields of political science and history, but the library holdings are also fairly strong on international relations, economics, and culture. The ISSS library receives many periodicals emanating from East Asia; 9 Japanese periodicals (e.g., *Chūō Kōron, Jiyū*, etc.), 1 from Korea, and 21 from China, Taiwan, and Hong Kong. Also, it contains the *FBIS* reports and *JPRS* translations; *Survey of China Mainland Press* (1953-1977); and *Selections from China Mainland Magazines* (1955-1977). Unquestionably, this is an excellent research library with many basic reference books and much periodical literature. Library hours are from 9:00 A.M. to 8:00 P.M. Monday through Friday and 9:00 A.M. to 1:30 P.M. Saturdays during the academic year. Serious researchers may make on-site use of the holdings without special permission.

8. As mentioned in point 6, the weekly colloquia meetings (1 on Russia and Eastern Europe and 1 on East Asia) provide important opportunities for scholars and qualified graduate students to participate. The ISSS also sponsors occasional lectures and other presentations by experts in the field of East Asian studies. Generally, these events are open to the interested public. A schedule of both colloquia is available on request from the ISSS office.

9. The institute members' individual monographs are published by academic and commercial presses. The ISSS offers reprint copies of selected articles and other publications of the staff.

10. The ISSS also works closely with the other universities in the Consortium of Universities of the Washington Metropolitan Area.

M16 Georgetown University—Center for Strategic and International Studies (CSIS)

1. *1800 K Street, NW, Suite 520*
    Washington, D.C. 20006
    833-8595

2. 1962

3. David Abshire, Chairman
    Dr. Ray S. Cline, Executive Director of Studies

4. The CSIS is staffed by about 30 senior research specialists and about 30 administrative support staff. Dr. Ray S. Cline coordinates the research programs and activities on East Asia.

5. The CSIS is an off-campus branch of Georgetown University.

6. The primary focus of the CSIS has been policy-oriented research into the strategic interests of United States foreign policy. The center engages in a broad range of studies on international affairs, including East Asia. While the center does not make specific policy recommendations, it attempts to collect, clarify, and circulate policy alternatives. Private briefings, public reports, and contributions to scholarship are among the center's most important activities.

    In order to facilitate ongoing research on a variety of important subjects, the CSIS maintains geographic and functional divisions of research, each with its own director. In addition to Pacific Basin Studies, for example, there are divisions on European, Middle Eastern, Latin American, and African studies; energy, food, and other resource projects; and public diplomacy, international communications, and military power-balance studies. The center intends to continue building a systematic study program on the Pacific Basin region.

    The CSIS benefits from many diverse contacts with foreign affairs specialists in government as well as in the academic community here and abroad; and a group of distinguished scholars from around the world serves on the center's International Research Council which assists and advises the CSIS on its research programs and activities.

8. The CSIS sponsors a number of important conferences and seminars, some of which deal with East Asia. For example, the CSIS sponsored a conference on "The Pacific Basin: Forces of Unity and Division" on October 23, 1976. In June 1977, the CSIS held the Sixth Sino-American Conference on Mainland China: "Mainland China After Mao" in Washington, D.C. In addition, the center has sponsored a series of meetings with Japanese scholars and leaders on maritime problems, especially the law of the seas. Eleven U.S. specialists participated under the CSIS auspices in a Tokyo conference on the law of the seas in November 1977.

9. The CSIS has an active publication program. Its monographic series entitled *Washington Papers* contains contributions from scholars worldwide on a variety of topics. Some recent books of interest to East Asian specialists are: Harold C. Hinton, *Peking-Washington: Chinese Foreign Policy and the United States* (1976); Young C. Kim, *Japanese-Soviet Relations* (1974); William F. Griffith, *Peking, Moscow and Beyond: The Sino-Soviet Triangle* (1973); and Robert Scalapino, *American-Japanese Relations in a Changing Era* (1972).

Other monographs from staff members and outside researchers plus conference reports and proceedings are also regularly published: e.g., Harland Cleveland's *China Diary* (1976); Charles Ebinger's *Great Power Rivalry in the Far East: The Geopolitics of Energy* (1977); and *Mainland China After Mao: Proceedings of the Sixth Sino-American Conference on Mainland China* (1977).

M17 Georgetown University—Department of Chinese and Japanese

1. *483 Nevils Building*
   School of Languages and Linguistics
   Georgetown University
   Washington, D.C. 20057
   625-3964

2. 1946

3. Dr. Michael J. McCaskey

4. The teaching staff consists of 5 full-time faculty members and 6 part-time members.

6. The department offers a broad range of courses in Chinese and Japanese languages, literature, linguistics, and East Asian civilization and culture. The academic program leads to the degrees of B.A. and M.A. in Chinese or Japanese and the Ph.D. in Chinese language and literature. Both undergraduate and graduate students may take a summer semester of study in Taiwan, Hong Kong, and Japan.

7. For students studying Chinese and Japanese, the department provides a language laboratory with excellent audio and video equipment.

8. The department has 2 East Asian clubs: the China Forum and the Japanese Club. They are open to students interested in either Chinese or Japanese language and culture. In addition to the general meetings, the China Forum sponsors several banquets and parties to fulfill its

social as well as academic functions. The Japanese Club, too, sponsors lectures, discussions, social gatherings, and films. Scholars should contact the department for further information about upcoming meetings or events that they might wish to attend.

10.   The School of Languages and Linguistics publishes occasional *Working Papers in Linguistics*, to which faculty members of the Chinese and Japanese department contribute.

M18   Georgetown University East Asian Studies Program

1.   *c/o Department of History*
Georgetown University
Washington, D.C. 20057
625-4509

2.   1950

3.   An East Asian studies committee is expected to be established in the future (probably by 1980).

4.   Approximately 14 faculty members from 5 different departments offer over 50 different courses on East Asian politics, history, economics, international relations, religions, culture, language and linguistics.

6.   Georgetown University does not have an independent program in East Asian studies except for the degree programs in the Chinese and Japanese language (see entry M17). However, students enrolled in the departments of economics, government, and history can concentrate on East Asia as a part of their graduate degree programs. For further information, contact Rev. Joseph Sebes, S.J., or Rev. John D. Witek, S.J. (625-4509).

7.   For the Georgetown University Lauinger Library, see entry A19.

M19   Georgetown University—Foreign Service School

1.   *Walsh Building, Main Lobby*
Georgetown University
Washington, D.C. 20057
625-4218

2.   1919

3.   Dr. Peter F. Krogh, Dean
Dr. Matthew M. Gardner, Jr., Assistant Dean, for information on East Asian area studies.

4.   The teaching faculty of the school is drawn from various departments of the Georgetown University, especially from economics, history, government, sociology, and geography. Of the approximately 21 full-time and 49 part-time members of the faculty, about 5 are specialists in East Asian studies.

6.   The Edmund A. Walsh School of Foreign Service is designed to educate students in international affairs; this includes the social sciences, humanities, and foreign languages. The undergraduate curriculum is multidisciplinary, designed to prepare students for further academic or professional study and for public and private international careers. The school's program covers most aspects of East Asian affairs, including history, politics, economics, international relations, and religion. The graduate program offers professional training in the social sciences. A B.S. and an M.S. degree are available in Foreign Service.

8.   In addition to the regular curriculum, the School of Foreign Service offers a number of co-curricular activities such as seminars, conferences, and special lectures, which are usually accessible to all serious scholars. Many of these events deal with East Asia either directly or indirectly. For more information about these activities, scholars should contact the dean's office of the Foreign Service School (625-4218).

9.   The *School Foreign Service Globe* (monthly) carries news of the school and schedules of co-curricular events. Copies of this publication are free on request.

M20 Government Research Corporation (GRC)

1.   *1730 M Street, NW*
      Washington, D.C. 20036
      857-1400

2.   1969

3.   Anthony Stout, President

4.   GRC's Research Division staff consists of about 20 analysts, researchers, and librarians. GRC's Publications Division is staffed by about 20 editors and reporters.

6.   GRC is a private nonprofit organization primarily concerned with the study of domestic economic and political affairs. The Research Division serves about 40 domestic and foreign clients. Recently the Research Division carried out a major multivolume "U.S.-Japan Policy Study" with the emphasis on United States-Japanese economic relations. The *National Journal*, produced weekly by the Publications Division, covers trade and international affairs along with domestic political subjects.

7.   The GRC has a small library with total holdings of 1,500 volumes, mostly in politics and government and on aspects of the American and international economics. Subscribing to 270 periodicals, 170 newsletters and 9 newspapers, the library is for staff use only. A limited reference service is available to *National Journal* subscribers.

8.   The Publications Division sponsors occasional conferences on important policy issues, including international trade and investment. Transcripts from the international trade conferences are available. Scholars interested in attending these conferences should call or write GRC for further information.

9.   The GRC's main publication is *National Journal* (weekly) which covers United States government activities, policy development, and political trends. It periodically features articles on international matters. Special subscription rates are available to students, faculty, and libraries.

M21   Historical Evaluation and Research Organization (HERO)

1.   *2301 Gallows Road*
Dunn Loring, Va. 22127
(703) 560-6427
Mail to: P.O. Box 157, Dunn Loring, Va. 22127

2.   1962

3.   Col. Trevor N. Dupuy, USA (ret.), President and Executive Director

4.   The staff consists of about 12, including an editor and a director of research.

6.   HERO is a private research organization specializing in the military history of all nations, past and present. Most work is done under contract for the Department of Defense.

9.   The organization has recently begun publication of a quarterly *History, Numbers and War*. Another quarterly issued by HERO is the *Combat Data* which contains statistics and combat data analysis for many countries, including the People's Republic of China, Japan, and Korea.

10.   HERO is a division of T. N. Dupuy Associates, Inc., Washington, D.C.

M22   Institute for Defense Analyses (IDA)

1.   *400 Army-Navy Drive*
Arlington, Va. 22202
(703) 558-1000

2.   1956

3.   Dr. Alexander H. Flax, President

4.   The IDA has a staff of approximately 420, one-half of whom are trained specialists in the natural, life, and social sciences or engineering. Administrative and other support staff members comprise the remainder. These professionals are joined by outside experts either as consultants or short-term employees when appropriate and necessary.

5.   Originally formed by the Massachusetts Institute of Technology and 4 other universities, IDA has evolved into an independent research organization.

6.   Six branches of the IDA carry out its research programs: the Science and Technology Division, the Systems Evaluation Division, the Program Analysis Division, the Communications Research Division, the International and Social Studies Division, and the Cost Analysis Group. The

fields researched by IDA staff encompass primarily military affairs, weapons, defense, and related matters. Most of the institute's work is done on contract for the United States Department of Defense, but some projects are for other agencies of the federal government. In recent years, IDA has broadened its scope to include studies for other government agencies such as the Departments of Transportation; Housing and Urban Development; Justice; and Health, Education, and Welfare.

In addition, IDA encourages its staff to engage in independent non-contract research and to participate in professional societies, publish independently, and teach or lecture at local universities.

7.   IDA facilities are available only to its own staff members. Library services are provided by Technical Information Services to IDA staff. No unique collections are maintained. Neither the document nor the book collection is available to outsiders.

IDA also has a computer facility operated by the Computer Group which supports the research of other branches of the institute.

9.   IDA does not maintain a list of its publications since the circulation of its work is restricted. Most of its classified work goes to the Defense Documentation Center (entry G3), and its publicly released studies are available from National Technical Information Service (NTIS) at the Commerce Department (entry K5). IDA publications (sponsored by the independent research program) that are available at the National Technical Information Service (NTIS) include: *China's Detente Policy: Elements of Stability and Instability* by P. W. Colm (1975); *Preliminary Analysis of Japan's Dependence on Selected Imported Raw Materials* by N. N. White (1973); *Soviet and Japanese Interests in Joint Siberian Development* by R. Hayes and N. N. White (1975); and *Political Viability of the U.S. Base System in Asia After a Vietnam Settlement* by A. M. Fraser (1970).

M23   International Food Policy Research Institute (IFPRI)

1.   *1776 Massachusetts Avenue, NW*
Washington, D.C. 20036
862-5600

2.   1975

3.   John W. Miller, Director

4.   The professional research staff numbers about 20; the support staff, 21.

6.   The IFPRI was organized to study the world food situation, especially as it affects developing countries; and to conduct research on how to increase the availability of food in developing countries. The IFPRI's research focuses on alternative ways to reduce the great disparities in food supplies between developed and developing countries. Specifically, its research program analyzes: (1) trends in the production, exchange, and consumption of food in developing countries; (2) policies that affect agricultural production in developing countries; (3) programs and

policies to improve distribution of available foodstuffs; and, (4) policies to increase the effectiveness of international trade to cope with the food problem.

7. The IFPRI has a small research library (about 2,000 volumes) with emphasis on current periodicals and research reports. On-site use of the library is available to serious researchers.

8. Seminars and workshops are frequently sponsored by the institute; and a "Food Policy Seminar" is held once a month with participants from governmental and academic communities. Scholars interested in the seminar should contact the institute for further information. The IFPRI planned an international conference on the "Question of Food Security in the Developing Countries" in the fall of 1978.

9. In addition to its annual report, the institute has published the following research reports: *Meeting Food Needs in the Developing World* (1976); *Recent and Prospective Development in Food Consumption: Some Policy Issues* (1977); and *Food Needs of Developing Countries: Projections of Production and Consumption to 1990* (1977). The People's Republic of China and South Korea are covered in these publications.

10. The IFPRI has been granted nongovernmental observer status by United Nations organizations that deal with food policies.

M24 Johns Hopkins University—School of Advanced International Studies (SAIS)—East Asian Studies Program

1. *1740 Massachusetts Avenue, NW*
    Washington, D.C. 20036
    785-6200

2. 1943

3. Dr. Nathaniel B. Thayer, Director

4. Currently, there are 2 full-time and 5 part-time faculty members who offer courses in the Asian studies program at the SAIS and 5 language instructors in Chinese and Japanese.

6. Candidates for the M.A. degree may select Asian Studies as one of the 3 areas of concentration. (International economics and general instruction studies are the other 2.) Asian studies majors are required to take 5 1-semester courses in this area during their 2 years of study at the SAIS. In addition, they are urged to study either the Chinese or Japanese language, although a European language is sometimes accepted in lieu of an East Asian language. The SAIS offers intensive courses in elementary and intermediate Chinese and Japanese. Students with prior training may take advanced courses.

8. The SAIS sponsors a variety of conferences, lectures, and discussion sessions on Asian and American-Asian relations. For example, as part of the annual Christian A. Herter Lecture Series, a 4-part program on

"China and the Great Powers" was held in 1973. In December 1975, the SAIS hosted "Peking Summit: The Future of U.S.-China Relations." Also, the SAIS sponsored a 2-day conference on "The Changing Asian Market" in the fall of 1975.

M25 Johns Hopkins University—School of Advanced International Studies (SAIS)

1. *1740 Massachusetts Avenue, NW*
   Washington, D.C. 20036
   785-6200

2. Established as an independent graduate school in 1943, the SAIS was incorporated as a graduate division of the Johns Hopkins University in 1950.

3. George R. Packard, Dean of the SAIS

4. The SAIS faculty consists of approximately 30 full-time and 30 part-time members. Part-time members are drawn largely from the academic, governmental, and international organizations in Washington, D.C.

5. The Johns Hopkins University, Baltimore, Maryland. The school has a branch in Bologna, Italy.

6. The primary purpose of the SAIS is to provide an advanced professional education for students seeking international careers in government, private business, teaching, and research. The SAIS offers a 2-year program leading to the M.A. To a smaller number of students, it offers a program leading to the Ph.D. To a group of special students, chosen from government and business communities in the United States and abroad, it offers a year of study leading to a Master of International Public Policy. Over 300 full-time students are enrolled at SAIS.

   Other activities of SAIS include organizing and conducting a series of 4 or 5 conferences annually for business executives, government officials, scholars, and diplomats on the overseas operations of American industry. Two "Seminars in Diplomacy" are also held each year for young diplomats from Third World countries.

   The Washington Center of Foreign Policy Research (founded in 1957) is an organization within the SAIS which conducts research on American foreign policy. It is comprised of 9 members of the SAIS and several associates from the SAIS faculty and visiting fellows from the United States and abroad. The center holds weekly discussions on current trends and issues with visiting officials, politicians, scholars, and others from the Washington area.

7. The SAIS has its own library with total holdings of about 80,000 volumes. The library receives over 800 current periodicals and newspapers. It is well stocked in secondary source materials, especially monographs on history, political and social sciences, economics, and international relations. Several East Asian language periodicals, such as *Jenmin jih-pao, Asahi Shimbun,* and *Shimbun Geppō,* are available at the

library. Scholars can use the library facilities on a short-term basis. For further information about current schedules and arrangements, call Peter Promen, Head Librarian (785-6296).

8. The SAIS sponsors a number of lectures, seminars, and conferences during the academic year on a variety of topics in international affairs. Scholars should contact the dean's office for current schedules and for permission to attend functions.

9. The SAIS has no publication program of its own; faculty members publish their research findings in non-SAIS scholarly journals and monographs. The school's catalog as well as *The Johns Hopkins University Circular* are available free on request.

M26 National Planning Association (NPA)

1. *1606 New Hampshire Avenue, NW*
   Washington, D.C. 20009
   265-7685

2. 1934

3. John Miller, President

4. Approximately 25 professional research specialists and about the same number of administrative and support workers comprise the staff.

6. The NPA is an independent, private, nonprofit, nonpartisan organization that conducts research and policy studies relating to the efficient use of the productive resources of the United States and the operation of the international economy. The NPA is engaged primarily in the development of policy-oriented reports and studies through committees made up of leaders from American business, labor, agriculture, and education. These efforts are concerned with general planning and economic policy formulation as well as specific policy issues. In addition, NPA's professional staff undertakes a wide variety of technical research designed to provide data and ideas for policymakers and planners in government and the private sector. The NPA's International Division conducts research on various international economic problems.

7. The NPA has a small research library (with about 1,000 volumes) for staff use only.

8. Seminars and conferences on international economic problems (e.g., trade and monetary issues) are held regularly. Attendance is by invitation only.

9. The NPA has a publication program focusing on national and international economic problems. In addition to its quarterly, *Development Digest,* its publications include monographs on international economic issues, such as Harold Van B. Cleveland and W. H. Bruce Tritam, *The Great Inflation* (1976); and Neil McMullen, *The Debt-Service Problems of Certain Important Developing Countries* (1977).

M27 Overseas Development Council (ODC)

1.   *1717 Massachusetts Avenue, NW*
   Washington, D.C. 20036
   234-8701

2.   1969

3.   James T. Grant, President

4.   The office has a staff of 25 professional and support members.

6.   ODC was established in 1969 to enhance American understanding of the economic and social problems confronting developing countries. The ODC seeks to achieve its objectvies through research, publications, conferences, and liaison with organizations. ODC programs are funded largely by grants from foundations and corporations, with some support from individuals and government agencies.

      Most ODC research projects deal with specific issues such as trade investment, food, and energy rather than a specific country or region. Nevertheless, developing countries of East Asia are covered in many of these studies.

7.   ODC has a small research library for staff use only.

8.   To promote "North-South" understanding, ODC has sponsored a series of conferences for American specialists and their counterparts from Asia, Africa, and Latin America. In addition to these "Transnational Dialogues," the council sponsors frequent seminars on international issues related to development. Food, energy, agricultural research, trade, monetary reforms, and human rights have been subjects of recent meetings attended by business executives, academics, and development specialists in many fields.

9.   ODC publishes its research findings both through commercial publishers and its own series of monographs, development papers, and communiques. In addition to its annual book-length review, *The United States and World Development: Agenda*, ODC has recently published *Women and World Development* (1976); *Beyond Dependency: The Developing World Speaks Out* (1975); *Energy and Development: An International Approach* (1976); and *Development in the People's Republic of China: A Selected Bibliography* by Patricia Blair (1976).

M28 Population Reference Bureau, Inc.

1.   *1337 Connecticut Avenue, NW*
   Washington, D.C. 20036
   785-4664

2.   1929

3.   Robert M. Avedon, President

4.   The bureau has about 21 staff members: 12 professional and 9 administrative support members.

6. The bureau is primarily concerned with the study, analysis, and reporting of "population problems." It endeavors to increase public knowledge of and interest in issues relating to national and international population trends, including population growth, migration, and the effect of increasing population on the environment. For nearly 50 years, it has functioned as a unique source of up-to-date, factual, unbiased demographic information for leaders, teachers, students, and the interested public. It has Non-Governmental Organization (NGO) status with the United Nations and is one of the oldest ongoing population reference organizations in the United States.

7. The bureau has a specialized research library (total 15,000 volumes) with an excellent collection of scholarly works as well as government documents from the United States and the United Nations on population problems. It maintains over 450 periodicals with an emphasis on demographic and social sciences. In addition, it has a collection of conference papers and vertical file materials.

   The library is open to scholars from Monday to Friday (8:30 A.M.-4:30 P.M.) For further information, call Bruce A. Knarr, director of the bureau's library and information services (785-4664).

8. The bureau sponsors special seminars and occasional meetings on population-related topics, which are open to nonmembers.

9. The bureau has an ongoing publication program. It publishes *Intercom* (international population news magazine) once a month; *Interchange* (4 times during the school year, intended primarily for educators); *Population Bulletin* (monograph series; 6 per year); and *World Population Data Sheet* (annual). It also publishes an occasional paper series called *PRB Report*.

10. It is registered as a Non-Governmental Organization with the United Nations.

M29 Potomac Associates

1. *1740 Massachusetts Avenue, NW*
   Washington, D.C. 20036
   785-6234

2. Incorporated as a profit-seeking organization in 1970, Potomac Associates became a tax-exempt, nonprofit group in 1975.

3. William Watts, President

4. Research projects are carried out on a contractual basis by experts recruited for specific studies. For information concerning East Asia, researchers should contact William Watts.

6. Potomac Associates specialize in research on public policy issues, both domestic and international. One major area of research has been United States public opinion toward foreign policy issues relating to China, Japan, and Korea.

7. One valuable source of information that a researcher can secure from the organization is the computerized attitudinal data (i.e., opinion polls) which have been utilized in its *Policy Perspectives* series as well as its other publications. Researchers interested in utilizing the data should contact William Watts for further information.

9. The group issues papers entitled *Policy Perspectives*. In 1977, *The United States and China: American Perceptions and Future Alternatives,* jointly authored by Ralph N. Clough, Robert B. Oxnam, and William Watts, was published under the *Policy Perspectives* series; and similar studies on Japan and Korea (i.e., *The United States and Japan: American Perceptions and Policies* and *The United States and Korea: American Attitudes and Policies*) were published in 1978. A book containing the 3 reports and updated material is scheduled to be published by D.C. Heath and Company, Lexington, Massachusetts, in 1979 under the title, *Japan, Korea and China: American Perceptions and Policies*. In addition to Clough, Oxnam, and Watts, George R. Packard is a contributor to the volume.

M30 Rand Corporation—Washington Office

1. *2100 M Street, NW*
   Washington, D.C. 20037
   296-5000

2. 1948

3. Dr. George Tanham, Vice President, Washington Operations

4. The Rand Corporation's Washington Office is staffed by approximately 50 researchers and 50 other full- and part-time support workers (e.g., research assistants, secretaries).

5. The Washington Office is a part of the Rand Corporation of Santa Monica, California.

6. The Rand Corporation is a private, nonprofit institution engaged in research and analysis on issues of national security and the public welfare of the United States. Rand conducts its research with support from federal, state, and local governments; from private foundations; and from its own funds generated from fees.

   Although professional staff members are grouped into 7 research departments (e.g., Computer Services, Physical Sciences, Social Sciences, etc.), specific research programs are managed within 3 divisions: National Security Programs, Project AIR FORCE, and Domestic Programs. National security programs focus on the planning, development, acquisition, deployment, support and protection of military forces, and include international affairs that may affect United States defense policy and strategy. Domestic research programs pertain to public health, housing, labor, population, and urban policy. Rand also conducts research programs in applied science and engineering and computer technologies. The corporation runs a computation center and the Rand Graduate Institute in California.

7.   The Washington Office has a library (ext. 329/330) but is it closed to non-RAND personnel. Holdings of the library are relatively small—only a few thousand volumes—and mostly in social sciences. Nonclassified materials may be used through interlibrary loan service.

9.   The Rand Corporation has an extensive publication program. Several hundred technical reports and professional papers are published by the corporation. These publications are available at Rand, government documentation centers, and more than 350 subscription libraries here and abroad. Subscription libraries in the Washington area include: Army Library, Department of the Army; George Washington University Library; Howard University, School of Engineering Library; Fort Belvoir, USAES, Learning Resources Center; and the Mitre Corporation, McLean, Virginia. The Rand Corporation also produces a large number of classified reports and working papers which are not available to the general public.

A bibliography of selected Rand publications on Asia (1978) lists titles as well as abstracts of the important recent Rand publications on Asia. Copies of the bibliography may be obtained free from the Washington Office.

M31 Resources for the Future (RFF)

1.   *1755 Massachusetts Avenue, NW*
      Washington, D.C. 20036
      462-4400

2.   1952

3.   Dr. Charles J. Hitch, President

4.   There are about 100 professional and support staff members working for RFF.

6.   RFF is a private nonprofit organization which is primarily concerned with research and education in the development, conservation, and use of natural resources and the improvement of the environment. Established in 1952 with the cooperation of the Ford Foundation, most of its subsequent work has been supported by grants from the Ford Foundation. Specific fields of interest encompass the basic resources of land, water, minerals, and air, and the goods ond services derived from them. Most RFF studies are in the social sciences and are broadly concerned with the relationships of people to the natural environment. Because of the growing importance of energy, RFF is particularly active in this field of study.

There are 3 research divisions: (1) The Center for Energy Policy Research which examines all aspects of energy policy, including the technical, economic, institutional, and human health and safety. The center also analyzes supply and demand of nonfuel minerals and other materials; (2) the Quality of the Environment Division which deals with management of air, water, and land pollution, and with the conservation of natural and environmental resources and related policy studies; and

(3) the Renewable Resources Division which conducts research on inte-
grated management of the land, including studies of agriculture and
forestry, and of fresh water, oceans, and the atmosphere.

8.   The organization sponsors occasional seminars and workshops; however,
such seminars are by invitation only.

9.   RFF's research is disseminated largely through the publication of books
and monographs, mostly by the Johns Hopkins University Press in Baltimore. In addition, book-length research papers are published by RFF
from the author's typescript. Members of the research staff also publish
frequently in professional journals, some of which are issued in RFF's
reprint series. A bulletin entitled *Resources* is published 3 times a year.
Relevant RFF's publications include: *The Pacific Salmon Fisheries: A
Study of Irrational Conservation* by James A. Crutchfield (1969); *Population and Development: The Search for Selective Interventions* edited
by Ronald G. Ridker (1976); *Fisheries of the Indian Ocean: Issues of
International Management and Law of the Sea* by Arlon R. Tussing
(1974); *Fishery and Resource Management in Southeast Asia* by John
C. Marr (1976); and *The World Food Situation: Resource and Environ-
mental Issues in the Developing Countries and the United States* by
Pierre R. Crosson and Kenneth D. Frederick (1977).

M32   SRI International—Strategic Studies Center—Washington Area Office (formerly Stanford Research Institute)

1.   *1611 North Kent Street, Rosslyn Plaza*
Arlington, Va. 22209
(703) 524-2053

2.   Stanford Research Institute (SRI) was founded in 1946 at Menlo Park,
California, and the Strategic Studies Center (SSC) in 1954. In 1956
SRI International began operations in Washington, D.C., and SSC began
in 1967.

3.   Charles A. Anderson, President, SRI International
R. B. Foster, Director, Strategic Studies Center (SSC)

4.   SRI International's Washington staff numbers approximately 170, including the SSC research staff of about 25 who are mostly political scientists,
economists, or foreign area specialists. In addition, a limited number of
senior scholars from the academic community are employed by the SSC
on a joint appointment basis. The center also maintains a pool of approximately 100 consultants, about 50 of whom are used on a regular
basis to handle specialized research projects.

5.   The SSC is an affiliate of the main SRI International located in Menlo
Park, California. SRI is no longer associated with Stanford University.

6.   SRI's research programs encompass broad fields, including the physical
sciences, life sciences, industrial and developmental economics, management and systems sciences, and engineering sciences. It gives major
emphasis to the advancement of worldwide peace and prosperity, and

its research is supported by federal, state, and local government agencies as well as from the private sector. The institute undertakes more than 1,000 new research projects each year with revenue from contract research exceeding $100 million annually. (The SRI staff totals about 3,000).

The SSC does broad interdisciplinary research and analysis on political, economic, and military topics relating to national security and foreign policy planning and on international relations. The primary focus of the center's research activities has been on all aspects of Soviet strategy, foreign policy, and economics. Recently, the center has also undertaken research on the strategic problems of Northeast Asia with special reference to the withdrawal of the United States ground troops from South Korea. Through briefings and publication programs, the SSC aims to improve the quality of discussion on defense and strategic policy issues among opinion leaders and policymakers.

7.   The SSC maintains a specialized library, including certain classified governmental materials, for its research staff. The collection has works on the Soviet Union, Western European powers, and the foreign policies of the major powers, as well as data on special strategic problems of Asia and the Middle East. The total holdings of the library in Washington number about 8,000 (i.e., 6,000 Russian and 2,000 English titles). Its holdings on East Asia are relatively small, not more than a few hundred titles.

Outside researchers must secure special permission from the SSC to use the library facilities. For further information, call the library (ext. 215).

8.   The SSC regularly holds symposia on a variety of topics. With respect to East Asia, the center held "Seoul Symposium on Northeast Asia" in cooperation with the Asian Institute for Public Policy (Korea) in Seoul on January 24-26, 1977; "Northeast Asian Security 1977—with Focus on the Korean Peninsula" in Tokyo on January 30-31, 1977 (in cooperation with the Committee of Defense Policy Analysis [Japan]); and "Strategic Studies Center Symposium on Northeast Asia Security" in Washington, D.C., on June 20-22, 1977.

9.   The SSC has an extensive publication program. Besides the dissemination of published material to government agencies, congressional staffs, university personnel, and the public, center members also contribute ideas directly to government studies through contract projects. One of its recent (1975) studies was titled *U.S. Strategy in Northeast Asia* (authored by William M. Carpenter et al.). The SSC also began the publication of a new quarterly, *Comparative Strategy: An International Journal* in 1978.

10.   The SSC is not formally affiliated with other organizations, but maintains relationships with a number of other research institutes around the world, such as the International Institute of Strategic Studies (London), the French Institute of Strategic Studies (Paris), the Norwegian Institute of International Affairs (Oslo), the Research Institute on Swedish National Defense (Stockholm), the Stockholm International Peace Research Institute, the Asian Institute for Public Policy (Korea), and the Center for Study of Security Issues (Tokyo). In the United States,

relationships are maintained with the Foreign Policy Research Institute (Philadelphia), the Center for Strategic and International Studies (Georgetown University), the Washington Center for Foreign Policy Research (Johns Hopkins University, SAIS, Washington, D.C.), and the Hoover Institute for War, Revolution, and Peace (Stanford University).

M33 University of Maryland East Asian Studies Program

1. *c/o History Department*
    University of Maryland
    College Park, Md. 20742
    (301) 454-2843

2. 1969

3. Marlene J. Mayo, Chairperson, East Asian Studies Committee

4. Currently about 18 faculty members from 8 different departments (i.e., art, architecture, history, government and politics, music, horticulture, anthropology, and language and literature) offer courses on China, Japan, and Asia. In the fall semester, 1978, 30 courses were offered: 13 on China, 11 on Japan, and 6 on East Asia or Asia.

    Chinese and Japanese language courses are offered regularly and East Asian history and culture courses occasionally in the evening by University of Maryland University College (see entry M34).

6. A degree program in East Asian Studies as such does not exist on the College Park campus at the undergraduate level. However, students may specialize in various aspects of China or Japan by taking an Individual Studies major under the auspices of the Office of the Undergraduate Dean. In a few departments, such as History or Government and Politics, graduate students can specialize in East Asia at the M.A. and Ph.D. level.

    The Committee on East Asian Studies coordinates the overall academic activities of the College Park campus in the field of East Asian studies with the hope that it may eventually be able to establish a coherent East Asian degree program for undergraduates. It is also supporting efforts to create a Department of East Asian Language and Literature in the Division of Arts and Humanities. In addition, it seeks to promote overseas programs for Maryland students in Hong Kong, Japan, the People's Republic of China, and Taiwan and has been instrumental in setting up the Keio-Maryland student-exchange program.

    The activities involved in the field of Asian studies are intimately connected with those of the individual departments represented on the committee and the East Asia Collection. The committee, whose membership comes from the faculty, staff, and student body, either sponsors on its own or cosponsors with departments such activities as lectures, films, recitals, and concerts. It has recently carried out fundraising to expand the curriculum and to assist the East Asia Collection. The Committee on East Asian Studies has also been instrumental in organizing and launching the "Traditional China Colloquium of the Metropolitan Washington Area" which will meet several times a year at various campuses in the area starting in 1979.

7. See the East Asia Collection, McKeldin Library, University of Maryland (entry A42).

8. Since 1974, the Washington and Southeast Regional Seminar on China has been held at the University of Maryland University College under the joint auspices of the Social Science Research Council (SSRC) and the American Council of the Learned Societies (ACLS). The seminar has been chaired by Professor Chun-tu Hsueh, Department of Government and Politics, University of Maryland (College Park campus) and emphasizes aspects of modern China, especially in the period after 1949. Four seminars are held each year (2 in the spring and 2 in the fall).

    Also, since 1973, the University of Maryland at College Park has hosted the Washington and Southeast Regional Seminar on Japan with funding from the SSRC and the ACLS. It is currently co-chaired by Dr. Edward Griffin (United States Department of State) and Professor Marlene J. Mayo at the University. Three seminars are held each year on Saturday afternoon for members of the seminar and their guests. Seminar papers are distributed to members only.

M34 University of Maryland University College (UMUC)

1. *University Boulevard at Adelphi Road*
    College Park, Md. 20742
    (301) 454-4756 (Overseas Program)

2. 1947

3. Dr. Julian S. Jones, Assistant Dean for Overseas Programs

6. University of Maryland University College (UMUC) is one of the 5 campuses and 7 professional schools that make up the University of Maryland. It offers degree and nondegree programs (including some undergraduate courses with an East Asian focus) in the late afternoon and evening for adults in the Maryland and Washington, D.C., areas, as well as 24 foreign countries including Japan, South Korea, and Taiwan.

    The college's Far East Division administers an undergraduate overseas program for United States military and civilian personnel in Japan, South Korea, and Taiwan. The division's administrative headquarters are located in Tokyo. Recently, UMUC has established a University of Maryland-Keio University student-exchange program. Also, it is raising funds for an Asian Garden to be laid out at UMUC's Center of Adult Education. Occasionally, the University College sponsors lectures on East Asian affairs or related cultural events.

7. For the University of Maryland's McKeldin Library, see entry A42.

M35 Woodrow Wilson International Center for Scholars (WWICS)

1. *Smithsonian Institution Building*
    1000 Jefferson Drive, SW
    Washington D.C. 20560
    381-5613

2. 1968

3. Dr. James H. Billington, Director

4. A 16-member Board of Trustees appointed by the president of the United States oversees the operations of the center which is run by a staff of 21 full-time, permanent employees.

6. The Woodrow Wilson International Center for Scholars was created by the United States Congress as the nation's official living memorial to its 28th president. As a national institution with international interests, the center seeks to encourage the creative use of the unique human, archival, and institutional resources in the nation's capital for studies illuminating man's understanding of his past and present.

    The center's programs attempt to commemorate the Wilsonian connection between ideas and affairs, between intellect and moral purpose. At the heart of the center stands its Fellowship Program, which enables the institution to appoint annually up to 40 fellows from the United States and abroad to conduct research on major projects at the center for periods ranging from 4 months to 1 year or more. The center has no permanent or tenured fellows. The center's Fellowship Program consists of 2 broad divisions and 4 specific study programs. In general, it is divided between the Social and Political Studies Division and the Historical and Cultural Studies Division. The 4 special programs are devoted to research on Russia and the Soviet Union, on Latin America and the Caribbean, on international security issues, and on environmental problems.

    In addition, the center also operates a Guest Scholar Program for the short-term use of the center's facilities by a small number of visiting scholars and specialists.

    Through these programs, several scholars specializing in East Asian affairs are brought into the center annually to carry out research. The number varies from year to year. During 1977-78, the center's fellows and guest scholars with East Asian specialties included: Chiaki Nishiyama, Ralph N. Clough, Sukehiro Hirakawa, Joseph Sebes, Ikuhiko Hata, Ambassador Heishiro Ogawa, and Eiichi Shindo. George R. Packard, former deputy director, was the coordinator of the center's activities relating to East Asia from 1976 to 1979.

7. The Wilson Center has a working library containing 15,000 volumes of basic reference works, bibliographies, and essential monographs in the social sciences and humanities. The library subscribes to and maintains the backfiles of about 300 scholarly journals and periodicals. As part of a National Presidential Memorial, the library has special access to the collections of the Library of Congress and other government libraries. The librarian is Dr. Zdeněk David (381-5850).

8. The center's activities include frequent colloquia, evening seminars, and other discussions designed to foster a true intellectual community among the participants. The scheduled events are announced in the monthly *Calendar of Events*. During the spring and fall of 1978, Ralph N. Clough led a series of evening seminars on North and South Korea.

    A core seminar based upon a critical policy issue in East Asian affairs is planned for each of the years from 1979-82. These seminars bring together leading scholars, journalists, diplomats, political leaders, and policymakers to consider policy choices facing the United States and other nations in the region. Their purpose is to illuminate and enrich both the scholarship and the decision-making process in the nation's capital.

9. The *Wilson Quarterly* carries occasional articles on East Asia: The summer 1977 issue included 3 articles on Japan; and the summer 1978 issue covered "Korea and America, 1950-1978" with 4 articles devoted to the subject. The center also sponsors a series of *Scholars' Guides to Washington, D.C.,* which survey the collections, institutions, and organizations pertinent to the study of particular geographic areas, such as Russia/Soviet Union, Latin America and the Caribbean, and other world regions.

N Publications and Media

Entry Form for Publications and Media (N)

1. *Address, telephone*
2. Founding date
3. Sponsoring organization
4. Editor
5. Frequency
6. Principal subjects covered

Introductory Note

To economize on space, a large number of publications which are listed elsewhere in this *Guide* are not covered in this section. Readers should check under Associations and Government Agencies for such titles.

N1 *American Journal of International Law*

1. *2223 Massachusetts Avenue, NW*
   Washington, D.C. 20008
   265-4313

2. 1906

3. American Society of International Law (see entry I).

4. Oscar Schachter and Louis Henkin, Co-Editors-in-Chief

5-6. This quarterly journal features occasional articles on subjects relating to East Asia. In addition, articles dealing with various aspects of international law and relations (e.g., foreign trade, the law of the sea, etc.) are frequently pertinent to East Asia.

N2 *Armed Forces Journal*

1. *1414 22d Street, NW*
    Washington, D.C. 20037
    296-0450

2. 1863

3. Army and Navy Journal, Inc.

4. Benjamin F. Schemmer

5. Once a month.

6. The journal occasionally carries articles on various aspects of the Chinese and Japanese military establishments. Subjects covered include the Chinese defense effort and buildup, the armed forces of the People's Republic of China, the United States-Japanese alliance system, United States security policy toward East Asia, and the like.

N3 *Asia Mail*

1. *128 S. Royal Street*
    Alexandria, Va. 22314
    (703) 548-2881

2. 1976

3. Potomac-Asia Communications, Inc.

4. Edward Neilan

5. Monthly

6. The *Asia Mail* is a forum designed to present diverse opinions and ideas about Asia to executives, businessmen, academicians, and others interested in Asian affairs in the United States. It endeavors to present essentially "American prespectives on Asia and the Pacific." The Journal's editor and publisher, Edward Neilan, is a syndicated columnist on Asian affairs with 12 years reporting experience in Asia. Co-author of *The Future of the China Market,* he won an Overseas Press Club Citation for reporting from the People's Republic of China in 1973. The journal features not only in-depth analyses of major issues by East Asia specialists, but also timely information on business trends and travel tips for Americans interested in Asia. It has a circulation of over 30,000 worldwide.

N4 *Asian-American Journal of Commerce*

1. *National Press Building (Suite 767)*
    Mail: P.O. Box 1933
    Washington, D.C. 20013
    638-7171

2. 1962

3. Association of Asian-American Chambers of Commerce

4. Editor: K. Nakatsukasa; Managing Editor: Edward von Rothkirch

5. Quarterly (supplemented by 8 newsletters each year).

6. The main focus is on the trade and commerce of Asia; it reports changes in import and export regulations, joint ventures, living costs, patents, and business climates of various nations. In addition, the *Journal* also presents information on travel, culture, and other subjects.

Asian Student See entry H16.

N5 Carrollton Press Incorporated and U.S. Historical Documents Institute, Inc.

1. *1911 North Fort Myer Drive*
    Arlington, Va. 22209
    (703) 525-5940 (Carrollton)
    (703) 525-6035 (USHDI)

6. The Carrollton Press puts out a number of significant titles. For East Asian specialists interested in previously classified and restricted materials of the United States government, this company provides a Declassified Documents Reference System. Since 1975 the Carrollton Press has issued quarterly catalogs of abstracted declassified documents from the CIA, the presidential libraries, the Departments of State and Defense, the National Security Council, and other agencies which became available in accordance with the Freedom-of-Information Act of 1974, executive orders, and/or mandatory review procedures. Excluded are materials declassified automatically or published elsewhere. At present the annual collections contain about 1,100 documents (available in microfiche at Carrollton). Each annual collection also contains a cumulative subject index. A 2-volume collection of pre-1975 materials contains about 8,000 abstracts. Microfiche of the documents themselves are also available.

    Other important reference and bibliographic publications of the 2 presses include:

    Combined Retrospective Index Sets to more than 530 journals (350,-000 articles) in history, political science, and sociology in the English language (arranged by subject and author) dating back to 1838, 1886, and 1895 respectively;

    Cumulative Subject Index to the P.A.I.S. Annual Bulletin, 1915-1974.
    Checklist of United States Public Documents, 1789-1976.

N6 Chase World Information Corporation—Washington Bureau

1. *2000 L Street, NW (Suite 502)*
    Washington, D.C. 20036
    785-3976

4. Bureau Chief: Donald C. Winston

5. The bureau's 2-man staff contributes to the publication of the corporation's biweekly *East-West Markets,* which is published in New York.

6. *East-West Markets* contains a section dealing with the People's Republic of China. The office has a file of its own publications with annual indexes plus some outside journals and materials. As time permits, the staff may be able to serve scholars' requests for information and data pertaining to East-West trade and new developments in the Sino-American trade.

N7 *Congressional Quarterly Weekly Report*

1. *1414   22d Street, NW*
   Washington, D.C. 20037
   296-6800

2. 1945

3. Congressional Quarterly, Inc.

4. Eugene Patterson

5. Weekly

6. This weekly publication is indispensable for any serious researcher interested in the American legislative process in general and Congress's role in foreign policymaking in particular. Congressional action on both domestic and foreign policy issues is covered in detail.

   Note: The Editorial Reports Library of the Congressional Quarterly, Inc. is described in the Libraries section (see entry A14).

East Asian Ethnic Media in the Washington Area. For a list of East Asia ethnic media operating in Washington, D.C., see Appendix II.

East Asian Press. For a list of East Asian press and their correspondents accredited to Washington, D.C., see Appendix I.

N8 *Foreign Policy*

1. *11 Dupont Circle, NW*
   Washington, D.C. 20036
   797-6420

2. 1970

3. Carnegie Endowment for International Peace

4. Editor: Richard H. Ullman; Managing Editor: Sanford J. Ungar

5. Quarterly

6.   This journal offers in-depth analyses of and provocative insights into the intricacies of international relations. It covers the whole range of political, economic, military, and human issues of concern to policy makers and laymen alike. Articles on East Asian subjects since 1976 include "Concensus in Japan" by Kei Wakaizumi; "Human Rights: What About China?" by Susan L. Shirk; and "The Puzzles of Chinese Pragmatism" by Lucian W. Pye. *Foreign Policy* is published by the Carnegie Endowment for International Peace (see entry H20).

N9   Government Printing Office and Office of the Federal Register (General Services Administration)

1.   *U.S. Government Printing Office*
Superintendent of Documents
Washington, D.C. 20402
275-2091

GPO's primary function is to provide printing and binding services required by Congress and other government agencies. All of these titles (currently about 24,000) are listed in 270 different *Subject Bibliographies*. Annually, about 3,000 new titles enter the sales inventory; and new titles are listed in the *Monthly Catalog of Government Publications* which has semiannual indexes. Orders for all titles listed in the *Monthly Catalog* can be placed by telephone (783-3238) or by writing to the Superintendent of Documents, GPO.

National Archives and Record Service
Office of the Federal Register
Washington, D.C. 20408
523-5240

This office publishes a number of important publications, mostly concerned with the operations of the United States government: *United States Government Manual* (annual); *Weekly Compilation of Presidential Documents; Public Papers of the Presidents of the United States;* and *Federal Register* (daily, on weekdays) and *Code of Federal Regulations*. These publications should be ordered from GPO. Sample copies of some may be requested by writing to: Director, Office of Federal Register, National Archives and Records Service, Washington, D.C. 20408.

N10   Organization for Economic Cooperation and Development (OECD)—Washington Publications and Information Center

1.   *1750 Pennsylvania Avenue, NW (Suite 1207)*
Washington, D.C. 20006
724-1857

2.   1961

3.   Organization for Economic Cooperation and Development (main headquarters are located in Paris, France).

4. Eric N. Ekers, Head of the OECD Washington Publications Center.

6. The OECD has an extensive publication program with emphasis on economic and financial affairs, agriculture, the environment, sociopolitical developments, energy, education, and science and technology. Many of its publications deal with Japan either directly or indirectly, since Japan is a member of the OECD. Some of the more important OECD publications include: *Manpower Policy in Japan* (1973); *Economic Survey, Japan* (1978); *Social Sciences Policy in Japan* (1977); *Monetary Policy in Japan* (1972); *The Industrial Policy of Japan* (1976); *Educational Policy and Planning: Japan* (1973); *Environmental Policies in Japan* (1977); and *Major Air Pollution Problems: The Japanese Experience* (1974). All of the OECD publications are available at the center's library (see entry A37).

N11 *Problems of Communism*

1. *1776 Pennsylvania Avenue, NW*
    Washington, D.C. 20547
    632-4887

2. 1951

3. International Communication Agency (U.S.)

4. Editor: Paul A. Smith, Jr.; Managing Editor: Marie T. House

5. Bimonthly

6. *Problems of Communism* provides analyses and significant information about current political, social and economic affairs of the Soviet Union, China, and comparable states and related aspects of the world Communist movement. It is designed to provide a forum for in-depth analyses of the pace and direction of change in the Communist countries and parties. In addition to frequent coverage on the PRC, the journal also presents articles dealing with other Communist parties and states in Asia. For example, the March-April 1977 issue of the journal was devoted to the analysis of "Asian Communism" by presenting "China after Mao" by Harry Harding, Jr.; "The JCP's Parliamentary Road" by Hong N. Kim; "Vietnam since Reunification" by William S. Turley; and "New Paths for North Korea" by Chong-Sik Lee. It has a circulation of over 35,000 in nearly 100 countries. It is extensively reprinted, and back issues are available on microform through commercial firms.

N12 *Strategic Review*

1. *1612 K Street, NW (Suite 1204)*
    Washington, D.C. 20006
    331-1776

2. 1973

3. United States Strategic Institute

4.   Walter F. Hahn, Editor-in-Chief

5-6.   *Strategic Review,* the quarterly publication of the U.S. Strategic Institute (a private nonprofit organization) provides a forum for the discussion of matters of current significance in the politico-military field. It carries occasional articles relating to East Asia (e.g., "Withdrawal from Korea: A Perplexing Decision" by Ernest W. Lefever in its winter 1978 issue).

N13 University Press of America

1.   *4710 Auth Place, SE*
       Washington, D.C. 20023
       (301) 899-9600

4.   James Lyons, Editor

       University Press of America has developed a more cost-efficient approach to scholarly publishing by simplifying the entire publishing process. All books published under the program are printed directly from a type-written manuscript and other author-provided materials via the photo-reproduction process. Publications are geared for the academic community and cover a wide range of subjects, including history, religion, political science, philosophy. A number of scholarly works on East Asia are published annually.

N14 University Publications of America, Inc. (UPA)

1.   *5630 Connecticut Avenue*
       Washington, D.C. 20015
       362-6201

       University Publications of America publishes both printed and micro-film copies of original works as well as reprints and collections of government documents. UPA publications are designed for the scholarly community, and publications cover a wide range of subjects such as law, history, economics, foreign affairs, and the sciences. Of special interest to East Asian specialists are the following titles (microfilm) published by UPA: *O.S.S. State Department Intelligence and Research Reports on Asia:* (1) *Japan and Its Occupied Territories during World War II;* (2) *Postwar Japan, Korea, and Southeast Asia;* (3) *China and India;* (8) *Japan, Korea, Southeast Asia, and the Far East Generally: 1950-1961 Supplement;* (9) *China and India: 1950-1961 Supplement.* Also published in microfilm by UPA are *The MAGIC Documents: Summaries and Transcripts of the Top Secret Diplomatic Communications of Japan, 1938-1945* and *Manhattan Project: Official History and Documents.* In book form UPA has published 34 titles of *Japan Studies,* 42 titles of *China Studies,* and the 2-volume set entitled *Marshall's Mission to China: The Report and Appended Documents.*

N15 Voice of America (VOA)

1. *HEW Building (Room 2137)*
   300 Independence Avenue, SW
   Washington, D.C. 20547
   755-4749

2. Voice of America broadcasts to East Asia began in 1942.

3. As of April 1, 1978, the United States Information Agency (USIA) was reorganized into the International Communication Agency (ICA). VOA is 1 of 4 parts of this new agency.

4-5 East Asian-Pacific Division (VOA/PF)
   Edward J. Findlay, Division Chief
   755-4840

   The division provides daily vernacular language broadcasts to East and Southeast Asian countries. The daily number of broadcast hours in various languages is as follows: Mandarin Chinese, 8½; Korean, 1½; Vietnamese, 3; Khmer, 1; Lao, 1; Burmese, 1; and Indonesian, 3, for a total of 19 hours.
   Scholars interested in details of programming or tapes of these broadcasts should consult *Content Report,* which lists program titles and indicates in-house sources. See also the brief quarterly VOA "Broadcast Schedule" for pertinent languages. Tapes of most broadcasts are kept for about 2 to 3 months, unless they are of particular significance. On-site use of these materials can be arranged through the VOA Public Information Office, room 2137, of the HEW Building (755-4744).

N16 *Washington Post*

1. *1150 15th Street, NW*
   Washington, D.C. 20071
   334-6000

2. 1877

4. Executive Editor: Benjamin Bradlee; Managing Editor: Howard Simons.

5-6 The *Washington Post* is a leading American daily newspaper which covers international affairs extensively. Its correspondents in East Asia report on the politics, diplomacy, and economies of East Asian nations, as well as other important developments of the region. Currently, Jay Mathews is stationed in Hong Kong; William Chapman in Tokyo. Don Oberdorfer, who was formerly stationed in Tokyo, is now working as national reporter for the *Washington Post,* covering diplomatic affairs. He would be happy to discuss East Asian affairs with scholars. For further information concerning the newspaper's personnel resources on international affairs, contact Peter Harris, Foreign Desk (334-7371).

The *Washington Post* has a reference library which contains over 5 million newspaper clippings, 600,000 photographs, and 20,000 books. Items are arranged by names and subjects. An index covering the period from 1940 to the present is available. The library is restricted to staff use; for outsiders interlibrary loan and photoreproduction services are available. Those seeking access to the collections should contact Mr. Simons for permission. The library is open from 10:30 A.M. to 7:00 P.M. during the weekdays and for a few hours on weekends.

N17 *Washington Star*

1. *225 Virginia Avenue, SE*
    Washington, D.C. 20003
    484-5000

2. 1852

4. Editor: Murray J. Gart; Executive Editor Sidney Epstein

5-6 The *Washington Star* is a major daily newspaper which covers national and international news relating to East Asia. Henry Bradsher, who reported on East Asian affairs from Hong Kong (for several years in the late 1960s and early 1970s) is willing to confer with scholars concerning his experiences and observations in East Asia. For further information on the newspaper's coverage of international affairs, contact Walter Taylor, National Editor of the *Washington Star* (484-4303).

The *Washington Star* has a library containing books, clippings, photographs, and other items. An index from 1894 to the present is available on cards at the library and on microfilm. The use of the library is restricted to the staff. Those seeking access to the library's materials should make such a request to Mr. Epstein. The facility is open from 11:00 A.M. to 3:00 P.M. during weekdays.

N18 *World Affairs*

1. *4000 Albemarle Street, NW*
    Washington, D.C. 20016
    362-6195

2. 1828. Originally called *Advocate of Peace,* it was renamed in 1932.

3. American Peace Society

4. Cornelius W. Vahle, Jr., Managing Editor; and Evron M. Kirkpatrick, chairman of the editorial board.

5-6 This quarterly journal carries articles on international relations, law, foreign policy, comparative politics, and diplomatic history, frequently bearing on East Asia.

APPENDIXES

Appendix I. East Asian Press—Washington, D.C., Area

JAPANESE PRESS LIST

The Asahi
477 National Press Building
783-0523/0524
Kensaku Shirai
Katsuji Miyazaki
Yoshio Murakami
Hiroshi Ando

The Asahi National Broadcasting Co.
477 National Press Building
347-2933
Makoto Ishihara

The Chunichi Tokyo
877 National Press Building
783-9479
783-1689
Tatsuo Oe
Fumiyasu Endo

Fuji Telecasting Co., Ltd.
274 National Press Building
347-6070
Yuzo Kumamoto

The Hokkaido
877 National Press Building
783-9479
783-1689
Takeo Mizukami

The Jiji Tsūshin
383 National Press Building
783-4330/4331/4332
Chichi Yone
Shigebumi Sato
Kenji Sekiguchi
Yasushi Tomiyama

The Kyōdo
1229 National Press Building
347-5787/5048
Yuichiro Hayashi
Atsuo Kanoko
Kotaro Nogami
Kazuyoshi Hishiki
Shotaro Kobayashi
Hideaki Sakamoto
Hideo Yamashita

Mainichi Shimbun
377 National Press Building
737-2817/2818
Mitsuaki Nakao
Soji Teramura
Yoshihisa Komori
Toshiji Ari

N.H.K.
935 National Press Building
393-1076/1077
Hiroshi Narita
Hiroto Oyama
Hatsuhisa Takashima
Hiroshi Iwamoto
Toshio Kobayashi

Nihon Keizai Shimbun
741 National Press Building
393-1388
Teruo Tsutsumi
Yutaka Ichiki
Mitsuhisa Yoshino
Norimichi Okai

Nihon Shimbun Kyokai
c/o ANPA
P.O. Box 17407
Dulles International Airport
Washington, D.C. 20041
860-3208

Nippon Television Network Corp.
763 National Press Building
638-0890
Masanobu Fujimoto

Nishi Nippon Shimbun
877 National Press Building
783-9479/1689
Hidetoshi Yoshimoto

Sankei Shimbun
274 National Press Building
347-9718/5772
Yoichi Kitazume
Yasunori Abe
Yoneo Sakai

T.B.S. (Tokyo Hōsō)
CBS Building, No. 311
2020 M Street, NW
223-5562
457-4321/4599
Kyo Suzuki

Yomiuri Shimbun
973 National Press Building
783-0363/0186
Jiro Yokoyama
Takemoto Iinuma
Shoichi Oikawa
Akira Saito

KOREAN PRESS LIST

Chosun Ilbo
Dae-Joong Kim
3626 Barcroft View Terrace, No. 402
Arlington, Va. 22041
(703) 578-0026

Dong-a Ilbo
In Sup Kang
1042 National Press Building
347-4097

Hankook Ilbo
Soon Whan Cho
831 National Press Building
783-2674

Hapdong News Agency
Tae Myung Kwon
761 National Press Building
783-5539

Joong-ang Ilbo
Kun Jin Kim
1123 National Press Building
347-0121

KBS-Radio-TV
Doh-Jin Kim
1046 National Press Building
347-4693

Kyunghyang Shinmun and
  MBC-TV-Radio
Kang-Gul Lee
720 National Press Building
347-4013

Orient Press
So-Whan Hyon
730 National Press Building
347-8931

Seoul Shinmun
Young-mo Ahn
922 National Press Building
638-2151

TAIWAN PRESS LIST

Central Daily News
Brice Wang, Washington
   Correspondent
214 Normandy Hill Drive
Alexandria, Va. 22304
(703) 751-9380

Central News Agency, Inc.
549 National Press Building
529   14th Street, NW
Washington, D.C. 20045
628-2738
C. K. Li, Director

China Times
1276 National Press Building
529   14th Street, NW
Washington, D.C. 20045
347-1162
Norman C. C. Fu, Bureau Chief

Economic Daily News
6200 Springhill Drive
Apt. 203
Greenbelt, Md. 20770
(301) 345-5314
James Wang, Washington
   Correspondent

United Daily News
2000 Cradock Street
Silver Spring, Md. 20904
(301) 384-1091
Comet K. M. Shih, Washington
   Correspondent

Appendix II.   East Asian Ethnic Media

CHINESE PUBLICATIONS

Hua-fu Chun-chiu (monthly)
P.O. Box 57039
Washington, D.C. 20037

Hua-fu Lun-tun (quarterly)
P.O. Box 4730
College Park, Md. 20740

KOREAN PUBLICATIONS AND MEDIA

Donga Ilbo and Miju Donga (daily)
2267 Lewis Avenue
Rockville, Md. 20851
(301) 770-2510/2511
Jung Hyun Kim, Representative

Hankook Shinbo (weekly)
927 S. Walter Reed Drive, No. 3
Arlington, Va. 22204
(703) 979-8350/51/52
Sung Woun Hong, Representative

Hanmin Shinbo (weekly)
2732 N. Washington Boulevard
Arlington, Va. 22201
(703) 528-8880
Kee Yong Chung, Representative

Joong Ang Ilbo and Miju Pan (daily)
102 Wilson Boulevard, No. 2314
Arlington, Va. 22209
(703) 525-2176/2177
Tae Hee Yoo, Representative

Korean Broadcasting of
   Washington, D.C.
807 Lawton Street
McLean, Va. 22101
(703) 893-3030
Kwang Jae Lee, Representative
Broadcast Time: 8:00-9:00 A.M.
   Sunday
Frequency: AM 900

Korean Culture Broadcasting Station
1026 University Boulevard, No. 112
Silver Spring, Md. 20903
(301) 439-1353
Broadcast Time: 12:00 P.M. Sunday
Frequency: AM 75

Radio Korea
12004 Gordon Avenue
Beltsville, Md. 20705
(301) 939-8223 or (202) 484-9339
Young Ho Kim, Representative
Broadcast Time: 4:00-5:00 P.M.
   Saturday
Frequency: AM 780

U.S.-Asia News Service
986 National Press Building
14th and F Streets, NW
Washington, D.C. 20045
638-1117
Myung Ja Moon, Representative

Voice of Hope
3330 Lauriston Place
Fairfax, Va. 22030
Broadcast Time: 3:00 P.M. Sunday
Frequency: FM 102.3

Appendix III. East Asian Ethnic Churches and Religious Organizations

CHINESE CHURCH

Chinese Community Church
1011 L Street, NW
Washington, D.C. 20001
Rev. Manking Tso
232-9495
Service—11:00 A.M. Sunday

KOREAN CHURCHES AND TEMPLE

Bul Guk Sa Temple (Buddhist)
5015   16th Street, NW
Washington, D.C. 20011
Zen Master Gosung
829-3700
Service—10:30 A.M. Sunday

Calvary Korean Church
1900 N. Glebe Road
Arlington, Va. 22207
Rev. Tae Ku Lee
(703) 560-8325
Service—1:30 P.M. Sunday

First Korean Baptist Church
13421 Georgia Avenue
Silver Spring, Md. 20906
Rev. Huyn Chil Kim
(301) 871-8949 and 460-1656
Service—11:00 A.M. Sunday

First Korean Presbyterian Church of
    Maryland
6513 Queens Chapel Road
Hyattsville, Md. 20782
Rev. Choong Ho Huh
(301) 864-7938 and 927-4194
Service—2:00 P.M. Sunday

Full Gospel Washington Korean
    Church
3895 Massachusetts Avenue, NW
Washington, D.C. 20016
Rev. Paul Kim
937-1122 and 321-7870
Service—2:00 P.M. Sunday

Galilee United Methodist Church
814   20th Street, NW
Washington, D.C. 20006
Rev. Samuel D. Shinn
223-5933 and 243-6923
Service—11:00 A.M. Sunday

Groveton Korean Baptist Church
6511 Richmond Highway
Alexandria, Va. 22036
Rev. Moon Yo Chang
(703) 698-8937
Service—2:00 P.M. Sunday

Kent Korean Baptist Church
7006 E. Flagstaff Street
Landover, Md. 20785
Rev. Paul Y. Shin
(301) 773-8299
Service—2:00 P.M. Sunday

Korean Assembly of God
4501 N. Pershing Dr.
Arlington, Va. 22203
Rev. Sung Kwa Kim
(703) 532-1651
Service—3:00 P.M. Sunday

Korean Baptist Church of Washington
3850 Nebraska Avenue, NW
Washington, D.C. 20016
Rev. Wonse Yeo
363-2282
Service—1:30 P.M. Sunday

Korean Catholic Church of Greater
   Washington
4200 Harewood Road, NE
Washington, D.C. 20017
Rev. Francis Wang
635-7044/2578
Service—10:30 A.M. Sunday

Korean Central Baptist Church
7000 Arlington Boulevard
Falls Church Va. 22042
Rev. Moon Sup Song
(703) 532-6118 and 671-5308
Service—2:00 P.M. Sunday

Korean Central Baptist Church of
   Washington
7808 Marlboro Pike
Forestville, Md. 20028
Rev. Yong Dae Kim
(301) 420-3617
Service—11:00 A.M. Sunday

Korean Central Presbyterian Church
22d and P Streets, NW
Washington, D.C. 20037
667-2092
Service—2:00 P.M. Sunday

Korean Church in Washington, D.C.
1500   16th Street, NW
Washington, D.C. 20017
Rev. Peter Y. Sun
593-6818
Service—2:00 P.M. Sunday

Korean Eastminster Presbyterian
   Church of Greater Washington
Randolph Street and 56th Place
Villa Heights
Hyattsville, Md. 20784
Rev. Jong Sun Kim
(301) 588-3325 and 439-7226
Service—2:00 P.M. Sunday

Korean First United Methodist
   Church
Queens Chapel and Queensbury Roads
Hyattsville, Md. 20782
Rev. Thomas J. Ahn
(301) 277-7689/7081
Service—2:00 P.M. Sunday

Korean Presbyterian Church of
   Washington
204 East Del Ray Avenue
Alexandria, Va. 22301
Dr. Taek Y. Kim
(703) 548-3620 and 323-7221
Service—11:00 A.M. Sunday

Korean United Methodist Church of
   Washington
Glebe Road and S. 8th Street
Arlington, Va. 22204
Rev. Young Hoon Kim
(703) 370-9523
Service—11:00 A.M. Sunday

Maryland Korean Presbyterian
   Church
6301 Greenbelt Road
College Park, Md. 20740
Rev. Il Hyung Chang
(301) 459-1135 and 587-9644
Service—2:00 P.M. Sunday

McLean Korean Presbyterian Church
7144 Old Dominion Drive
McLean, Va. 22101
Rev. Sang Mook Kim
(703) 821-0676
Service—2:00 P.M. Sunday

Montgomery Korean Baptist Church
55 Adclare Road
Rockville, Md. 20850
Rev. Sung Hak Kim
279-9222 and 460-6421
Service—1:00 P.M. Sunday

Northern Virginia Korean Church
3846 King Street
Alexandria, Va. 22302
Rev. Su Pong Hwang
(703) 244-4760 and 256-6164
Service—1:00 P.M. Sunday

United Korean Church of Virginia
Grace and Bath Streets
Springfield, Va. 22150
Rev. Yong C. Chung
(703) 726-0244 and 946-3818
Service—11:00 A.M. Sunday

United Korean Church of Washington
16th and Kennedy Streets, NW
Washington, D.C. 20011
Rev. Yong Chul Chung
726-0244 and 946-3818
Service—2:00 P.M. Sunday

University United Korean Church
3621 Campus Drive
College Park, Md. 20740
Rev. Wha Jung Choi
(301) 773-5219
Services—2:00 and 7:00 P.M. Sunday

Virginia Korean Church
1125 N. Patrick Henry Drive
Arlington, Va. 22205
Rev. Kwan Bin Park
(703) 533-8988 and 323-9716
Service—11:00 A.M. Sunday

Virginia Korean Church of the
  Nazarene
5900 Wilson Boulevard
Arlington, Va. 22205
Rev. Young Y. Kim
(703) 532-2576
Service—11:00 A.M. Sunday

Washington Korean Seventh Day
  Adventists' Church
Columbia Union College
Takoma Park, Md. 20012
Rev. Young Lin Lee
(301) 434-7133
Service—11:00 A.M. Saturday

RELIGIOUS ORGANIZATIONS

Chinese Community Church
  Chinatown Service Center
803 H Street, NW
Washington, D.C. 20001
638-1041
Theresa Lau, Director

Council of Korean Churches
Rev. Mun Sop Song
7000 Arlington Boulevard
Falls Church, Va. 22402
(703) 671-5308
Rev. Kwan Bin Park, President

Korean Bible Institute of Washington
5005 Gainsborough Drive
Fairfax, Va. 22030
(703) 323-7221 and 548-3620
Dr. Taek Yong Kim, President

Korean Christian Chorus
11209 Woodson Avenue
Kensington, Md. 20795
(301) 933-5454

Korean Christian Mission in America
3509 Leesburg Court
Alexandria, Va. 22302
Joo Bok Suh, President (703) 931-6098

Korean Pastor's Council
14009 Rippling Brook Drive
Silver Spring, Md. 20906
(301) 460-6421
Rev. Sung Hak Kim, President

Korean World Mission of Washington
7003 E. Forest Road
Landover, Md. 20785
(301) 341-5321

Youth Christian Association in
  Washington
7614 Matera Road
Falls Church, Va. 22043
(703) 790-0798

Appendix IV. East Asian Ethnic Organizations, and Social/ Recreational Clubs

CHINESE ORGANIZATIONS

Chinese Consolidated Benevolent
  Association
803 H Street, NW
Washington, D.C. 20001
638-1041
Tom L. Fong, President

Organization of Chinese-Americans
1443 Rhode Island Avenue, NW
Suite 6
Washington, D.C. 20005
Hayden Lee, President

Chinese Cultural Center
755 8th Street, NW
Washington, D.C. 20001
727-2158

Chinese Cultural Service Center
742 6th Street, NW
Washington, D.C. 20001
347-0739

On-leung Merchants Association
620 H Street, NW
Washington, D.C. 20001
347-3208
Chung-suey Lee, President

JAPANESE ORGANIZATIONS

Japan-America Society of Washington
1302 18th Street, NW (Suite 704)
Washington, D.C. 20036
233-1772
Arthur K. Dornheir, Executive
  Secretary

Japan Commerce Association of
  Washington, D.C.
c/o Japan Airlines (Suite 203)
1666 K Street, NW
Washington, D.C. 20006
Mitsutake Okano, Chairman

Koyukai
2430 Pennsylvania Avenue, NW
Suite 3208
Washington, D.C. 20037
659-3850
Paul Ishimoto, President

Washington-Tokyo Women's Club
536-7268
Mrs. Morris E. Coon, President

KOREAN ORGANIZATIONS

First Korean School
10409 Juliet Avenue
Silver Spring, Md. 20902
(301) 460-1656
Han Il Lee, President

Korea Amateur Sports Association—
  Eastern Region in U.S.A.
9317 Riggs Road
Adelphi, Md. 20783
(301) 439-2583
Myong Yop Chu, President

Korean-American Political
  Association
6115 Thomas Drive
Springfield, Va. 22150
(703) 971-3286
Dr. Won Taik Moon, President

Korean-American Wives Club
3300 Chicamuxen Court
Falls Church, Va. 22041
Mrs. Sooyoung Lim Whitaker,
  President
(703) 820-8558 and 532-3325

Korean Architects' Association
10704 Great Arbor Drive
Potomac, Md. 20854
(301) 299-3402
Young Whan Park, President

Korean Artists Association
722 Anderson Avenue
Rockville, Md. 20880
(301) 340-0728
Mrs. Hong Ja Kim, President

Korean Association of Greater
  Washington
1741 Connecticut Avenue, NW
Washington, D.C. 20009
387-2200
Do Young Lee, President

Korean Businessmen's Association
441 P Street, NW
Washington, D.C. 20005
Han Yong Cho, President
(703) 671-5462

Korean Christian Social Services of
  Greater Washington
Queens Chapel and Queensbury Roads
Hyattesville, Md. 20782
277-7081/7689
Man Choon Kang, Director

Korean Community Service Center
7720 Alaska Avenue, NW
Washington, D.C. 20012
882-8270/8271
Rev. Y. C. Chung, Chairman

Korean Musicians Association
4437 Rena Road, No. 103
Forestville, Md. 20023
(301) 735-1109

Korean Scholarship Foundation in
  America
P.O. Box 50005
F Street Station
Washington, D.C. 20004
(301) 460-8512
Dr. Yo Taik Song, President

Korean School
P.O. Box 1084
Rockville, Md. 20855
(301) 424-4299
Dr. Cheol Park, President

Korean School of Kent
2374 Vermont Avenue
Landover, Md. 20785
(301) 341-1585
Jun Sang Rim, President

Korean Scientists and Engineers
  Association
802 Crystal Plaza 1
2001 Jefferson Davis Highway
Arlington, Va. 22202
(703) 979-2230

Legal Aid for Korean Families
1105 Highland Drive
Silver Spring, Md. 20910
(301) 587-7449
Mrs. Soon Young Rhee, President

Minority Legal Rights Foundation
733 15th Street, NW
Washington, D.C. 20005
393-6666
Choon Y. Chung, President

Washington Metropolitan "Go"
  Association
7016 Heatherhill Road
Bethesda, Md. 20034
(301) 229-6990
Dr. Jong Soo Lee, President

Appendix V. Bookstores

Since there is no local bookstore specializing in East Asian language materials (except possibly for some reference works, dictionaries, learning aids, etc.), a selective list of bookstores, which may prove useful to East Asian specialists, is included below. Unless indicated otherwise, these stores carry mostly English-language textbooks and monographs with a good selection of works on East Asian affairs. Scholars should contact individual stores for further information on service hours, discount rates, and other related subjects.

Discount Records and Books
1340 Connecticut Avenue, NW
Washington, D.C. 20036
785-1133

Globe Book Shop (Foreign)
1700 Pennsylvania Avenue, NW
Washington, D.C. 20006
393-1490

Maryland Book Exchange
4500 College Avenue
College Park, Md. 20740
(301) 927-2510

Savile Book Shop
3236 P Street, NW
Washington, D.C. 20007
338-3321 or 338-3325 (paperbacks)

Sidney Kramer Books, Inc.
1722 H Street, NW
Washington, D.C. 20006
298-8010

OTHERS (Used, Publishers' Overstock, etc.)

Horizon Bookshop
3131 M Street, NW
Washington, D.C. 20007
965-8865

Kramer Books, Inc.
1347 Connecticut Avenue, NW
Washington, D.C. 20036
293-2072

Second Story Books
5017 Connecticut Avenue, NW
Washington, D.C. 20008
244-5550

Note:
The bookstores of the local universities generally carry a good selection of reference works, textbooks, and other publications. Also, scholars should look into the several book sales held in the Washington area each year, including that of the Association of American Foreign Service Wives, held annually in the fall in the Department of State Building. The Brandeis University and Vassar College book sales are held in the spring. Advertisements for these sales are carried in local papers such as the *Washington Post*. Finally, some of the popular East Asian vernacular magazines can be purchased at local ethnic grocery stores.

Appendix VI. Library Collections: A Listing by Size of East Asian Holdings

500,000 volumes or more:
   Library of Congress (A30)

25,000-100,000 volumes:
   Georgetown University Library (A19)
   National Library of Medicine (A34)
   University of Maryland (A42)

10,000-25,000 volumes:
   Freer Gallary of Art (A16)
   State Department Library (A38)
   U.S.D.A. Technical Information Systems (A41)

Appendix VII.   Housing, Transportation, and Other Services

(Prices quoted are those available in January 1979 and are subject to change)

This section is prepared to help outside scholars who come to Washington, D.C., for short-term research in finding suitable housing facilities as well as in the use of local transportation facilities and information services.

HOUSING INFORMATION AND REFERRAL SERVICE

For any one interested in leasing an apartment or house, *Apartment Shoppers Guide and Housing Directory* (ASGHD) (updated every 3 months) is a valuable source of information. The directory which quotes current rental prices, terms of leases, and directions to each of the facilities listed is available at various People's Drug Stores in the Washington area. It is published by an organization bearing the same name as the directory and is located at 35 Wisconsin Circle, Suite 310, Washington, D.C. 20015. The ASGHD staff provides a housing referral service, free of charge, from 9:00 A.M. to 5:00 P.M. Monday through Friday. An up-to-date list of available apartments and houses is maintained at the office. For further information, call 652-1632 or 652-1633.

Scholars can also get help from the following local universities' housing offices:

George Washington University Off-Campus Housing Resources Center
676-6688
2121 I Street, NW (Rice Hall), 4th Floor
Washington, D.C. 20052

Summer: 9:00 A.M.-7:00 P.M.   Monday-Friday
Winter: 9:00 A.M.-5:00 P.M.   Monday-Friday

This office has listings of apartments and other housing in the Washington area. Open to the public, the office also distributes the *Apartment Shoppers Guide and Housing Directory* (see immediately preceding), maps of Washington, D.C., and *Guide to Off-Campus Housing* (annual) prepared for the students by the office.

Georgetown University Off-Campus Housing Office
625-3026
Healy Building Basement, Room G08
Georgetown University
37th and O Streets, NW
Washington, D.C. 20057

1:00 P.M.-4:30 P.M.   Monday-Friday

Open to the public, this office offers services similar to those of the George Washington University Housing Resource Center.

Catholic University of America Off-Campus Housing Office
635-5618
St. Bonaventure Hall, Room 106
Catholic University of America
Washington, D.C. 20064

9:00 A.M.-2:00 P.M.   Monday-Friday

Open to the public, this office provides services similar to those of George Washington University.

Northern Virginia Community College—Annandale Campus Housing
Office: (703) 323-3143
Student Activities Center
Science Building, Room 225-A
8333 Little River Turnpike
Annandale, Va. 22003

8:30 A.M.-5:00 P.M.   Monday-Friday

Its services are similar to those listed above.

The off-campus housing offices of American University, Howard University, and the University of Maryland handle inquiries and requests from their own students and faculty members only.

HOUSING—SHORT-TERM

For those scholars who intend to stay for a short period of time (i.e., a few weeks to several months), the following facilities may be useful.

International Guest House
726-5808
1441 Kennedy Street, NW
Washington, D.C. 20011

Rates: $8.50 per bed per day or $51.00 per week—breakfast with shared rooms; $4.25 for a child under 10; $3.25 per cot; and $2.00 per crib (daily rate).

International Student House
232-4007
1825 R Street, NW
Washington, D.C. 20009

Rates: $220 to $315 per month for room and board (2 meals, 7 days). Single, double, triple rooms are available. The House maintains a nationality quota policy that limits no more than 10 Americans or 3 from any one country at any time. For further information, see entry H27.

The Woodner Hotel
483-4400
3636   16th Street, NW
Washington, D.C. 20010

The hotel has furnished efficiency and 1-bedroom or 2-bedroom apartments.

Rates: $265 and up for efficiency; $335 and up for 1-bedroom; and $575 and up for 2-bedroom apartments.

Hunting Towers
(703) 548-8484
1204 South Washington Street
Alexandria, Va. 22314

Rates: For short-term (1-month) lease, $268.08 for furnished efficiency; $328.00 for furnished 1-bedroom apartment; and $428.76 for 2-bedroom apartments. All rates are reduced somewhat after 3-month stay.

The Capitol Park
484-5400
800   4th Street, SW
Washington, D.C. 20024
(Near the Library of Congress)

Rates: Furnished 1-bedroom apartment: by the week $115, by the month $430; and furnished 2-bedroom apartment (3-month lease required), $510 per month including maid service.

The Coronet Apartment
547-6300
200 C Street, SE
Washington, D.C. 20003
(Near the Library of Congress)

Rates: Furnished efficiency, $375 per month for 1; $425 for 2; furnished 1-bedroom apartment, $425 for 1; $475 for 2, including maid service and linen 6 days a week and utilities. (Add $24.80 occupancy tax per month).

HOUSING—LONG-TERM

Those wishing to rent an apartment or house for 1 year or more should consult with not only the *Apartment Shoppers Guide and Housing Directory* and the local university housing offices, but also the following rental agents:

Milicent Chatel   338-0500
Lynch   232-4100
Greenbelt Realty Co.   474-5700
Edmund Flynn Co.   554-4800
H. A. Gill   338-5000
Shannon & Luchs   659-7000
Norman Bernstein   331-7500

Home and apartment rents vary greatly from one section to the other in the Washington area. Normally, rents are lower in suburban Virginia and Maryland than in Washington, D.C. One should also remember that it is difficult to find furnished apartments in the Washington area through regular real-estate agents. People who need furnished quarters may have to take unfurnished apartments and rent furniture. Such an arrangement can be negotiated with the real-estate brokers. To be sure, even under such an arrangement linen, blankets, dishes, silverware, and cooking utensils must be furnished by the tenant.

TRANSPORTATION IN THE WASHINGTON AREA

Scholars should be advised that the parking space in the nation's capital is limited, and that it is relatively expensive to park at commercial lots (e.g., $1.25 per hour). It may be useful, therefore, to use either bus, METRO-subway, or taxi to get around the downtown Washington area.

To National Airport
Metro-bus No. 11 leaves every ten minutes from 10th and Pennsylvania Avenue, NW. Also there is a Metro-subway train that leaves every seven minutes from various downtown stations for National Airport.

To Dulles International Airport
Airport bus leaves from Capital Hilton Hotel, 16th and K Streets, NW, Washington, D.C., at the frequency of once every hour in the morning and every 30 minutes in the afternoon until 9:30 P.M. (Fare: $4.25). Also, there is a Metro-bus (only one per day) departing at 8:25 A.M. from 11th and E Streets, NW, downtown Washington and arriving at the Dulles Airport at 9:45 A.M. Also, there is a 24-hour limousine service to National Airport and Dulles International Airport. For further information, call Greyhound Airport Service (471-9801).

To Baltimore-Washington (Friendship) International Airport
All buses leave from 16th and K Streets, NW, downtown Washington, making stops at various points in the metropolitan area. For further information call (301) 441-2345.

Taxi

Fares in Washington, D.C., are based on a zone system and are reasonable as compared with other large cities in the United States. Taxi fares crossing state lines into and out of Virginia and Maryland are, however, fairly expensive.

Metro-Subway System

Although the subway system is still under construction, various parts of the system have been completed with the remainder to be operational within the next year or two. It is by far the most economical and efficient means of transportation that is available in Washington, D.C. Maps of the subway can be obtained at the National Visitors' Center, located at the site of the old Union Station. For further information, call Washington Metropolitan Area Transit Authority (637-2437).

Metro-Buses

In order to get around the town by METRO-bus, which links just about every major corner of the metropolitan Washington area, scholars should get a copy of "Getting About by Metro-bus" which is available at the Metro Headquarters, 600 5th Street, NW, Washington, D.C. 20001. For routes and schedule information, call 637-2437.

Train

Union Station is the terminal for all trains serving Washington, D.C. Located near the Capitol, it is within minutes of the downtown hotel area. More detailed information pertaining to Washington, D.C., can be obtained from the National Visitors' Center which is located at Union Station.

INTERNATIONAL VISITORS' INFORMATION SERVICE (IVIS)

IVIS is a private, nonprofit community organization that offers a diversified program of services to international visitors to the Washington area. Its programs are operated with the support of over 1,200 volunteers living in the Washington area. IVIS has two locations:

Main Information and Reception Center
801 19th Street, NW
Washington, D.C. 20006
872-8747
Information Booth
Dulles International Airport

Multilingual staff and volunteers are available to help the visitor with sightseeing arrangements, hotel accommodations, and bilingual medical assistance. IVIS also provides tour brochures, maps and information, and telephone language assistance in 47 languages (operating 24 hours a day, 7 days a week). Persons in need of language assistance (e.g., Chinese, Japanese, Korean) may call 872-8747. For further information, see entry H28.

For the foreign students enrolled in United States institutions of higher education, it may be useful to contact the Foreign Student Service Council of Greater Washington (FSSC), located at 1623 Belmont Street, NW, Washington, D.C. 20009 (Tel. 232-4979). Its staff and volunteers provide home hospitality, sightseeing, and other services to the foreign students (local and transient). For further information, see entry H25.

SOURCES OF FURTHER INFORMATION

Among several guidebooks on Washington, D.C., *Newcomers Guide to Metropolitan Washington*, edited and published by the *Washingtonian Magazine*, is highly useful. It is updated annually. Also useful is *The Best of Washington, the Washingtonian Magazine's Guide to Life in the Nation's Capital* (Washington, D.C.: Washingtonian Books, 1977). Dated somewhat, but still useful is *The Washington Post Guide to Washington* edited by Laura L. Babb (New York: McGraw-Hill Book Co., 1976).

MAP

Free copies of the metropolitan Washington area map are available from the District of Columbia Department of Transportation. Also, one can get a copy of the same from the Map Office, Room 519, 415 12th Street, NW, Washington, D.C. 20004. Mail requests must include a stamped self-addressed, 8 x 10-inch envelope. The office is open from 8:15 A.M. to 4:45 P.M. on weekdays.

Appendix VIII.   Standard Entry Forms

Entry Form for Libraries (Government, Academic, Public, Private, Special) (A)

1.   Access
  a. *Address; telephone number(s)*
  b. Hours of service
  c. Conditions of access, including interlibrary loan; and reproduction facilities)
  d. Name/title of director and heads of relevant divisions

2.   Size of collection

3.   Description and evaluation of collection
  a. 18 subject categories
  b. Evaluation of subject strength on a scale from A to C

4.   Special collections
  a. Periodicals
  b. Newspapers
  c. Government documents
  d. Books and monographs
  e. Archives and manuscripts
  f. Maps
  g. Films
  h. Tapes

5.   Noteworthy holdings

6.   Bibliographic aids (catalogs, guides, etc.) facilitating access to collection

---

Entry Form for Archives and Manuscript Depositories (B)

1.   Access
  a. *Address; telephone number(s)*
  b. Hours of service
  c. Conditions of access
  d. Reproduction services
  e. Director; heads of relevant divisions

2. Size of holdings pertaining to East Asia

3. Description of holdings

4. Bibliography of materials facilitating access to the collection (inventories, finding aids, catalogs, guides, descriptions)

Entry Form for Museums, Galleries, and Art Collections (C)

1. Access
   a. *Address; telephone number(s)*
   b. Hours of service
   c. Conditions of access
   d. Reproduction services
   e. Director; heads of relevant divisions

2. Size of holdings pertaining to East Asia

3. Description of holdings

4. Bibliography of materials facilitating access to the collection (inventories, catalogs, guides, descriptions)

5. Exchange programs and fellowships

Entry Form for Collections of Music and Other Sound Recordings (D)

1. Access
   a. *Address; telephone number(s)*
   b. Hours of service
   c. Conditions of access; special requirements or restrictions on use
   d. Director; heads of relevant divisions

2. Size of collection pertaining to East Asia

3. Description of holdings

4. Facilities for study and guidance for use
   a. Listening equipment
   b. Reservation requirements
   c. Fees charged
   d. Copies available for purchase

5. Bibliography of materials facilitating access to the collection (inventories, catalogs, guides, descriptions)

Entry Form for Map Collections (E)

1. Access
   a. *Address; telephone number(s)*
   b. Hours of service
   c. Conditions of access
   d. Reproduction services
   e. Director, heads of relevant divisions

2.   Size of holdings pertaining to East Asia

3.   Description of holdings

4.   Bibliography of materials facilitating access to the collection (inventories, guides, descriptions)

Entry Form for Film and Still-Picture Collections (F)

1.   General Information
   a. *Address; telephone number(s)*
   b. Hours of service
   c. Conditions of access
   d. Name/title of director and key staff members

2.   Size of holding pertaining to East Asia

3.   Description of holdings pertaining to East Asia

4.   Facilities for study and use
   a. Availability of audiovisual equipment
   b. Reservation requirements
   c. Fees charged
   d. Reproduction services

5.   Bibliographic aids facilitating use of collection

Entry Form for Data Banks (G)

1.   General information
   a. *Address; telephone number(s)*
   b. Hours of service
   c. Conditions of access (including fees charged for information retrieval)
   d. Name/title of director and key staff members

2.   Description of data files (hard data and bibliographic reference)

3.   Bibliographic aids facilitating use of storage media

Entry Form for Associations (H)

1.   *Address; telephone number(s)*

2   Founding date

3.   Chief official and title

4.   Staff

5.   Number of members

6.   Program or description

7.   Sections or divisions

8. Library
9. Conventions/meetings
10. Publications
11. Affiliated organizations

Entry Form for Cultural Exchange Organizations (J)

1. *Address; telephone number(s)*
2. Founding date
3. Chief official and title
4. Staff
5. Budget and its source
6. Affiliation with other organizations
7. Program or description
8. Publications

Entry Form for United States Government Agencies (K)

1. General information
   a. *Address; telephone number(s)*
   b. Conditions of access
   c. Name/title of director and heads of relevant divisions
2. Agency's programs and research activities
   a. In-house research
   b. Contract research
   c. Research grants
   d. Employment of outside consultants
   e. International exchange programs
3. Agency libraries and reference facilities
4. Agency's publications and records
5. Detailed description of relevant divisions

Entry Form for International Organizations (L)

1. General information
   a. *Address; telephone number(s)*
   b. Hours of service
   c. Name/title of director
2. Description of services
3. Library
4. Publications
5. Description of relevant divisions

Entry Form for Research Centers, Academic Programs and Departments (M)

1. *Address; telephone number(s)*
2. Founding date
3. Chief official and title
4. Staff; research and/or teaching personnel
5. Parental organizations
6. Principal fields of research and other activities
7. Library/special research facilities (including specialized collections and unique equipment; availability to nonmember)
8. Recurring meetings sponsored by the center (open or closed)
9. Publications or other media of dissemination
10. Affiliated organizations

Entry Form for Publications and Media (N)

1. *Address; telephone number(s)*
2. Founding date
3. Sponsoring organization
4. Editor
5. Frequency
6. Principal subjects covered

Bibliography

These publications were among the sources of the original basic lists of collections and organizations investigated for this *Scholars' Guide.*

American Association of Museums. *Official Museum Directory.* Washington, D.C.: American Association of Museums, 1975.

American Council of Voluntary Agencies for Foreign Service, Inc. *U.S. Non-Profit Organizations in Development Assistance Abroad Including Voluntary Agencies, Missions, and Foundations.* New York: Technical Assistance Information Clearing House of the American Council of Volunteer Agencies for Foreign Service, Inc., 1971.

Ayer Press. *'77 Ayer Directory of Publications.* Philadelphia: Ayer Press, 1977.

Benton, Mildred. *Federal Library Resources: A User's Guide to Research Collections.* N.Y.: Science Associates/International, 1973.

————. ed. *Libraries and Reference Facilities in the Area of the District of Columbia.* 9th ed. Washington, D.C.: American Society for Information Science, 1975

Brownson, Charles B. (comp.). *Congressional Staff Directory.* Mount Vernon, Virginia, 1976.

Center for Voluntary Society. *Voluntary Transnational Cultural Exchange Organizations of the U.S.; A Selected List.* Washington, D.C.: Center for a Voluntary Society, 1974.

Chamberlin, Jim, and Hammond, Ann, eds. *Directory of the Population-Related Community of the Washington, D.C. Area.* 3d ed. Washington, D.C.: World Population Society—D.C. Chapter, 1978.

Committee of the Association for Recorded Sound Collections. *A Preliminary Directory of Sound Recordings Collections in the United States and Canada.* New York: The New York Public Library, 1967.

Congressional Quarterly, Inc. *Washington Information Directory, 1977-1978.* Washington, D.C.: Congressional Quarterly, Inc., 1977.

Encyclopedia of Library and Information Science. New York: Marcel Dekker, 1977. Vol. 21.

Fisk, Margaret, ed. *Encyclopedia of Associations.* 11th ed. Detroit: Gale Research Co., 1977.

Grant, Steven A. *Scholars' Guide to Washington, D.C. for Russian/Soviet Studies.* Washington, D.C.: Smithsonian Institution Press, 1977.

Grayson, Cary T., Jr., and Lukowski, Susan. *Washington IV: A Comprehensive Directory of the Nation's Capital . . . its People and Institutions.* Washington, D.C.: Potomac Books, Inc., 1975.

Green, Shirley L. *Pictorial Resources in the Washington, D.C., Area.* Washington, D.C.: Library of Congress, 1976.

Hamer, Philip M., ed. *A Guide to Archives and Manuscripts in the United States.* New Haven: Yale University Press, 1961.

International Visitors Service Council of Greater Washington Organizations, *Organizations Serving International Visitors in the National Capital Area.* 4th ed. Washington, D.C.: International Visitors Service Council of Greater Washington Organizations, 1973.

Joyner, Nelson T., Jr. *Joyner's Guide to Official Washington.* 3d ed. Rockville, Maryland: Rockville Consulting Group, 1976.

Korean Association of Greater Washington, *Directory of Korean Association of Greater Washington.* Washington, D.C.: Korean Association of Greater Washington, 1978.

Mason, John Brown, ed. *Research Resources: Annotated Guide to the Social Sciences.* Santa Barbara, Calif.: American Bibliographical Center, 1968-1971.

Palmer, Archie M., ed. *Research Centers Directory.* 5th ed. Detroit: Gale Research Co., 1975.

Ruder, William, and Nathan, Raymond. *The Businessman's Guide to Washington.* Rev. ed. N.Y.: Macmillan Publishing Co., 1975.

Schmeckebier, Laurence Frederick, and Eastin, Roy B. *Government Publications and their Use.* 2d rev. ed. Washington, D.C.: Brookings Institution, 1969.

Schneider, John H.; Gecham, Marvin; and Further, Stephen E., eds. *Survey of Commercially Available Computer-Readable Bibliographic Data Bases.* Washington, D.C.: American Society for Information Science, 1973.

Sessions, Vivian S., ed. *Directory of Data Bases in the Social Behavioral Sciences.* New York: Science Associates/International, 1974.

Smith, David Horton, ed. *Voluntary Transnational Cultural Exchange Organizations of the U.S.: A Selected List.* Washington, D.C.: Center for a Voluntary Society, 1974.

Tsien, Tsuen-hsuin. *Current Status of East Asian Collections in American Libraries.* Washington, D.C.: Center for Chinese Research Materials, Association of Research Libraries, 1976.

U.S. Government Documents Round Table, American Library Association. *Directory of Government Document Collections and Libraries.* Chicago: American Library Association, 1974.

U.S. Department of State, Office of External Research. *Foreign Affairs Research: A Directory of Governmental Resources.* Washington, D.C.: U.S. Department of State, 1977.

————. *Government-Supported Research on Foreign Affairs: Current Project Information, 1976.* Washington, D.C.: Government Printing Office, 1977.

U.S. Library of Congress, National Referral Center for Science and Technology. *A Directory of Information Resources in the United States: Federal Government.* Washington, D.C.: Library of Congress. 1974.

————. *A Directory of Information Resources in the United States: Social Sciences.* Rev. ed. Washington, D.C.: Library of Congress, 1973.

U.S. National Archives and Records Service. *United States Government Organization Manual, 1977/78.* Washington, D.C., 1977.

Washington Booksellers Association. *Metropolitan Bookstore Guide.* Washington, D.C.: Washington Booksellers Association, 1975.

Washington, D.C., area telephone directories.

Weber, Olga S. (comp.). *North American Film and Video Directory; A Guide to Media Collections and Services.* New York: Bowker, 1976.

Wynar, Lubomyr R. *Encyclopedic Directory of Ethnic Newspapers and Periodicals in the United States.* Littleton, Colorado: Libraries Unlimited, 1976.

————. *Encyclopedic Directory of Ethnic Organizations in the United States.* Littleton, Colorado: Libraries Unlimited, 1975.

Name Index

(Organizations and Institutions)

Notes:

(1) The alphabetic code represents the following sections of the *Guide:*

Guide:

A—Libraries
B—Archives and Manuscript Depositories
C—Museums, Galleries, and Art Collections
D—Collections of Music and Other Sound Recordings
E—Map Collections
F—Film and Still Picture Collections
G—Data Banks
H—Associations
J—Cultural Exchange Organizations
K—United States Government Agencies
L—Foreign Government Agencies and International Organizations
M—Research Centers, Academic Programs and Departments
N—Publications and Media

(2) For information on the following, see Appendixes: East Asian Press List (Appendix I); East Asian Ethnic Media (Appendix II); East Asian Ethnic Churches and Religious Organizations (Appendix III); East Asian Ethnic Organizations and Social/Recreational Clubs (Appendix IV); Bookstores (Appendix V).

Academic Travel Abroad, Inc. J1
Advanced International Studies Institute M1
Agency for International Development (AID) A1, F1, K1
  Bureau for Asia K1
  Bureau for Program and Policy Coordination K1
  Bureau of Development Support K1
  Bureau of Private and Development Cooperation K1
Communications and Records Management Division K1
Development Information Center A2
Economic and Social Data Bank K1
Office of American Schools and Hospitals Abroad K1
Office of Food-for-Peace K1
Office of Labor Affairs K1
Office of Public Affairs K1

Personal Papers Index

(See the section entitled "How to Use This Guide")

Library Subject Strength Index

This index is prepared to identify the most useful Washington area library collections by subject-category (i.e., 14 subjects and 4 geographic areas). The method of rating the collections (A, B, and C) is explained in the introductory section of this book entitled "How to Use this *Guide.*" Some ratings are based on only part of a subject category, for no other method could be found to cope with a few exceptionally fine specialized collections. The reader's attention is also called to Appendix VI—"Library Collections: A Listing by Size of East Asian Holdings."

1. Philosophy and Religion
   - A collections:
       - China—A30
       - Japan—A30
       - Korea—A30
   - B collections:
       - Japan—A42
   - C collections:
       - China—A8, A19, A24, A38, A42

2. History
   - A collections:
       - China—A30
       - Japan—A30
       - Korea—A30
   - B collections:
       - China—A16, A18, A38, A42
       - Japan—A16, A38, A42
   - C collections:
       - China—A19, A24
       - Japan—A19
       - Korea—A19, A38, A42

3. Geography and Ethnography
   - A collections:
       - China—A17, A30

- Japan—A17, A30
- Korea—A17, A30
   - B collections:
       - China—A32, A41, A42
       - Japan—A32, A41, A42
       - Korea—A32
   - C collections:
       - China—A8, A19
       - Korea—A41

4. Economics
   - A collections:
       - China—A30, A41
       - Japan—A30, A41
       - Korea—A30, A41
   - B collections:
       - China—A10, A15, A25, A28, A38
       - Japan—A10, A15, A25, A28, A38, A42, H95
       - Korea—A10, A15, A28, A41
   - C collections:
       - China—A19, A42, H37

5. Sociology
   - A collections:
       - China—A9, A12, A30

Japan—A9, A30
Korea—A9, A30

B collections:
China—A12, A38
Japan—A42

C collections:
China—A6, A18, A19, A29, A42
Japan—A18, A29, A38

6. Government and Politics

A collections:
China—A30
Japan—A30
Korea—A30

B collections:
China—A38, A42
Japan—A38, A42

C collections:
China—A6, A18, A19
Korea—A38, A42

7. Foreign Relations

A collections:
China—A30
Japan—A30
Korea—A30

B collections:
China—A18, A19, A38, A42
Japan—A19, A38, A42

C collections:
China—A8, A24
Japan—A6, A18, A24
Korea—A38, A42

8. Law

A collections:
China—A30
Japan—A30
Korea—A30

C collections:
China—A38
Japan—A38
Korea—A38

9. Fine Art

A collections:
China—A16, A30
Japan—A16, A30
Korea—A16, A30

B collections:
China—A5, A8, A42
Japan—A5, A23, A42

C collections:
China—A6
Japan—A6
Korea—A42

10. Education

A collections:
China—A30, A42
Japan—A30
Korea—A30

B collections:
Japan—A42

C collections:
China—A6, A38
Japan—A6, A38

11. Language

A collections:
China—A30
Japan—A30
Korea—A30

B collections:
China—A19, A42
Japan—A19, A42

C collections:
China—A16
Japan—A16
Korea—A19

12. Literature

A collections:
China—A30
Japan—A30
Korea—A30

B collections:
China—A19, A42
Japan—A19, A42

C collections:
China—A18
Korea—A38

13. Military Affairs

A collections:
China—A30
Japan—A30
Korea—A30

B collections:
China—A7, A36
Japan—A7, A36, A42
Korea—A7, A36, A38, A42

C collections:
China—A19

Subject Index

A24, A26, A30, A36, A38, A41, A42, G5, G6, K5, K31; (Japan) A4, A6, A7, A8, A9, A10, A15, A18, A19, A24, A26, A36, A37, A38, A39, A42, G5, G6, K5, K31, L5; (Korea) A4, A6, A7, A8, A10, A15, A18, A19, A24, A26, A30, A36, A38, A39, A42, G5, G6, K31, L5

Intelligence Activity A3, K4, K8, K21, K30

International Exchange H16, H25, H27, H28, H30, H33, H34, H35, H36, J1, J2, J3, J4, J5, J6, J7, J8, J9, K14, K17, K29, K31

International Law H12, N1, N8, N18

International Relations A6, A7, A8, A14, A19, A22, A24, A26, A30, A36, A38, A41, A42, B5, B8, G3, H12, H20, H47, H48, H49, K7, K8, K28, K30, L1, L2, L3, L4, L5, L7, M1, M2, M3, M5, M7, M8, M9, M10, M12, M15, M16, M18, M19, M25, M29, M32, N3, N7, N8, N12, N16, N17, N18

Immigration and Naturalization K23

Investment A6, A7, A8, A9, A10, A11, A12, A15, A18, A19, A24, A30, A38, A41, A42, B8, K22, K26, M27

Jesuits A19, A20, A41

Korean War A3, A6, A7, A8, A9, A10, A18, A19, A24, A26, A30, A31, A36, A38, A42, B3, B5, B6, B8, B9, C11, F2, F3, F5, F6, F7, F8, F9, F11, G3, H15, H20, H40, K3, K6, K7, K8, K25

Labor A4, A6, A8, A12, A18, A19, A24, A26, A27, A29, A30, A38, A41, A42, B8, H18, M14, M15, M16, M24
See also Trade Unions

Language (Chinese) A6, A8, A12, A16, A18, A19, A24, A27, A30, A38, A41, A42, H20, H22, K30, M14, M18, M24, M33; (Japanese) A6, A8, A18, A19, A24, A30, A38, A42, H29, K20, K30, M13, M18; (Korean) A6, A7, A8, A18, A19, A30, A38, A42, K20, K27

Law (Chinese) A6, A7, A8, A18, A19, A24, A30, A38; (Japanese) A6, A18, A19, A24, A30, A38, H5;

(Korean) A6, A7, A8, A18, A19, A24, A30, A38

Literature (Chinese) A6, A8, A18, A19, A24, A30, A41, A42, M13, M17; (Japanese) A6, A8, A18, A19, A24, A30, A38, A42, M18; (Korean) A6, A8, A18, A19, A24, A30, A38, A42

Media A30, H41, K17, K18, N2, N3, N12, N16, N17, N18
See also Appendix I (East Asian Press List) and Appendix II (East Asian Media in the Washington Area)

Medicine A35, K14
See also Health

Military Affairs (China) A3, A6, A7, A8, A9, A10, A18, A19, A24, A30, A36, A42, B5, B6, B8, B9, C9, C11, F1, F3, F5, F6, F7, F8, F9, F11, G3, H15, H20, H40, K3, K6, K7, K8, K25, M1, M5, M15, M16, M21, M22, M30, M32, N2; (Japan) A3, A6, A7, A8, A10, A18, A19, A20, A24, A26, A36, A38, A42, B3, B5, B6, B8, B9, C9, C11, C12, D2, F3, F5, F6, F7, F8, F9, F11, G3, H15, H20, H40, K3, K6, K7, K8, K25, K29, M2, M7, M12, M16, M21, M22, M32, N2; (Korea) A3, A6, A7, A8, A9, A10, A18, A19, A24, A26, A30, A36, A38, A42, B3, B5, B6, B8, B9, C11, F2, F3, F5, F6, F7, F8, F9, F10, F11, G3, H15, H20, H40, K3, K6, K7, K8, K25, M2, M5, M10, M12, M16, M22, M32, N2

Mining and Mineral Resources A17, A25, A30, C8, K17

Monetary Affairs
See Finance

Mongolia A6, A7, A8, A12, A16, A18, A19, A24, A30, A38, A40, B8, E3, E4, F6, H17, K18

Multinational Corporations A10, A15, A19, A28, A30, A37, A38, A42, K5

Music (Chinese) A6, A8, A19, A30, A42, D1, D2, D4, H21; (Japanese) A6, A8, A30, A42, C6, D1, D2, D4, H17, K19; (Korean) A30, A42, C8, D1

Narcotics A30, B9

National Security K24, K30, M1,

The author, Hong Nack Kim, is Professor of Political Science at West Virginia University. After graduating from Seoul National University (B.A., 1956) and Georgetown University (M.A., 1960; Ph.D., 1965), he taught at Georgetown and North Texas State universities. Formerly editor of *Asian Forum*, he has written widely on Japan's politics and international relations, contributing articles to such journals as *Asian Survey, Asia Quarterly, Asian Forum, Asia Mail, Asian Profile, Current History, Journal of Asian Affairs, Korea and World Affairs, Problems of Communism, World Affairs, World Politics,* and *Collier's Encyclopedia Yearbook* (1977, 1978, and 1979). His other publications include *Essays in Political Science* (co-editor, 1971) and numerous review articles.

The consultant, Frank Joseph Shulman, is the Head of the East Asia Collection, McKeldin Library, University of Maryland's College Park Campus.

The consultant, Dr. Warren M. Tsuneishi, is the Acting Director for Area Studies, Research Services, Library of Congress.

The series editor, Dr. Zdeněk V. David, has been librarian of the Wilson Center since 1974. Previously he served as the Slavic Bibliographer of the Princeton University Library, and as Lecturer in the Department of History at Princeton University.